Hindenburg, Ludendorff and Hitler

For
Ross, Alex & Kay
the best of colleagues

Hindenburg, Ludendorff and Hitler

Germany's Generals and the Rise of the Nazis

Alexander Clifford

Pen & Sword
MILITARY

First published in Great Britain in 2021 by
Pen & Sword Military
an imprint of
Pen & Sword Books Ltd
Yorkshire – Philadelphia

Copyright © Alexander Clifford 2021

ISBN 978 1 52678 333 2

The right of Alexander Clifford to be identified as Author of this work has been asserted by him in accordance with the Copyright, Designs and Patents Act 1988.

A CIP catalogue record for this book is available from the British Library.

All rights reserved. No part of this book may be reproduced or transmitted in any form or by any means, electronic or mechanical including photocopying, recording or by any information storage and retrieval system, without permission from the Publisher in writing.

Typeset by Mac Style
Printed and bound by CPI Group (UK) Ltd,
Croydon, CR0 4YY

Pen & Sword Books Limited incorporates the imprints of Atlas, Archaeology, Aviation, Discovery, Family History, Fiction, History, Maritime, Military, Military Classics, Politics, Select, Transport, True Crime, Air World, Frontline Publishing, Leo Cooper, Remember When, Seaforth Publishing, The Praetorian Press, Wharncliffe Local History, Wharncliffe Transport, Wharncliffe True Crime and White Owl.

For a complete list of Pen & Sword titles please contact

PEN & SWORD BOOKS LIMITED
47 Church Street, Barnsley, South Yorkshire, S70 2AS, England
E-mail: enquiries@pen-and-sword.co.uk
Website: www.pen-and-sword.co.uk

Or

PEN AND SWORD BOOKS
1950 Lawrence Rd, Havertown, PA 19083, USA
E-mail: Uspen-and-sword@casematepublishers.com
Website: www.penandswordbooks.com

Contents

Acknowledgments — vii
List of Illustrations — viii
Glossary — xiii
Political Parties of Weimar Germany — xv
Cast of Characters — xx

Prologue	The Double Act: The Emergence of Hindenburg and Ludendorff	xxii
	Contrasting backgrounds	xxiv
	The Great War	xxvi
	The new Germany	xxxiii
Chapter 1	The Stab in the Back: Hindenburg and Ludendorf as Liars-in-Chief	1
	Origins	1
	Ludendorff as architect: The excuses of a broken man	8
	Hindenburg as cheerleader: The myth becomes mainstream	14
Chapter 2	Conspirator: Ludendorf as Public Enemy Number One	28
	Paramilitary politics	28
	The Kapp Putsch	33
	Munich – the far right's playground	53
	1923: Year of crisis	64
	The Beer Hall Putsch	71
Chapter 3	Figureheads: Hindenburg and Ludendorff as Leadership Contenders	87
	On trial	87
	The struggle for control	97
	The 1925 presidential election	106

Chapter 4	Constitutionalism and Conspiracy Theories: Hindenburg Ascends, Ludendorff Fades	119
	Hindenburg: Father of the nation	119
	Ludendorff's withdrawal	128
	Hindenburg and the Grand Coalition	134
Chapter 5	The Hindenburg Republic: Hindenburg as the Arbiter of German Politics	143
	Presidential government	143
	The president looks to the right	154
	The field marshal versus the lance corporal	164
	A cabinet of 'my friends'	177
	Hindenburg digs Weimar's grave	196
Epilogue	The One-Man Show: Hindenburg and Ludendorf in Eclipse	222
	Hindenburg: Willing collaborator	222
	Ludendorff's final retreat	233
	Hindenburg, Ludendorff and German history	238
Appendix I	Elections in the Weimar Republic	242
Appendix II	Governments of Hindenburg's Presidency	245
Appendix III	Hindenburg's Cabinets	246
Notes		252
Further Reading and Bibliography		281
Index		285

Acknowledgements

The genesis of this book was a conversation during a departmental meeting at my school several years ago, the topic of which I have long since forgotten. Somehow, I managed to divert discussion away from data, curriculum or pedagogy to Erich Ludendorff and his pernicious influence on twentieth-century history. One of my colleagues suggested, perhaps in jest, that I write a book about him and that, in contrast to my work on the Spanish Civil War, it would be a book they would actually read. This planted a seed which, alongside my pre-existing interest in Paul von Hindenburg, eventually flowered into the present volume.

The book could not have been written without the remarkable scholarship that already exists on these two controversial figures and several of the creators of that scholarship have been immensely helpful and kind in assisting me during my research and writing. Larry Eugene Jones's works have been instrumental in shaping my picture of the period and he was very generous in providing me with both answers to many naïve questions and granting me access to some of his latest research. Jay Lockenour was equally forthcoming in directing me to essential source material on Ludendorff and our conversations, which were released as a podcast (episode 34 of *History's Most*), were very instructive and certainly altered some of my conclusions, to this volume's benefit. Equally, George Vascik was kind enough to talk to me about the Stab-in-the-Back myth, a discussion which was also immortalised in podcast form (episode 31 of *History's Most*) and deepened my understanding of the *Dolchstoss* considerably.

I am indebted to Jack Arscott, whose translation skills I leaned on many times in helping me decipher difficult texts and better render peculiarly Germanic phrases in English. Our conversations about German nationalism also helped me form my arguments presented in this book. I must thank Rupert Harding at Pen & Sword for once again putting enormous trust and faith in me, and for his understanding when the Coronavirus pandemic derailed my research schedule. Linne Matthews has edited the book magnificently and worked wonders in preparing it for publication. As in the past, it has been a pleasure to work with her.

Finally, my partner Róisín, amidst the adversity of lockdown, had to tolerate my attentions at times being unforgivably given over to Paul von Hindenburg and Erich Ludendorff. I thank you for your tolerance.

Alex Clifford, March 2021

List of Illustrations

Page xiv Diagram 1. States of the Weimar Republic. *(Wikimedia user shadowfox, CC By-SA 3.0)*
Page xv   Diagram 2. Political Spectrum of the Weimar Republic. *(Alexander Clifford)*

Plate section

Page 1
1. Field Marshal Paul von Hindenburg (left) and General Erich Ludendorff (right) as Chief of the General Staff and First Quartermaster General respectively, pose with Kaiser Wilhelm II, 1917. *(Public domain)*
2. & 3. The making of an icon: the famous wartime 'Iron Hindenburg' statue in Berlin and one of the countless examples of Hindenburg kitsch – the field marshal decorates an ashtray. *(Public domain & Author's collection)*

Page 2
4. Wartime portrait of Erich Ludendorff from 1918, when his grand plans failed, his mental health collapsed, and he devised the Stab-in-the-Back myth. *(Public domain)*
5. Postcard to raise money for the Ludendorff-Spende, a charity for wounded war veterans that ran from 1918 to 1923, of which the general was honorary president. The inscription reads: 'No victory without sacrifice, no peace without victory.' *(Author's collection)*
6. One of many visualisations of the poisonous Stab-in-the-Back myth that pervaded German perceptions of the Great War thanks to Hindenburg and Ludendorff. *(Public domain)*

Page 3
7. Two protagonists of the Kapp Putsch farce – General Walther von Lüttwitz (centre) converses with Defence Minister Gustav Noske (right). *(Bundesarchiv)*
8. Corvette Captain Hermann Ehrhardt (second from left), commander of the key Freikorps milita Marine Brigade Ehrhardt, during the Kapp Putsch. *(Bundesarchiv)*

List of Illustrations   ix

9. Early twentieth-century postcard of Berlin. The Reichstag building dominates the Tiergarten park, with the Siegesallee running up to the Brandenburg Gate, just visible in the distance. This is where Ludendorff supposedly ran into the putschists while he was out on a morning walk through the park. *(Public domain)*

Page 4
10. & 11. The Kapp Putsch, 1920: Freikorps troops of Marine Brigade Ehrhardt march into central Berlin. Note the swastika decal painted onto their helmets. *(Bundesarchiv)*
12. The Erhardt Brigade that occupied Berlin was heavily armed and highly experienced, making the government's decision to flee the capital rather understandable. *(Bundesarchiv)*

Page 5
13. Ludendorff in Bavaria: the general (centre) with Bavarian premier Gustav von Kahr (left) and Munich Chief of Police Ernst Pöhner (right), 1921. *(Bundesarchiv)*
14. Ludendorff as Nazi leader, reviewing SA troopers of the newly formed *Kampfbund* at the German Day rally, 2 September 1923. *(Bundesarchiv)*
15. A Nazi meeting at the Munich Bürgerbräukeller, sometime in 1923. The same beer hall would play host to von Kahr's address on 8 November 1923 that Hitler hijacked to proclaim the National Revolution. *(Bundesarchiv)*

Page 6
16 & 17. The Beer Hall Putsch: *Kampfbund* paramilitaries guarding the Bavarian War Ministry, where Ludendorff wasted the early hours of 9 November 1923, and the central Munich Marienplatz that morning, where the general made the fateful decision to march on the same ministry. *(Bundesarchiv)*
18. The Feldherrenhalle in 1915, a martial monument that stands on the southern edge of Munich's Odeonsplatz. The fateful march that Ludendorff and Hitler led through the city on 9 November 1923 ended bloodily when they ran into a police cordon at the end of the narrow Residenzstrasse (left). *(Public domain)*

Page 7
19. Ludendorff is chauffeured to the final day on the putsch trial, 1 April 1924, greeted by cheering crowds. *(Bundesarchiv)*
20. The final day of the Beer Hall Putsch trial, 1 April 1924. Ludendorff (wearing the uniform he swore never to put on again) stands to the left of Hitler and is joined by: (from left to right) his stepson Pernet, Weber, Frick, Kriebel, Brückner, Röhm and Wagner. *(Bundesarchiv)*

21. The nationalist veterans' association *Der Stahlhelm* campaign for Hindenburg, April 1925. Note the Imperial colours and the distinctive posters which mirrored wartime propaganda. *(Bundesarchiv)*

Page 8
22. A giant bust of Hindenburg is ferried around Berlin during the 1925 campaign. *(Bundesarchiv)*
23. The newly elected Reich President von Hindenburg (approaching the podium) is presented to the Reichstag. *(Author's collection)*
24. The Weimar era Presidential Palace on the Wilhelmstrasse, Berlin. *(Public domain)*

Page 9
25. Hindenburg attending the grandiose dedication of the Tannenberg Memorial, where the Nazis would eventually bury him, September 1927. This was the scene of the president's painful public break with Ludendorff. *(Bundesarchiv)*
26. Hindenburg's eightieth birthday celebrations – 40,000 schoolchildren watch the conclusion of the presidential motorcade at the Grunewald Stadium, 2 October 1927. *(Bundesarchiv)*
27. Hindenburg as father of the nation: star-struck children welcome him to a sporting event, February 1930. His son and aide-de-camp Oskar is behind him. *(Bundesarchiv)*

Page 10
28. Postcard featuring the official portrait of Hindenburg as Reich president, late 1920s. *(Author's collection)*
29. Last gasp of parliamentary democracy – the Grand Coalition cabinet: (front row, left to right) Economics Minister Julius Curtius, Foreign Minister Gustav Stresemann, Chancellor Hermann Müller, Defence Minister Wilhelm Groener, Minister for Occupied Territories Joseph Wirth; (back row, left to right) Postal Minister Georg Schätzel, Justice Minister Theodor von Guérard, Transport Minister Adam Stegerwald, Interior Minister Carl Severing, Agriculture Minster Hermann Dietrich and Finance Minister Rudolf Hilferding. *(Bundesarchiv)*
30. First experiment in presidential government – the 'Hindenburg Cabinet': (front row, left to right) Interior Minister Joseph Wirth, Finance Minister Hermann Dietrich, Chancellor Heinrich Brüning, Foreign Minister Julius Curtius, Postal Minister Georg Schätzel; (back row, left to right) Minister for Occupied Territories Gottfried Treviranus, Justice Minister Johann Viktor Bredt, Labour Minister Adam Stegerwald, Economics Minister Paul Moldenhauer, Justice Minister Theodor von Guérard. *(Bundesarchiv)*

31. The House of Hindenburg – State Secretary Otto Meissner (centre, on steps) watches as Oskar von Hindenburg helps his father into a car at the Neudeck estate. *(Public domain)*

Page 11
32., 33. & 34. Re-electing the Saviour: Berlin posters during the 1932 presidential campaign. At the famous Potsdamer Platz, voters are told to 'Vote for a man, not a party', a skyscraper tells voters, 'Against the system of eternal strife', while passers-by at the Brandenburg Gate are simply told, 'Vote Hindenburg!' *(Bundesarchiv)*

Page 12
35. Innovative Hindenburg pamphlet for the second ballot. 'Awake', the front cover implores, in an echo of the famous Nazi slogan 'Germany awake'. *(Author's collection)*
36. The reader is bombarded by images of British and French betrayal on disarmament and trade, while the stereotypical voter Michel sleeps, oblivious to Germany's plight. The caption informs voters that Germany will continue to be cheated so long as 'we wear ourselves out in useless, tiresome party strife' and so long as Michel sleeps.
37. Meanwhile, Michel is dreaming of a fantasy world in which poverty is ended by printing money, credit is available on tap, the world disarms and the French cancel reparations – an implicit criticism of the Nazi and Communist utopian visions.

Page 13
38. But as he wakes, Michel realises both that miracles only happen in dreams and that 'If everyone pulls in the same direction, we're strong!' Therefore, in order to save the work of Bismarck and prove Germany's enemies wrong, the nation must unite behind Hindenburg.
39. Finally, Michel casts his vote for the president under the slogan 'Away with radicalism! Do not leave the rudder of state to the inexperienced! Only Hindenburg deserves your vote.'
40. Heinrich Brüning addressing a mass rally during the 1932 Hindenburg campaign. *(Bundesarchiv)*

Page 14
41. Hindenburg election poster proclaims 'A hero's burden calls for heroes' as the 84-year-old appears as Atlas, lifting a globe emblazoned with the German imperial eagle. Hitler is protesting: 'But I'm still much stronger.' *(Bundesarchiv)*
42. The *Illustrated London News* reports on Hitler versus Hindenburg, the presidential second round. *(Author's collection)*

43. & 44. Two 1932 Hindenburg pamphlets: one in the Imperial colours of black-white-red tells military veterans to stay loyal to Hindenburg as Hindenburg had stayed loyal to them, while the other tells voters, 'Hindenburg must remain Reich President' to protect Germans' freedoms. *(Author's collection)*

Page 15

45. The 'cabinet of barons', or 'my friends', as Hindenburg called them: (front row, left to right) Agriculture Minister Magnus von Braun, Interior Minister Wilhelm von Gayl, Chancellor Franz von Papen, Foreign Minister Konstantin von Neurath; (back row, left to right) Justice Minister Franz Gürtner, Economics Minister Hermann Warmbold, Defence Minister Kurt von Schleicher. *(Bundesarchiv)*
46. The Reichstag, 12 September 1932 – an impotent Papen (standing, centre-left) is ignored by the speaker, Hermann Göring, as he attempts to dissolve the Reichstag and avoid an embarrassing vote of no confidence. He lost the resulting vote by 512–42. *(Bundesarchiv)*
47. The Hitler Cabinet: (front row, left to right) Minister without Portfolio Hermann Göring, Chancellor Adolf Hitler, Vice Chancellor Franz von Papen; (back row, left to right) Labour Minister Franz Seldte, Commissioner for Works Günther Gereke, Finance Minister Lutz Schwerin von Krosigk, Interior Minister Wilhelm Frick, Defence Minister Werner von Blomberg, Economics and Agriculture Minister Alfred Hugenberg. *(Bundesarchiv)*

Page 16

48. Goebbels's dramatic Day of Potsdam ceremony, 21 March 1933, put the president centre stage and tied Hindenburg's mythos and prestige to the new Nazi regime in a deliberate attempt to win over Hitler sceptics. *(Bundesarchiv)*
49. Hindenburg and Hitler, field marshal and lance corporal, *Ersatzkaiser* and heir apparent. *(Bundesarchiv)*
50. NSDAP election poster for the March 1933 Reichstag elections, Hitler's proclaimed 'final election', in which the Nazis won their best-ever result with Hindenburg's image at the centre of their appeal. *(Bundesarchiv)*
51. The lavish Hindenburg funeral held at the gigantic Tannenberg Memorial, East Prussia, 7 August 1934. *(Bundesarchiv)*
52. Ludendorff's grave, which stands to this day, in the town cemetery of Tutzing, Bavaria. *(Public domain)*

Many images from the German Bundesarchiv have been reproduced in the plates section and on the cover under the Creative Commons ShareAlike licence 3.0 (which can be viewed here: https://creativecommons.org/licenses/by-sa/3.0).

Glossary

ADGB	Free Trade Unions
BEF	British Expeditionary Force
BVP	Bavarian People's Party
CNBL	Christian-Nationalist Farmers' and Peasants' Party
CSVD	Christian Social People's Mission
DAP	German Workers' Party
DDP/DStP	German Democratic Party/German State Party
DNVP	German Nationalist People's Party
DVFP	German Völkisch Freedom Party
DVP	German People's Party
GVG	Grossdeutsche Volksgemeinschaft
KPD	German Communist Party
KVP	Conservative People's Party
NSFB	National Socialist Freedom Movement
NSFP	National Socialist Freedom Party
NSDAP	National Socialist German Workers' Party
OC	Organisation Consul
OHL	Oberste Heeresleitung (Supreme Army Command)
RLB	Reich Rural League
SA	Sturmabteilung
SPD	Social Democratic Party of Germany
UHC	United Hindenburg Committees
USPD	Independent Social Democrats
VSB	Völkisch-Social Bloc
WP	Economic Party/Reich Party of the Middle Class
Z	Centre Party

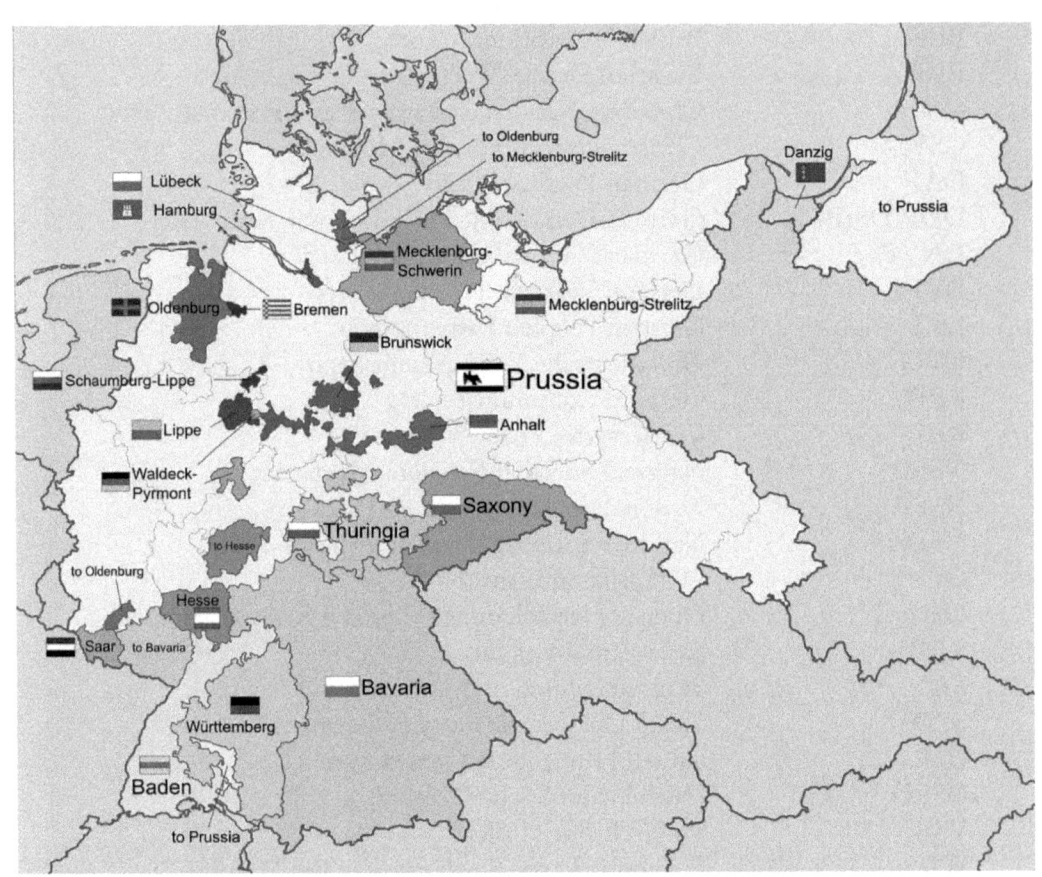

States of the Weimar Republic.

Political Parties of Weimar Germany

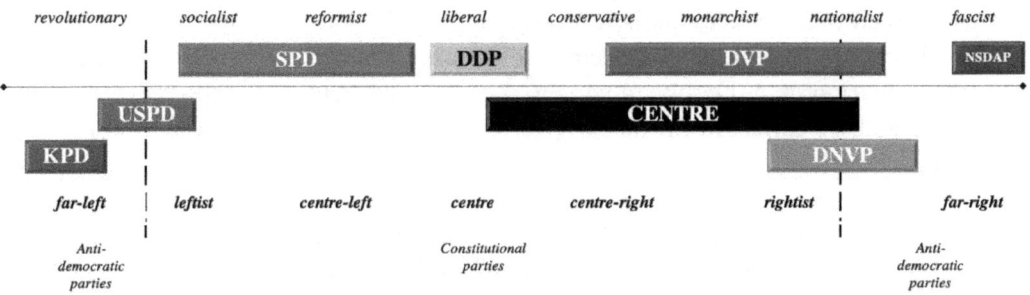

Political Spectrum of the Weimar Republic.

Major Political Parties

Communists (KPD) – the Moscow-directed German Communist Party was formed by the Spartacists, a radical far-left splinter group which left the USPD in 1918. The bloody suppression of their attempted uprising in January 1919 by the Social Democratic government led to a bitter hatred within the SPD which never healed. Further failed uprisings in the Ruhr and central Germany in 1920 and 1923 only added to the acrimony between the two major parties of the left, preventing meaningful cooperation.

Independent Socialists (USPD) – the pacifist wing of the SPD left the party in 1917 over the leadership's support for the war effort. The USPD fought for the creation of a socialist state based on workers' councils during the German Revolution, rather than the parliamentary democracy that the SPD favoured. Their star soon faded after the revolution died down and the party folded with radicals joining the KPD and moderates reunifying with the SPD in 1922.

Social Democrats (SPD) – At the time, Europe's largest political party and the biggest party in the Reichstag until 1932, the Social Democrats represented the interests of organised labour and were affiliated with the Free Trade Unions (ADGB). The Social Democrats were the key party in the foundation of the Weimar Republic and were successful in retaining working-class support throughout the period, though they seldom appealed beyond their base. Despite being the party most committed to the Republic, they rarely took on the burden of office after 1920, with many party figures seeing nothing to be gained from compromise in coalitions with bourgeois parties.

Democrats/State Party (DDP/DStP) – A middle-class liberal party founded by the pre-war Progressives. The Democrats were centrists who participated in most Weimar cabinets and were willing to work with the SPD on the left and, at a push, the DNVP on the right. In 1930, with their electoral fortunes fading, they merged with the nationalistic Young German Order and rebranded as the State Party in an unsuccessful attempt to distance themselves from the failing parliamentary system. Despite moving to the moderate right in subsequent years, the party's base collapsed in the early 1930s as middle-class voters deserted to the Nazi Party.

Centre Party (Z) – the party of Germany's Catholic minority, the Centre was a broad church representing all Catholic opinion from Christian democrats and trade unionists through to traditional social conservatives. As a result, it contained politicians both committed to the new democracy and ardent monarchists, making it an essential component of Weimar coalition governments. It was generally more conservative than centrist, especially in the latter years of the Republic under Brüning's leadership, more at ease working with the right than the SPD. Even as the Nazis reached their peak, the Centre managed to retain strong support among Catholic communities and a Nazi-Centre coalition government was touted for a time during 1932, highlighting how far the party had moved to the right.

People's Party (DVP) – The German People's Party developed out of the old National Liberal tradition, an ideology which combined a nationalistic worldview with liberal, laissez-faire economic policies that would benefit big business. Their links to the industrial elite rendered collaboration with the trade union-orientated SPD difficult and prevented them ever becoming a mass party. As monarchists, the DVP initially opposed the Republic, but leader Gustav Stresemann took a more pragmatic position over the course of the 1920s, seeing participation in government as the only way to protect right-wing interests. After his death in 1929, the party gradually adopted an authoritarian stance, opposing Weimar democracy.

Bavarian People's Party (BVP) – a conservative and reactionary Catholic party, the BVP was a Bavarian breakaway from the Centre Party. More right-wing and monarchist than the Centre, the party was opposed to interference from Berlin and even displayed separatist tendencies in the early 1920s. Similarly, Bavaria's branch of Angela Merkel's modern Christian Democratic Union operates independently as the more conservative Christian Social Union.

Nationalists (DNVP) – the largest party of the right before the rise of Hitler, the German National People's Party was a monarchist, conservative and nationalist organisation that, other than during a brief spell in the mid-1920s under Westarp, vehemently opposed the Republic. Collaboration in several coalition governments only brought electoral defeat and in 1928 the reactionary media magnate Alfred Hugenberg became leader and shifted the party dramatically rightwards. Under Hugenberg the anti-Semitic DNVP sought closer ties with Hitler and worked hard to bring unity to the far right in the form of the so-called National Opposition and the Harzburg Front.

National Socialist Freedom Party/Movement (VSB/NSFP/NSFB) – formed in 1924 by the merger of the Völkisch Freedom Party (DVFP, a far-right splinter of the DNVP) and the remnants of the Nazi Party, banned after the Beer Hall Putsch. The parties ran a joint ticket in the two federal elections of 1924 as first the Völkisch-Social Bloc (VSB), then the National Socialist Freedom Movement (NSFB) and achieved some success on the back of the Hitler trial. They were unified in their allegiance to Ludendorff and sat as the National Socialist Freedom Party (NSFP) in the Reichstag, but factional infighting soon destroyed any semblance of harmony. Despite the strident anti-Semitism of all concerned, by 1925 both the Nazi and Völkisch Freedom parties had been reconstituted.

National Socialists (NSDAP) – The Nazis were one of a plethora of far-right groups to emerge in Bavaria after the crushing of a short-lived Soviet regime in 1919. In the nationalist greenhouse that was Munich in the early 1920s, the Nazis grew to be the most powerful of the Bavarian völkisch groups, although up to 1925 their activities were often in collaboration with the rest of the far right. After being banned following their failed uprising in 1923, Hitler rebuilt the party from 1925 as an independent force, loyal solely to their Führer. Electoral success followed as the party gained prominence as part of the National Opposition and as Nazi propaganda, offering simple solutions to the Republic's growing problems, increasingly cut through from 1929.

Other Political Parties of the Right

Conservative People's Party (KVP) – a moderate right group led by Westarp and Treviranus that broke away from the DNVP once Hugenberg moved the Nationalists into intransigent opposition to democracy in the late 1920s. Although insignificant electorally, Hindenburg was sympathetic to their standpoint and they therefore played a role in his presidential cabinets.

Christian Social People's Mission (CSVD) – a conservative party that broke away from the DNVP in 1929 in response to Hugenberg's radical nationalism. It attempted to become a Protestant version of the Catholic Centre Party and was loyal to Hindenburg and Brüning.

Christian-Nationalist Peasants and Farmers' Party (CNBL) – agrarian party founded by smallholders who walked out of the DNVP in 1928 over the latter's preference for the interests of large estate owners. Ran in the 1930 election on a joint ticket with the moderate conservative KVP but moved further to the right after this, breaking from the pro-Hindenburg parties to join the National Opposition in 1932.

Economic Party/Reich Party of the Middle Class (WP) – special interest party representing small business owners. On the moderate right of the political spectrum, the WP initially participated in the Brüning government but soon switched to a policy of toleration. The grassroots favoured joining the National Opposition, but the party leadership continued to support Hindenburg's presidential government.

Reich Rural League (RLB) – right-wing pressure group representing landowners and farmers that also ran candidates in Reichstag elections. The Rural League was closely aligned with the DNVP until 1928, after which, under the leadership of Martin Schiele, the League adopted a more moderate stance to Hugenberg. However, Schiele was forced out in October 1930 and the League sided with the National Opposition, joining the Harzburg Front the following year.

Coalitions and Alliances

Weimar Coalition – refers to the three parties who founded and were most committed to the Weimar Republic (at least until 1930), namely the Social Democrats, Democrats and Centre. These three parties combined won a majority in the 1919 elections to the National Assembly and therefore were able to nominate the Republic's first president (Ebert) and write its constitution. The wax and wane of the vote share attained by these parties roughly indicates the level of support for democracy.

Bürgerblock – literally Bourgeois Bloc, this expression refers to the coalition governments of Chancellors Hans Luther (1925) and Wilhelm Marx (1927–28), which consisted of all the middle-class parties of the right and centre-right, namely the DNVP, DVP, BVP and Catholic Centre, and in the case of the Luther government, the DDP. Participation in the *Bürgerblock* cost the DNVP votes and seats in the 1928 election and resulted in Alfred Hugenberg seizing control of the party and taking it in a more anti-democratic direction.

Hindenburg Bloc – a term used in this volume to describe the collection of moderate right parties that supported the presidential government Henrich Brüning led in 1930–32, which relied on the authority of President Hindenburg rather than the approval of the Reichstag. The parties that participated in and supported this presidential administration were the Centre, BVP, DVP, KVP, DStP, CNBL, CSVD and WP. The increasingly right-wing DVP left the Brüning government in 1931 and moved into the National Opposition, but supported Hindenburg's re-election in 1932. The SPD carried out a policy of parliamentary toleration towards Brüning's presidential government, viewing it as a bulwark against Nazism.

National Opposition – a term used to describe the right and far-right nationalist parties unequivocally opposed to the Weimar Republic. After taking over the DNVP in 1928, Alfred Hugenberg sought greater unity among the anti-democratic right and used the phrase National Opposition to describe this loose alliance, which was first brought together in the Young Plan Referendum and included Hitler's Nazis, the Stahlhelm and Pan-German League.

Harzburg Front – a development of the National Opposition, the Harzburg Front was a more formal alliance of the far right, made up of the DNVP, NSDAP, Stahlhelm, Pan-German League and Reich Rural League. The aim of the Front, founded in Bad Harzburg in October 1931, was to present President Hindenburg with a unified nationalist coalition who could be trusted to assume office and attract other parties such as the DVP to the anti-democratic banner. In reality, Hindenburg's concerns about nationalist disunity proved accurate, as the presidential elections of March 1932 shattered this fragile coalition.

Note: When the terms Nationalist or Democrat are capitalised in this volume, it is referring specifically to the political parties denoted by these terms, namely the DNVP and DDP respectively. On the other hand, terms such as nationalist or democratic that are not capitalised refer to wider ideologies, movements or political positions. Additionally, the names of political parties are translated into English but paramilitary groups retain their German titles as many translate poorly.

Cast of Characters

Colonel Max Bauer (born 31 January 1869)
Staff officer in German High Command during the First World War, the main mind behind the 'Hindenburg Programme' industrial plan and Ludendorff's chief political fixer, with links to the far right. Participated in Kapp Putsch.

Otto Braun (born 28 January 1872)
The 'strongman' of social democracy, Braun was prime minister of Prussia, Germany's largest state, for virtually the entire Weimar period at the head of an SPD-Centre-DDP coalition. Social Democratic candidate for the presidency in the first round of the 1925 election. One of the few 'Marxists' that Hindenburg respected personally.

Heinrich Brüning (born 26 November 1885)
Catholic conservative of the Centre Party who won the Iron Cross as a machine gun commander in the Great War. Entered the Reichstag in 1924 and gained reputation for financial expertise. Made chancellor at the head of the 'Hindenburg Cabinet' in March 1930, serving until his relationship with the president collapsed in May 1932, having been dubbed the 'hunger chancellor' for his austerity policies.

Lieutenant Colonel Theodor Duesterberg (born 19 October 1875)
Professional soldier. After his military career, he became involved in nationalist politics, becoming deputy leader of the right-wing veterans' association Der Stahlhelm. Candidate for the DNVP and Stahlhelm in the 1932 presidential election.

Friedrich Ebert (born 4 February 1871)
Tailor's son and leading Social Democrat, Reich chancellor November 1918 to Febrary 1919, Reich President 1919 to 1925. A political moderate of the centre-left, he sought to rein in the German Revolution through cooperation with the army and Freikorps.

Captain Hermann Ehrhardt (born 29 November 1881)
Torpedo boat commander in the Great War, founder of an infamous Freikorps formation, the Marine Brigade, and played a leading role in the Kapp Putsch. Fleeing to Bavaria, his Organisation Consul undertook a campaign of domestic terrorism in the early 1920s.

Cast of Characters xxi

Albrecht von Graefe (born 1 January 1868)
Nationalist politician who broke with the DNVP in 1922 to found the DVFP, a far-right völkisch party that aligned itself with the Nazis. Participated in the Beer Hall Putsch, and during Hitler's time in prison, strived for a merger between the DVFP and Nazi Party, helping to create the NSFB.

General Wilhelm Groener (born 22 November 1867)
Brilliant staff officer succeeded Erich Ludendorff as First Quartermaster General at OHL in October 1918. Hindenburg leaned on him heavily in the abdication of the Kaiser and signing of Versailles. Concluded a famous pact with the first republican chancellor, Friedrich Ebert, putting the army at the government's disposal. In 1928, Hindenburg ensured his appointment as defence minister, a post he held until 1932, as well as interior minister from October 1931 to May 1932. Mentor of Kurt von Schleicher.

General Kurt von Hammerstein-Equord (born 26 September 1878)
Close ally of Schleicher, who used his influence to promote Hammerstein to first head of the Troop Office (1929–30), then Chief of the Army Command (1930–33). Suspicious of the Nazis.

Adolf Hitler (born 20 April 1889)
Austrian son of a customs official, Hitler moved to Munich in his twenties and joined the German Army in 1914, being promoted once to the rank of lance corporal (Gefreiter) and winning the Iron Cross in four years of service. After the war, the army asked him to observe the German Workers' Party (DAP), a small nationalist faction in Munich, and he swiftly rose to be leader of the rebranded NSDAP.

Alfred Hugenberg (born 19 June 1865)
Successful businessman and Germany's leading media magnate. Held extreme nationalist and anti-democratic views and used his influence to become chairman of the DNVP in 1928. He took the party away from compromise with the system and into collaboration with the far right, chiefly the Nazis, in the 1929 Young Plan referendum and 1931 Harzburg Front rally. Became minister of economics and agriculture in the 1933 Hitler cabinet.

Gustav Ritter von Kahr (born 29 November 1862)
Civil servant and monarchist, installed as prime minister of Bavaria (1920–21) by nationalists in the wake of the Kapp Putsch, later appointed State Commissioner General of Bavaria with dictatorial powers, September 1923 to February 1924. Formed a power triumvirate during this period with General von Lossow and Colonel von Seisser.

Wolfgang Kapp (born 24 July 1858)
Experienced civil servant in the Second Reich and founder of the wartime far-right Fatherland Party. Became involved in Ludendorff's National Association and was briefly chancellor during the abortive Kapp Putsch.

Dr Mathilde von Kemnitz (born 4 October 1877)
An eccentric physician and psychiatrist, Kemnitz was a significant political and philosophical influence on Ludendorff after 1923 and in particular turned him against Christianity in favour of a neo-Pagan faith. Ludendorff divorced his wife to marry Kemnitz in 1926, after which the pair worked together on their conspiracy theories, cultivating an esoteric circle of followers.

Lieutenant Colonel Hermann Kriebel (born 20 January 1876)
Retired officer, served in the Freikorps and as chief of staff of the Bavarian Civil Guard, later military leader of the Kampfbund and prominent in the Beer Hall Putsch.

General Otto Ritter von Lossow (born 15 January 1868)
German military attaché to the Ottoman Empire in the First World War, senior Reichswehr officer after the war, commander of Wehrkreis VII, the military region of Bavaria, January 1923 to March 1924. Formed a power triumvirate in Bavaria with Commissioner General von Kahr and Colonel von Seisser.

Hans Luther (born 10 March 1879)
Technocrat who served as chancellor 1925–26 at the head of two centre-right coalitions, later appointed head of the Reichsbank by Hindenburg.

General Walther von Lüttwitz (born 2 February 1859)
Senior Reichswehr officer and Freikorps leader with far-right sympathies, became involved with the plotting around Ludendorff in 1919 and triggered the Kapp Putsch in 1920 by organising a march on Berlin.

Wilhelm Marx (born 15 January 1863)
Dour lawyer and moderate politician of the Catholic Centre Party, he served as chancellor 1923–25, was first the Centre, then the People's Bloc candidate for president in the 1925 election, and after defeat to Hindenburg, served as chancellor again 1926–28.

Otto Meissner (born 13 March 1880)
Served as State Secretary of the Presidential Office 1920–45, making him the leading civil servant in the Presidential Palace and the right-hand man of Ebert and Hindenburg, often representing the head of state in cabinet meetings.

Hermann Müller (born 18 May 1876)
Senior Social Democrat and foreign minister 1919–20, Müller was chancellor of the Grand Coalition 1928–30, breaking with his own party on a number of issues to ensure the survival of the cabinet.

Gustav Noske (born 9 July 1868)
First defence minister of the Weimar Republic, self-proclaimed 'bloodhound' of the revolution, his use of Freikorps formations made him a controversial figure. The Kapp Putsch undermined his position and forced him to resign.

Franz von Papen (born 29 October 1879)
Catholic aristocrat and former staff officer who had been military attaché in the United States during the war. Kicked out of the Centre Party for replacing Brüning as chancellor, served as the head of the cabinet of barons May to December 1932. Struck up a personal friendship with Hindenburg and returned as vice chancellor of the Hitler cabinet.

Ernst Pöhner (born 11 January 1870)
District judge and prisoner governor with links to the Pan-German League and Thule Society. Munich chief of police 1919–21, during which time he sheltered far-right groups such as Organisation Consul. Fell into Nazi orbit and participated in the Beer Hall Putsch.

Captain Ernst Röhm (born 28 November 1887)
Great War veteran, Freikorps organiser and Reichswehr staff officer in Bavaria until September 1923. Röhm aided various right-wing paramilitary groups, was an early supporter of Hitler and led the Reichskriegsflagge militia in the Beer Hall Putsch. Reichstag deputy for the NSFB in 1924 but split with Hitler 1925. Returned to Nazi fold in 1930, chief of staff of the SA 1931–34.

Max Erwin von Scheubner-Richter (born 21 January 1884)
Baltic German and Great War veteran, early adherent to Nazi Party with good connections on the far right, including with General Ludendorff and White Russians.

Martin Schiele (born 17 January 1870)
Agrarian, Nationalist politician and chair of the Reich Rural League, 1928–31. A Hindenburg favourite, he pioneered DNVP coalition participation, serving as interior minister January to October 1925 and agriculture minister January 1927 to June 1928. Hindenburg ensured his appointment as minister of agriculture again in March 1930 to oversee Eastern Aid and he soon after left the DNVP for the Christian-Nationalist Farmers' and Peasants' Party (CNBL).

General Kurt von Schleicher (born 7 April 1882)
Rose through the ranks of the German General Staff thanks to the patronage of Wilhelm Groener, becoming army liaison with the government in 1919. Grew in influence through the 1920s as a 'political general', especially after the appointment of Groener as defence minister, who promoted him to major general and made him head of the Office for Ministerial Affairs. From 1929 to 1932 he was the most influential member of Hindenburg's inner circle, becoming defence minister himself in June 1932 and then chancellor in December that year.

General Hans von Seeckt (born 22 April 1866)
Chief of staff to Mackensen during the Great War, became head of the Troop Office in 1919 and then Chief of the Army Command in 1920. Worked to turn the army into an independent force within the Weimar state and famously refused to allow the army to intervene in the Kapp Putsch.

Colonel Hans Ritter von Seisser (born 9 December 1874)
Army staff officer, made chief of Bavarian Police October 1919 and built up the state police as a powerful armed force. Formed a power triumvirate in Bavaria with Commissioner General von Kahr and General von Lossow.

Gregor Strasser (born 31 May 1892)
Bavarian soldier, Freikorps fighter and early adherent to the NSDAP. Rose quickly due to his organisational abilities. Allied himself with Ludendorff and Graefe during 1924, becoming part of the leadership triumvirate of the National Socialist Freedom Movement (NSFB). Reconciled with Hitler in spring 1925 and eventually became Reich organisation leader for the Nazis, heading up the party machine. Differed sharply with Hitler over strategy in the crucial year of 1932.

Gustav Stresemann (born 10 May 1878)
Leader of the DVP, chancellor during the height of the hyperinflation crisis and Beer Hall Putsch, August to November 1923, then foreign minister until his death in October 1929. Pursued a controversial policy of fulfilment, i.e., fulfilling the terms of the Treaty of Versailles but negotiating for improvements with the Allied powers.

Gottfried Treviranus (born 20 March 1891)
Youthful conservative politician, friend and confidant of Heinrich Brüning. Led a defection of moderates from the DNVP in 1929 and allied with Westarp in 1930 to form the Conservative People's Party (KVP). Held various ministerial posts in the 'Hindenburg Cabinet'.

Friedrich Weber (born 30 January 1892)
Great War veteran and lecturer in veterinary medicine, served in the Oberland Freikorps and eventually led its paramilitary successor, Bund Oberland, which formed a component of the Kampfbund and participated in the Beer Hall Putsch, during which he was earmarked to serve as Bavarian prime minister.

Count Kuno von Westarp (born 12 August 1864)
Right-wing civil servant and politician who Hindenburg respected. Parliamentary leader of the Conservative Party in the Second Reich, then led its successor, the Nationalist DNVP, in the Weimar Republic. In the mid-1920s moved the DNVP away from hostility to the system but was then deposed as party chairman by Hugenberg. Eventually split with the DNVP in 1930 to join Treviranus and form the KVP. Ally of Brüning and key figure in the 1932 Hindenburg campaign team.

Prologue

The Double Act: The Emergence of Hindenburg and Ludendorff

A strong case can be made that few men had as great an impact on European twentieth-century history as Paul von Hindenburg and Erich Ludendorff, Germany's First World War leaders. Their dynamic partnership resurrected their military careers from retirement and obscurity respectively, to the supreme command and the assumption of near-dictatorial authority in the Kaiserreich during the Great War. Defeat in 1918 brought an end to their 'silent dictatorship', yet each was to play a decisive role in the turbulent politics of the new Weimar Republic.

A common depiction of these generals in the English-speaking world is of guardians of the old order – competent and conservative, honourable soldiers who served their country well. Essentially, they are viewed as 'Good Germans', and indeed this was literally the phrase used by Norman Stone in his portrait of Hindenburg in the 1976 compendium *The War Lords*.[1] The reality is quite different, for both Hindenburg and Ludendorff, in markedly diverse ways, were intensely political men, whose ideas and beliefs would shape the new Germany and ultimately lead to the Nazi dictatorship. In English-language history, their pivotal role in the Weimar era has often been overlooked. Their poisonous wartime legacy was the infamous 'Stab-in-the-Back' myth. According to the generals, the true cause of the disastrous defeat in the Great War was the betrayal of the army by politicians, leftists and Jews on the home front. This toxic conspiracy theory polluted Weimar politics and has been labelled the beginning of 'the twisted road to Auschwitz'.[2]

Hindenburg and Ludendorff's political fortunes contrasted starkly. Ludendorff inhabited the far-right fringes and engaged in plots, assassinations and conspiracies, playing a leading role in failed uprisings such as Hitler's 1923 Beer Hall Putsch. Meanwhile, Hindenburg, residing in the mainstream nationalist right, was a vastly more successful politician, winning two presidential elections and serving as head of state for nine years. Arguably he bore even more responsibility for the destruction of democracy for he, and the political faction he led, sought, through Hitler, to remould the Weimar system towards authoritarianism.

The popular image of Hindenburg in Britain and the US, such as it exists, could be epitomised by his portrayal by Peter O'Toole in the 2003 docu-drama

Hitler: The Rise of Evil. O'Toole plays a benevolent old man doing his best to prevent Nazi takeover and living to regret the beast he unleashes. In the same drama, Ludendorff makes a brief appearance at the Beer Hall Putsch, portrayed as a bumbling fool, although there is at least a nod to his attempt to bring the far right under his own control while Hitler was imprisoned. The 2019 BBC documentary series *Rise of the Nazis* repeated the familiar trope of a 'good' Hindenburg manipulated by those around him, with the talking head selected to discuss the field marshal being former British army general Mike Jackson rather than an historian. Needless to say, Jackson's picture of Hindenburg was sympathetic; a noble military man doing his best in confusing political circumstances, longing for the certainties of army life.

Ludendorff meanwhile is almost invisible in popular history. His appearance at the Beer Hall Putsch often gets a mention, but usually totally devoid of the context that the general was arguably the leading figure on the far right of German politics at the time. The 2017 Netflix documentary *Hitler's Circle of Evil* asserts that Ludendorff was recruited by Hitler during the final preparations for the Beer Hall Putsch as a convenient figurehead, ignoring the fact that the general and Hitler had been building a united far-right movement together for months. Ludendorff's name is also often omitted from accounts of the Kapp Putsch, despite him being a leading light behind the 1920 coup, with such classic histories as Evans's *The Coming of the Third Reich* and Weitz's *Weimar Germany* failing to mention his involvement.[3] A 2015 school textbook the author has used even claimed that Ludendorff had refused to join the Kapp Putsch, contributing to its collapse![4] Ludendorff's portrayal as an evil genius determined to continue the war at all costs in the recent *Wonder Woman* film (2017), while mildly entertaining, likely did little to enlighten the general public as to the true nature of this forgotten figure.

It goes without saying that professional historians have long been aware of the political impact the two men had, although such views rarely make it onto the shelves of high street bookshops or Amazon bestseller lists. Notable exceptions include Ian Kershaw's brilliant biography of Hitler and David King's account of the Beer Hall Putsch and subsequent trial, both of which show Ludendorff as the significant political actor he was in the early 1920s.[5] There have been many excellent studies of Hindenburg, not least Wolfram Pyta's unsurpassed biography (which sadly has not yet been translated into English) and Anna van der Goltz's PhD thesis on the Hindenburg myth, which was published as *Hindenburg: Power, Myth and the Rise of the Nazis*. Why then do these two figures, essential to understanding interwar German history, continue to be overlooked or mischaracterised? The answer could well lie in the lack of good biographies in English, especially ones addressing the generals' respective political careers.

On Field Marshal von Hindenburg, there are two reasonable political biographies that are sadly long out of print and naturally, given their publication date, now rather dated – John Wheeler-Bennett's 1936 *The Wooden Titan* and Andreas Dorpalen's 1964 *Hindenburg and the Weimar Republic*. William J. Astore and Dennis E. Showalter wrote a fine pocket biography of Hindenburg in 2005, but with the book extending only to a little over 100 pages, the treatment of his political career is necessarily brief, if incisive.[6] Ludendorff is unfortunately even less well served, with the three English-language biographies of the general all being rather unsatisfactory and providing scant coverage of his political adventures. Goodspeed's *Ludendorff: Genius of World War I* (1966) and Parkinson's *Tormented Warrior* (1978) are both out of print and, as their titles suggest, somewhat sympathetic, with Ludendorff's post-war politics receiving fleeting attention and being portrayed as an aberration. More recently, a Ukrainian businessman, Alex Rovt, wrote (apparently with the help of Will and Denise Drace Brownell) *The First Nazi: Erich Ludendorff, The Man Who Made Hitler Possible* (2016). While the title may sound promising for those looking for a political history of the man, *The First Nazi* is a travesty of a book which provides virtually no information on Ludendorff's political career and even gets the date of the Beer Hall Putsch wrong, never mind failing to detail Ludendorff's decisive role in it. As one reviewer put it, Wikipedia provides better accuracy than this book and the authors requested that *The First Nazi* be withdrawn from sale in North America.[7] The deficiency in English-language scholarship on Ludendorff has only begun to be addressed in 2021 with the publication of Jay Lockenour's *Dragonslayer*, a fine study of the general and his legend after 1918.

The aim of the present volume is to drag Paul von Hindenburg and Erich Ludendorff out of the shadows and place them centre stage. The story of the failure of Weimar democracy and the rise of the Nazis is a familiar one, but the essential role Hindenburg and Ludendorff played in first destabilising the Republic and then bringing Hitler to power has for too long been obscure. The author hopes he has succeeded in synthesising the brilliant scholarship of the likes of Larry Eugene Jones, Anna van der Goltz, Roger Chickering, Wolfram Pyta, William Patch, Harold Gordon and many others in bringing the arguments and conclusions of these academics to a wider audience, thereby going some way to correct the popular perception of two of twentieth-century history's most significant figures.

Contrasting backgrounds

Paul Ludwig Hans Anton von Beneckendorff und von Hindenburg was as aristocratic as his name suggested. Born in 1847 into an ancient family of the Junker class of landowners, Hindenburg was very much a product of the nineteenth-century Prussian nobility. Able to trace his descendants back to the thirteenth century, Hindenburg, or Beneckendorff, as was his given surname at that time, was staunchly conservative and sincerely religious, in an understated Lutheran way. Aged 11 he was already at cadet school and after a spell at the Prussian court in his teenage years, he was commissioned as a lieutenant at the age of 18 in the Third Regiment of Foot Guards.[8] The 1860s was a decade of war and conquest for Prussia as Bismarck undertook German unification by force of arms, and Beneckendorff fought bravely in the Austro-Prussian War of 1866 and the Franco-Prussian War of 1870–71, being decorated for his leadership under fire. He was present in the Versailles Palace's Hall of Mirrors when, after victory over the French, the Prussian king was crowned Kaiser Wilhelm I of Germany.

Standing over 6 feet tall, with broad shoulders, a square jaw and blue eyes, it was little wonder that the young von Beneckendorff caught the eye. Far from being the slow-witted figure he was later portrayed as, Beneckendorff won entry by exams to the War Academy in Berlin and after three years of study his grades earnt him a posting with the Great General Staff, the famous institution that had made Prussia, and now Germany, the dominant military power on the Continent. He then quickly rose through the ranks, performing well in both command postings and in General Staff roles and eventually teaching at the academy for five years. He reached the rank of major general in 1897 and commanded first a division, then a corps over the next decade. In 1909, Albert von Schlieffen, under whom he had served in the 1880s, recommended him as the next Chief of the General Staff, the most senior position in the army, but he was passed over. In 1911, after a 46-year army career, Lieutenant General von Beneckendorff und von Hindenburg quietly retired to Hanover, aged 63. He had been a successful if unremarkable officer, but, as he put it, it was now time to make way for younger men.[9]

Although, like Hindenburg, Erich Friedrich Wilhelm Ludendorff was from Posen in eastern Prussia, he had a considerably less prestigious background than his wartime partner and was a generation younger, born in 1865. Ludendorff was in many ways a contrasting character to Hindenburg – he lacked his chief's composure and self-confidence but was single-minded, extremely hard-working and ambitious. He also lacked a martial tradition in his family, having a merchant father and a mother from a bankrupt aristocratic family. At 12, the young Ludendorff, who had shown considerable promise at school, was shipped off to a cadet school, where he once again impressed, although throughout his childhood he was reportedly a loner.

Success at a military academy brought his first commission in 1885 and after eight years as a junior officer he was accepted for the War Academy, as Hindenburg had been. His industrious mind marked him out as a staff officer and finally, in 1904, he was posted to the Great General Staff in Berlin. Ludendorff became an increasingly influential figure in the General Staff, drawing up the plans for German war mobilisation and pushing for greater preparations for a future conflict, most notably through expanding the army.[10] His agitation, however, was to be his undoing. Frustrated by the Reichstag's 1911 rejection of army expansion plans, Ludendorff, by now a colonel, reached out to retired officers and the far-right Pan-German League in an attempt to create a network to pressure politicians into granting the army its wishes. For this breach of protocol Ludendorff was severely reprimanded and his choice of political allies revealed the political direction in which his militarist life had taken him.

Ludendorff continued his political medalling, the following year persuading his superior at the General Staff to bypass the minister of war and appeal directly to the chancellor and Kaiser for increased military spending. Playing politics proved to be Ludendorff's undoing, however, for the unhappy war minister ensured his removal from the Great General Staff in January 1913, and he was sent into semi-exile in the form of command of an infantry regiment in Düsseldorf. On the eve of war, he was promoted to major general but remained in infantry command rather than staff work, his career seemingly at a dead end before he had even turned 50.[11]

The Great War

There is a wealth of literature on Hindenburg and Ludendorff's conduct of the First World War, not least in that the conflict takes up the majority of the existing biographies on the two generals, but there are also specialist studies by the likes of Asprey, Kitchen, Lee and Watson. In order for us to understand the political careers of the two men, however, it is necessary to provide a cursory overview of their more famous exploits in the Great War. Von Beneckendorff und von Hindenburg was of course retired and so, although he contacted the army to inform them of his readiness to serve at the outbreak of war in summer 1914, he was initially uninvolved in the conflagration that was rapidly engulfing Europe. Ludendorff, on the other hand, was attached to Second Army, which was tasked with punching through Belgium and into France, the key element of the Schlieffen Plan to win the war in six weeks.

Here, the general won almost instant fame, for, under enemy fire for the first time in his life, he led an assault on the fortresses around the city of Liege and supposedly captured the citadel almost single-handedly by banging on the door with his sword hilt.

With the war literally days old, Ludendorff was quickly trumpeted as one of Germany's first war heroes and was awarded the Pour le Mérite, the highest military honour in the Kaiserreich.[12] All was not well on the Eastern Front, however, where the Russians had mobilised faster than expected and made tentative incursions into East Prussia, the heartland of the traditional Prussian landowning classes and therefore of particular symbolic importance. There is now evidence that the military situation in East Prussia was not quite as dire as it has often been reported but the commander of the defending forces, Eighth Army, had certainly lost his head and needed to be replaced.[13] The Supreme Command (OHL, the wartime iteration of the Great General Staff), therefore dispatched Ludendorff, fresh from his Liege triumph, to get a handle on the situation in the east. However, as a 'commoner', he was not suited to lead an army and would therefore be Eighth Army's chief of staff. Instead, Paul von Beneckendorff und von Hindenburg was the OHL's fateful choice as the new Eighth Army commander.

Meeting on a train platform on their way east, von Beneckendorff and Ludendorff soon struck up an understanding that would blossom into a highly effective working relationship.[14] Hindenburg would describe the relationship as like a 'happy marriage' in the sense that their personal characteristics complemented each other well; Hindenburg the delegator, man-manager and broad-shouldered frontman, Ludendorff the temperamental genius, who needed to be reined in and calmed down on occasion, but ultimately should be left to do what he does best without interference.[15] Upon taking up their post on 23 August 1914, Ludendorff, with the help of Lieutenant Colonel Max Hoffmann (who would become a long-term collaborator), rapidly drew up a daring plan to defeat in detail the two Russian armies advancing into German territory. Hindenburg served as the charismatic figurehead, whose cool, calm demeanour steadied the ship and when Ludendorff lost his nerve during the battle, Hindenburg's composure and reassuring words restored the confidence of his brilliant but unstable chief of staff.[16] The plan was a stunning success and by 31 August, the Russian Second Army had been encircled and almost completely destroyed, suffering 50,000 casualties, with a further 92,000 captured by the Germans. The Russian First Army only escaped the same fate with a rather panicked retreat.[17]

Showing an uncanny knack for public relations, von Beneckendorff now became von Hindenburg, a catchier name certainly, but one that also had links to the medieval Teutonic Knights that had battled the Slavs in Eastern Europe. He also may have named the battle he was fighting, calling it Tannenberg, after a famous 1410 battle in which the Teutonic Knights had been heroically crushed by Polish-Lithuanian forces.[18] Thus, this modern Tannenberg, the first major German victory of the war, could be sold by the press and propagandists as avenging the fallen knights, and the distinctive name of Hindenburg provided a direct connection to the past. For a nervous nation, desperate for positive news, this seemingly miraculous turnaround in the east was like manna from heaven. Hindenburg became a national hero overnight. His unmistakable image – square head, clipped hair, stern eyes, bold moustache – filled the newspapers and newsreels and Tannenberg would remain throughout the conflict the most famous and celebrated German victory.

While Ludendorff, to some extent, remained in the shadows, Hindenburg very quickly became an icon. During the course of 1915, wooden statues of the general appeared in most major cities and eager citizens made cash contributions to the war effort in return for an iron nail to hammer into him. The largest of these statues was erected in Berlin, stood 13 metres tall and was inaugurated by the Kaiser himself on 4 September 1915, with 20,000 nails sold and driven into the statue that same day.[19] These 'Iron Hindenburgs' were not the only way his image penetrated the public sphere; Hindenburg's face was soon seen on everything from war propaganda to matchboxes, from cigars to mouth organs, from china tea sets to ashtrays. His portrait was soon hanging in millions of homes.[20]

Historians Vascik and Sadler have noted that the emergence of Hindenburg as a hero of near-mythical status, the saviour of the nation who had delivered Germany from the peril of Russian incursion, is one of the strangest phenomena of the war. Effectively, with Kaiser Wilhelm II being an inadequate war leader, both due to his physical defects and his divisive personality, Hindenburg became a surrogate symbol for the nation to unite behind – a symbol of German militarism yes, but also of duty, honour and quiet, steadfast determination.[21] The story of his returning from retirement to serve his country in its hour of need only added to the romanticism and reinforced the reassuring perception that the conflict was a defensive war. For the rest of his life, he would bear the moniker 'the Victor of Tannenberg', and remarkably quickly, his name and image would become a ubiquitous feature of German life and remain so for the next twenty years. Nothing less than a cult of personality was established around Hindenburg in the war's opening months, a development in which he was certainly not passive.

Such hero worship would not have been so enduring were it not for the fact that in 1914 and 1915, Hindenburg and Ludendorff built on the success at Tannenberg and achieved a series of impressive victories over the Russians, forcing them out of what would become Poland and driving into European Russia. In many ways, the duo were fortunate to be posted to the east, as the vast expanses of the Steppe allowed them to win manoeuvre battles in a way that simply was not possible on the stalemated Western Front. Now the politicking began. Increasingly, the two generals used their growing power and influence as the country's leading war heroes to put pressure on both their military superiors and the Kaiser to divert more resources to the war in the east. Petty squabbling over troop allocations developed into full-blown intrigue as Hindenburg and Ludendorff in particular sought to remove Erich von Falkenhayn, the Chief of the General Staff since autumn 1914, and a convinced 'westerner' – i.e. an advocate of focusing on the Western Front over the east.[22]

The year 1916 would prove to be one of crisis for Germany and her ally Austria-Hungary as Falkenhayn's offensive at Verdun descended into a prolonged bloodbath and simultaneous Entente offensives at the Somme in France, the Isonzo in Italy and the Russian Brusilov Offensive in Galicia stretched their resources to breaking point. This was Hindenburg and Ludendorff's great opportunity. In August, they got their wish. Having undermined the Kaiser's confidence in Falkenhayn, they were put in charge of OHL, Hindenburg (now a field marshal) was Chief of the General Staff, Ludendorff's post was created for him – First Quartermaster General, although he effectively remained Hindenburg's chief of staff and the mastermind behind their schemes.[23] Now that they were in supreme command, the duo set about altering Germany's war policy in a more radical and ruthless direction, and over the coming months OHL was to acquire so much power that Hindenburg and Ludendorff became de facto military dictators. In the west, the scale of casualties at the Somme and Verdun necessitated a strategic withdrawal, and they therefore oversaw the construction of the mighty Siegfried Line (known in English as the Hindenburg Line), a huge network of fixed defences, concrete fortifications and seas of barbed wire that was to preserve lives and serve as an 'insurance policy'.[24] At home, efforts to mobilise the economy for war were redoubled with the so-called Hindenburg Programme and control over the vital aspects of the economy passed to OHL, which increasingly used forced labour and prisoners of war to try to increase production.[25]

War propagandists made even greater usage of Hindenburg's reputation now he was directing the war effort. A Hindenburg museum was opened, massive public celebrations accompanied his seventieth birthday in October 1917 and the Reichsbank's seventh war loan centred its appeal on the field marshal, the posters featuring simply his distinctive head with the slogan 'Those who subscribe to the war loan give me my most beautiful birthday present.'[26] Political domination soon came too. Hindenburg and Ludendorff used the power of the threat of their resignation to compel politicians and even the Kaiser to bend to their will, for to lose the legendary Hindenburg would surely imperil civilian morale. In particular, they strongarmed the deeply reluctant chancellor, Bethmann-Hollweg, into accepting unrestricted submarine warfare (the sinking of all ships destined for Entente ports, including those from neutral nations), a policy that was to prove calamitous. As a result of his resistance to OHL's wishes, Hindenburg and Ludendorff intrigued throughout the spring and summer of 1917 for the chancellor's sacking, which they eventually secured, and thereafter the situation became one where the chancellor had to enjoy the confidence of the military, rather than the Kaiser, to remain in post.[27] As a result, a series of weak chancellors who were little more than puppets for the Supreme Command came and went and ever more power was concentrated in OHL's hands. Not satisfied to merely dominate high politics, the duo also sought to influence the Reichstag, which that same year had passed a resolution calling for peace without annexations – effectively a return to 1914 borders. In response, Ludendorff and his political fixer Colonel Max Bauer helped establish the Fatherland Party, a far-right nationalist organisation that parroted OHL policy in parliament, in particular regarding war aims.[28] Meanwhile, the victory that Hindenburg and Ludendorff had longed for in the east arrived in 1917 thanks to the Russian Revolution.

Ludendorff himself, in a remarkably offhand decision earlier in the year, had organised for Vladimir Lenin to be secretly smuggled from his exile in Switzerland to Russia. The October Revolution had seen Lenin's Bolsheviks seize power and a ceasefire descend on the Eastern Front. In subsequent peace negotiations, Hindenburg and Ludendorff's war aims became clear. They sought nothing less than German domination over the Continent, not just through extensive annexations in east and west, but also through the economic subjection of Europe to German control in a scheme known as Mitteleuropa.[29] In the face of opposition from the Foreign Ministry, the OHL demanded huge swathes of territory and the establishment of German puppet states over much of Eastern Europe. When asked why Germany needed control over the Baltic States, Hindenburg replied simply, 'I need them for the manoeuvring of my left wing in the next war.'[30] This comment reveals an extreme militarist, almost proto-fascist, culture at OHL in which war is not a means to an end, but an end in itself. Perhaps also it was a tacit admission from Hindenburg that the terms of Brest-Litovsk were so harsh that they would inevitably cause a new conflict with Russia in the future. If Hindenburg truly believed this, his approval of the treaty and Germany's maximalist war aims was both illogical and morally reprehensible. The final terms of the Brest-Litovsk treaty were eyewatering: Russia was to lose more than a third of its population, more than half its industry and almost 90 per cent of its coal reserves, all ceded to the Central Powers.[31] Brest-Litovsk was an act of extreme hubris, for while OHL could move around a million men to the west for an all-out offensive in the new year, many hundreds of thousands of troops had to remain in the east, pursuing the generals' imperialist fantasies by garrisoning vast expanses of hostile, revolutionary territory and forcibly extracting material resources.[32] Even when Germany was on her knees in the west in autumn 1918, huge forces would remain tied down in the east thanks to OHL's territorial greed and imperialist dreams of Lebensraum (living space) for the German people in the vast expanses of Eastern Europe.

Rather than opting for the very real possibility of securing peace in the west with the exhausted and demoralised Allies in the winter of 1917/18, OHL, and particularly Ludendorff, insisted on going for broke – either total victory or total defeat would be the result.[33] With the entry of the United States into the war (thanks to OHL's disastrous decision to pursue unrestricted submarine warfare), Ludendorff realised Germany was in a race against time of her own making. He hoped to knock France out of the war and push Britain out of continental Europe before US manpower and material resources tipped the scales irreversibly in the Allies' favour. Hence, OHL now planned an all-out offensive in the west for spring 1918. It was sold to the troops as the Kaiserschlacht (Kaiser's Battle) or peace offensives, the final effort required to secure German victory. Beginning on 21 March 1918 with Operation Michael, the Germans at first achieved a remarkable breakthrough, thanks to a massive concentration of troops and artillery, as well as innovative stormtrooper infiltration tactics. However, Michael lacked any objective whatsoever – it was simply a diversionary push to draw Allied reserves away from Flanders, where Ludendorff wanted to launch his main offensive. The troops were therefore simply to advance, with no target in mind, and too late OHL realised they could have pushed for the vital rail junction at Amiens. Additionally, the German Army lacked any weapon of exploitation; with all their cavalry policing the eastern conquests, the Spring Offensive would advance at the pace of the infantryman. Although Michael gained a stunning amount of territory and had had the Allies in disarray for a time, German forces suffered such heavy casualties that the follow-up push in Flanders had to be downscaled, from Operation George to Georgette.[34]

Ludendorff continued to hammer away at the Allies in April, May and June, but he never came close to his true objective of capturing the Channel ports in order to force a British evacuation and each new attack soon became an exercise in diminishing returns, despite German forces getting dangerously close to Paris. The final stage of the Spring Offensive was actually launched in mid-July on the Marne River, but just three days into the attack, the Germans were stunned by a major Allied counter-attack spearheaded by hundreds of tanks that sent their forces reeling. It was now evident that the Allies could not be knocked out of the war and, having raised expectations among the troops that this would be the decisive moment, Hindenburg and Ludendorff soon realised that army morale was melting away. The failure of this 'last push' to win the war had a devastating effect on the fighting spirit of the German Army, not to mention the material damage done by the roughly 1 million casualties they had sustained during the Spring Offensive.[35]

Far from being on their knees, the Allies now engaged in a series of massive mechanised offensives known as the Hundred Days, driving the Germans back from all the gains they had made, and indeed back to the battlefields of 1914 by the end of the war. The Battle of Amiens, on 8 August 1918, was labelled by Ludendorff as the 'black day' of the German Army and 'the worst experience I had to go through' as a British and Commonwealth assault near Amiens drove the depleted Germans back 8 miles in a single day.[36] Both Hindenburg and especially an increasingly dislocated Ludendorff had been seriously shaken by the surprise Marne counter-attack in July and by this stage, historian John Terraine argues, Ludendorff's nerve and judgement were 'seriously impaired'.[37] The 'Black Day' of Amiens was therefore a tipping point and OHL was particularly disturbed by reports of mass surrenders and frontline soldiers greeting their reinforcements with cheers of 'blacklegs' and 'war-prolongers'. Ludendorff therefore informed the government that an end to the war was needed urgently and offered his resignation.

At an Imperial Conference, held on 13–14 August, Ludendorff had to some extent regained his nerve, but Hindenburg was, as ever, calm and confident, insisting a defensive war could still be fought in order to extract good peace terms from a position of strength. In fact, both men were out of touch with army and civilian morale and military realities.[38] The First Quartermaster General's mental health was failing at this point as he approached what was likely at the very least to be a nervous breakdown; he had been becoming increasingly prone to fits of rage and dramatic mood swings. In mid-August, members of the OHL staff had arranged for a psychiatrist, Dr Hochheimer, to come to the Supreme Headquarters and observe Ludendorff. He diagnosed him with 'overwork', which had damaged his 'drive and creative power'.[39] On 3 September, Hochheimer was asked to return as Ludendorff's condition worsened. He had a frank conversation with the general, and Ludendorff, whom Hochheimer found to be a virtual husk of a man, agreed to a programme of treatment that included breathing exercises, singing, moving to more pleasant quarters, taking walks in the nearby gardens and woodland, and overall adhering to a new and less strenuous daily routine, including taking more than his usual 1–5 hours sleep. Apparently, it worked, as a fellow officer noted some weeks later: 'Ludendorff is much quieter and friendlier on the telephone.'[40]

The military situation had only deteriorated, however. By September, German forces had been pushed back to the formidable Siegfried (Hindenburg) Line, which Ludendorff had ordered in 1916–17 as an 'insurance policy'. On 26 September, the Allies launched their 'Grand Offensive': four sequential operations to smash the Siegfried Line at different points, designed to put maximum pressure on the overstretched German forces. Within days it was clear that the Germans could not plug the multiple gaps emerging and that the insurance policy had failed. At this point, with certain defeat now looming, Ludendorff finally lost his nerve and cracked under the immense pressure, flying into another fit of rage as he realised the inevitable: that his life's work had come to ruin.

In what historian Roger Chickering calls a 'psychological catastrophe' for the general, he informed an emotional Hindenburg on the evening of 28 September that Germany had to seek an immediate armistice or face total military collapse.[41] OHL then shrewdly began shifting responsibility, advising the Kaiser to carry out democratising reforms and appoint a government based, for the first time, on the political parties in the Reichstag, both so that the democratic nations of the Allies might be inclined to provide more favourable peace terms, and so that the odious task of requesting an armistice be undertaken by a purely civilian and parliamentary government under the liberal Prince Max of Baden, appointed chancellor on 3 October. The Prince's 'peace note', sent under heavy pressure from OHL, to President Wilson of the United States on 4 October came as an immense shock to the German people, fed on a diet of relentlessly positive war propaganda.[42] By mid-October, however, it became clear that the ceasefire terms Wilson was offering would be highly unfavourable; in essence, the Allies wished to ensure their advantageous position would be maintained and any armistice could not simply be used by the Germans as a 'breathing space' to reorganise, dig in and resume the fight in a few months' time. Additionally, Wilson's condemnation of 'arbitrary power' in Germany effectively meant he regarded the Kaiser and OHL as a barrier to peace. Now, in an extraordinary volte-face, Ludendorff, with Hindenburg in tow, demanded that the civilian government reject the peace terms and fight on.[43] This was a totally unrealistic demand, as army morale had further been undermined by the announcement that the government was seeking a ceasefire and the civilian population was now expecting a swift end to the nightmare that they had endured for four years. Seeing their previously unassailable power melt away, on 24 October OHL issued an order to the troops (in Hindenburg's name, but almost certainly written by Ludendorff) condemning the negotiations and demanding the army fight on. The First Quartermaster General had gone too far this time, defying the Kaiser and the government, and seemingly seizing control of German foreign policy.[44]

In the subsequent power struggle, Prince Max used Hindenburg and Ludendorff's tactic of threatening resignation if he did not get his way. As a result, in an audience with the Kaiser on 26 October, in what he described as 'the bitterest moments of my life', Ludendorff was sacked – he had once again threatened to resign but on this occasion, the Kaiser called his bluff and accepted his resignation.[45] Hindenburg's offer of resignation was rejected – by now the Hindenburg myth was too vital a national asset to lose. The 'happy marriage' was at an end.

The new Germany

Defeat remained imminent and the masses longed for peace. Although Ludendorff's sacking had been warmly received, the Kaiser, thanks to Wilson's peace notes, was now seen as a barrier to peace and popular pressure for his abdication began to grow. Mutiny broke out in the Imperial Navy when vainglorious officers attempted to take the fleet out in a suicidal confrontation with the British in order to go down fighting. By early November, revolutionary sailors had seized control of the port of Kiel and the uprising began to spread like wildfire. Although the vast majority of Germany's would-be revolutionaries merely wanted peace and the departure of the Kaiser, the establishment of Workers' and Soldiers' councils across the major cities gave the revolution the appearance of a Bolshevik takeover.[46]

On 9 November 1918, bowing to the inevitable, Prince Max announced the abdication of the Kaiser and resigned as chancellor, handing over control of the Reich to a 47-year-old former saddler, trade unionist and leader of the Social Democratic Party (SPD), Friedrich Ebert. At the same time, the Kaiser was at the OHL headquarters in Spa, Belgium, hoping to lead his army home and crush the rebels who had dethroned him. It was the responsibility of his generals to dispel any illusions that such a scheme had any hope of success. Wilhelm II addressed Hindenburg directly, asking whether it would be possible to reconquer his kingdom, but the field marshal choked and could not speak. It fell to Ludendorff's replacement as First Quartermaster General, Wilhelm Groener, to explain the impossibility of such an undertaking; not only would the field army be cut off from supplies from the homeland, but the army itself could no longer be relied upon to fight for their Kaiser against the people. Failing to get through to the deluded emperor, Groener dramatically informed the Kaiser, 'Sire, you no longer have an army ... in circumstances like these, oaths are but words.'[47] Hindenburg finally broke his silence and half-heartedly backed his new partner. Later, he had to ask the Kaiser to leave OHL as he could no longer guarantee his safety. The events of 9 November and his perceived responsibility for his monarch's abdication and exile would haunt Hindenburg for the rest of his life.[48]

Meanwhile, the new chancellor in Berlin, Ebert, desperately tried to maintain control. Ebert was a decidedly moderate leftist, who hated revolution 'like sin' and would have preferred to retain the monarchy.[49] Unexpectedly carried to power by revolution, he set about attempting to restore order and establish a parliamentary democracy. The civilians, at Hindenburg's instance, signed the armistice offered by the Allies and it came into force on the morning of 11 November. With the war at a close, internal battles followed as the army, still under Hindenburg's command, defended Ebert's precarious regime from communist insurrection. Elections to a National Assembly were held in January 1919 and produced a coalition government of the three parties most committed to the new democratic order – Ebert's SPD, the Democrats (DDP) and the Centre, a Catholic confessional party.

With revolutionary violence in Berlin, the Assembly could not meet in the Reichstag building and instead convened during the Republic's early months in the quiet town of Weimar in central Germany, leading to the christening of the new regime as the Weimar Republic. The Assembly elevated Ebert to head of state as Germany's first president in February and set about writing a new constitution. Adopted in August that year, the Weimar Constitution remains a highly controversial document. There can be no doubt that the constitution was irreproachably democratic and guaranteed many freedoms and rights that the German people had never enjoyed before, such as gender equality, collective bargaining, basic welfare provision, universal suffrage and freedom of speech.[50]

At its heart, the new Germany was supposed to be a parliamentary democracy in which the chancellor and his government were directly responsible to the Reichstag, which was to be elected by all men and women over 20 at least once every four years. Elections used a party list system of proportional representation, which meant the percentage of seats awarded to any given party very closely mirrored the percentage of votes won. While this was exceedingly fair and democratic, it did mean that no single party could ever win a majority and that a myriad of minor and extreme parties could easily win Reichstag representation in the polarised political climate of post-war Germany. A chancellor and his government had to enjoy the support of a majority in the parliament (both to pass legislation and avoid a vote of no confidence) and would therefore have to build coalitions, which would soon prove unstable. There was an upper house, the Reichsrat, made up of representatives of Germany's federal states, although its role was mainly advisory. A strong head of state, as there had been in the Kaiserreich, was intended to counterbalance the strength of the Reichstag. The president was to be directly elected by the people every seven years and he held the power to hire and fire chancellors, although his choice had to command the support of the Reichstag for the system to function. The president was the commander-in-chief of the armed forces and also had considerable emergency powers under Article 48 of the constitution. These powers permitted the president and his government to suspend civil liberties and rule by decree, bypassing the Reichstag in times of crisis – the only problem was, the constitution did not define when or how often these emergency powers could be deployed and President Ebert soon came to routinely use Article 48 to pass legislation.[51] Although the Reichstag had the authority to overturn presidential decrees through a simple majority vote, the president also held power over the Reichstag, for he had the capacity to dissolve the parliament and call fresh elections at any time. Considerable power also remained in the hands of Germany's eighteen federal states, each of which was to have its own elected parliament, government and prime minister, with control over substantial aspects of local life, not least the police, education and welfare.

Prussia was far and away the largest state in Germany following its conquests in the nineteenth century. It contained 57 per cent of the Reich's population, the important Ruhr industrial region and the capital Berlin.[52] The Prussian government therefore represented a significant counterweight to the central Reich administration in that it directly ruled the majority of Germans despite only nominally being a regional authority. German nationalists would be particularly offended by the fact that the demographics of Prussia (which contained many industrial, urban centres and also a significant Catholic population) meant the state that had always embodied traditional Junker landowner values of conservatism and Protestantism would be governed by a 'red-black' coalition of socialists and Catholics of the SPD and Centre parties throughout the 1920s.

A final flaw with the constitution was that it left most of the old Wilhelmine institutions untouched, in the hope of maintaining stability. Thus, the civil servants, bureaucrats, judges, policemen, professors and army officers who had loyally served the Kaiser and were therefore often reactionary and anti-democratic in their politics, remained in post, undermining the Republic from within.[53]

German political life was highly fragmented and party allegiance was often determined by narrow class, occupational or confessional interests. Most major parties also fragmented the public sphere further by having a myriad of organisations and associations that divided Germans in their leisure time; from party youth, sports and paramilitary clubs, to choirs, libraries, pubs, festivals and newspapers, party allegiance often led to segregation of communities along political and religious lines.[54] The German left was divided between three major parties initially. The revolutionary Spartacist League soon became the German Communist Party (KPD), which was an implacable enemy of the Republic and democracy, especially after the first republican government had violently crushed their January 1919 uprising. The biggest political party in the world at the time was the Social Democratic Party of Germany (SPD), the political arm of Germany's massive organised labour movement. The Social Democrats represented the trade unions and working classes and had a complex and well-organised party machine rooted in most urban centres. Given they had founded the Republic in November 1918, it is little surprise the SPD was the only party consistently and unequivocally committed to both the Weimar Republic and the concept of parliamentary democracy throughout the period 1918–33. The Social Democrats were, for the most part, subscribers to the evolutionary strand of Marxism that advocated peaceful reform and the gradual construction of socialism rather than violent revolution. From 1917 to 1922, the Independent Social Democrats (USPD) existed to the left of the SPD, before the party was dissolved and its members either re-joined the mother party or joined the Communists. The Catholic Centre Party represented the interests of Germany's substantial Catholic minority (around a third of the population). The party was a broad church, encompassing all Catholics of left and right, ranging from Christian trade unionists and relatively liberal figures through to conservatives and monarchists. Generally speaking, the party began the republican era as a firm supporter of democracy, but as the system began to crumble from 1930, the more right-wing and authoritarian aspects of the Centre came to predominate.

German liberalism meanwhile was divided and had a limited support base, mostly restricted to the urban, well-educated middle classes. The pre-war Progressives had founded the German Democratic Party (DDP). Initially left-leaning, the Democrats were strong advocates of parliamentary democracy and individual rights, but they formed closer associations with the *Bürgerblock* bourgeois parties of the centre-right as the 1920s wore on, undergoing a full rebrand and a drastic political shift rightwards when they changed their name to the German State Party in 1930. At the same time, the pre-war national liberal tradition was taken up by the new German People's Party (DVP) of Gustav Stresemann. The People's Party were what might be labelled today neo-liberals;

they were patriotic and even nationalistic, and promoted capitalist interests, especially those of big business and heavy industry. In both the early and late phases of the Weimar Republic, they were openly opposed to democracy and remained a monarchist party throughout, despite cooperating in a number of coalitions.

The largest party of the right was the German National People's Party (DNVP), usually referred to as the Nationalists. Monarchist and opposed to the republican order, the Nationalists eventually relented in their intransigence and cooperated in a couple of coalition administrations before again rapidly returning to the anti-Semitic far right from 1928 under the leadership of media magnate Alfred Hugenberg. The party was especially strong in rural parts of northern and eastern Germany, being associated with agricultural interests (especially those of the Junker landowners) and Protestant values. The Nationalists would fragment by the end of the 1920s, leaving a clear path for a new force to capture the radical right. The Nazis, or National Socialists, a tiny far-right group with less than a hundred members in 1919, would by 1932 be the biggest political party in Germany. Their story will unfold later in the text.

As we have seen, not only were there many more major parties than in most modern democracies, but each was relatively limited in representing a single class, religious or economic special interest and there were many more minor parties proclaiming to be the voice of, for instance, small business owners, peasants or individual regions or states, such as the Bavarian People's Party (BVP). Most parties had only a limited appeal and rarely attracted supporters from outside the class or interest group they represented, for instance the Social Democrats never won the support of the rural poor, while the Centre's electorate was limited to the Catholic population. This made the obtaining of a parliamentary majority impossible in a proportional electoral system. The extreme political fragmentation of Weimar politics, the weakness of German liberalism and the confining of political parties to special interest or class groups all undermined the Republic and led to persistent instability, as did the lack of firm commitment to the Republic on the part of most of the political right. One of the most potent aspects of the Nazi message would be both their pledge to sweep away the myriad parties and their conscious and, in the context of Weimar, fairly unique effort to appeal across class lines.

The Weimar Republic is often characterised as a disastrous and markedly brief experiment in democracy, unstable and doomed to failure. Yet the fourteen-year republican regime lasted longer than Hitler's thousand-year Reich and the latter wrought far more chaos and trauma on the German people. There was nothing inevitable about the fall of Weimar democracy, nor the remarkable rise of the small, provincial Nazi Party and its maverick leader. Rather, the actions of powerful individuals and groups, as well as societal forces, both catapulted the Nazis to prominence and led to establishment conservatives seeking to actively undermine democracy and build an authoritarian system from at least 1930 onwards. Hindenburg and Ludendorff were two of the most important individuals in these dangerous trends and shaped Germany, and German opinion, in the turbulent decade and a half that followed defeat in the Great War. It is to their story that we now turn.

Chapter 1

The Stab in the Back: Hindenburg and Ludendorff as Liars-in-Chief

The Stab-in-the-Back myth, or *Dolchstosslegende*, was one of the most important, and damaging, lies of modern history. Indeed, historian Laird Easton calls it 'perhaps most baleful myth of the twentieth century'.[1] Even before the fighting finished, an insidious effort to shift the blame for defeat had started in OHL and among the right. The myth would come in various forms, some more virulently anti-Semitic, others merely anti-democratic, but the essential notion that the German military was undefeated and that traitors on the home front had brought about the nation's downfall took hold remarkably quickly. This early example of 'fake news' would irrevocably poison the politics of the Weimar Republic and was a keystone of Nazism.[2] Its chief architect was Erich Ludendorff and its most famous proponent was Paul von Hindenburg.

Origins

Hindenburg and Ludendorff displayed, in their promulgation of the Stab-in-the-Back myth, the very human fallacy of wishing to avoid responsibility and blame. Their attempts to explain away the High Command's failings to themselves and others had begun much earlier than the signing of the armistice and revolution in November 1918 but would have long-reaching consequences for Germany. In order to protect their reputations, and preserve the 'honour' of the army, it became necessary to find a scapegoat for the cataclysmic defeat in the Great War. The public and right-wing politicians took the idea that OHL created and ran with it. It was a welcome comfort blanket for a bewildered and defeated people, embittered by years of hardship and dislocated by the sudden collapse and revolution. Claude Levi-Strauss once said that 'The purpose of myth is to provide a logical model capable of overcoming a contradiction', and the *Dolchstosslegende* is a perfect example of this conception of myth in practice.[3] For nationalists, convinced of German superiority and having eagerly consumed propaganda throughout the war years extolling German successes, the Stab-in-the-Back myth made perfect sense; it logically explained the seemingly illogical German defeat and was therefore both believable and reassuring.

For the wider populace also, the information they had received about the war effort had been uniformly positive, especially in the spring and summer of 1918 when the great offensives had seemingly brought Germany to the brink of victory. The news that Germany was on the brink of defeat in autumn 1918 was therefore incomprehensible to a vast swathe of the population. Amidst the 'physiologically devasting' events of October and November, Germans had to build a narrative to explain the apparently inexplicable, and many settled on the theme of betrayal.[4] In its various forms, responsibility was doled out to different groups in different measures but essentially, rather than the military, the defeat became the responsibility of politicians (both the weak men of the Kaiserreich and, more pertinently, the democratic politicians who succeeded them and built the subsequent Republic), socialist and/or communist agitators (who had spread discontent and unrest resulting in the revolution), and unpatriotic, scheming Jews.

Before we trace the myth's origins, we should first debunk the *Dolchstoss* and demonstrate the true cause of German defeat. In so doing, we can see even more starkly the moral bankruptcy and treacherous nature of Hindenburg and Ludendorff's efforts to cover their tracks. There is no doubt that Germany's defeat in the First World War was a military one, rather than merely a political capitulation; the German Army was beaten on the Western Front.[5] From 1916 onwards, morale in the German Army was in decline; a 1917 patriotic education programme was, even in the opinion of some senior officers, ineffective and flawed, while stories of 'abuses' (mistreatment of soldiers) and an increasingly broken relationship between the officers and men, and especially the staff and the front, meant that the grinding attrition and horrendous conditions of trench warfare began to tell on the German soldiery.[6] German historian Boris Barth dates the beginning of the disintegration of the German Army to the Passchendaele campaign of August-November 1917 (also known as the Third Battle of Ypres), a battle that Ludendorff himself described as ripping the heart out of the army and turning it into a mere 'militia'.[7] Clear signs of demoralisation were evident in the winter of 1917/18 and one in ten German soldiers transferred from the Eastern to the Western Front following the defeat of Russia took the opportunity to desert.[8] Then came the Spring Offensive, which, while gaining much ground and restoring movement to the war in the west, crippled the German Army in terms of both fighting strength and morale, yet failed to knock the Allies out of the war. From March-July 1918, the Germans suffered 1 million casualties and those losses were disproportionately high among the best and most motivated men who had been selected for the stormtrooper units. There is much evidence that not only were the Germans literally running out of men, but those who remained were showing increasing signs of crumbling morale. From the spring of 1918 onwards, not only were soldiers generally referring to the war as 'the Great Swindle' but already during April and May the army was having trouble with looting, riots, and units refusing to return to the front.[9] The failure of the Spring Offensive and the subsequent Allied counter-attacks of July and August would prove the tipping point for German Army morale as victory became an impossibility. Historian Tim Travers has convincingly shown why the Germans lost in 1918 and his analysis is worth quoting at length:

> The German army was really defeated by the summer of 1918. This was due partly to the cumulative effects of wearing out the German army from 1914 to 1917, and partly to the desperate efforts of the BEF in bringing the German offensives to a halt. But it can also be argued that to a considerable extent the German army defeated itself through its own offensives from March to July, because these offensives led to excessive casualties due to poor tactics, and because the OHL employed an unwise strategy that did not maintain its objectives. German morale also suffered a crippling blow in spring and summer 1918 because of heightened expectations from these 'peace offensives' that were not fulfilled. This defeat was hammered home by the French counter-attack of 18 July and the Amiens offensive of 8 August, followed by the constant attacks and mobile warfare of late August, September and October… In the end, German casualties were so heavy, and the loss of morale so decisive as a result of the German 1918 spring and summer offensives, that the German army began to disintegrate in mid-July.[10]

In fact, as historian Wilhelm Deist has shown, the exact opposite of a stab in the back had occurred. The primary cause of defeat was the OHL's decision to go onto the offensive in 1918. The failure of this strategy caused the German Army, not the home front, to disintegrate and as morale collapsed, a 'covert strike' took hold as soldiers surrendered, deserted or 'shirked' in ever greater numbers; from the summer of 1918 onwards, replacement units regularly arrived at the front 20 per cent depleted due to desertion.[11] The argument that Ludendorff would deploy in late October 1918, shortly before his sacking, that the armistice terms should be rejected and that the army simply needed time to withdraw to more defensible positions, can be readily dismissed. Firstly, the Allies had just broken through the most impressive defensive positions of the entire war in breaking the Hindenburg line in late September 1918, and second, when put on the spot by the civilian government as to whether there was any chance the military situation could be stabilised, even temporarily, Ludendorff refused to give a straight answer.[12] The German Army was broken, and military defeat was inevitable *before* power was handed to democratic politicians at home, and revolution took hold. In many ways, it was the recklessness of Ludendorff and Hindenburg in launching all-out offensives in the first half of 1918, and in selling them to the troops as decisive, win-or-die battles, that triggered the dramatic military collapse in the second half of the year. There can be no doubt that the army's defeat came before, and indeed played the major part in precipitating, collapse on the home front and revolution in October–November 1918.

As the supreme directors of Germany's war effort, Hindenburg and Ludendorff were of course well aware of the military realities of 1918. Their efforts to abdicate responsibility for the disaster, however, long predated the abdication of the Kaiser and signing of the armistice. Hindenburg apparently believed that internal enemies, not least members of the Kaiser's privy council and the chancellor himself, were working to sabotage the German war effort.[13] Already in March 1918, as the initial offensive gained ground rapidly, Hindenburg wrote to his wife that he would prefer a 'good and advantageous peace … It is not my fault in any case if the struggle ends unfavourably for us.'[14] Such an abdication of responsibility from the head of the Supreme Command is hardly credible and yet it helps us understand why the field marshal so readily embraced the *Dolchstoss*.

By May, as the Spring Offensive increasingly ran out of steam, all OHL could do was accuse local commanders of doom-mongering.[15] As spring turned to summer, Ludendorff desperately sought a scapegoat for the failure of his grand plan, blaming everyone from the ordinary troops to the staff of the High Command: 'Ludendorff [is] terribly excited. Everybody else is to blame,' an aide wrote in August.[16] As we have seen, at the end of September 1918, the military situation became critical and Ludendorff lost his nerve. He persuaded first Hindenburg and then the Kaiser that an armistice was an immediate necessity with his infamous declaration that the front could no longer be guaranteed for two hours. President Woodrow Wilson of the United States, it was reckoned, would offer the best terms if approached, and Ludendorff believed he could be 'wooed' by domestic reforms in Germany.[17]

The October Reforms, or 'Revolution from Above', transformed Germany, on paper, into a parliamentary democracy under a constitutional monarch – retaining the Kaiser but handing real power to the parties of the Reichstag. The new chancellor, the liberal Prince Max of Baden, was immediately besieged by requests from the High Command to seek peace; the army was 'at the end of its tether' and a delay of forty-eight hours was described as potentially catastrophic.[18] From the OHL's perspective, the fact that civilians would now be responsible for peace negotiations was more than a happy by-product; Ludendorff was already telling his fellow officers on 29 September: 'now those circles must be brought into the government … whom we have above all to thank for having brought us to this point … Let them now eat the broth they have cooked for us.'[19] In Goltz's evocative phrase, Ludendorff's Revolution from Above 'planted the seed' for the Stab-in-the-Back myth, for it would now be the pro-democracy politicians of the Reichstag who would bear the outward responsibility for seeking an armistice and terminating the war effort – not the army High Command.[20]

There was a logical sequencing to events that hid the truth; Germany had handed power to the politicians *and then* the government had requested an armistice, the war effort had collapsed and revolution broken out. Due to wartime censoring, the populace did not know what Hindenburg and Ludendorff knew, that defeat was imminent and that it had been coming for some time. A confused chronology developed among many Germans that mixed up the events of the revolution and military collapse, and blame for the army's defeat became associated with the revolution that brought an end to the monarchy and democracy to Germany.[21] The pro-democracy politicians and parties (SPD, DDP, Centre) that signed the armistice, founded the Republic and later assented to the Treaty of Versailles became forever, for millions of Germans, the 'November Criminals' – traitors who had sold out their country, betrayed their kaiser and stabbed their own army in the back.[22] There can be no doubt that the real responsibility for the armistice lay with the military rather than the civilian government, for while it was Prince Max who sent the so-called peace note to President Wilson, he acted at the behest of the OHL and Ludendorff in particular, who had dragged the civilian government into opening negotiations.[23] Ludendorff and Hindenburg knew it was military necessity – they had asked for the armistice and strong-armed reluctant civilians into beginning negotiations. Their 29 September letter to the Kaiser requesting a peace makes no mention whatever of the home front or civilian government, instead explaining their decision in purely military terms, making it clear that there was no way a peace could be enforced on the enemy by military action, i.e. that defeat was inevitable.[24] Similarly, in a letter to his wife at the time, Hindenburg conceded that a ceasefire was 'militarily necessary. We shall soon be at the end of our strength.'[25] And yet, both men had already demonstrated a desire to shift responsibility and escape retribution for their own cataclysmic errors of judgement. The Stab-in-the-Back myth would merely be the crystallisation of this effort.

That is not to say that only Hindenburg and Ludendorff bear responsibility for the legend, although they were amongst its chief instigators. There are many different versions of who used the catchy, succinct phrase *Dolchstoss*, or back-stab, first. Already, in July 1917, when a majority in the Reichstag voted for the Peace Resolution calling for a peace without annexations, General Hans von Seeckt had written, 'What are we really fighting for? The home front has attacked us from behind, and therefore the war is lost.'[26] The best answer historians have come up with to trace the phrase 'stab in the back' in referring to Germany's defeat is a public meeting in a Munich beer hall on 2 November 1918. A liberal politician, Ernst Müller-Meiningen, told a receptive audience: 'As long as the front holds, we damn well have the duty to hold out in the homeland. We would have to be ashamed of ourselves in front of our children and grandchildren if we attacked the battlefront from the rear and stabbed it in the back.'[27] Clearly, before the armistice was even signed, the disorientated German populace were looking for an explanation for defeat. Even before the phrase 'stab in the back' was used, some had begun to consider the potential of using defeat as a political weapon, foreshadowing the myth's later application. On 19 October, the chairman of the far-right Pan-German League (an organisation with links to Ludendorff) had told his executive committee that 'the situation should be used for a fanfare against Jewry and the Jews as lightning conductors for all injustices'.[28] Further foundations for the myth were laid by the leaders of the new republic that replaced the monarchy.

On 9 November, as the Kaiser abdicated and Prince Max resigned, Friedrich Ebert and his Social Democratic Party found themselves inheriting the state, with all its manifold problems. Despite being the largest party in the Reichstag since 1912, the SPD had only been given a share in governmental power with the October Reforms the previous month, but the revolution had put paid to Ludendorff's scheme for a constitutional monarchy and unexpectedly thrust Ebert into the chancellorship. It was immediately clear to the Social Democratic government of soon-to-be-president Ebert that they would face violent insurrection from radical socialists and communists determined to push the revolution further than merely the creation of a parliamentary democracy. Keen to re-establish order and secure the new republic, Ebert sought to ensure the loyalty of the army to his regime with the so-called Ebert-Groener Pact of 10 November 1918. The new chancellor, terrified of the perceived revolutionary threat, did a deal with General Wilhelm Groener, the doughty, practical and quite brilliant south German who had replaced Ludendorff as First Quartermaster General. Groener wrote of the fateful call between the two:

> In the evening I telephoned the Reich Chancellery and told Ebert that the army put itself at the disposal of the government, that in return for this the Field Marshal [Hindenburg] and the officer corps expected the support of the government in the maintenance of order and discipline in the army. The officer corps expected the government to fight against Bolshevism and was ready for the struggle. Ebert accepted my offer of an alliance. From then on we discussed the measures which were necessary every evening on a secret telephone line between the Reich Chancellery and High Command. The alliance proved successful.
>
> We [the High Command] hoped through our actions to gain a share of power in the new state for the army and the officer corps. If we succeeded, then we would have rescued into the new Germany the best and strongest elements of old Prussia, despite the revolution.[29]

Thus, the moderate left who found themselves in control of the government machinery did a deal with the conservatives and reactionaries of the Imperial Army leadership in order to fight a common foe, albeit for different reasons – Ebert et al. to defend their new republic, the officers to preserve both their power and the institution of the old army. It was in the interests of both OHL and the democratic politicians in the new government that Hindenburg's nimbus be protected and preserved. The German people and army needed a figurehead to unite behind and a hero to cherish from an otherwise disastrous war. The field marshal's prestige conferred legitimacy on an otherwise vulnerable government and temporarily silenced right-wing critics of the SPD, and it was held that his presence would prevent the collapse of the army, the support of which Ebert needed to regain control of the nation and tame the revolution.[30]

Social Democrats were keen to extoll Hindenburg's virtues and dissociate him from both Ludendorff and the Kaiser. When the OHL headquarters moved on 14 November to Wilhelmshöhe, the local council leader and future SPD minister Albert Grzesinski proclaimed, 'Hindenburg belongs to the German people and the German Army. He led his armies to glorious victories and did not leave his people in a difficult hour. Never has Hindenburg in the greatness of the fulfilment of his duty been closer to us than today. He stands under our protection.'[31] Such hero worship was almost incompatible with believing that the German Army had lost the war. The Social Democrats had therefore coopted the Hindenburg myth in the hope of ensuring stability and loyalty but in so doing had legitimised and justified the burgeoning Stab-in-the-Back myth. How could Germany's saviour, the victorious war leader, have led the army to defeat? If Hindenburg's reputation was to be preserved, then blame for the loss of the war had to fall elsewhere. This meant, as Goltz has pointed out, that the Hindenburg and Stab-in-the-Back myths were to a large extent mutually reinforcing – a liberal journalist would reflect: 'The unfortunate scapegoat theory could not emerge if the infallibility theory had not risen on the other side.'[32] Fuel was added to the fire when, as chancellor of the Reich, Ebert welcomed returning troops with the words 'Your sacrifices and actions are unprecedented. No enemy has overcome you!'[33] In popular memory, this speech would be remembered for a phrase that Ebert never actually used but would become a watchword for nationalists and *Dolchstoss* proponents: *im Felde unbesiegt* (undefeated in the field).[34] The reassuring official story was thus that the German Army remained unbeaten, occupying enemy soil at the war's end, and that their field marshal, the venerated, untarnished Hindenburg, had led his army home in good order. This phrase would soon find its way onto war memorials across the Reich that commemorated the fallen of an undefeated army.[35]

Within the context of this narrative, it is easy to imagine how the Stab-in-the-Back myth took hold. The Social Democrats, in their embrace of Hindenburg and championing of the army, as well as their failure to criticise the army and OHL, had helped ensure the *Dolchstosslegende* became accepted fact. Endorsing the Hindenburg myth and venerating an undefeated army would come back to bite the SPD, for they would bear the odium of being 'November Criminals' for the rest of the Weimar period, regularly being accused of treachery and cowardice. Hindenburg was of course not a passenger in all this – he had actively cultivated his myth from 1914, as we have seen, and he, Groener and the High

Command continued to protect his reputation in the delicate months from October 1918. In letters after the sacking of Ludendorff in late October, he had emphasised that his 'heart was bleeding' but that 'duty' meant he would keep going, and after the armistice, Hindenburg's remaining at the head of the army was sold by OHL as the actions of a man devoted to his people, standing by them in their hour of greatest need.[36] Thus, by 'bravely' remaining at his post at the head of the Supreme Command and through the lack of any critical analysis of his role on the part of the democratic parties, the Hindenburg myth survived military defeat in 1918. A year later, this would ensure the Stab-in-the-Back myth would become the dominant narrative in explaining Germany's downfall.

Ludendorff as architect: the excuses of a broken man

The mental health of Erich Ludendorff had been in crisis since the military situation had significantly worsened in August 1918. His sacking as First Quartermaster General on 26 October came as a hammer blow. It marked the beginning of what Chickering has labelled 'a long emotional and intellectual odyssey, whose goal was to make sense of the disaster, both collective and personal, that the armistice of November 1918 had signalled. The quest for discovery and self-justification occupied him for the rest of his life.'[37] For days on end after his sacking, he sat in silence at his desk in his family's Berlin apartment, simply staring and brooding, 'utterly depressed and sunk in the gloomy silence of despair'.[38]

The general was desperately trying to come to terms with nothing less than the collapse of his life's work and, indeed, his world. The calamitous failure of his war strategy would surely have terrible personal and geopolitical consequences, ruining his life and reputation, destroying the army to which he had dedicated his whole life since the age of 12, and maybe also the nation he had served all that time. The millions of lives he had sacrificed, the hardships he had imposed on the German people, the huge personal effort he had made – all were for nothing. Even worse, Ludendorff faced the wrath of an angry and restless people. The political left and centre were deeply hostile to the general (unsurprising given his known links to the far right) and whipped up public anger against him as a warmonger and charlatan who had led his nation down the garden path. Prince Max of Baden's liberal government had engineered his dismissal and the response of the press to his removal was wholly positive, with commentators condemning the general's political meddling and authoritarian ambitions.[39] Perhaps even more galling was the fact that the Kaiser, the government and the press (even the Social Democratic *Vorwärts*) all demanded Hindenburg remain and praised him for 'bravely' doing his duty in continuing at the head of OHL.[40]

As revolution rapidly engulfed the country in early November, Ludendorff felt increasingly under threat. The revolutionary crowds that had swept Ebert to power on 9 November reportedly chanted Ludendorff's name as one of the guilty and friends began to advise him to flee.[41] Eventually, he was compelled to leave by his landlady, who did not want any trouble, and he went briefly, in disguise, to his brother's in Potsdam and then to the Berlin home of Wilhelm Breucker, a friend and former member of his staff. Breucker did his best to find a safe haven for the general and it was soon decided he should go with a newly appointed member of the German legation to Copenhagen, and then on to Finland.[42] Although he made it to Denmark on 16 November, rather than Finland he instead ended up moving on to rural Sweden in early December, where he was soon joined by his wife Margarethe, who was increasingly worried by the disturbances in Berlin.[43] Ludendorff's fragile mental state, as well has his burgeoning sense of victimhood, is revealed by a letter he sent his wife when he first departed:

> My heart was torn at leaving you and having to leave you alone, and what made me saddest of all was the memory of my harsh words to you shortly before I left. ... To me it all seems like a bad dream. I do not know if I was right to go away. Things cannot go on like this forever. I say 'forever', though the whole thing has only just begun. ... For four years I have fought for my country and now when so much is hanging in the balance I must stand aside. I am at war with myself and the whole world. Dearest, it isn't easy to pull myself together again. ... My nerves are too much on edge and sometimes my speech gets out of control. There is no help for it, my nerves have simply gone to pieces! ... Tell everybody how like my fate was to that of Hannibal. That will teach them to understand. Keep these letters, dearest, in time they will form my memoirs.[44]

Once in Sweden, his mental state remained unstable. His wife remembered that he was constantly murmuring and whispering to himself, seemingly lost in another world.[45] Later recalling their reunification in Sweden, Margarethe wrote: 'The moment I saw Ludendorff again I realised how very great his mental agony had been. ... Hidebound, as he always was, by his temperament, he was unable to give any outward sign of his pleasure at my arrival.'[46] He used German mythology to help explain Germany's (and his own) predicament, turning to the ancient *Nibelungenlied* with its story of the betrayal of the tragic hero Siegfried, whom he came to identify himself with.[47] Around this time he wrote a testament for Germany, directly linking current events to the *Nibelungenlied*, arguing that the High Command had been deprived of the necessary manpower and willpower from back home and that if traditional values were restored, the disastrous end of the Nibelungs could be averted.[48] Despite his fragile state, Ludendorff rapidly found purpose in exile, beginning work on his memoirs almost immediately. As well as tragic heroes such as Hannibal and Siegfried, he may have drawn inspiration from a story widely circulated in the German press from mid-December 1918. The British general Sir Frederick Maurice had written a series of articles on the end of the war for the *Daily News* in which he had noted that 'moral forces have had greater influence than the physical'. A Swiss newspaper had carried on 17 December a summary of Maurice's articles and views from London in which the unnamed correspondent stated that there was a consensus that the civilian population stabbed the German Army in the back.[49] It remained unclear in the article whether this was Maurice's view or a common view in Britain. However, the following day, the German right-wing newspaper *Deutsche Tageszeitung* carried a single-paragraph article quoting the Swiss report as its source but totally distorting the message further like a game of Chinese whispers. Under the headline 'The Stabbed-in-the-Back German Army', the paper told its receptive readers:

> Our correspondent reports: According to the Neue Zürcher Zeitung, General Maurice has written in the Daily News, 'Before the war, the German Army was the strongest in Europe. At the time of the armistice, the ratio of Allied to German forces on the Western Front was five to three and a half. The civilian population stabbed the German Army to death from behind. The behaviour of the sailors of the German fleet was disreputable. They chose to surrender their ships to the enemy, rather than to defy death. They were the ones who saved Paris.'[50]

This was the Stab-in-the-Back myth in black and white, complete with the delusion that victory, i.e. the fall of Paris, was imminent had it not been for the revolution. This was not actually General Maurice's view; he published a book several months later on the end of the Great War that emphasised Germany's military defeat, but it was too late. *Deutsche Tageszeitung* had a news wire service that distributed their articles and in the days after 18 December this remarkable headline was carried in numerous local and regional papers. Word was out that the British believed the revolution had handed them victory and that the Germany Army was indeed undefeated in the field. Furthermore, German nationalists were quick to claim that Maurice's book was an attempt to rewrite his previous statements and hide his 'true' opinion.[51] It was fake news and the claims had been fairly rapidly debunked, but that did not matter. This reassuring falsehood found popular acceptance, especially on the German right.

Lies can often be disproven with the help of experts, but Germany's foremost military expert Erich Ludendorff was at the same time working feverishly to reinforce the *Dolchstoss* distortion. As we have seen, Ludendorff had already been actively looking for scapegoats for the German defeat months before his removal. Ludendorff was single-minded and closed to alternative perspectives. His lack of self-reflection and ducking of responsibility were essential elements of his character.[52] His grasp of the possible, one could argue, had been slipping ever since his disastrous decision to launch an all-out offensive in the west. His mental state was questionable. Little wonder then that the memoirs he was now feverishly composing were aimed solely at shifting the blame. The German public were primed to receive such a message due to the rapidly developing narrative of betrayal surrounding the events of October-November 1918. Indeed, Ludendorff's long-time collaborator Colonel Max Bauer produced a pamphlet in spring 1919 entitled *Could We Have Avoided, Won, or Broken Off the War?* in which he stated that the war could easily have been won, but that 'It was lost only and exclusively through the failure of the homeland. The revolution especially sealed Germany's fate in the most difficult moment.'[53] Ludendorff told an aide in January 1919 that 'It is essential to salvage the honour of the fatherland, the army, and my own honour and my name.'[54] With this clear objective in mind and his characteristic focus and feverish work ethic employed to full effect, Ludendorff had completed his 270,000-word manuscript, written largely from memory, by the time he left Sweden in February 1919 – a stunning achievement for less than three months' work.[55] *My War Memories*, published in August 1919, ran to 628 pages and went through five editions in as many months. A mass-market version of just 218 pages was later published in 1921.[56] Ludendorff's book was both extensive and expensive, and despite the fact extracts were trailed in the right-wing press, Matthias Farhrenwaldt estimates less than 100,000 copies were sold.[57] However, those who read it were the educated middle class, who could both afford it and played a disproportionately significant role in shaping public opinion. As was to be expected, his memoirs included a full-blooded condemnation of the revolution and new republic that sat easily in the rapidly developing Stab-in-the-Back narrative:

> On November 9 Germany, lacking any firm hand, bereft of all will, robbed of her princes, collapsed like a house of cards. All that we had lived for, all that we had bled four long years to maintain, was gone. We no longer had a native land of which we might be proud. Order in State and society vanished. All authority disappeared. Chaos, Bolshevism, terror, un-German in name and nature, made their entry into the German Fatherland. Soldiers and workmen's councils, prepared in long, systematic underground work, were now established. Men had occupied themselves with these matters who, if they had served at the front, might have insured victory. Many of them were classified as fit only for garrison duty; others were deserters, but all were indispensable. ...
>
> The proud German Army, after resisting victoriously its superior enemies for four years, achieving feats of unprecedented greatness, and keeping our enemies clear away from our frontiers, disappeared in a moment. Our victorious fleet was handed over to the enemy. The authorities at home, who had not fought against the enemy, could not hurry fast enough to pardon deserters and other military criminals, including in part among these themselves and their nearest friends.

> They and the soldiers' councils worked with zeal, determination and purpose to destroy everything military. This was the gratitude of the newly formed homeland to the German soldiers who had bled and died for it in millions. The destruction of the German power, achieved by these Germans, was the most tragic crime the world has witnessed. A tidal wave had broken over Germany, not by the force of nature, but through the weakness of the Government represented by the Chancellor and the crippling of a leaderless people. ...
>
> What the revolution thinks that it has achieved might have been won on constitutional lines without self destruction. It was a terribly criminal game that they played with Germany in her hardest hour, and Germany is paying for it with her life and her ideals.
>
> Before all these events the world has stood astonished; it could not believe its eyes when it saw the collapse of this proud and mighty Germany, the terror of her foes. The Entente feared us even in our destruction, and could not do enough in using the opportunity to weaken us still further internally by propaganda and to force a helots' peace upon us.
>
> Germany, by her own fault, has been brought low. She is no longer a great Power; she is not even an independent state. Her very existence is in danger.[58]

The general closed his account with a nationalist call to arms which demanded a return to traditional values and 'unselfish submission' to authority.[59] At this stage, however, Ludendorff still described his enemies with innuendo and indirect, dog-whistle language. The Social Democrats were 'Those who for decades had confused the people and made them false promises, who have all the time agitated against authority in State and army', while references to the Jews hid behind familiar tropes of disloyalty and power exercised in the shadows: 'The Government allowed the conduct of affairs to slip more and more from its grasp; and the worst of it was, it abandoned them, not to the people as a whole, but to certain groups which, through their history, had always displayed critical and never constructive faculties.'[60] Most of all, Ludendorff laid the blame for defeat with civilian politicians, who, he claimed, had been weak and indecisive throughout the conflict. The lack of firm leadership at home was his key theme and he argued it had undermined the efforts of the OHL, eaten away at morale and ultimately allowed revolution to sweep the country.[61] Ludendorff hinted towards his future ambitions by mentioning that many people had approached him to take up the chancellorship during the war, but that the all-encompassing nature of his military role had prevented him from doing so.[62] He did, however, say that he had desired a minister of propaganda who would essentially be a dictator, with oversight over military, political and economic affairs, as well as the government's messaging.[63]

For many reasons, blaming the politicians was disingenuous and simply inaccurate, for until Ludendorff had initiated the October Reforms and demanded an armistice, the politicians, and especially the pro-democracy parties in the Reichstag, had had little power or influence over the direction of the war in comparison to OHL. It was Hindenburg and Ludendorff, not the Reichstag, who had made and unmade chancellors, and despite the Peace Resolution the Reichstag had passed in July 1917 calling for no annexations, the OHL had got their way at Brest-Litovsk and annexed vast swathes of Eastern Europe. The hugely significant decision to gamble on an all-out offensive in spring 1918 was OHL's alone; parliament was not consulted and all branches of the German government were strongarmed into agreement by Hindenburg and Ludendorff – their plans had not been frustrated, rather their plans had been pushed through without toleration of dissent and the results were catastrophic. As Deist has argued, the beginning of 1918 was one of the few moments where the Germans had an almost completely free hand strategically speaking and Ludendorff got his way – diplomatic solutions were not even considered, discussions of other options were shut down and the whole German war effort was geared to Ludendorff's vision of an offensive victory in the west.[64] A fellow officer, Admiral Georg von Müller, put it best when he wrote:

> But who were our politicians during the war? Hindenburg, Ludendorff and the political branch of the Great General Staff ... Mistake after mistake had been made, above all the casual handling of peace with Russia, whose collapse had been a boon of immeasurable value and should have been exploited to release troops for the West. But instead of this we conquered Latvia and Estonia and became involved with Finland – the results of an excess of megalomania. Very seldom did the actual political leaders manage to prevent the acts of violence planned by the High Command.[65]

The publication of Ludendorff's war memoirs in the summer of 1919 did not end the criticism he had been subjected to since the previous autumn. Arriving back in Berlin in February 1919, the general had for a time resided in the Hotel Adlon under a false name. He dined with the liberal Jewish journalist Theodor Wolff, one of his more prominent critics during the war, although in their discussion of the defeat, Ludendorff made no mention of the *Dolchstoss*. Wolff did note, however, that the war leader was 'permeated by a deep, passionate resentment [which] gnawed at him incessantly, burrowed in him'.[66] There is a story, which appears to originate in a 1938 essay by John Wheeler-Bennett and has been repeated in the English-language biographies of Ludendorff, that the general also dined with the head of the British Military Mission in Berlin, General Sir Neill Malcom. As Ludendorff attempted to explain the manner in which Germany lost the war, Wheeler-Bennet wrote that Malcolm asked him: '"Do you mean, General, that you were stabbed in the back?" Ludendorff's eyes lit up and he leapt upon the phrase like a dog on a bone. "Stabbed in the back?" he repeated. "Yes, that's it, exactly, we were stabbed in the back."[67]

Although this has been cited as the origin of the fateful phrase, as we have seen, it had already been in use in Germany in November and December 1918. The general's return was not, however, consumed entirely with dinner dates. Just as at the moment of his sacking, Ludendorff was attracting much criticism and negative press in the spring and summer of 1919, especially from the left, who regarded him as the symbol of the arrogant and incompetent military caste who had brought defeat on Germany. The new chancellor, the Social Democrat Philipp Scheidemann, even called Ludendorff a reckless gambler in an official statement and it was noted that there was now a fashion to 'piss on' the general.[68] Most stinging of all must have been the reception of his memoirs from Germany's most prominent military historian, Hans Delbrück. In a scathing review of the general's masterpiece, and a subsequent review of another war memoir, Delbrück was uncompromising in his critique of both Ludendorff's actions and analysis. He shot down Ludendorff's criticism of the civilian leadership, lauding the wartime chancellor Bethmann-Hollweg's moderation and, most damning of all, explained the German Army's defeat thus: 'It was their leader [surely Ludendorff himself], who could not accommodate himself to feasible objectives and this rendered all their heroism null and void.'[69] The resentment and bitterness that Wolff had observed in Ludendorff, alongside his sense of victimhood, were clearly entrenched during the months of exile and his unwelcome return, helping to create a man hell-bent on exonerating himself and righting perceived wrongs. Ludendorff the wounded tiger would be a great threat to the new Germany.

Hindenburg as cheerleader: The myth becomes mainstream

What of Paul von Hindenburg? During Ludendorff's exile and vilification, the field marshal had remained as Chief of the General Staff at OHL, nominally overseeing the return home of the German Army and its deployment in the first half of 1919 in defence of the new government against leftist revolt. In reality, most of the credit for the difficult operation of bringing a defeated army home and then mobilising it in defence of the new republic must go to Ludendorff's successor as First Quartermaster General, Wilhelm Groener. Hindenburg meanwhile remained essentially a passive figurehead at the new OHL headquarters at Wilhelmshöhe, outside Kassel, then from February at Kolberg.[70] As Astore and Showalter have pointed out, Hindenburg's mere presence at the head of the army was enough to forestall the likelihood of a military coup against Ebert's vulnerable administration and meant Germany avoided the fate of similar new republics in Hungary and Poland that rapidly succumbed to rightist dictatorship in the immediate post-war years.[71] On the other hand, the retention of Hindenburg and the aforementioned Ebert-Groener

Pact that had ensured his continuation as chief of staff meant that the German Army went unreformed and Hindenburg's myth remained undiminished despite military defeat. With his reputation intact and as a figure respected by both sides of the political spectrum, the field marshal was able to expound the Stab-in-the-Back fiction with far greater authority than the discredited Ludendorff.

Hindenburg's final act at the head of the army would serve to add fuel to the fire of the burgeoning Stab-in-the-Back perception of Germany's defeat. Since January, the Allied powers had been negotiating a peace treaty in Paris, without permitting German representatives to take part in any of the serious discussions. Just as with the armistice the previous autumn, when German envoys were invited to view a draft of the treaty, it was the military leaders rather than the civilians who were notable by their absence. When the government got to see the peace terms in May, they were appalled.[72] The Treaty of Versailles (as it would come to be known) was moderate in comparison to OHL's Brest-Litovsk outrage, yet was a crippling blow to German national pride, especially as the revolution and President Wilson's Fourteen Points had raised unrealistic hopes of a 'fair peace'.[73] In fact, Germany lost a tenth of its population, 13 per cent of its territory, plus all its overseas colonies, East Prussia stood cut off from the rest of the country, union with Austria (presumed inevitable after the dissolution of the Habsburg Empire) was forbidden and millions of Germans or German speakers now found themselves in Poland, Czechoslovakia, Denmark, France, Belgium and Lithuania. The German military was crippled – the army, which just a few months before had numbered 6 million, was limited to 100,000 men and forbidden from possessing tanks, the navy was allowed just six outdated battleships and no U-boats, while no air force was permitted whatsoever. Finally, Germany had to accept the hated War Guilt Clause, in which German responsibility for the outbreak of war in 1914 was implied, meaning they were liable to cover the cost of damage done to Allied nations – a figure still to be calculated. Signing the treaty therefore represented a blank cheque for the German government and the final total for war reparations was eventually 132 billion gold marks or £6.6 billion.[74]

While historians might still debate how fair or otherwise Versailles was, of more relevance was the perception of the treaty in Germany. Brest-Litovsk, *Mitteleuropa* and Ludendorff's war of conquest were swiftly forgotten, and Versailles became one of the few unifying aspects of Weimar politics – everyone hated it, believed it disgracefully unjust, and across the political spectrum all parties wanted either to revise it or ignore it completely.[75] The German press condemned this *Diktat*, labelling Versailles a dictated peace because Germany had not been allowed to negotiate. However, they had been deceived by the 'undefeated in the field' and *Dolchstoss* rhetoric. The Germans were so enraged about being treated as a defeated power, having terms imposed on them, precisely because they were living under the misconception that they were *not* a defeated power. Therefore, a large portion of the furore and bitter hatred that Versailles stoked up can be regarded as the whirlwind harvest of the comforting denial of defeat the previous autumn. The final text, which had ignored almost all of Germany's suggested amendments, was presented on 16 June 1919 alongside an ultimatum: sign or else hostiles will resume. Naturally, the government sought the advice of the OHL at Kolberg. Groener knew signing was a military necessity and that rejection would bring only total defeat and even harsher terms. Yet Hindenburg, despite having advocated peace at any price on multiple occasions in October and November the previous year, now wavered, providing an ambiguous answer to the anxious politicians in his letter to President Ebert of 17 June:

> In the event of a resumption of hostilities we can reconquer the province of Posen and defend our frontiers in the east. In the west, however, we can scarcely count upon being able to withstand a serious offensive on the part of the enemy in view of the numerical superiority of the Entente and their ability to outflank us on both wings.
>
> The success of the operation as a whole is therefore very doubtful, but as a soldier I cannot help feeling that it were better to perish honourably than accept a disgraceful peace.[76]

With this equivocal advice to guide them, the cabinet failed to come to a consensus and Ebert's successor as chancellor, Philipp Scheidemann, resigned rather than face the odium of signing. He was replaced by another Social Democrat, Gustav Bauer, but the problem facing the government had not changed. On 22 June, Bauer, with the backing of the National Assembly, indicated to the Allies that he would sign if certain clauses were withdrawn, not least the War Guilt Clause, but the Allies were unwilling to negotiate. Their message was simple: sign the treaty as it is, or else hostilities will restart in forty-eight hours, and indeed it was no empty threat; the Allied Generalissimo Ferdinand Foch had made detailed preparations for an advance into Germany from the Rhine bridgeheads they had established after the armistice, aiming to split the country in two with an advance along the Main River before occupying and disarming the south.[77] Nevertheless, both President Ebert and his government remained highly reluctant to acquiesce, not least because there had been rumblings from officer associations that they would refuse to serve an administration that assented to the terms dictated by Versailles. Indeed, a telegram from Hindenburg himself had hinted in that direction.[78] In a series of indecisive cabinet meetings on 24 June, with the deadline creeping closer, the coalition government remained divided on the issue and political chaos reigned. In one break in the lengthy negotiations that morning, a senior general, Maercker, approached Defence Minister Gustav Noske and suggested the army make him dictator and reject the terms – a hairbrained scheme the minister rejected but which illustrated the extent to which OHL was losing its grip on its own generals in the crisis.[79]

The Stab in the Back: Hindenburg and Ludendorff as Liars-in-Chief 17

As the government continued to vacillate, President Ebert telephoned the High Command at Kolberg just after noon, with less than seven hours remaining before the Allied ultimatum expired. Ebert was clear with Groener, who immediately reported his conversation to Hindenburg: if the OHL believed there was even the smallest possibility of successful armed resistance, the president was willing to reject the treaty and fight on. Effectively, Ebert was throwing down the gauntlet to the military, suggesting that Germany reject the Versailles terms and take up arms against the Allies once more unless the military believed it to be out of the question. He informed the First Quartermaster General that before the government made any decision, they must have the opinion of Hindenburg and that he would call back at 4.00 pm to receive it.[80] Hindenburg again found himself with enormous power and responsibility placed in his hands, for he now had the final say as to peace or war, whether to accept Versailles or fight on. The politicians, far from stabbing the army in the back, had handed the baton to OHL and offered exactly what Ludendorff had demanded in late October 1918 and what Hindenburg had called for in his letter just a few days previously – a fight to the death rather than a meek surrender. Groener knew resistance was pointless and the break-up of the Reich would be the inevitable outcome of Allied conquest. Hindenburg knew this too but was, as we have seen, tempted to go down fighting. After several hours of discussion, he agreed that signing was the only option. Once again, however, he abdicated responsibility. Around 3.45 pm, Groener asked the Chief of the General Staff what he should tell Ebert. 'You know as well as I do that armed resistance is impossible,' was Hindenburg's evasive reply. 'There is no need for me to stay. You can give the answer to the President as well as I can,' said Hindenburg, and he left the room, leaving Groener to make the fateful telephone call.[81] Groener was careful not to mention Hindenburg's name in his conversation with the head of state, and Ebert did the same in conveying OHL's advice to the cabinet, ensuring, as they saw it, that the field marshal and his mythical status was kept well away from this shameful moment.[82] Yet such a momentous decision would likely not have been taken without Hindenburg's implicit backing; Groener's words carried so much weight with the politicians because they implicitly indicated the opinion of the field marshal.[83]

Right up to the last moment, a majority in the government and Ebert himself favoured rejection, meaning OHL's intervention was decisive. The following day, Hindenburg submitted his resignation to Ebert, keen to distance himself from the controversial acceptance of the treaty.[84] By leaving immediately, he could, by implication, suggest that he had been opposed to signing, even though he actually lacked the resolve to take as decisive a step as rejecting the treaty. Again Hindenburg could reap the plaudits while avoiding responsibility for his actions. A final insult to German sensibilities came with the signing of the treaty in the Hall of Mirrors in the Palace of Versailles, the same room where, in 1871, Wilhelm I had been proclaimed Kaiser of Germany, formally achieving German unification after the defeat of France in the Franco-Prussian War. On the day the treaty was signed, 28 June 1919, Hindenburg retired from the army for a second time. His final army order issued to all troops that day, as well as many emotional sentiments about the welfare of the Fatherland, also included the line: 'Soldiers, I recently informed the Government that as a solider I would rather perish in honour than sign a humiliating peace.'[85] Once more, the truth was bent and Hindenburg's reputation was preserved. The field marshal would thus avoid the blame for the conditions that were about to be imposed despite his decision being decisive in Germany's reluctant acceptance of the treaty. There is an argument to be made that had the Germans at least put up token resistance, it would have dispelled the burgeoning *Dolchstoss* and 'undefeated in the field' narrative as Allied superiority would have been made patently clear and Versailles would have been seen for what it was – a peace imposed on a defeated power.[86] Naturally, Hindenburg and Groener had no interest in restarting hostilities as they knew it would only bring shame and total defeat on the German Army they had worked so hard since the armistice to preserve. Despite being well aware of this sad reality, and advising the politicians to behave accordingly, Hindenburg would in just a few short months be promoting the myth that the German Army had never been beaten and betrayal at home was responsible for the disasters that had befallen the Reich.

As Goltz has argued, had Hindenburg retired peacefully and made no further interventions in political life, the efforts of both Groener and democratic politicians to insulate his hero status from responsibility for 1918 and Versailles may not have been so disastrous for the new republic.[87] As it was, Hindenburg would use his untarnished reputation to catapult the Stab-in-the-Back myth into the mainstream and ensure it became the dominant narrative of German defeat in the Great War. The Weimar government had convened a public inquiry to investigate the war. It had three aims: to forestall Allied demands for the extradition of war criminals, to establish responsibility for starting the war in 1914 in light of the infamous Versailles War Guilt Clause, and to establish responsibility for Germany's disastrous defeat.[88] The pro-democracy parties hoped that the inquiry would bolster the Republic, for they had advocated a peace without annexations in 1917, yet Germany had instead been humiliated, therefore blame for both starting the war and its disastrous end could be assigned elsewhere and they could secure the moral high ground.[89]

Almost immediately after the inquiry opened on 21 October 1919, it became clear that hopes of debunking the *Dolchstoss* and discrediting the military and the Kaiser's government would be dashed. The questioning of many witnesses, such as former chancellor Bethmann-Hollweg, proved to be unenlightening, while the right went onto the offensive with the testimony of Karl Helfferich, a former civil servant, wartime vice chancellor (during which time he had become a vocal supporter of OHL's policies) and now a leading figure in the new Nationalist party (DNVP). Helfferich contemptuously ignored the questions of the parliamentarians on the panel and instead launched a vitriolic attack against the 'November Criminals', denouncing pro-democracy politicians who had betrayed the nation and accusing the panel of treason.[90] The inquiry had now become a prominent public platform from which to attack the Republic, dig up old graves from the revolution the previous year and promote the Stab-in-the-Back fiction. Right-wing tempers were raised further when it was revealed that the nation's hero, Paul von Hindenburg, was to be, as they saw it, dragged out of his retirement in Hanover to be interrogated by traitors in Berlin.[91] The committee had intended on leaving the field marshal alone; Hindenburg was only called because Erich Ludendorff, who republican politicians were more than willing to denounce, had refused to attend his hearing unless accompanied by his chief.[92]

Hindenburg's presence in Berlin in November soon proved politically explosive. For the first time since the left-wing revolution a year before, right-wing and nationalist demonstrators flooded the streets upon his arrival on the morning of 12 November, the crowds being so large the field marshal struggled to get to his car. As well as expressing their devotion to the war hero, the gathering had clear nationalist, anti-democratic and anti-Semitic overtones.[93] The presence of leftist counter-demonstrations in which Hindenburg was condemned as a 'mass slaughter' resulted in fights and angry clashes that continued throughout the week, despite the field marshal's public call for calm, and increasingly the government began to fear that Hindenburg's presence in the capital might spark a coup.[94] On 14 November, a crowd of some 3–4,000 nationalist students mobbed the old man's car in central Berlin, expressing their outrage that their hero had been summoned like a schoolboy to answer to a 'Jewish government'.[95]

For the duration of his visit, Hindenburg stayed at the villa of Karl Helfferich, where they were joined by Erich Ludendorff. The trio planned out how the forthcoming testimony of Germany's two wartime leaders could be used for maximum political advantage. It was agreed that Hindenburg would not accept any of the questions asked by the panel, even though they had courteously submitted six to him in advance for him to prepare. Instead, the field marshal would read from a prepared statement that was written by Helfferich and Ludendorff. In this text, the Stab-in-the-Back myth was codified and the *Dolchstoss* would become a matter of public record. Ludendorff would address any subsequent technical questions the panel may have in order to avoid the undignified cross-examination of the field marshal. As Helfferich had done earlier in the month, the plan was that Hindenburg and Ludendorff would turn an essentially defensive situation, in which they had been summoned to answer questions, into an offensive one in which they would use the inquiry as a platform to give their version of the story and attack their political enemies.[96]

Almost certainly in Hindenburg's mind was the fact that he had already been approached by the main rightist parties, the DVP and DNVP, to run for president in elections that were expected in the new year.[97] It was vital therefore that at the inquiry he both protected his reputation by distancing himself from Germany's defeat and showed himself capable of combatting the political left. We can dismiss Wheeler-Bennett's assertion that Hindenburg was indoctrinated or hoodwinked by Ludendorff and Helfferich; as we have seen, he had benefited from and contributed to the Stab-in-the-Back myth from the beginning and he had clear personal motives for safeguarding the legend's credibility.[98]

Hindenburg again drew large crowds as he travelled with Ludendorff on the morning of 18 November 1919, with the field marshal contemptuously dismissing these well-wishers when they encouraged him not to appear with the curt phrase, 'Don't bother me, I am on duty.'[99] The Reichstag was heavily guarded and the inquiry committee had tried to ensure no one could doubt as to their deference for the old man; his podium was decorated with flowers and ribbons in the Imperial German colours, while it was agreed in advance that he would not be questioned by any of the Social Democrats on the panel, but rather a former Prussian civil servant of the DDP, Georg Gothein.[100] The two generals appeared in plain clothes and adopted a decidedly cool attitude towards their hosts, despite the warm reception, informing the press afterwards that they had not wished to pay the committee the compliment of appearing in the uniform of Prussian officers.[101] Gothein opened proceedings by apologising on behalf of the inquiry for inconveniencing the field marshal:

> The Committee would have been glad to spare you the great trouble of appearing before it and, above all, would gladly have spared you the difficulties of your journey in the winter time, but since General Ludendorff placed great importance upon having his testimony taken at the same time as yours was, we could not avoid the necessity of requesting you to appear before us.[102]

Hindenburg replied:

> I may be permitted to state that I felt it incumbent upon myself to take my place at the side of my faithful companion in arms during great and troubled days, and that I am grateful that the opportunity has been afforded me to do so. I am also grateful for having had my journey made easier for me.[103]

The two generals had to be sworn in, but at this point Ludendorff interrupted. The former Quartermaster General read a statement which denied the two were obligated to testify as, according to the criminal code, witnesses need not testify if they endanger incriminating themselves. Ludendorff insisted that they were testifying merely to help establish the historical truth. 'It is only by learning the truth that the German people can recover, and it is for this reason, and for this reason alone, that we are ready to give our testimony under oath.'[104] Gothein dismissed this intervention as a 'private expression of will' and then proceeded to ask Hindenburgh the first of the prepared questions, which regarded OHL's decision to demand unrestricted submarine warfare in spring 1917, a decision that had of course brought the United States into the conflict: When and why had the decision been taken? Hindenburg, as agreed beforehand with Ludendorff and Helfferich, completely ignored Gothein's line of enquiry. Instead, he took his statement from his pocket and requested that he be allowed to read it. The chairman, a Social Democrat, refused on the grounds that this would be an expression of personal opinion rather than fact.[105] Hindenburg ignored the chairmen entirely and started to read. His delivery was calm but not especially impressive. At various points, the chairman and Gothein attempted to interrupt the field marshal, the chairman ringing his bell and decrying expressions of opinion. Hindenburg completely ignored these interventions, offering only contemptuous stares before continuing.[106] In a lengthy address, he stated that the German people, as well as the Kaiser, the government and the army, had not wanted war in 1914, but that thanks to the military's preparedness:

> In spite of the superiority of the enemy in men and materiel, we could have brought the struggle to a favourable issue if determined and unanimous co-operation had existed between the army and those at home. But whereas the enemy showed an ever greater will for victory, divergent party interests began to manifest themselves with us. These circumstances soon led to a disintegration of our will to conquer… [Gothein interrupted as this was an expression of opinion on internal politics. Hindenburg continued regardless.] Owing to this, our will to victory was undermined. I looked for energy and co-operation, but found pusillanimity and weakness.[107]

Finally, the field marshal concluded with a closing statement that left the committee room in stunned silence:

> History will judge what I say to you today … When we [meaning Ludendorff and himself] assumed leadership of the Supreme Command, we proposed that the government combine all forces at its disposal for the successful prosecution of the war. What became of these proposals is known … I wanted complete and willing co-operation. Instead, as a result of party competition, we encountered failure and defeatism … We were constantly concerned whether we would maintain the support of the Home Front until the war could be successfully concluded. At this time [Hindenburg does not indicate a date, seemingly the last year of the war] the intentional undermining of the army and navy began. Those troops who remained loyal had to carry the additional burden of those, inspired by revolutionary ideas, who did not … Ultimately, we could no longer expect that our commands would be executed. We asked that we be allowed to enforce strict discipline

to counter this subversion but our appeals were fruitless. We were no longer able to control the forces at our disposal. The collapse was inevitable. The revolution was only the capstone.

An English general rightly said, 'The German army was stabbed in the back.' The solid core of the army remained true. Like the officer corps, it stood firm. Where the true guilt lay has been demonstrated. If you need any more proof, I need only refer you to the statement that I quoted earlier and our enemies' amazement that they had won.

That is the general trajectory of the tragedy that befell Germany. We succeeded brilliantly on many fronts and achieved unsurpassed victories. The accomplishments of our army and people deserve nothing but the highest praise.[108]

With this, Hindenburg folded up his statement and reclined in his chair. Gothein attempted to get the hearing back on track by repeating his original question about unrestricted U-boat warfare. Hindenburg replied briefly about the necessity of ending the naval blockade of Germany before referring Gothein to Ludendorff for more detail. Now the examination became more bad-tempered as Ludendorff fired off a rapid series of accusations and denials under the committee's questioning, with the Berlin correspondent of *The Times* writing:

Hindenburg was calm, massive, and impassive, making his observations without excitement. Even when he expressed indignation he did not do it indignantly. Ludendorff, on the other hand, was excited, and raised his voice to a shout when he declared that a certain article put in evidence by the Commission was an infamous lie. He repudiated part of Count Bernstorff's testimony, declaring it to be an insult to his honour – in short, making scenes generally that raised the temperature, if not to fever heat, at least to a pitch which made both Press and public declare that the proceedings for once were really interesting. Count Bernstorff was cool and collected. In a brush between him and Ludendorff the latter declared that 'he was the defender of his own honour'.[109]

Hindenburg sat quietly throughout these fiery exchanges, intervening in proceedings just once more to comment that his and Ludendorff's views had always coincided during the war.[110] The cross-examination closed around noon and the generals left, returning to Helfferich's villa and addressing the press outside. After requesting and receiving permission from the government to leave, Hindenburg returned to his home in Hanover the next day, receiving another mobbing and honour guard on his way to the railway station. From the perspective of the two generals, their appearance at the inquiry would prove a triumph.

Given their wholehearted endorsement of the Hindenburg myth, it was now next to impossible for the democratic parties to condemn the war hero, despite his explosive and damaging testimony. The impact of Hindenburg's testimony on 18 November cannot be underestimated. The field marshal was loved and respected, considered a brilliant military leader and the epitome of honour and duty; he was unquestionably the most popular living German at the time.[111] His word carried enormous weight and his message to the German people on the most public stage conceivable was clear: under oath he told them they had been betrayed, that they had been stabbed in the back. Telford Taylor would label Hindenburg's statement 'among the most politically effective words ever uttered'.[112] What had been a conspiracy theory was, at least for a significant portion of German society, now a statement of fact. Hindenburg's was the decisive evidence in turning the *Dolchstoss* into the dominant explanation for German defeat. Furthermore, Hindenburg's appearance at the inquiry was a major news story, so his accusations of treachery were printed and debated in the newspapers repeatedly over the coming days, bringing the legend to a far greater audience, with right-wing columnists proclaiming 'a victory of the truth'.[113] Wheeler-Bennett concluded that Hindenburg's evidence did immeasurable harm, 'contributed materially' to the subsequent far-right terrorist campaign that would see the assassination of several high-profile democratic politicians and reckoned that 'the marshal's desire for exculpation had overridden his sense of justice and truth'.[114] Dorpalen calls the hearing the 'official birth' of the Stab-in-the-Back legend and maintains that once Hindenburg had thrown his weight behind this version of events, 'all contrary documentary evidence and expert opinion were to prove utterly ineffective'.[115] The analysis of historian Anna van der Goltz probably put it best and is worth quoting at length:

> Hindenburg thus lent his mythical authority to the 'stab-in-the-back' allegation. His endorsement popularised the narrative immediately … Hindenburg had not invented the narrative, but broadened its dissemination considerably… He was therefore midwife to an idea German society had been pregnant with since the revolution – an idea that burdened the young republic with accusations of treachery, thereby intensifying political polarisation and shifting the political climate decisively to the right.[116]

Chickering argues that the testimony was also Ludendorff's greatest contribution to the Stab-in-the-Back myth, for Hindenburg's words came from his pen and were clearly building on the themes established by his recent memoirs – indeed, certain points of the testimony could be interpreted as a direct riposte to the stinging critiques his book had received.[117] Furthermore, Matthias Farhrenwaldt has traced direct connections between passages of Ludendorff's earlier writings and the Hindenburg testimony, and Ludendorff's book would be cited and even directly quoted by later witnesses in the parliamentary inquiry in defending the *Dolchstoss* interpretation of defeat.[118]

Before long, Hindenburg was to make another significant contribution to the *Dolchstoss* canon in the form of his memoirs. Negotiations had already begun in the first half of 1919 and eventually Hindenburg agreed a contract with Leipzig publisher, S. Hirzel. The book was quite consciously, as Hindenburg himself described it to a friend, *volkstümlich* (sentimental, dewy-eyed), written with a mass audience in mind and designed to showcase Hindenburg the man and personality and be an inspirational read rather than getting bogged down in military and political detail, as Ludendorff's tomes had been guilty of doing.[119] The title, *Out of my Life (Aus meinem Leben)*, pointed to the book's spiritual and personal focus. As usual with the old man, Hindenburg took a back seat, merely advising a team of ghostwriters as to what the memoirs should, and indeed should not, include. The writing, for the most part, was done by a former OHL aide who had written the official history of the war, Colonel Hermann Mertz von Quirnheim, and DNVP politician Otto Hoetzsch. The contract drawn up ensured that the ghostwriters would not be credited or even mentioned anywhere in the text and that the book should be modelled on the wildly popular, bestselling memoirs of Bismarck.[120] While Ludendorff's earlier memoirs, a 270,000-word, two-volume tome, had relatively limited appeal outside of fervent nationalists and military specialists, Hindenburg consciously requested of his ghostwriters that his own war memoirs be accessible and easy to read. As a result, *Out of my Life* would have genuine mass market, popular appeal. Hindenburg the self-publicist was in evidence again. The writers were careful to avoid any controversial topics or contributions to the debates surrounding the war and so OHL's intervention in politics, the sacking of Bethmann-Hollweg, Ludendorff's loss of nerve at Tannenberg and his final sacking are either glossed over or ignored entirely.[121] The only contentious aspect of the conflict that was addressed in *Out of my Life* was, of course, responsibility for Germany's defeat. The Stab-in-the-Back myth was emphasised in dramatic terms:

> We were at the end! Like Siegfried under the deceitful javelin thrust of the grim Hagen, our weary front collapsed; in vain she had tried to drink fresh life out of the dried up spring of our homeland's strength. Our task now was to save the life of the remaining forces of our army for the reconstruction of the fatherland. That left much hope for the future.[122]

The final part of the book was entitled 'Beyond Our Powers' and several passages alluded to the betrayal of both politicians and revolutionaries at home:

> The homeland collapsed sooner than the Army. In these circumstances we were unable to offer any real resistance to the ever-increasing pressure of the President of the United States. Our Government cherished hopes of moderation and justice. The German soldier and the German statesman went different ways. The gulf between them could no longer be bridged.[123]

The revolution, naturally, was portrayed as a disaster that had brought about collapse while the army remained 'undefeated in the field':

The German battle line was then still connected with the lines of communication, the life-nerve which kept it in touch with the homeland. Gloomy pictures were certainly revealed here and there, but generally speaking the situation was still stable. Yet this could not last for long. The strain had become almost intolerable. Convulsions anywhere, whether at home or in the Army, would make collapse inevitable.

Our fears of such convulsions began to be realised. There was a mighty upheaval in the homeland. The Revolution was beginning. As early as November 5 General Gröner hastened to the capital, foreseeing what must happen if a halt were not called, even at the eleventh hour. He made his way to his Emperor's presence and described the consequences if the Army were deprived of its head. In vain! The Revolution was now in full career, and it was purely by chance that the general escaped the clutches of the revolutionaries on his way back to Headquarters. This was on the evening of November 6.

The whole national organism now began to shake with fever. Calm consideration was a thing of the past. No one thought any longer about the consequences to the whole body politic, but only of the satisfaction of his own passions. These passions in turn began to foster the craziest plans. For could there be anything more crazy than the idea of making life impossible for the Army? Has a greater crime ever had its origin in human thought and human hatred? The body was now powerless; it could still deal a few blows, but it was dying. Was it surprising that the enemy could do what he liked with such an organism, or that he made his conditions even harder than those he had published?[124]

Interestingly, the memoirs end abruptly after this with the close of the Great War and omit any link between Hindenburg and the revolution and subsequent democratic regime, brushing over entirely his advice to the Kaiser to abdicate and the field marshal's service for the Republic from November 1918 to June 1919, including his reluctant acceptance of the Versailles treaty and advice to Ebert to sign it. Naturally, Hindenburg was ensuring his reputation would be protected from any association with the defeat, revolution and shameful peace, but the book's dishonesty on these counts played into the *Dolchstoss* trope that it was republican politicians who were to blame, not the military leadership. Hindenburg clearly was careful about ensuring his memoirs would continue to preserve and indeed enhance his mythical reputation and he was consciously attempting to further his cult status. Deliberately simple, uplifting and easy to read, *Out of my Life* proved to be a best-seller, with several hundred thousand copies being sold on publication in 1920, resulting in the book running into many editions.[125] Despite adding very little to the literature on the conflict, it was a popular Christmas and birthday gift and the author's prestige ensured its commercial success. With sales came the ever-wider dissemination of the Stab-in-the-Back myth. Dangerous conspiracy theories and disinformation were thus making their way onto the bookshelves of countless German homes thanks to the perfidiousness of Germany's most venerated hero.

As in all their previous collaborations, Ludendorff was the chief architect of the *Dolchstoss*, while Hindenburg, with his prestige and untarnished hero status, was the frontman who leant the myth vital legitimacy and credibility. It is easy to see why Ludendorff promulgated the Stab-in-the-Back legend. He had been blamed, vilified and ultimately sacked for German defeat in the autumn of 1918 and he clearly sought a scapegoat for his own failings. Having long been associated with far-right and Pan-German politics, ideas of left-liberal or Jewish conspiracies and subversion sat comfortably with his worldview. The cognitive dissonance between his own knowledge of the military situation and his promotion of the *Dolchstoss* can perhaps be explained by the severe mental collapse Ludendorff suffered in 1918–19. The Stab-in-the-Back was essential to Ludendorff's own sense of self in the new reality brought about by military catastrophe; it was his way of making sense of the changed world in which he found himself. On the other hand, no such excuses can be made for Hindenburg's acceptance and propagation of the *Dolchstoss*. Like Ludendorff, he was well aware of the military realities of the second half of 1918 and the scale of the German defeat. Yet for purely selfish reasons – the defence of his own and his army's reputation – he became not just a subscriber to but the cheerleader-in-chief for the myth of a German army undefeated in the field betrayed by the home front. Through his famous testimony in November 1919 and his best-selling memoirs, he did even more than Ludendorff to sell the *Dolchstosslegende* to the German public at large. While Ludendorff was the brains, working from as early as September 1918 to devise the strategy to exonerate the military and immediately after the war constructing a false narrative through his writings, Hindenburg was the PR man who was crucial in convincing millions of Germans that the army had been wronged and that the Republic – and implicitly, therefore, leftists and Jews – were to blame. Like many political lies, the Stab-in-the-Back myth was relatively easy to debunk, and indeed it was, in detail, in 1919 by progressive journalists. However, Germany's two most famous and influential military experts in Hindenburg and Ludendorff denied that the army had been beaten and instead proclaimed the opposite. Furthermore, the new republican administration not only publicly venerated Hindenburg and adhered to his myth, but also promoted the 'undefeated in the field' fiction, preventing a national self-reflection on the defeat and its true causes. Little wonder then that the majority of Germans believed at least some version of the *Dolchstoss* myth, from the virulent Jewish-Bolshevik conspiracy strain through to the milder undefeated-in-the-field variant.

There can be no doubt that the defeat, and its attribution to a stab in the back, brought about a huge spike in anti-Semitism in German society. American historian Larry Eugene Jones notes an 'explosion' in anti-Semitism in these years and points to the fact that the German right became so imbued with anti-Semitism that even politically moderate candidates of the leading right-wing party, the Nationalists (DNVP), felt it necessary to address the 'Jewish question' in their electoral platforms.[126] The most notable example would be that the fledging Nazi Party, born and nurtured in the post-war atmosphere of suspicion and hatred, was 'deeply committed' to the Stab-in-the-Back myth, which in many ways was instrumental to the Nazi worldview and of course central to their interpretation of the Great War and subsequent revolution.[127] Holger Herwig has posited the not-unreasonable theory that a direct link can be drawn from the Stab-in-the-Back lie to the later anti-Semitism of the Nazis and the Holocaust: 'Is it too far off the mark to suggest that the "twisted road to Auschwitz" began with the *Dolchstosslegende*?'[128] Indeed, Nazi racial policy during the Second World War makes some logical sense when viewed through the prism of the *Dolchstosslegende*. The decisions taken to carry out a 'final solution' of the Jewish question in late 1941 and early 1942 can sadly be justified by the Stab-in-the-Back notion that a Jewish-Bolshevik conspiracy was responsible for defeat in the First World War. As Germany engaged in a life-or-death total war with the Soviet Union, it made sense, according to the twisted Nazi worldview, that measures be taken to ensure the home front was not undermined once again by internal enemies who (according to Hindenburg and Ludendorff) had destroyed the German war effort last time around. In crafting and promoting this malicious lie for purely selfish reasons, Hindenburg and Ludendorff helped ensure their nation would be riven by political polarisation for over a decade, that the new republic would be regarded as the creation of traitorous 'November Criminals', that the majority of the German right would become implacable opponents of democracy and that the populace would embrace the conspiracy theories of Hitler and the Nazis. It was a poisonous political legacy with far-reaching consequences and while the two Great War generals tried to escape responsibility for their own military defeat, they must be held accountable by historians now for spreading such a potent and dangerous falsehood.

Chapter 2

Conspirator: Ludendorff as Public Enemy Number One

'The most dangerous man in Germany for the last four years' – that was how the *New York World* described General Erich Ludendorff in 1923.[1] Given his leadership of two putsches and patronage of countless far-right paramilitary groups and conspiratorial circles in the first years of the Weimar Republic, the sensationalist headline hides a remarkably accurate assessment. Little wonder that in 1921 the army High Command felt it necessary to alert both senior officers and the rank and file to the threat of a Ludendorff-led coup d'état.[2] Nationalists and reactionaries frequently sought Ludendorff's support in this period to lend their projects credibility and wider appeal, and the devious general wasted little time after his brief exile to begin proactively aiding and organising plots to overthrow Germany's first democracy.

Paramilitary politics

Unsurprisingly, just as the convulsions of the German Revolution were beginning to tail off, by mid-1919, many on the right began to dream of a nationalist counter-revolution. The immediate reaction of the German right to the establishment of the Republic and social democratic triumph was to mourn the loss of the monarchy and old army and begin to plot for their restoration. Both the source of and primary vehicle for much of this nationalist plotting was the Freikorps. The Freikorps (literally Free Corps) were paramilitary militia bands formed in the immediate aftermath of the armistice as a response to the revolutionary uprisings of the left. While the majority of returning soldiers in late 1918 wished more than anything else to return home to spend Christmas with their families, a significant minority soon decided to retain their uniform, weapons and equipment and enlist in the various Freikorps militia units quickly established by right-wing army officers. These veterans were understandably distressed by the collapse of the Second Reich and frightened by the menace of Bolshevism, and the Freikorps volunteers were overwhelmingly nationalist, anti-communist, anti-democratic and, in many cases, völkisch in their politics. Völkisch is a rather untranslatable term that describes a racist, anti-Semitic, intensely German far-right worldview built on racial superiority, the ancient German 'blood and soil' and aggressive nationalism, a word Ludendorff described as something only the heart, rather than the head, can comprehend.[3] Naturally, the Freikorps also provided demobilised servicemen, especially those brutalised by war, with an opportunity to continue their military service in a less official capacity. The ranks were thickened by scores of patriotic students and teenagers, their formative years shaped by the Great War and its propaganda of duty and sacrifice, who resented having *just* missed out on joining the brave *Frontkämpfer* (frontline soldier) in fighting the Fatherland's foreign enemies. They now relished the opportunity to fight an internal foe alongside their heroes.[4] Veterans of the Freikorps would dominate the German far right for years to come; indeed, the early Nazi Party was essentially an amalgamation of these paramilitary elements with völkisch pseudo-intellectuals.[5] Captain Ernst Röhm, a staff officer in the Bavarian army and later a leading Nazi, was one of the chief organisers of the Freikorps in the south German state:

> After the ... government in Bavaria approved advertising for the Freikorps, volunteers from all trades and callings in Bavaria hastened to enlist. They included former officers volunteering as rank and file soldiers, students, high school boys, cadets, servicemen who had fought in the field, workers and farmers; all had one thought and inspiration which drove and bound them together. It was a quasi-military community which looked to its leaders and was prepared to follow them blindly.[6]

The Freikorps were not entirely a movement from below, however. Although anything from 25–50,000 diehards had already joined up by January 1919 (and the figure would eventually grow tenfold[7]), the key to the growth of the Freikorps was the benevolence and encouragement of military and civilian officialdom as a result of the Ebert-Groener Pact that had seen the new Social Democratic government cut a deal with OHL. The Freikorps blossomed in early 1919 due to the active support and endorsement of their activities by both the republican government and the army High Command in order to tame the revolution. The need for Freikorps troops to achieve the task in hand was paramount, given the parlous state the Germany Army was in at the end of 1918, the lacklustre performance of official troops in combatting revolutionaries and the unreliability of some war-weary units in fighting their fellow countrymen. With the rapid demobilisation, nay dissolution, from below of the old Imperial Army as soldiers hurried home from four years of war and the Kaiserreich collapsed, General Groener essentially built a new counter-revolutionary army from scratch in the first half of 1919, the essential component being the integration of up to half a million Freikorps troops; the new Reichswehr represented a rapid remobilisation of both hardened veterans and schoolboy recruits for the counter-revolutionary cause.[8] In giving Hindenburg and Groener free reign to establish the new army, Weimar's leaders missed the opportunity of building a democratic army loyal to the new regime. They believed they needed the Kaiser's officers to defend them against the revolutionary left, but the consequence was handing immense power to the enemies of democracy – both in maintaining the position of reactionary commanders and arming hundreds of thousands of ardent nationalists.

The most serious left-wing threat to the new republic came in January 1919 with the uprising of the Spartacist League – later the German Communist Party (KPD) – in the capital. The revolutionary leaders Karl Liebknecht and Rosa Luxembourg rallied 15,000 fighters, many of them ex-soldiers, to their cause and seized key parts of central Berlin with 2,000 machine guns and several local army units defecting to the cause.[9] Lacking the manpower in the official army, Defence Minister Gustav Noske (the self-proclaimed 'bloodhound' of the revolution) and the OHL were forced to call in the Freikorps to put down the revolt, which they did with infamous brutality – Liebknecht and Luxembourg were viciously beaten and executed, the latter dumped in Landwehr Canal.[10] Across Germany, similar scenarios played out on a smaller scale as the German Revolution was tamed by force, the Social Democrats and liberals of the new republic allied in a bloody marriage of convenience with the monarchists and nationalists of the Freikorps and army High Command, united only by their fear of communism. In March 1919, Noske effectively let the far-right paramilitaries loose with an order that all those opposing government forces with a weapon in their hands would be summarily shot.[11] The case of Bavaria is instructive of the consequences of this Faustian pact; a short-lived Soviet had ousted the SPD administration, whose Reichswehr troops failed to drive the revolutionaries from Munich. Noske dispatched government troops to the southern state, including many Freikorps units, who, alongside swiftly recruited Bavarian militias easily retook the state capital in May 1919. There they indulged in an orgy of counter-revolutionary violence against suspected 'Reds', including the massacre of a meeting of Catholic craftsmen, twenty-one of whom were beaten to death.[12] In total, somewhere from 600 to 1,000 people were killed, most of them civilians, compared to just thirty-eight deaths among government forces, both regular army and Freikorps militia.[13] While the Social Democratic prime minister of Bavaria, Johannes Hoffmann, was able to resume his post, the local administration, especially the army and security forces, were firmly in the hands of Freikorps men, and soon they would make their political clout felt in the state. Freikorps brigades also fought less official campaigns, including running border battles in Silesia on the new German-Polish frontier and doomed attempts to protect German holdings in the Baltic states (gained at the Treaty of Brest-Litovsk) against the Red Army, a project that had the full support of Hindenburg, perhaps as an attempt to salvage some prestige for OHL from an otherwise disastrous war.[14]

This large and potentially dangerous armed force of reactionaries and rightist zealots began to become a political threat to the Republic in the second half of 1919. With the immediate danger of a Communist takeover crushed, the allegiance of the Freikorps to the democratic government rapidly disappeared. The burgeoning Stab-in-the-Back myth and the punitive terms of the Versailles peace treaty, made public in May, stoked nationalist passions, reigniting opposition to the Weimar politicians who right-wingers saw as first betraying the nation in November 1918 and now selling out to the Allies again by signing the hated treaty. Without doubt, German public opinion at large was outraged with the terms of the Versailles *Diktat*; famous sociologist and philosopher Max Weber, who had run as a DDP candidate in the January 1919 elections and had a hand in writing the new constitution, called for a national revolution against an imposed peace and praised General Ludendorff.[15] Interestingly, Weber, having helped draft the German response to the peace proposals, met with Ludendorff that summer to try to persuade him to hand himself over to the Allied war crimes tribunal in an attempt to secure more favourable terms. Although certainly not sharing his politics, Weber admired the general and, according to his wife, he *wanted* to believe that the supposed military genius was a great man. He was to be disappointed when they met in person.

Ludendorff (who knew about Weber's desire from his letter): Why do you come to me with this? How can you expect me to do a thing like that?

Weber: The honour of the nation can be saved only if you give yourself up.

Ludendorff: The nation can go jump in the lake! Such ingratitude!

Weber: Nevertheless, you must render us this last service.

Ludendorff: I hope to be able to render more important services to the nation.

Weber: Well, then your remarks are probably not meant so seriously either. Incidentally, it is not only a matter of the German people but one of restoring the honour of the officer corps and of the army.

Ludendorff: Why don't you go and see Hindenburg? After all, he was the General Field Marshal.

Weber: Hindenburg is seventy years old and besides, every child knows that at the time you were Number One in Germany.

Ludendorff: Thank goodness!

Having established that the general was not willing to give himself up for his nation (although Ludendorff had ominously hinted at other ways he would serve Germany), the conversation moved to the Weimar system:

Ludendorff (driven into a corner, and evading the issue): There you have your highly praised democracy! You and the *Frankfurter Zeitung* [a liberal newspaper] are to blame for it! What has improved now?

Weber: Do you think that I regard the *Schweinerei* [unholy mess] that we now have as democracy?
Ludendorff: If you talk that way, maybe we can have a meeting of the minds.
Weber: But the *Schweinerei* that preceded it was not a monarchy either.
Ludendorff: What is your idea of a democracy, then?
Weber: In a democracy the people choose a leader whom they trust. Then the chosen man says, 'Now shut your mouths and obey me. The people and the parties are no longer free to interfere in the leader's business.'
Ludendorff: I could like such a 'democracy'![16]

Predictably, as it turned out, Ludendorff's vision of how to save the nation from the ignominy of Versailles and party political chaos had more in common with the Freikorps view than Weber's presidential model. At the same time as army officers and paramilitaries were beginning to plot the overthrow of the new republic, Ludendorff, having returned to Berlin, re-engaged with the very highest circles of far-right nationalist politics. For men like Ludendorff, the peace terms were totally unacceptable and any government that adhered to them was illegitimate. A strong, authoritarian regime was required that would have the courage to defy the treaty and crush internal and foreign enemies ruthlessly. The remobilisation of the Fatherland that the recruitment of the Freikorps had represented would have to be extended to a *levée en masse* should the Allies attempt to enforce Versailles by military means.[17] Such a plan was a jingoistic fantasy; Germany's crippled military and economy was in no state to put up armed resistance, as Groener had concluded when the government had sounded out High Command over the possibility of refusing to sign at the peace conference. And popular support for a militaristic or monarchist regime simply did not exist, as exemplified by the recent revolution, in which above all else, the masses had demanded peace and the abdication of the Kaiser. But none of this stopped Ludendorff throwing himself into conspiracies to stage an army coup, overturn Versailles, and crush the 'reds' once and for all. That it was irrational or impossible did not especially matter; the desire of the Freikorps and a large portion of the army to 'turn back the clock', to erase or reverse November 1918, was an emotional response to the disorientating effects of the armistice, revolution and peace treaty. It is perhaps understandable that, given his mental state over the previous twelve months, Ludendorff was out of touch with political and military realities and, of course, public opinion. In the end, Max Weber concluded it was probably best that the infamous general had not handed himself over to the enemy:

Perhaps it is better for Germany that he does not give himself up. He would make an unfavourable personal impression. The enemy would find once again that the sacrifices of a war which put this type out of commission have been worthwhile. Now I understand why the world resists the attempts of men like him to place their heels upon the necks of others. If he should again meddle with politics, he must be fought remorselessly.[18]

Unfortunately for German democracy, meddling in politics was precisely what Ludendorff had in mind.

The Kapp Putsch

As we have seen, for his first weeks after returning from Sweden, Ludendorff resided in the exclusive Hotel Adlon in central Berlin. He soon moved to a more permanent home when he and his wife were lent a lavish flat on the leafy Viktoriastrasse, overlooking the Tiergarten Park, by a former colleague from OHL, furnished decadently with Impressionist artwork, including that of Manet and Von Gogh.[19] Soon, the Ludendorff residence became a hub for far-right figures, with near-constant visits from a diverse cast of characters; the former Fatherland Party leader Wolfgang Kapp, the commander of the Berlin garrison General von Lüttwitz, Ludendorff's political fixer from the old days Colonel Max Bauer, Freikorps leaders Captain Waldemar Pabst and Major Franz von Stephani, as well as Ludendorff's only surviving stepson, Heinz Pernet, who was now serving in the Cavalry Guards fighting Spartacists.[20] 'In the beginning, Ludendorff was surrounded by a small circle, but the number of his clientele increased from day to day, and finally it was like the consulting room of a fashionable physician.'[21] What Ludendorff created in 1919–20 (and maintained up to 1923) was a network of soldiers, paramilitaries, politicians and journalists that shared both a völkisch, nationalistic ideology, and in many cases a personal loyalty to the general, leading German scholar Bruno Thoss to label this shadowy web the 'Ludendorff Circle'.[22] It was clear that these were not merely social calls. Ludendorff declared to his wife at this time: 'The greatest blunder of the revolutionaries was to leave us all alive. If I once get back to power, there will be no quarter. I should string up Ebert, Scheidemann, and their comrades with a clear conscience and watch them dangle!'[23]

Chickering argues that Ludendorff and his clique of rebellious officers essentially viewed post-war politics as a civil war, one in which military authority must predominate.[24] As nationalist sentiment continued to smoulder in the wake of Versailles, conversations and aspirations became more concrete plans during the autumn and winter of 1919, and the conferences at Viktoriastrasse began examining the possibility of an armed seizure of power. As early as July 1919, conversations between Ludendorff, Kapp and others were working on the assumption of when – not if – a coup should be launched, and it was agreed that the circle should make their move within two years.[25] At this time,

Colonel Bauer, speaking in Ludendorff's name, met with officers from the British Military Government in Cologne (overseeing areas occupied by Allied troops) seeking to win British approval for the coup. Despite Bauer's insistence that Ludendorff would head merely a temporary military dictatorship, with the end goal being a constitutional monarchy, the British Foreign Office decided to ignore the military plotters.[26] As preparations gathered pace, Captain Pabst, after obtaining Ludendorff's consent (for he held the highest rank of the conspirators), took the first step in organising this coterie into a more formal, if secretive, body. The *Nationale Vereinigung* (National Association) took up offices in the old Fatherland Party headquarters on Schellingstrasse and Pabst, Kapp and Bauer set to work building up the organisation. As well as providing the Ludendorff Circle with structure, the National Association also managed to attract other less salubrious members including the Hungarian conman Ignaz Trebitsch-Lincoln and a journalist who went by the name of Dr Schnitzler. Trebitsch-Lincoln was a Christian missionary who had lived in Canada, the US and Britain and had talked his way into the Liberal Party, gained a seat in the British Parliament in 1910, been a German spy during the war and would end up converting to Buddhism and working for Chinese warlords. Dr Schnitzler meanwhile was an alias for a bizarre figure named Handke who claimed to be a political scientist, although his doctorate was in fact a mail-order dentistry qualification.[27] Rather more respectable figures such as the arch-conservative Count Kuno von Westarp and the former chaplain to the Kaiser, Dr Gottfried Traub, also lent their services to the Association. It must be said, the National Association appears to have been very poorly organised, with Margarethe Ludendorff later writing that its office had been run 'with almost criminal carelessness and entirely devoid of system'.[28]

Although not directly involved in the practical planning of the plot (Goodspeed alleges due to his erratic and brooding behaviour[29]), Ludendorff was central to the coming nationalist coup attempt that was to become known as the Kapp Putsch. Ludendorff's contacts in the military and civilian world were essential, tying together the disparate strands of the conspiracy. No one else on the far right had Ludendorff's clout or prestige, and it was the general himself who secured from the industrialist Hugo Stinnes the hard cash to finance the National Association and their schemes.[30] Ludendorff's involvement took up so much of his time that in the early months of 1920 his wife Margarethe essentially claims that their relationship began to fall apart, therefore historians who see him as a peripheral figure to the Kapp Putsch are clearly mistaken.[31] It was first and foremost a military operation, although there were significant connections between the officers and the political right; Wolfgang Kapp himself was a member of the presidium of the DNVP.[32] Documents pertaining to the coup attempt attest to Ludendorff's centrality to the plot, and there can be no doubt that, despite his omission from some accounts of the putsch, he was a decisive figure in the conspiracy.[33]

But who was to lead the coup? For whatever reason, Ludendorff did not become the figurehead of the military plot, despite being the senior general (albeit retired) in the circle and the patron of the National Association. In his later writings, the general would claim that he was prepared 'to accept full responsibility for a national dictatorship', i.e. that he held out hopes all this plotting might restore to him the power he had during the war, if not more, and that he was not prepared to play second fiddle.[34] It is unclear whether his co-conspirators shared this view or if he was deliberately sidelined as too divisive a figure in the army and wider country. Instead of Ludendorff, Wolfgang Kapp, the East Prussian civil servant, was to be civilian leader and candidate for chancellor, while the military leader was General Walther von Lüttwitz, head of Gruppenkommando 1 – the designation for forces east of the Elbe, including the Berlin region. Lüttwitz's credentials for leadership were strong; he had overseen the suppression of the Spartacist revolt, been a vocal supporter of the Freikorps and shared their ultra-nationalist beliefs, earning him the moniker 'father of the Freikorps'. While possessing the huge advantage of directly commanding the troops who would carry out the putsch, Lüttwitz lacked subtly; his behaviour in the days leading up to the coup attempt was less than discreet.[35] There remains another possibility as to why Ludendorff himself was not the slated leader. As will become clear over the course of this chapter, throughout his career as a revolutionary, Ludendorff took precautions to ensure he always had deniability; he never launched a coup in his own name, nor admitted to ever being involved in planning one – his participation, he always claimed, was due to his being coincidently present when a putsch broke out. The ludicrous explanations he would develop for his role in both the Kapp Putsch and Hitler's Beer Hall Putsch three years later betray Ludendorff's desperation to avoid accountability and repercussions; just as with German defeat in the war, he always sought to shift responsibility. Equally, in both cases, it appears that his reverential hero status with the far right meant that his fellow conspirators were keen to help Ludendorff avoid direct involvement so that he could escape scot-free. Whatever the truth of the matter, events moved quickly, and Ludendorff did not appear to be the master of them. Admittedly, neither did Lüttwitz or Kapp.

Despite months of plotting, plans for the putsch were not fully in place when the Freikorps and dissident officers finally made their move in March 1920. The trigger for the coup was the government's attempts to comply with the hated Versailles treaty. The Allies demanded that the Reichswehr be reduced to 200,000 men by 10 April 1920, in preparation for the final figure of 100,000, and so Freikorps troops began fearing for their livelihoods.[36] Additionally, the plotters must have been alarmed by the possibility that the very militias they hoped would propel them to power would soon be disbanded. It was now or never, and the cool response of other leading generals when Lüttwitz floated his intentions did not deter the putschists.[37] The reduction in the size of the military was an intensely political question because the government and Reichswehr command had to choose *which* units to disband. Both agreed on the desirability of starting the cutbacks with some of the most notorious Freikorps, namely the Marine Brigade Ehrhardt stationed just outside Berlin, as well as another Marine Brigade in Silesia. There were two reasons the Marine Brigades were prioritised by the Social Democratic defence minister, Gustav Noske. Firstly, the Allies were insisting that the navy be reduced to just 15,000 men by the deadline, and these particular Freikorps, as their names imply, were made up of naval personnel.[38] More importantly perhaps, Corvette Captain Ehrhardt's brigade was the key component of Lüttwitz's command. The Ehrhardt brigade had a ferocious reputation as one of the most radical and diehard Freikorps units; they were veterans of the Baltic campaign and the destruction of the Bavarian Soviet, they painted swastikas on their helmets, and with a strength of 5,000 they were the largest and most experienced unit in the vicinity of the capital.[39]

When the order was issued to disband the Marine Brigades on 29 February, Lüttwitz protested the decision vehemently, assured the paramilitaries he would not comply and decided the putsch, which it appears was pencilled in for April, would have to come sooner.[40] The Reichswehr at this time was headed by two men engaged in a protracted power struggle with one another: the Chief of the Army Command General Walther Reinhardt and the Chief of the Truppenamt (Troop Office) General Hans von Seeckt. Reinhardt was the most pro-republican of the senior army officers and was a close ally of Noske. He was determined to oppose any move Lüttwitz and his co-conspirators made with armed force. Meanwhile, Seeckt was Groener's protégé, protector of the army's interests above all else. The Troop Office was actually a front for the old General Staff, concealed due to the famous Prussian institution being forbidden by the Versailles treaty. Both opposed the putschists but for their own reasons and in very different ways.

Seeckt announced on 8 March that, despite Lüttwitz's objections, the order to disband still stood. The defence minister went a step further just two days later; Noske removed the Marine Brigades from Lüttwitz's command and transferred them to the navy in what he hoped would be a fait accompli to ensure their dissolution. General von Lüttwitz was furious and demanded an audience with President Ebert and his defence minister, which took place on the evening of 10 March. The general effectively attempted to carry out a soft coup in the Presidential Palace by outlining a stringent, and quite ridiculous, set of demands to the president, who, after all, was his commander-in-chief. Not only should the Marine Brigades be saved, but the president and government had to resign, Lüttwitz stipulated, and presidential and parliamentary elections be called. Reinhardt was to be dismissed and replaced with a retired DNVP sympathiser, while the government would be composed of non-party experts.[41] Unsurprisingly, Ebert, Reinhardt and Noske declined. Indeed, Noske reminded the maverick general that no officer was permitted to disobey direct orders, nor make demands of their superiors, and that he expected his resignation in the morning. The dramatic meeting effectively fired the starting gun on the Kapp Putsch, for Lüttwitz left enraged and with no intention of relinquishing his command.

On the morning of 11 March, Lüttwitz was formally relieved of his command of Gruppenkommando 1 and, belatedly, Noske ordered the arrest of leading figures from the National Association. Warrants were issued for Wolfgang Kapp, Colonel Bauer, Captain Pabst and Dr Schnitzler – Ludendorff was deferentially omitted from the list. However, sympathisers in the police warned the putschists and they all evaded the authorities, while a raid on the National Association offices found them deserted.[42] Upon hearing of the raid, Lüttwitz realised he had to act and fled to the Marine Brigade camp, 15 miles west of Berlin, and in a swift roadside conference agreed with Captain Ehrhardt to march on the capital at the earliest opportunity. Both men were effectively now mutinying against High Command and the government.

By 12 March, word was out in military circles that the coup was on. Reinhardt attempted to shore up support for the government, visiting various local military and police commanders, most notably the deputy (now acting) head of Gruppenkommando 1, General von Oven, and emphasising the necessity of armed resistance. However, the army chief of command was met mostly with a cool response – the troops would not fire on their own comrades.[43] The situation was looking increasingly grim for the government – they could count on just one Reichswehr regiment (3,000 men) and 9,000 police, a force unlikely to match Ehrhardt's well-armed veterans, even if they did remain loyal and resist. In desperation, late on 12 March Noske dispatched von Oven at the head of a delegation to the Marine Brigade camp at Döberitz to talk the Corvette captain out of his march. Ehrhardt received the two generals sent to him with a loaded pistol and said that things had gone too far to back down now (perhaps the putschists recognised that this was their only opportunity to strike). He repeated Lüttwitz's key demands – with the addition of the general being restored to his post – to which von Oven suggested Ehrhardt halt his brigade's march at the Siegesallee (the boulevard through the Berlin Tiergarten which leads to the Brandenburg Gate), so that the government could respond to his terms the following morning.[44]

At 1.00 am on 13 March, Noske held an emergency conference at the Defence Ministry, attended by Generals Reinhardt, von Seeckt, von Oven and seven other senior officers. First, von Oven and his colleague reported on their failure at Döberitz and listed Ehrhardt's demands. Noske was furious at his generals for not arresting or shooting the mutineer, and although military discipline had clearly broken down, one can sympathise with von Oven for not attempting to do so while surrounded by 5,000 murderous paramilitaries. The defence minister did make it clear that negotiation with the rebels was a non-starter –

the terms, after all, were ludicrous – and he now demanded armed resistance to defend the administration. However, Noske and Ebert's policy of cooperation with the old Imperial Army and its officer corps did not yield the desired fruit – the Ebert-Groener pact was undone in a few short sentences from General Hans von Seeckt. His exact words are different according to different witnesses but the sentiment of what he said is clear. The cool, aloof, monocle-wearing head of the Troop Office said simply that he could not permit 'Berlin to be presented with the spectacle of their soldiers fighting each other with live ammunition' and that 'Reichswehr do not fire on Reichswehr! How can you, Herr Minister, countenance a battle at the Brandenburg Gate between troops who have fought side by side against the enemy?'[45] Noske, playing his final card, asked who around the table would fight with him. Only Reinhardt and Noske's own adjutant, Major von Gilsa, replied in the affirmative. An emotional Noske said he would rely on the police, Seeckt claimed they were about to defect. In desperate straits, the defence minister berated the treacherous generals and lamented, 'Everyone has deserted me. Nothing remains but suicide,' before ending the meeting.[46]

At 4.00 am, Noske and Reinhardt convened with President Ebert, Chancellor Gustav Bauer and the cabinet to bring them up to speed with the situation. General Reinhardt and Noske remained belligerent and spoke in favour of gathering whatever loyal forces they could muster and leading the defence at the Brandenburg Gate. Unsurprisingly, the cabinet came to the same conclusion as Seeckt; that there was no hope of resisting the Ehrhardt brigade. As a result, the government opted for flight, first to Dresden, only to find the local commander unsympathetic, then to Stuttgart in south-western Germany. As a mediator, they left behind Justice Minister and Vice-Chancellor Eugen Schiffer, leader of the DDP.[47] As the Republic's political leadership ignominiously fled the capital, the Reich Chancellery press officer prepared a proclamation which was to decide the outcome of the putsch. On behalf of President Ebert, Chancellor Bauer, SPD chairman Otto Wels and the other Social Democrats in the government, the announcement boldly declared:

> Workers, Party Comrades! The military putsch has started. The Baltic mercenaries, fearing the command to dissolve, are trying to remove the Republic and to form a military dictatorship. Lüttwitz and Kapp at their head. … The achievements of a whole year are to be smashed, your dearly bought freedom to be destroyed. Everything is at stake! The strongest countermeasures are required. No factory must work while the military dictatorship of Ludendorff and Co. rules! Therefore down tools! Come out on strike! Deprive the military clique of oxygen! Fight with all means for the Republic! Put all quarrels aside! There is only one way against the dictatorship of Wilhelm II: paralysis of all economic life! No hand must move! No proletarian must help the military dictators! General strike all along the line! Proletarians unite! Down with the counter-revolution![48]

The Communists for the time being stood aloof, unwilling to cooperate with the party that had crushed them so brutally just months before. Soon, however, they would use the power vacuum as an opportunity to stage their own revolutionary activities. The parties of the right meanwhile, namely Gustav Stresemann's DVP and the Nationalists of the DNVP, were outside the governing coalition and adopted a far more ambivalent stance to the coup. Many party members were sympathetic; Kapp, after all, was one of their own.

At the same time as the cabinet was departing, Marine Brigade Ehrhardt was closing in on the capital. The 5,000 Freikorps troops had paused at 5.00 am at the Pichelsdorfer Bridge on Berlin's outskirts to take breakfast and, without having heard from either the government or von Lüttwitz, proceeded into the city, flying the flag of the Imperial Navy and singing the *Ehrhardt-Lied* as they marched through the Tiergarten.[49] By 7.00 am, they had reached the Brandenburg Gate at the end of the great park, the location where General von Oven had promised negotiations would be undertaken and just a short walk from the government quarter. It was now time for the other conspirators to join them. Excitement spread among the men, reclining on the grass after their early morning march; they had spotted the man regarded by many nationalists as the greatest leader of the war – General Ludendorff. Comically, Ludendorff claimed that he had simply left his Viktoriastrasse apartment, overlooking the Tiergarten, for a pleasant walk on a crisp spring morning. Upon seeing the assembled Freikorps in the park, delighted to see 'real soldiers', as he described them, he had unassumingly wandered over to see what was going on.[50] Here was Ludendorff's deniability, as ludicrous as it might appear. Given the fact that first Wolfgang Kapp, then General von Lüttwitz, also happened to appear at the Brandenburg Gate at seven o'clock, the rendezvous was evidently pre-arranged. The National Association was out of the shadows at last; Ludendorff, Lüttwitz, Ehrhardt – and Kapp, in a top hat and pinstriped suit, ready to assume the office of chancellor. With the national anthem playing and the old Imperial colours flying, the foursome now marched at the head of the Marine Brigade through the Brandenburg Gate, on to Unter den Linden, then to the Wilhelmstrasse, which was home to the Reich Chancellery, the Presidential Palace, the Foreign and Finance ministries and numerous Prussian State departments.[51] It had all been so easy – the putschists had seized Berlin without a shot being fired and now entered the corridors of power, ready to overthrow the Republic and defy Versailles. The plotters must have wondered why they had waited so long.

What was the Reichswehr's attitude to the putsch? While von Seeckt and his colleagues had not been prepared to defend the government they supposedly served, they also did not join the Freikorps march on Berlin. Seeckt simply retired to his apartment and awaited events, and most senior officers and regional commanders were equally non-committal. The army's neutrality is, at first glance, hard to understand. On the one hand, the vast majority of officers were sympathetic to either Kapp's dreams of restoring the monarchy or Ludendorff and Lüttwitz's vision of an authoritarian military regime. Either was preferable to the hated Weimar democracy in the eyes of the conservatives and nationalists that made up the unreformed officer corps. If political sympathies did not sway officers, then surely their duty and honour bound them through their oath of allegiance to the constitution and their commander-in-chief, the Reich President? And yet neither pull was sufficient to elicit a reaction from the Reichswehr as a whole. Most chose the course of von Seeckt – to wait things out and preserve the unity of the army by not taking sides. In all likelihood, they shared some of the objections that Seeckt and his ilk at the top of the new army had to the putsch. First and foremost, while sympathising with the objectives of the plotters, Seeckt and his close allies in the Troop Office such as Wilhelm Heye and Kurt von Schleicher (head of the Office's political department) saw the replacement of the Republic as a long-term objective; they had the perception to realise it was impossible in the current political climate. Given how recently the German people had overthrown their Kaiser and the clear working and middle-class support for democracy shown in the elections of 1919, Seeckt and the new generation of officers at the top of the Reichswehr bureaucracy knew they were playing the long game to achieve their political objectives. For now, their priority was the preservation and protection of the army, both from political interference and the sort of division that would be created by participating in or fighting the Kapp Putsch. That way, the Reichswehr would remain intact and independent as a vehicle that could help bring about the desired political change at a later date. Staging a coup that was doomed to fail would only serve to make leftist demands for thorough reform or a democratisation of the military more pertinent and increase the likelihood of a further Allied clampdown on German military activity. Colonel Heye, Seeckt's deputy at the Troop Office, surmised this point of view in his memoirs; although it meant avoiding an internal conflict within the army, he found his passive resistance to the putsch:

> very disagreeable, for Lüttwitz's final aim was also the wish of my heart. But I had to carry out my heavy task as was my duty, because the danger existed that, as the *only* result of the Putsch, a 'war' would break out between 'Reichswehr East' and 'Reichswehr West', to the joy of the triumphant third party, the Ebert government.[52]

If this big picture thinking was beyond some ordinary officers, perhaps they shared Seeckt et al.'s instinctive distaste for the Freikorps. For serious professionals like Seeckt and Schleicher, the Freikorps must have seemed little better than bloodthirsty mercenary bands, loyal first and foremost to their charismatic leaders and a political ideology rather than to military discipline and the chain of command. They had been a convenient tool with which to fight a dirty war against internal enemies, but they stood in the way of creating a modern, highly trained and disciplined professional force. This was especially true of units such as the Ehrhardt Marine Brigade, what Nigel Jones has described as the 'wild, savage fringes of the Freikorps'.[53] The late William A. Pelz, in his readable and iconoclastic history of the German Revolution, sees the army's stance in March 1920 as highlighting the bankruptcy of the military policy of Noske and Ebert and the Faustian pact with Groener in November 1918. Their naïve hope that by cooperating fully with the traditional officer elite, they could build a democratic army, in Pelz's eyes, proved to be a disastrous mistake, with inevitable consequences.[54] Effectively, the army was never going to support the Republic because the SPD had not overhauled it, therefore its stance during the putsch was no surprise. In contrast, Karen Schaefer's recent study of General von Seeckt argues that the enigmatic Reichswehr leader was in fact trying to construct an apolitical army that sought consensus rather than conflict with civilian authority. Schaefer attempts to explain the discrepancy between this stance and Seeckt's attitude to the Kapp Putsch in the following terms: if the Reichswehr had been compelled to fire on the rebels:

> Not only would it be a force void of comradeship, but it would be unable to secure the existence of the Reich either. It would no longer trust either the state or its politicians who had issued them the order to fire at soldiers alongside whom they had once fought in the trenches. Such a force would be able to protect neither the state nor its citizens, especially at the beginning of a change of system. It would be worn out politically and ultimately turn on itself.[55]

Therefore, Seeckt actually saved the Republic with his neutral stance – had he complied with Noske and Reinhardt's demands for armed resistance, the army would have been irreparably damaged and might perhaps have abandoned the government entirely. In Schaefer's view, had the orders been issued to the troops to fight the Ehrhardt Brigade, the army would have splintered and might never have cooperated with the government again. There is validity in both interpretations; it is easy to imagine the reaction of the army if they had been ordered to crush the Kapp conspiracy. While a few officers might have remained faithful to their oath, not least General Reinhardt, the majority would have rather thrown in their lot with the putschists than fire on their own comrades. The result could only have been full-scale civil war – as happened in Spain in 1936 when the army and security forces split over whether to support a nationalist coup or the sitting government – or else a swift triumph for the reactionary rebels. Equally, Pelz is right to point out the total lack of loyalty the officer corps felt to their Social Democratic allies, despite their bloodstained cooperation in 1918–19, and the innate flaws in SPD strategy which the putsch so cruelly exposed. Without a loyal army, the state could never survive in the long run. We might therefore conclude that Seeckt's infamous phrase 'Reichswehr don't fire on Reichswehr' was both the doom and deliverance of the Weimar Republic. The decision of the sphinxlike general and the army leadership to sit things out and back neither side in the Kapp Putsch both condemned the military policy of the Republic's founders as a catastrophic failure *and* saved the new democracy from total collapse just over a year into its existence by averting civil war.

To return to the narrative, the putschists, led by Ludendorff, Lüttwitz and Kapp, entered the Reich Chancellery early on the morning of 13 March 1920 to find the corridors of power deserted. It was a Saturday, so in normal circumstances only a skeleton staff would have been present, but the high civil service, the bureaucrats and mandarins who made the machinery of government tick, had stayed away and largely refused to cooperate with the new regime, hindering the conspirators from the get-go.[56] The same could be said of the Defence Ministry on Bendlerstrasse, where just a few officers remained, and those that did (such as Seeckt's deputy Colonel Heye) were in civilian clothes and following the neutrality policy.[57] Nevertheless, the putschists divided up the spoils of their success: Wolfgang Kapp was the new chancellor, Lüttwitz both defence minister and Chief of Army Command. In keeping with his hands-off, zero-liability approach, Ludendorff was not yet awarded a post, although the position of head of state was left alluringly vacant. Practical problems soon put paid to the lofty aspirations of the new government as Kapp could not find a typist to write up his proclamation of the new administration; instead he eventually had to ask his own daughter. The delay meant Kapp missed the crucial deadline for the Sunday papers to print his bold declaration. It was not until Monday therefore that the German public got to read what the putschists' intentions were:

> Reich and nation are in grave danger. We are speedily approaching the total collapse of the state and legal system. The people only vaguely sense the coming disaster. Prices soar without stopping. Misery is growing. Famine threatens. Corruption, usury, racketeering, and crime show up with ever greater audacity. The ineffective government, lacking authority and tied to corruption, is not capable of mastering the danger. Away with a government in which an Erzberger [the Catholic politician who had negotiated the armistice] is the leading spirit!
>
> Militant Bolshevism threatens us with devastation and violation from the east. Is this government capable of fending it off? How will we avoid external and internal collapse?
>
> Only by re-establishing the authority of a strong state. What concept should lead us in this endeavour?
>
> Nothing reactionary, instead a further free development of the German state, restoration of order, and the sanctity of law. Duty and conscience are to reign again in German lands. German honour and honesty are to be restored

> The National Assembly [the parliament elected in January 1919], continuing to govern without a mandate, has declared itself to be permanent. In violation of the constitution it is postponing elections until the autumn. Instead of protecting the constitution it recently issued with such ceremony, a tyrannical party government already wants to deprive the nation of the important basic right of electing the president.
>
> The chance to save Germany is disappearing; that is why there is no other way left but a government of action ...[58]

Clearly, the putschists did not see the irony in condemning the elected parliament as lacking a mandate, and while claiming to want 'nothing reactionary', the same proclamation also announced that strikes would be suppressed 'without mercy' and that they would end 'the working classes' hostility toward the state'.[59] Kapp signed off in combative fashion:

> Attempts to separate from the Reich will be dealt with as high treason according to martial law. We are strong enough not to have to begin our rule with arrests and other violent measures. But we will strike down any revolt against the new order with ruthless determination.
>
> We will not rule according to theories, but according to the practical needs of the state and the nation as a whole. According to the best German tradition the state must stand above all the struggles of occupational groups and parties. The state is the impartial judge in the current struggle between capital and labour. We reject every class preference, whether for the right or the left. We recognize only German citizens. Every German citizen who in this difficult hour gives to the fatherland what belongs to the fatherland can count on us.
>
> Let each person do his duty! Today work is the most noble duty for everyone. Germany is to be a moral working community! The colours of the German Republic are black-white-red![60]

As Goodspeed has wryly commented, the putschists were at least honest in proclaiming they would not govern according to any theory, because the new government soon descended into farce.[61] The announcement itself was a contradictory mess; it highlighted the plotters' hope that the coup would attract mass support, including from the working class, while simultaneously threatening military reprisals, condemning parliamentary democracy and hailing the black-white-red monarchist flag. This betrays the fact that the National Association's clandestine conferences had been almost entirely concerned with the military matter of seizing power. Perhaps unsurprisingly, the army and Freikorps officers who predominated amongst the conspirators failed to consider the political implications of success or develop a clear programme to implement once in power.[62] On the whole, the staff work and planning for the putsch was abysmally poor, as Ludendorff's first visit to the Defence Ministry later that morning would reveal. Colonel Heye, who was in constant touch with the absent Seeckt, was asked by Ludendorff of his opinion of 'our affair'. Heye's answer was non-committal, sticking to Seeckt's neutrality policy, but he did say pointedly that it seemed odd that they had not yet arrested the government they wished to overthrow. Ludendorff simply grinned and called out to the nearby Lüttwitz and Colonel Bauer, 'Bauer, Heye here is of the opinion we ought to arrest the government,' before hurrying off declaring, 'We shall finish the job!'[63] That such a move had not been carried out, nor an order for the government's arrest issued, perhaps not even considered in the planning of the coup, highlights the total lack of preparation and forethought on the part of the conspirators. Lüttwitz meanwhile appointed new officers to various posts in the ministry, including a new chief of the Troop Office, but Heye and the staff ignored both the new appointees and the orders of Lüttwitz himself, insisting their loyalty was to Seeckt.[64] Chancellor Kapp too was struggling to form a team; his hopes of appealing across class lines by appointing the Social Democrat Carl Severing as economics minister unsurprisingly foundered when Severing turned him down. In the end, the Kapp administration was full of National Association aristocrats and cronies; Traugott von Jagow became minister of the interior, the landowner Freiherr von Wangenheim was minister of agriculture, the conman Trebitsch-Lincoln was Kapp's press officer, while the shady Dr Schnitzler served as political advisor.[65]

The military picture across the country was confusing to say the least. In Berlin, the militarised police and army garrison had put themselves at the disposal of Lüttwitz, who had after all been their commander until his dismissal on 11 March. The district commanders in East Prussia, Breslau, Schwerin, Weimar and Hamburg all declared their support for the putsch.[66] The Marine Brigade von Loewenfeld, stationed in Silesia, sent their congratulations to their comrades in Berlin and seized the provincial capital Breslau, unleashing a reign of counter-revolutionary terror that was condemned by the Reichswehr in the aftermath of the putsch.[67] Regional commanders in Bavaria and the tiny state of Saxony-Weimar-Eisenach (which two months later was absorbed into Thuringia) took advantage of the temporary power vacuum to remove the Social Democrat prime ministers of their respective states, staging their own miniature coups and installing right-wing nationalist regimes.[68] The vast majority of the army did not move, however, neither supporting Ludendorff and Lüttwitz, nor defending the new government; they, like Seeckt, were simply waiting for the putsch to play out. Even General von Möhl, army chief in Bavaria, while in the very act of ousting the Social Democrats in his own state, did not come out in support of the coup in Berlin, instead conveying the Bavarian Reichswehr's neutrality on 14 March.

It is perhaps surprising that the Freikorps as a whole staged no coordinated effort in support of the putsch – Nigel Jones suggests these rootless mercenaries, loyal primarily to their own leaders, had no interest in subordinating themselves to Lüttwitz.[69] This was compounded by the fact that the National Association had completely failed to even make contact with Freikorps units outside the Berlin area before the putsch, meaning their potential supporters were caught off guard as much as anyone else by the revolt and had no plans in place to seize local power. This was very much the case for Captain Ernst Röhm, a staff officer in the Bavarian army and one of the most influential figures in the south German Freikorps movement. Although deeply sympathetic to their cause, Röhm did not hear of the plot until early March and his overriding reaction was one of concern at the lack of preparation and the failure to contact any senior officers in Bavaria.[70] Two of the most famous and powerful Freikorps leaders, Rudolf Berthold and Gerhard Rossbach, only found out about the putsch when the Ehrhardt brigade was already on the march.[71] To have built up a clandestine network of supporters and to draw up a plan for a local seizure of power was simply too great a task in the short time that men like these had to respond – not to mention the potential wounded pride at not having been consulted. Amidst so much uncertainty, with the putschists not making their programme clear for two days, it appears most Freikorps, while deeply unhappy at the lack of action, simply fell into line with their immediate superiors – the regional commanders. The only thing that was clear was the Reichswehr were not firing on Reichswehr. General Maercker, the commander in Dresden who sympathised with the rebels but did not openly back them, communicated to Chancellor Kapp on the night of Sunday, 14 March:

> Germany is at the moment divided into two parts. The one is the whole of western and southern Germany, and the other northern and eastern Germany [the regional commanders who did back Kapp were in the north and east of the country]. If this state of affairs is not terminated soon, a battle between Reichswehr and Reichswehr is inevitable, and that must be prevented at all costs.[72]

Only the navy backed the uprising unequivocally; the Chief of the Navy Command Rear Admiral von Trotha communicated his decision to his subordinates on the day of the putsch, resulting in even the naval officers on Defence Minister Noske's staff siding with Kapp.[73]

But what of the general strike called for by the SPD? The Social Democratic leaders who had fled Berlin early on the morning of 13 March had not had time to make any preparations for such a vast undertaking. They spent the remainder of the day in Dresden, where they were challenged by General Maercker about the potentially revolutionary consequences of their declaration and attempted to distance themselves from it before fleeing again to Stuttgart. Instead, it fell to the union movement, specifically Carl Legien, chair of the ADGB (the Free Trade Unions, affiliated to the SPD) to turn the call for a strike into reality. At noon that same Saturday, Legien proclaimed a general strike alongside a drastic nine-point reform programme which ensured the support of the more radical USPD, and by 15 March, the Communists also.[74] United working-class action – not seen since the first days of the revolution in November 1918 when the monarchy had been toppled – was about to become a reality. Not only had Kapp, Ludendorff and Co. failed to attract working-class support, many middle-class Germans were dismayed at the chaotic state of affairs and were reluctant to throw their weight behind the putsch, as the diary of the right-wing Jewish professor Victor Klemperer reveals:

> My inclination to the right has suffered greatly … as a result of permanent antisemitism. I would dearly like to see the current putschists put up against a wall, I truly cannot work up any enthusiasm for the oath-breaking army, and really not at all for the immature and disorderly students [opinion in German universities at this time was strongly nationalist] – but neither can I for the 'legal' Ebert government either and less still for the radical left. I find them all off-putting.[75]

Even big business failed to get behind the putsch; they were fearful the conspirators' stance on Versailles implied a renewed conflict with the Allies, which would be disastrous for the economy.[76] Sunday, 14 March was far quieter than usual in Berlin. Those shops that operated Sunday trading did not open. The trams and underground were not running. The taps ran dry and the lights would not turn on. By 5.00 pm, a shutdown of gas, electricity and public transport had come into full effect.[77] In a makeshift cabinet meeting of the leading putschists on 14 March, at which Ludendorff was present, it was agreed that despite the difficulties the general strike was creating, the coup should carry on.[78] But the next day, a Monday, was when the general strike really started to bite and the putschists began to realise the true scale of the challenge they were facing. The vast majority of working-class and many middle-class Germans simply did not turn up for work. The country, and especially Berlin, was in a state of shutdown and Kapp's power barely extended beyond the government quarter of the capital, still held by Ehrhardt's increasingly frustrated militiamen. The new regime could not even get posters printed. In various towns and cities across the Reich, workers seized key government and transport infrastructure and violence from pro-putsch forces failed to break the strike.[79] The working-class response to the call to strike and the failure of the rebels to get their message out over the weekend meant the Kapp Putsch was being strangled before it had even got off the ground. A tetchy Captain Ehrhardt saw Kapp that day to complain on behalf of his men – workers were beginning to clash with the troops and they still had not been paid. An exasperated Kapp suggested they break into the central bank (the administrators refused to hand over any funds to the putschists as they lacked the proper authorisation), only for Ehrhardt to proudly declare: 'Certainly not! I am not a bank robber!'[80] Even the infamous Freikorps leader was not ruthless enough to get the coup back on track. That same day, 15 March, a delegation of officers from the Ministry of Defence read to General von Lüttwitz and Kapp a resolution that confirmed the army would stand aloof while maintaining law and order and that they supported negotiations between the rebels and the 'old' government to form a new government that would enjoy the confidence of the 'majority of the nation'.[81] Without a formal title or position, Ludendorff appears to have played a nonetheless pivotal role in advising Kapp and attempting to cajole officers at the Defence Ministry and around the country to support the new regime. His centrality was recognised by the republican government, who sent a civil servant to try to convince him to talk Lüttwitz down, a request Ludendorff flatly refused on the 16th. Numerous 'reshuffles' were also considered by the putschists as their plot began to disintegrate, including an unlikely 'People's dictatorship' of Ludendorff and the radical left USPD.[82]

Essentially, while remaining neutral, the army (and surely Seeckt's hand can be seen behind this) hoped for a negotiated settlement that would incorporate some of the putschists' demands and result in shift to the right. Lüttwitz and Kapp welcomed the officers' resolution and a senior Troop Office official was dispatched to Stuttgart to convey it to the exiled Ebert government. However, Lieutenant Colonel Hasse found the president and his ministers in belligerent mood – the success of the general strike had restored their confidence; they would not entertain negotiations with the Kapp regime. Such was the determination of the government that Hasse opted not to read the resolution and instead assured the army's political masters that 'the officers and officials of the Defence Ministry had nothing to do with the putsch and continued their work in accordance with their oath'.[83]

Even in the navy, events were not going in the putschists' favour – at Kiel and Wilhelmshaven, the sailors arrested 400 officers for supporting the coup and elected their own, as they had done in 1918.[84] In desperation, Kapp's team tried to open negotiations with the trade unions and with Vice Chancellor Schiffer, who had remained in Berlin. Talks broke down on Tuesday, 16 March in both cases. General Maercker, the putsch sympathiser in Dresden, took the rebels' terms to Stuttgart, only to find the National Assembly convening in the temporary capital and in no mood to compromise.[85] That evening, a Reichswehr battalion in Berlin rebelled against their officers (who had supported Lüttwitz) and declared for the Republic. The waverers in the military were now firmly on the side of the government because supporting Kapp seemed to threaten the loyalty of the men and because general strike activity in the industrial Ruhr region seemed to have triggered a communist insurgency. More and more district commanders now began to declare for Ebert.[86] To further add to the woes of Lüttwitz and Kapp, both received emissaries informing them that the British government would not cooperate with their regime.[87] Without money, without an army, without a voice – in short, without power – the prospects for the nationalists in the deserted Wilhelmstrasse seemed grim.

On the night of 16/17 March, a lengthy conference took place in the Reich Chancellery between Ludendorff, Bauer, Ehrhardt and Captain Pabst, organiser of the National Association and the officer who had been entrusted to negotiate with the vice chancellor. The absence of both Kapp and Lüttwitz is intriguing and suggests the plotters had become divided. Certainly, the tone of the meeting was bitter and acrimonious, especially as more bad news came in during the course of the night, such as the previously supportive Berlin police calling on Kapp to resign.[88] Ludendorff blamed the failure of the coup on 'subversive elements' and the cowardly stance of the officer corps, especially those in conservative Bavaria.[89] Ehrhardt and Bauer castigated Lüttwitz for not following through on the putschists' proclaimed ruthlessness and refusing to allow the Freikorps to shoot striking workers. Bauer, apparently with tears rolling down his cheeks, pleaded with Ludendorff to seize the leadership; clearly this sub-faction of the conspiracy believed more decisive measures were needed to rescue the putsch. But true to form, Ludendorff shunned any responsibility, and, wisely it must be said, refused to take command of a rapidly sinking ship.[90] As dawn broke, the only thing the officers could agree upon was that a new leader was required and eventually they settled on a name which they surely hoped would be seen as a compromise candidate – von Seeckt. Unsurprisingly, however, when Colonel Bauer saw Seeckt in his home on the morning of 17 March, the Troop Office chief contemptuously declined the role of military dictator; instead that day he was negotiating with both Schiffer and senior officers to secure his appointment as Chief of the Army Command.[91]

What was clear by Wednesday, 17 March was that the coup had failed spectacularly and reports were coming in of anti-putsch protests across the capital. Wolfgang Kapp was well aware that his tenure as chancellor was, after just five days, at an end and therefore issued a proclamation that afternoon, bizarrely claiming his aims had been achieved and that he was resigning in favour of Lüttwitz. Then Kapp, attempting to disguise himself with a scarf and hat, climbed into a taxi with his daughter and made straight for the airport, flying to Sweden on a passport provided by police sympathisers.[92] General Walther von Lüttwitz served as military dictator of Germany for just a few hours. He gathered Ludendorff, Bauer and Ehrhardt at the Defence Ministry (Pabst had already fled for Hungary) to work out how to save the nationalist project. The bloodthirsty Freikorps leader Ehrhardt was all for purging the Reichswehr and massacring the strikers.[93]

As with most of the events of the Kapp Putsch, we do not know Ludendorff's contribution, but given his stance the previous night, it seems unlikely he believed there was much chance of success. Any fresh plotting was soon cut short, however. Colonel Heye, Seeckt's eyes and ears in the ministry, was asked to speak on behalf of the officer corps and Gruppenkommando 1 – the troops in the Berlin region. His message was stark: Lüttwitz no longer enjoyed the confidence of the army; in fact they were now opposed to him. It was time for him to resign.[94] Ludendorff and Bauer tried to convince Lüttwitz to remain and the officers present to back him, but although Lüttwitz appears to have at first resisted Heye's demands, then stipulated certain conditions to secure his departure (including, fancifully, on the composition of the next cabinet), Lüttwitz finally resigned at 6.00 pm.[95] At this moment, Seeckt's associates in the meeting ensured Lüttwitz appointed their man as placeholder commander-in-chief, selling it as a necessary step to avoid a power vacuum in the army.[96] Although Ehrhardt objected, the departing Lüttwitz consented, convinced by the argument it had been von Seeckt who had prevented the Reichswehr firing on the putschists on 13 March.

It was now time for the remaining putschists to escape. Ludendorff left his old aide Colonel Bauer with surprisingly optimistic words: 'we are richer for a bitter experience' he insisted, and now that they understood the 'complete unreliability of the officer corps … and the fickleness of the public' it was clear that more radical and ruthless action would be required in the future.[97] At the end of March, under a new false name, Herr Lange, Ludendorff boarded a train for the reactionary south German state of Bavaria, where a baron offered to shelter him on his rural estate close to Rosenheim, a short drive from the Austrian border. Lüttwitz and Bauer followed Pabst to Hungary using yet more passports supplied by supporters in the police. The slippery Dr Schnitzler and Trebitsch-Lincoln were also able to evade the authorities.[98] Gloomily, without bands playing or songs being sung, the Ehrhardt brigade marched out of the capital. Large crowds on Unter den Linden watched them go, observing the fruits of their successful strike action. Reportedly, a boy started laughing at the pathetic paramilitaries and two of the troopers broke ranks to silence him, beating him with their rifle butts. The crowd hissed and booed, only for the brigade to halt and do what they had been restrained from doing throughout the strike – open fire on the people.[99] The Unter den Linden was cleared and the Freikorps left twelve dead and thirty wounded on the street. Marine Brigade Ehrhardt may have entered Berlin without firing a shot, but they certainly did not leave in such peaceful fashion. Their leader and many of his men followed Ludendorff to the safety of Bavaria. Meanwhile, Margarethe Ludendorff, who remained at the Viktoriastrasse flat for several weeks, received numerous employees from the National Association office who had not been paid, but could do nothing to help them.[100] The vision of an authoritarian Germany that had been dreamt up in that flat and at the Schellingstrasse offices had been served a major setback, but malevolent schemers like Ludendorff were still at liberty and had not given up their dark ambitions.

Max Weber, the intellectual who had attempted to persuade Ludendorff to give himself up to the Allies, was deeply disturbed by the putsch and its aftermath. He feared the nationalist coup had threatened the stability and unity of the Reich and was concerned that:

> The prime minister here [Kahr, premier of Bavaria, where Weber was now living] is supposed to have spoken about 'separation from the Reich', because the fat bourgeois are afraid of the Spartacists. If the Reich breaks up, then it will have been the work of these people (Kapp, Lüttwitz, and I fear I must add Ludendorff). I am afraid they will not be shot and not be sentenced to hard labour as any workingman would be in the same circumstances, a worker who does not have their 'education'.[101]

Weber was unfortunately proven correct. President Ebert and the rest of the Weimar government returned to Berlin on 20 March and negotiated an end to the General Strike with the unions. However, the combination of a temporary collapse of state authority and mass proletarian action had triggered a second wave of the German Revolution. In the Ruhr region, the central state of Thuringia and numerous other localities, communists, anarchists and radical socialists had used the strike as a springboard for an uprising. The situation was especially serious in the Ruhr, where the large unionised industrial workforce had answered the call to arms and taken control of the region, demanding the nationalisation of industry and the return of the workers' councils.[102] A Red Army of the Ruhr had been established and rapidly recruited workers; like a left-wing Freikorps with as many as 50,000 men, it had driven the military out of Dortmund on 17 March, at the same time as Kapp was resigning in Berlin. The Red Army continued to advance, taking Essen on the 20th and forcing the local Reichswehr commander to order a general withdrawal from the entire region.[103] The bitter irony was that President Ebert was forced to call on the very Freikorps who had betrayed him to once again crush a left-wing insurrection. Paramilitary and army units from across the country were gathered to retake the Ruhr, including those that had been directly involved in the Kapp Putsch, such as Marine Brigade Loewenfeld. Von Seeckt was quite willing for the army to defend the government this time, now they were fighting a 'red' threat. Again, the Freikorps unleashed their counter-revolutionary terror, with over 1,000 workers being killed in the Ruhr compared to 250 government troops.[104] One student volunteer in the Bavarian Epp Freikorps wrote to his parents:

> If I were to tell you everything, you would say I was lying. No pardon is given. We shoot even the wounded. The enthusiasm is tremendous – unbelievable. Our battalion has had two deaths, the Reds two to three hundred. Anyone who falls into our hands first gets the rifle butt and then is finished off with a bullet. We even shot ten Red Cross nurses on sight

because they were carrying pistols. We shot those little ladies with pleasure – how they cried and pleaded with us to save their lives. Nothing doing! Anyone with a gun is our enemy.[105]

Meanwhile in rural Thuringia, student paramilitaries executed fifteen villagers without trial, only to be found not guilty at court martial.[106] The desperation of the government to protect itself from 'Bolshevism' meant that, as in 1918–19, there was no reckoning with the army elite after Kapp. Seeckt and the Freikorps were needed to defeat the Ruhr rebellion so neither the High Command nor the paramilitaries faced retribution for the attempt to overthrow the democratic system. All the senior figures involved in the coup escaped serious punishment; indeed most, such as Ludendorff, escaped any punishment at all. Traugott von Jagow, Kapp's interior minister, was the only civilian to be prosecuted, being sentenced to just two years, while of 775 army and Freikorps officers officially designated as participants, only six were dismissed and total gaol time for military men amounted to a measly five years.[107] Wolfgang Kapp returned to Germany in 1922 to face the music but died in prison while awaiting trial. An amnesty for those involved in the Kapp Putsch meant that in 1925 Walther von Lüttwitz was able to return and quietly live out his years on a full military pension.[108] Colonel Bauer was also able to return from exile in Hungary at the same time. Personnel from Marine Brigades Ehrhardt and Loewenfeld who did not flee were simply transferred to the navy, where the spirit of the Freikorps lived on undiminished – the only measure taken in retribution for the navy's full support of the putsch was the sacking of its chief, Rear Admiral von Trotha.[109] While the Freikorps were dissolved in the coming months in accordance with Versailles, many units were integrated into the Reichswehr and in the case of those more extreme elements that were not (such as Ehrhardt loyalists), paramilitary activity continued underground, especially in Bavaria.[110]

In the aftermath of the coup, Lüttwitz's demand for early elections was actually met, with the country going to the polls in June 1920. The results dismayed republicans; the so-called Weimar coalition of centre-left to centre-right parties most committed to democracy (the SPD, DDP and Centre) that had governed since January 1919 lost their majority in the Reichstag, never to regain it. Kapp had brought rightist opposition to democracy out into the open and support for the Weimar coalition dropped from 76 per cent to just 45 per cent. While Catholics mostly remained loyal to their Centre Party, huge numbers of working-class voters punished the SPD for its compromises with the establishment, its crushing of the revolution and its use of the Freikorps by switching their allegiance to the more radical USPD and KPD. Meanwhile, the middle class moved away from the liberal DDP (which lost nearly half its seats) in favour of the monarchist DVP and nationalist DNVP, parties with limited commitment to democracy. Henceforth, the Republic was to be almost exclusively governed by minority administrations of the right and centre-right, seriously undermining the long-term stability of the Weimar system.[111]

Perhaps the most long-lasting effects of the putsch were felt in the Reichswehr. Seeckt's neutrality policy had kept the army intact and he rapidly emerged as the compromise candidate to lead the military forward. On 24 March, Gustav Noske resigned his cabinet post, while Reinhardt quit as Chief of the Army Command the following day – both had been totally discredited by the events of the coup.[112] With the departure of Noske as defence minister, the hopes of close ties between the Social Democrats, the largest pro-republican party in the country, and the military were lost. Trust between the army and SPD was shattered; the army felt they were now devoid of allies in the republican establishment, and the Social Democrats from now on viewed the generals with suspicion.[113] Noske's successor as defence minister, the Democrat Otto Gessler, would hold the office for nearly eight years, but he soon became isolated within his own party thanks to his close relationship with the military elite.[114] Effectively, the dream of a republican army was over. This allowed General Hans von Seeckt to become the new army chief, consolidating far more power in the post than Reinhardt had held and dominating the Reichswehr for the next six years. Despite Karen Schaefer's recent attempt to rehabilitate the enigmatic general, the historical consensus is that Seeckt set about building a 'state within a state' – the Reichswehr became a law unto itself, devoid of civilian oversight and loyal only to the 'Reich' and not to the democratic system.[115] The army was now controlled by officers of the Groener school – the modernising faction of the military – not least his favourites Seeckt and Schleicher from the Troop Office. They saw political change as a long-term objective and prioritised preserving the army as an institution for the time being, all the while covertly building it up as a modern and professional fighting machine. While reactionaries and ultra-nationalists of the Lüttwitz and Ludendorff mould remained prevalent in the officer corps, the corridors of power in the Defence Ministry were dominated by the new generation, with Seeckt at the head and the up-and-coming Major Kurt von Schleicher as the army's chief political fixer. Officers and men who had shown themselves overly loyal to the Republic during the putsch were quietly purged through the reductions necessitated by Versailles. Gessler, the new defence minister, was too weak to influence these intelligent, calculating officers and lacked the force of personality and authority Noske had commanded. Indeed, it appears he did not especially want to meddle in army affairs – a monarchist at heart, he saw his duty above all as shielding the Reichswehr from political interference.[116] The big winner of the Kapp Putsch was neither the far right, nor the Republic – it was the Reichswehr. Ludendorff did not get his dictatorship, but Seeckt got his army.

Field Marshal Paul von Hindenburg, the country's greatest military hero, had remained completely silent throughout the Kapp debacle. He was certainly not part of the ring of nationalist malcontents who had prepared the putsch, who were, as we have seen, primarily disciples of Ludendorff. On the other hand, as the Kapp regime faltered, a delegation from the conservative People's Party had suggested to the short-lived chancellor that he stand aside in favour of Hindenburg to rescue something from the fiasco.[117] This scheme had come to nothing and although Dorpalen's claim that the putsch represented a 'direct disavowal of everything for which Hindenburg had stood' is rather a strong assertion to make of a lifelong monarchist and military man, it is clear that the old field marshal had no intention of supporting his former partner Ludendorff in attempting to overthrow the state.[118] The Hindenburg Freikorps, named after the war hero, also did not take part; like many Freikorps brigades, this Hanover based unit were taken completely by surprise by the coup and were in the middle of a three-day festival in their patron's honour, which Hindenburg was attending.[119] Much more important to the wartime generalissimo, however, was that it had scuppered any hopes he had of winning the presidency.[120] It had been assumed that presidential elections would be held sometime in 1920. Friedrich Ebert had been provisionally appointed head of state by the National Assembly in February 1919, but the new constitution passed in August that year declared that the Reich President was to be directly elected by the people. Hindenburg was being touted seriously as a potential candidate of the right and even Colonel Max Bauer had spoken in favour of such a move, arguing a Hindenburg presidency would facilitate a restoration of the monarchy.[121] The DVP had first approached the war hero the previous August and, despite his initial reluctance, the idea was soon taken up by a powerful right-wing pressure group. On 6 March 1920, the two largest parties of the German right, the Nationalist DNVP and capitalist DVP, formally proposed Hindenburg as a cross-party candidate for the highest office in the land. The announcement put the Weimar Coalition parties, who publicly shared in the national reverence for Hindenburg, in a difficult position, and the next few days saw a lively public debate about a potential Hindenburg presidency.[122] However, the Kapp Putsch just days later both convinced Hindenburg against the idea of standing (he believed his candidacy would be too polarising in the wake of a military coup) and put paid to any hopes of holding a presidential election at such a delicate time; republican parties considered the situation too unstable and through a series of laws extended Ebert's term to 1925.[123] The actions of Ludendorff and his co-conspirators had destroyed the very real chance of a Hindenburg presidency in 1920 and ensured Ebert, the bogeyman of the right, would remain in office until his death.

Munich – the far right's 'playground'

Bavaria had suffered an especially tumultuous strain of the German Revolution. On 7 November 1918, a mass peace demonstration in Munich led by Independent

Socialist (and, significantly for the right, Jewish) Kurt Eisner turned unexpectedly into a march on the royal residence of Bavarian King Ludwig III. With the subsequent flight of the Wittelsbach dynasty that night, on 8 November Bavaria became the first German state to see the fall of the monarchy and declaration of a republic under Eisner and the USPD and SPD.[124] The fact that Catholic and conservative Bavaria was siding with the revolution indicated that change was inevitable and served as a final trigger for the abdication of the Kaiser and collapse of the Second Reich. Bavarian nationalists and monarchists were horrified at the events of November 1918 and wasted no time in opposing the new regime with Eisner being assassinated by the far-right nobleman and officer Anton Arco-Valley the following February.[125] His successor as Bavarian premier was the Social Democrat Johannes Hoffmann, but Hoffmann's moderation and commitment to parliamentary democracy angered left-wing revolutionaries and triggered a fresh revolt in April 1919. Hoffmann was deposed in favour of a Bavarian Soviet Republic, led at first by an unlikely band of socialist and anarchist intellectuals, such as the playwright Ernst Toller. Toller and co. were soon deposed themselves by communists, inspired by the recent revolution in Hungary. Prime Minister Hoffman fled to Bamberg and ordered the Bavarian Reichswehr to retake Munich, only for them to be defeated by the revolutionary Red Guards. This resulted in the rapid recruitment of large Bavarian Freikorps units, as well as the deployment of Freikorps and Reichswehr troops from elsewhere, in order to crush the Munich Soviet. As we have seen, this they did, quickly and with much brutality in May 1919.

The result of all this turmoil was that the political atmosphere in Bavaria, and Munich specifically, was super-charged, even in the context of the turbulent Weimar Republic.[126] Although the Freikorps' triumph had allowed Hoffmann and the SPD to return to the state capital, the prime minister found that the army and security forces in Bavaria were infested with far-right Freikorps figures, who, in the chaos of the collapse of the Soviet, had established themselves in positions of power. Unlike Captain Ehrhardt in the north, the Bavarian Freikorps generalissimo, Franz Ritter von Epp, ensured he and his brigade were not disbanded but instead integrated into the local Reichswehr. His chief of staff Ernst Röhm became one of the most influential army officers in the region and one of Röhm's main roles was procuring arms for right-wing militia units.[127] A prison governor who had sided with the counter-revolution, Ernst Pöhner, became Munich chief of police and he quickly set up a political department under Wilhelm Frick, one of the earliest members of the Nazi Party. The head of the Bavarian Reichswehr, General von Möhl, approved the controversial creation of an Einwohnerwehr, or Civil Guard. Headed by the monarchist Georg Escherich, ably assisted by Röhm, the Civil Guard was a civilian militia which had been recruited to help defeat the Munich Soviet. Its stated purpose was to defend Bavaria against any future uprising. Given that known leftists were expelled from its ranks, it could hardly claim to be a genuine citizens' defence organisation; evidently, the Civil Guard would not intervene against a rightist putsch.[128] Soon it mushroomed into the largest rightist militia in the Reich, with 400,000 members and 2.5 million weapons, and, unsurprisingly, its very existence was a source of political conflict – in the words of Ernst Röhm, it's huge strength made it 'a decisive power factor in Bavarian politics'.[129]

In March 1920, with the Weimar government temporarily powerless due to the Kapp Putsch, the Bavarian right opportunistically made their move. Pöhner, Escherich and von Möhl told Prime Minister Hoffmann that he and his administration no longer enjoyed their confidence and that failure to resign would result in civil war in Bavaria.[130] The Social Democrats were swiftly hustled out of power by the police, army and militia acting in unison and contrary to the democratic concept of civilian authority. In their stead, the right appointed as premier Gustav Ritter von Kahr, a civil servant and advisor to the ousted Wittelsbach dynasty. As a committed nationalist and bureaucrat who had spent his career serving the monarchy, Gustav von Kahr was very much in the mould of a Wolfgang Kapp. Kahr's appointment was soon granted the veneer of legality with his investiture by the Bavarian Landtag (State Parliament); he gained the backing of the Catholic reactionaries of the Bavarian People's Party (BVP), the conservative DVP and various smaller right-wing groups such as the Peasants' League. The collapse of the SPD in the aforementioned elections of June 1920 that followed the Kapp Putsch (which were simultaneously held for both the Reichstag in Berlin and state parliaments such as the Bavarian Landtag) ensured that Kahr's position was secure.

Kahr's policy was to transform Bavaria into a self-styled 'Cell of Order' within the chaotic Weimar Republic. Munich was to be the antithesis of Berlin and the new system it represented; if Berlin and Prussia were modern, progressive and liberal – even 'red', Munich and Bavaria were to be traditionalist, Christian, conservative – even reactionary.[131] While Prussia was a 'bulwark' of republicanism and social democracy, Bavaria was Weimar Germany's deep south. Effectively, the clock was turned back to before the revolution; Bavaria was to be returned to a rose-tinted vision of the Second Reich where the left was suppressed, order and deference prevailed and Munich was semi-independent of Berlin.[132] The new constitution had stripped the German states of some of their rights and privileges. Bavarian nationalists in particular were angered by the removal of their former kingdom's right to control its own railways, postal service and tax collection.[133] Kahr's regime sought to restore Bavarian sovereignty, for instance by building up the green-uniformed Bavarian State Police as a strong, locally controlled armed force full of army officers and military veterans with combat experience, not least their head, Colonel Hans Ritter von Seisser.[134] But Kahr's Bavaria was not just independent from Berlin and fiercely anti-Prussian; the premier and his successors relied on the support of a broad coalition of rightists, from Catholic conservatives to radical völkisch nationalists. Bavaria therefore became a greenhouse for far-right politics and ideas. Propaganda posters were littered with slander and fearmongering against the left, portraying their political opponents as an evil, foreign, even Asiatic enemy bent on destroying the Bavarian way of life. Fierce anti-Semitism also pervaded the political climate, merging with anti-communism to create the seductive bogeyman of Jewish Bolshevism, which was embodied in Bavaria by Kurt Eisner and Ernst Toller – Jewish leftists who had both briefly held the regional premiership.[135] The anti-communist, anti-democratic 'cell of order' also cultivated anti-Semitic, völkisch, Social Darwinist pseudo-intellectuals, such as Alfred Rosenberg, Dietrich Eckart, and Gottfried Feder, whose publications fomented racial hatred and rabid nationalism. All three would fall into the Nazi orbit in the early 1920s.

Munich was also home to the geopolitics professor, Karl Haushofer, who from 1919 promoted the idea of Lebensraum – the living space that the German race supposedly required in the east. Rudolf Hess was one of his students at Munich University and Adolf Hitler would accept the professor's theories wholesale.[136] The Bavarian capital also rapidly became a centre for the study of eugenics and 'racial hygiene', with the nationalist publisher J.F. Lehmann founding the Munich Society for Racial Hygiene in 1921 and the city's university playing host to a world-leading eugenics department.[137] Two prominent völkisch organisations, the Thule Society and the Schutz-und Trutzbund (Protection and Defiance Federation), were both established in the state and soon had followings in the thousands. Prime Minister Kahr himself indulged in racist, anti-Semitic policies, for instance ordering the expulsion of the Ostjuden, the Yiddish-speaking Eastern European Jews (as opposed to well-integrated German Jews) from Bavaria.[138] When the Versailles treaty necessitated disarmament, nationalists in the Bavarian Reichswehr and Freikorps instead created illegal hoards of weapons across the state and even in Munich itself. Ernst Röhm became known as the 'machine gun king' as he had could provide ready supplies of arms for paramilitary groups and he also recorded gleefully in his memoirs that those who tried to report these illegal arms dumps to the authorities 'get their deserts behind the prison wall'.[139]

Admittedly, there were strong factional divides in this right-wing utopia, most notably between 'white-blue' nationalists, such as Kahr himself, who were essentially Bavarian nationalists interested primarily in the affairs of their state (and its independence), and 'black-white-red' nationalists such as Ludendorff, Röhm and the emerging Nazi Party, who wanted to use Bavaria as a base to spearhead a Reich-wide counter-revolution and were totally opposed to Bavarian separatism.[140] Nevertheless, the most rabid and dangerous figures of Germany's blossoming far right were attracted to the 'cell of order' and were aided rather than molested by the police, making Munich a 'playground' for extremists.[141] Ludendorff fled to the south German state as the Kapp Putsch was disintegrating and found the Bavarian countryside to be a safe haven from potential recriminations over the failed coup. Even more surprisingly, Bavaria received the disgraced Captain Ehrhardt and much of his Freikorps brigade after their notorious role in the putsch. Astonishingly, the Munich police chief Ernst Pöhner actually invited Ehrhardt and his men to his city so that they might escape justice – a policeman, and indeed a federal state, were sheltering and sponsoring men who had attempted to overthrow the Reich government. At first, Ehrhardt and his marines had to hide on the rural estates of aristocratic patrons, but by spring 1921, the Freikorps leader felt confident enough to restart his activities.[142] Working through a front company in the Bavarian capital and with both protection and aid from Pöhner, Ehrhardt set up training camps for Organisation Consul, a secret paramilitary group of his most diehard supporters. The strategy now was not coup d'état but assassination and terror. OC's stated purpose was both 'warfare' against Jews and the left, and the hope that their actions would provoke chaos and unrest that would result in the overthrow of the Republic.[143] Under Kahr and Pöhner, Bavaria became a base for domestic terrorism under the benevolent eye of officialdom. This unique nationalist echo chamber served to radicalise both Adolf Hitler, discharged from the army on 31 March 1920, and General Ludendorff, fresh from his failure in Berlin, who would both choose Munich as the base for their political careers.

Ludendorff, having arrived in his Bavarian sanctuary, kept his head down for the remainder of 1920 and most of 1921, licking his wounds after the Kapp debacle and steering clear of frontline politics. His plotting was limited to writing a lengthy letter in April 1920 to the Hungarian dictator Admiral Horthy in support of Colonel Bauer's latest scheme; a joint Bavarian-Hungarian conquest of Germany, Austria, Czechoslovakia, Poland and Bolshevik Russia.[144] Despite his seeming prosaic reaction to the failure of the putsch, labelling it a lesson learnt, it must be remembered that Ludendorff's mental health was fragile, and the events of March 1920 had been another catastrophic failure for the general. The last few years had seen all his best-laid plans end in disaster and so a short-term reluctance to engage in plots and intrigue is understandable. At first, the general was in hiding, moving every few weeks to a new castle or mansion of supportive aristocrats, while his wife Margarethe remained temporarily in Berlin. It was not until August 1920, five months after the failed putsch, that he put down roots, purchasing a walled mansion in the salubrious Munich suburb of Prinz-Ludwigs-Höhe, a hilltop village (referred to in German as a villa colony) some 8km from the city.[145] He claimed he had moved to Munich to be closer to his sister. Despite Ludendorff keeping his head down for the time being, Prinz-Ludwigs-Höhe soon became a place of pilgrimage for German nationalists; the 'Ludendorff Circle' were soon visiting their leader in his new safe space in the 'cell of order' and they were joined by scores of Bavarian rightists, paying homage to the heroic general. His new mansion played host to patriotic students, esteemed officers such as Admiral von Tirpitz and a rising star on the Bavarian right, Adolf Hitler.[146] One such visitor, Ernst Röhm, later wrote of his 'honour' at being a visitor at '[Ludendorff's] fine home on Prinz-Ludwigs-Höhe' – Ludendorff was a celebrity and a war hero, and being invited into his presence clearly conferred kudos.[147] Ludendorff even appeared in public with Hindenburg again when the latter visited Munich in 1921 and the pair were lauded as national heroes by cheering crowds and assembled civilian, military and paramilitary leaders, including von Kahr.[148]

As Chickering has argued, now that the centre of gravity of right-wing politics had moved south to Bavaria, Ludendorff remained the most prominent figure of the nationalist opposition to the Weimar Republic, at the heart of a sprawling network of army officers, veterans, politicians and conspirators.[149] As well as holding court and once more making his home a hub for far-right figures, Ludendorff was writing again. At first, he returned to familiar themes, looking back at the First World War and assigning blame to civilians rather than the military (and indeed himself). While still in Berlin, he had compiled an array of hundreds of documents from his personal papers and military records that were to serve as an addendum to his memoirs. This effort had begun in connection to his appearance before the parliamentary enquiry into the defeat, but now Ludendorff chose to publish this carefully curated collection, along with his own commentary, as further proof for his version of events and justification for his actions. Published in two tome-like volumes, the English title, *The General Staff and its Problems: The History of the relations between the High Command and German Imperial Government as revealed by official documents*, rather betrays the story one receives from the documents Ludendorff chose to present. The first volume addressed questions around the war economy and the decision to wage unrestricted submarine warfare, while the second was intended to dispel suggestions that a compromise peace was ever possible, thereby justifying Ludendorff's reckless, all-or-nothing approach in 1918.[150] The message presented by the general was clear: he had done all he could to win the war but his efforts had been frustrated by indecisive civilian politicians who had not conducted the war ruthlessly enough, by unrealistic hopes of a peace settlement and by domestic agitation. Naturally, he also sought to prove the High Command was still in control of the military situation to the very end – that the army had been stabbed in the back by 'revolution from above *and* below'.[151] His victory and his army had been sabotaged, or so he claimed, and the general had high hopes for the impact his publications would have: 'May these records, like "My War Memoirs", fill the German people with fresh national resolution and open their eyes to truth.'[152] With the Stab-in-the-Back legend firmly ensconced in the German psyche, Ludendorff now focused on research – and the future rather than the past. He announced that he was 'occupying [himself] with the Jewish question' and read *The Protocols of the Elders of Zion* as well as numerous anti-Semitic tracts, from Henry Ford to Dietrich Schäfer.[153]

As we have already seen, Ludendorff clearly already possessed anti-Semitic and anti-Marxist views, but by immersing himself in conspiracy theory and pseudo-science, he found rational justification for his instinctive prejudices. He also revealed in his letters that he had made the mental connection between Judaism and the left that was such a keystone of far-right and Nazi thought, writing, 'I see the work of the Bolsheviks in the writing of the Jews.'[154] In late 1921 he published the first edition of his *Military Leadership and Politics*, his third book, which, as well as providing yet another analysis of the Great War, also strayed away from the realm of history and memoir towards ideological musings and guidance on the conduct of a future war. Ludendorff was able to dovetail what he had learnt from his research into conspiratorial anti-Semitism to his own theories about defeat in 1918. Gone were the hints to 'subversive elements' seen in his memoirs, replaced by open, rabid anti-Semitism: Germany's politicians had:

> put themselves mainly under Jewish influences, which were completely alien to the people and were in strict contrast to the Germanic nature ... The Jewish people wanted to rule over the people who had admitted them ... to castrate us as men and people, so that others with a stronger national will can rule us.[155]

Ludendorff claimed to have found the link between all who undid Germany at the end of the war, between war profiteers, pacifists, Social Democrats, revolutionaries and republicans – the Jew. In the book, he argued that to succeed in the coming European conflict, Germany would have to be free of Jews, or *judenrein*, a phrase, and indeed a policy position, adopted by the Nazis.[156] The reasons were predictable enough: Jews were an internal enemy who had destabilised the Reich at a crucial moment before. Germany must act to stop such a disaster happening again. *Military Leadership and Politics* also took aim at the great military theorist Clausewitz and his famous adage that 'war is politics by other means'. Instead, Ludendorff presented an apocalyptic, Social Darwinist vision of the modern world in which conflict is inevitable and war a necessity; 'politics, as a whole, have to serve war' was his bleak interpretation.[157] The state, therefore, should be geared to total war at all times. Perhaps most pertinently, Ludendorff laid the foundations for his claim to leadership of the nation. He reflected that, with hindsight, the military (and therefore he) should have seized dictatorial power during the war and that in the future, Germany would need a new breed of leaders who had studied the mistakes of the past and were 'free of every vanity and selfish instinct ... who are conscious of their Germanness, their racial heritage, their obligations, and the realities of power'.[158] The general was clearly making a pitch for his own suitability for the role of supreme leader and emphasised the belief he shared with many on the far right – that civilians should be subordinate to the military in future. Clearly, spending time in Munich's völkisch echo chamber, surrounded by sycophants, radicalised Ludendorff, but it also allowed him the time and space he had been denied in the frantic war years and their immediate aftermath in order to clarify and rationalise his views. This allowed him to move into politics with more confidence in the next few years, aided by the fact that all the other senior leaders of the Kapp Putsch (General von Lüttwitz, Colonel Bauer and Kapp himself) were either in prison or exiled, leaving Ludendorff unassailable as the far right's potential dictator of choice.

Although Ludendorff shied away from public life in 1920–21, this was not the case for other extreme nationalists. Captain Ehrhardt's Organisation Consul continued its campaign of terror unabated from the safety of their Bavarian base. In total, this shadowy group carried out at least 354 political murders in 1921–22, their victims ranging from leading republican politicians to ordinary citizens who reported illegal arms caches to the authorities.[159] All the while, the Bavarian police and military not only turned a blind eye to their activities, they provided active assistance, ranging from arms to forged documents. OC's campaign of murder was bookended with their most high-profile victims. Their first target was the Catholic Centre politician and Finance Minister Matthias Erzberger, whose crime was signing the November 1918 armistice on behalf of the German government. The last victim of OC was Foreign Minister Walther Rathenau, a liberal of the DDP and Jewish industrialist, who, ironically, had done a huge amount to help mobilise German industry during the Great War. As well as being a Jew and a Democrat, Rathenau as foreign minister had committed the deadly sin of accepting the terms of Versailles. Despite the acrimony over the collapse of the Kapp Putsch, Ludendorff remained in contact with OC's leader, Captain Ehrhardt, after both had moved to Bavaria and Ehrhardt's men guarded Ludendorff's villa around the clock.[160] The general not only tacitly supported their terrorist campaign, but can also be tentatively linked to both of OC's most infamous murders. Erzberger was the collateral damage of Ludendorff's Stab-in-the-Back myth, for he more than any other politician embodied the 'November Criminals' who had betrayed the army and Fatherland by agreeing to peace. Erzberger was, for disciples of Ludendorff's lies, the human incarnation of the *Dolchstoss*; the man who had agreed to the dishonourable ceasefire that had denied Germany final victory. Similarly, Walther Rathenau's acceptance of the shameful Versailles *Diktat*, as well as his Jewish background and democratic politics, made him a guilty man for those who subscribed to Ludendorff's version of the truth. Even worse, Rathenau had recently concluded an accord with the Soviet Union that had renounced the expansionist fantasies of Ludendorff's Brest-Litovsk treaty of 1918. Ludendorff himself had directly linked Rathenau to the 'Stab in the Back' in his own public statements, calling him a 'Jewish traitor and defeatist'.[161] Crown Prince Rupprecht, the heir to the vacant Bavarian throne, seems to have believed Ludendorff knew of Rathenau's murder in advance, although the general denied this.¹⁶² Nevertheless, Ludendorff endorsed both killings in his writings, describing Erzberger as a 'representative of Rome' and his murder merely an 'expression of German misery' and 'will to defend itself', while Rathenau, the wealthy industrialist, was:

> the Red Prophet of world revolution. Consciously, he wanted to Bolshevise the German people, with the help of the German intelligentsia. The Germans who executed the people's judgement on Walther Rathenau have acted with the thought that they have freed the German nation from vermin.¹⁶³

Perhaps the most shocking aspect of this campaign of underground nationalist violence was the ambivalence of the Bavarian authorities – the murderers of Erzberger for instance were sheltered in Munich and then issued false passports by the local police to leave for Hungary.¹⁶⁴ According to Ernst Röhm, when a concerned citizen went to see Munich Police Chief Ernst Pöhner to warn him about the 'political murder organisations' active in the city, Pöhner replied that he knew about their existence but there were 'far too few of them!'¹⁶⁵ Even on the occasions when the culprits were caught, they seldom faced real justice. Of the 354 cases of far-right murder in the early 1920s, 326 resulted in no punishment whatsoever, while for the remainder, the average sentence was just four months. The bias of the unreformed judiciary, a hangover from the Kaiserreich, was made evident by the fact that twenty-two leftist political murders in the same period resulted in ten executions and an average gaol term of fifteen years.¹⁶⁶ Unsurprisingly, in response to the high-profile killings, the Berlin government cracked down on paramilitary groups; Erzberger's death in August 1921 promoted the declaration of a state of emergency by President Ebert. Bavarian Prime Minister von Kahr, already embittered by Berlin forcing the dissolution of the Civil Guard in the spring, refused to enact the state of emergency in his state. As a result, he and Pöhner were forced to resign in September, although the dissolution of the large and heavily armed Civil Guard only served to create a plethora of new paramilitary organisations in the state.¹⁶⁷ After Rathenau's murder the following year, Organisation Consul was banned and Captain Ehrhardt, having hidden in a Bavarian monastery and across the border in Austria for a time, was arrested (although soon released).¹⁶⁸ With Kahr and Ehrhardt pushed to the sidelines of Bavarian far-right politics in 1921–22, a vacuum opened up for new figures to emerge.

The Nazi Party of course needs no introduction and it is not the purpose of the present volume to provide a history of the early movement. Suffice to say that the tiny German Workers' Party (DAP), insignificant in the kaleidoscopic world of nationalist politics in Bavaria in 1919, rapidly transformed in the early 1920s into a potent regional force, in large part due to the charisma of Adolf Hitler. After attending his first party meeting on army orders in September

1919, the young Hitler quickly became the fledging movement's 'publicity spokesman' as his talents for oratory were recognised. Just five months later, he told an audience of 2,000 supporters that the party was rebranding as the National Socialist German Workers' Party (NSDAP) and presented the twenty-five-point programme he had helped draw up.[169] Many of the programme's points, and indeed the new name, suggested a left-wing, socialist approach, but in reality, the party was decidedly a part of Munich's flourishing radical right. National Socialism or 'German Socialism' was a political idea found on the far-right fringes of politics in Germany and Austria in the early twentieth century. It must be noted that *national* in German generally meant 'nationalist' rather than nationwide – for the latter Germans used *Reich* (and today *Bundes*), e.g. Reich Chancellor. To give an example, the paramilitary groups in Bavaria swore allegiance to the Bavarian government on the condition that it remained *national* – not that it governed the entire nation, but that it was nationalist in character.[170] Essentially, parties such as the NSDAP, DSP and Austrian DNSAP tied extreme nationalism, anti-Marxism, Pan-Germanism, anti-Semitism and völkisch ideas to populist anti-capitalism and the successful political methods of Social Democracy and other worker movements in the hope of drawing the masses to the far right. The anti-capitalist rhetoric was itself laced with anti-Semitism and riled against big business on behalf of the independent trader or small farmer. Moreover, the core aim of left-wing socialism – a reducing of class inequality through the radical redistribution of society's wealth – was simply never on the Nazi's policy radar. Essentially, this particular strain of rightist politics was politics by and for the lower-middle class, the *Mittelstand*, or petite bourgeoise – craftsmen, traders, small business owners, famers, civil servants, clerks and junior army officers.[171] This class felt they suffered at the hands of banks, powerful corporations and international markets, while also feeling threatened by the rising power of the revolutionary working class and the growing economic clout of unionised workers. For all the rhetoric, the anti-capitalist measures in the twenty-five-point party programme would actually never be implemented once total power was achieved – hardly surprising given Hitler wrote the manifesto just five months into his nascent political career and a full thirteen years before he entered office with the assistance of big business and the conservative establishment. Hitler himself fitted the party's class profile almost perfectly; the son of an undistinguished customs official in rural Austria, his fears of both 'Jewish' international finance and impending Bolshevism mirrored those of his class and were combined into the grand Jewish Bolshevik conspiracy. Added to this lethal cocktail was huge resentment about defeat and revolution in 1918, the fall of the monarchy, the disgrace of Versailles and the betrayal of the *Dolchstoss*, all of which intensified middle-class opposition to the Weimar system and tied the Nazis ideologically to conspirators in the army and the wider radical right.

Hitler was very soon the heart and soul of the growing party, designing their red, white and black swastika banner, borrowing the Freikorps swastika, appropriating the colour red to provoke the left while retaining the red-white-black colours of German nationalism.[172] Nazi meetings had a unique appeal, both due to Hitler's undoubted skills as a public speaker and demagogue, and the confrontational clashes with leftists that necessitated the foundation of a paramilitary wing, the infamous stormtroopers of the SA, who were trained by Röhm and Ehrhardt and led by flying ace Hermann Göring. Like Ehrhardt's organisation, the young party enjoyed the benevolence of the authorities, especially from police chief Pöhner and his political assistant Wilhelm Frick, and the party newspaper, *Völkischer Beobachter*, was bought in part with money lent by sympathisers in the Bavarian Reichswehr.[173] In summer 1921, Hitler seized the party leadership and geared the organisation around himself as Führer. Amidst feverish political activism and scores of meetings attended by thousands in Munich's beer halls, party membership more than doubled from 3,300 when Hitler took over to 8,000 by the end of 1922, spread across over a hundred party branches, forty-four of which were in Bavaria.[174]

While still very much a regional figure, Hitler was now a serious force in the crowded Munich rightist scene. This rising star was brought to the attention of General Ludendorff in March 1921. Their paths had nearly crossed before; Hitler and another early Nazi, Dietrich Eckart, had flown to Berlin during the 1920 Kapp Putsch to update the new nationalist regime on the situation in Bavaria. When they arrived on 17 March, however, Kapp had already resigned and fled and the putsch was falling apart, so they beat a hasty retreat, perturbed by the presence of the Jew Trebitsch-Lincoln.[175] A year on, Hitler was introduced to Ludendorff by Max Erwin von Scheubner-Richter, an early adherent to the Nazi Party with good connections in aristocratic circles; he had persuaded Ludendorff to join his nationalist secret society Aufbau.[176] By all accounts, the two struck up a positive relationship during 1921–22; just as Ludendorff embarked on his 'research' into the Jewish question, he was coming into contact with Hitler and his supporters. Undoubtedly, Hitler was sycophantic in his praise for the general (he said Ludendorff's *Military Leadership and Politics* helped him understand the modern world) and Ludendorff enjoyed the adulation, but they clearly shared similar political beliefs and could be useful to one another.[177] Scheubner-Richter, a Baltic German, was well known among White Russian emigres through whom he acquired funds for Ludendorff, and by extension, the Nazis. The steel magnate Fritz Thyssen also donated 100,000 gold marks to Ludendorff at this time, and again, Hitler's movement was a likely beneficiary.[178]

As well as money, Ludendorff brought clout to the early Nazi Party. As Ian Kershaw has stated, while Ludendorff may not have been directing the disparate far-right parties and paramilitary groups of Bavaria, he was the common link between them; Ludendorff was a figurehead they could all get behind, a man who could unite bickering völkisch leaders in a common cause.[179] His connections and wide circle of contacts, both in the military and right-wing politics, was an invaluable asset and he was therefore courted by Hitler and other nationalist leaders. Winning Ludendorff's endorsement would open doors in wealthy establishment circles that the rabble-rouser Hitler may have otherwise found barred. Not only that, but Ludendorff brought prestige and notoriety to those he collaborated with – he was *the* leading personality on the radical right. If Hitler wanted to be a serious player in Bavaria's völkisch scene, winning the general's confidence was essential. As Chickering has argued, there was genuine mutual respect and admiration between Hitler and Ludendorff when they became acquainted.[180] For Hitler, being introduced to the world-famous general and becoming his confidant must have been a privilege and a moment of triumph as his star continued to rise. In the meantime, Ludendorff, like so many others, was entranced by the young Hitler, impressed by his uncompromising rhetoric and apparent popularity with the people. However, from the beginning, their aims were divergent and both Hitler and Ludendorff saw each other as tools to be utilised for their own ends. Hitler, while initially seeing himself as serving under Ludendorff in some future dictatorship, saw the general's prestige as a bandwagon to which he could hitch his own fledgling career and movement. Ludendorff meanwhile hoped he could use Hitler – that the demagogue could be an effective civilian face for a government controlled by the general himself and the military more broadly; Hitler would be the master propagandist, whipping up the masses in support of Ludendorff's militarist policies.[181]

1923: Year of crisis

The year of 1923 was to severely test the Weimar democratic system. On 9 January, 60,000 French and Belgian troops occupied the industrial Ruhr region of Western Germany in a move that caused outrage across the political spectrum. The rather flimsy pretext used by the French premier Poincaré, an avid nationalist, was that Germany had been found to be behind on her reparation payments, in particular timber and coal, and therefore Allied troops would take what they were owed by force.[182] At the time, Germany was being governed by a centre-right cabinet, led by the non-party businessman Wilhelm Cuno as chancellor. A political truce was called, known as the National Unity Front, which encompassed all parties except the Communists and gave the chancellor a free hand to tackle the crisis. Cuno, inspired by the spirit of patriotic unity that had swept the nation, initiated a campaign of passive resistance; the entire Ruhr region was ordered out on strike, their pay to be met by central government in a scheme reminiscent of the furlough arrangements seen during the coronavirus pandemic. As tax revenue slumped, huge coal imports became necessary and government spending increased exponentially, the administration meeting its rising costs by printing money – with devastating economic consequences. The German mark was already weak, and inflation had been a major concern since the war ($1 bought 8,000 marks in December 1922) and as a result, the value of the currency collapsed in dramatic fashion in the autumn.[183] The story of German hyperinflation has been told many times, but simple facts do bear out the genuine chaos and suffering it caused; a kilo of bread cost 163 marks in January 1923, over 1,600 by July, 9 million marks by October, 78 billion on 5 November and 233 billion on 19 November.[184] The worst affected and most embittered were the middle class and pensioners, who saw their savings, investments and pensions become worthless practically overnight. Understandably, therefore, the entire year of 1923 was defined by an acute sense of crisis and in this turbulent atmosphere, as the poverty rate in Munich more than trebled, Nazi Party membership surged from 8,000 in late 1922 to 55,000 by November 1923.[185]

Unsurprisingly, German nationalist opinion had been inflamed by the Ruhr occupation. Exaggerated horror stories about atrocities and abuses committed by Allied troops against the Ruhr residents circulated with reports of the very real brutality wielded in response to the civil disobedience undertaken by the local populace. With enemy troops on German soil and the Reich seemingly united in its will to resist, nationalists clamoured for a radical response to the crisis, preferably a people's war against the invaders consisting of a *Levée en masse* and a total mobilisation of society, as advocated by Ludendorff in *Military Leadership and Politics*. Ernst Röhm remembered:

> A military altercation with France was not without its prospects at that time. Perhaps it was our only possibility of salvation. Of course, one would have had to brace for the decision; the whole German people would have had to fight for freedom and existence. We should not have shrunk back from ceding voluntarily, temporarily and without a fight, great tracts of German territory to the enemy.[186]

The Nazi Party gained its first martyr, as a Freikorps veteran and Hitler convert was executed by French troops for sabotaging a railway bridge.[187] As the year wore on and hyperinflation devastated the economy and seemed to presage societal collapse, nationalist circles began to sense the time was ripe for a new putsch. Since 1920, thanks to the terms of Versailles, the failure of Kapp and the crackdown following the murders of Erzberger and Rathenau, paramilitary groups had been disbanded across Germany and peacetime conditions had slowly begun to return. However, 1923 would see an explosion of right-wing paramilitary activity, not least because President Ebert allowed Reichswehr commander General Hans von Seeckt to activate the 'Black Reichswehr', in effect mobilising former Freikorps units in preparation for a potential declaration of war.[188] Predictably, Hitler ramped up Nazi Party activities, holding twelve mass rallies in January and outmanoeuvring the Bavarian authorities' attempts to shut him down by enlisting the support of the regional commander of the Reichswehr, General Otto von Lossow, as well as the ex-premier Gustav von Kahr, to intercede on his behalf.[189]

With paramilitary politics back on the agenda, Erich Ludendorff returned to the political stage, as the figurehead to whom all the disparate Bavarian militias deferred. After the dissolution of the Bavarian Civil Guard in 1921, the various right-wing paramilitary groups in the state had been grouped into the Bund Bayern und Reich. However, this organisation was split by both personal jealousies and differences in politics; moderates such as Otto Pittinger were essentially loyal to the Bavarian government, as the Civil Guard had been, while the radicals around Röhm were intent on using paramilitary power for revolutionary ends. At the start of the year, Ludendorff had used his influence among the radicals to bring about a split in the organisation and in February, Captain Röhm (at this point still a serving army officer) brought together the far-right Bavarian paramilitary groups into a rival association.[190] With a strength of 15,000 under the command of the former chief of staff of the Bavarian Civil Guard, Lieutenant Colonel Hermann Kriebel, the association included the Nazi SA, the former Freikorps unit and Ludendorff devotees Bund Oberland, the Reichsflagge under Adolf Heiss, and Ehrhardt's successor to OC, Bund Wiking, amongst others and received training and arms from Lossow's Bavarian Reichswehr.[191] The army could use these troops to help fight the French, or perhaps to stage a military coup.

The patronage of both Röhm and Ludendorff ensured that Hitler was now at the top table in the conspiratorial discussions that followed in Bavaria, even meeting Reichswehr supremo von Seeckt in Berlin that March. Germany's top general was not impressed with the Führer; several days after meeting Hitler he prohibited army personnel from engaging in National Socialist activities.[192] The previous month, von Seeckt had held secret talks with Ludendorff in Wannsee, with some senior officers hoping the two could come to an agreement to form a military directory that would seize power and fight the French. Seeckt reportedly assured Ludendorff that he would step aside as Chief of the Army Command in favour of the war hero on the condition that Ludendorff respect the constitution.[193] Perhaps this was a deliberate attempt from the wily von Seeckt to play both sides, for he could appease the nationalist right by meeting their figurehead, but his one condition was almost perfectly designed to ensure cooperation between the two men would be impossible, and indeed Ludendorff rejected these terms. Seeckt had also helped scotch plans for a Reich-wide confederation of paramilitary groups. On 26 February a conference of northern 'pro-Fatherland' groups with Ludendorff and other Bavarian representatives had ended in failure, despite the general's advocacy of a nationwide alliance, in part due to Seeckt's meddling.[194] It must be said that as Ludendorff re-emerged into public life, he was not universally welcomed by the right – von Seeckt was not alone in having reservations about him. His chief opponent was Crown Prince Rupprecht, the heir to the vacant Bavarian throne, who was still resident in the state. Rupprecht had been an army group commander in the Great War and Ludendorff had heavily criticised him in his memoirs, and the animosity between them would eventually end in a libel suit. Both men attended a military celebration in Ingolstadt in July 1923 and Rupprecht's attitude towards Ludendorff was 'painful', in the words of Röhm – torn between his hero and his monarch.[195] Furthermore, the prince had strong connections with the conservative, Catholic and monarchist Bavarian People's Party (BVP) which governed the region and not only opposed Ludendorff's radical brand of politics but also instinctively disliked his Prussian background.[196] In fact, Ludendorff had crossed swords with senior BVP politician Heinrich Held in the Bavarian press during the spring of 1923, with the latter accusing the general of violating Bavarian hospitality with his critical public pronouncements.[197] There was a strong feeling in the BVP that Ludendorff, and indeed Hitler, were dangerous extremists who needed careful watching.[198]

Hitler, clearly influenced by Ludendorff's teachings, was warning of a second *Dolchstoss*, predicting weak politicians would capitulate to the Allies over the Ruhr occupation, and emotively arguing that patriots would 'bleed out of the same stab wounds as killed off the resistance of the heroic armies on the soil of France' unless the nationalist right came to power.[199] As tensions rose in Bavaria, paramilitaries underwent training and Hitler continued to whip up his supporters into a nationalist frenzy, and the labour movement's annual May Day marches became an issue of contention. The Nazis demanded a counterdemonstration and, in effect, an armed confrontation with the left in the streets of Munich as 1 May was also the anniversary of the crushing of the Bavarian Soviet in 1919. Instead, the commander of the Bavarian Reichswehr, von Lossow, who had backed Hitler in January, refused to arm the rightist paramilitaries (the militias' arms were being held in safekeeping by the army) and instead, the Nazis were forced into an embarrassing climbdown, holding a small rally of 2,000 uniformed militiamen outside the city while 25,000 trade unionists gathered in Munich.[200] The incident proved that the nationalist paramilitaries could achieve little without the backing of the army, but this was not a lesson that Hitler was to heed.

The Nazi leader was more cautious over the summer, although links with Ludendorff were intensified; clearly their politics were now closely aligned – Ludendorff gave a speech straight from the Nazi wheelhouse in which he talked of class divisions being replaced by a *volksgemeinschaft* and the age of monarchy being over.[201] The general's villa became 'the political centre of the National Socialists' that summer, with continual coming and going and conferences 'every hour', although Ludendorff made a point of busying himself with gardening to avoid direct liability for the schemes being hatched in his home.²⁰² On 27 August, Ludendorff, Hitler, Göring and sympathetic officers held a conference near Dortmund in which the general agreed to subordinate himself on political matters to Hitler and the conspirators were reassured of Reichswehr support, not least by Ludendorff's own declaration that von Seeckt would back them.²⁰³ The next major stepping stone for the general and the lance corporal who fancied themselves dictators was the so-called German Day rally on 1–2 September. A hundred thousand rightists and paramilitaries gathered at the Bavarian city of Nuremburg for two days of speeches and parades on the anniversary of the Prussian victory over the French at Sedan in 1870, which, given current events, seemed particularly pertinent.²⁰⁴ In a two-hour march-past, the radical right paramilitary groups presented themselves to Ludendorff, Hitler, their commander Kriebel and a member of the Bavarian royal family. In appearing shoulder to shoulder with Ludendorff on the platform, Hitler was gaining considerable credence and legitimacy as the general's clear political 'favourite'. Another crucial aspect of the rally was the formalisation of the loose paramilitary association Röhm and Kriebel had established in February into the Kampfbund. The Kampfbund swore loyalty to Adolf Hitler as their political leader and General Ludendorff as their military chief, thereby consolidating the duo's hold over the völkisch militias. Kriebel oversaw the military organisation while Scheubner-Richter was business manager and wrote up a political programme that openly advocated the armed overthrow of the government in Berlin.²⁰⁵ The Kampfbund brought together Göring's SA stormtroopers with Bund Oberland under Freidrich Weber, the Reichsflagge of Adolf Heiss and several smaller groups, although not Captain Ehrhardt and his Bund Wiking, who now saw Hitler as a rival. This large and powerful militia was the vehicle Hitler and Ludendorff planned to use to assert their strength in Bavarian politics, and indeed the wider Reich, although Hitler's role in the organisation was more ambiguous; Ludendorff was envisaged as the future dictator of the new Germany. The Kampfbund leaders hoped to use Bavaria as a vanguard for a nationalist revolution, the base from which to launch a successful putsch. Much inspiration was drawn from Mussolini's famous March on Rome the previous year and the central aspect of their plan was a march on Berlin to start in Munich which would draw in nationalists, paramilitaries and soldiers from across the Reich. In order to get their plans off the ground, however, they needed the backing of the Bavarian authorities, in particular the local army forces under General von Lossow. Fortunately for Hitler and Ludendorff, further crisis was about to bring about a shift in regional politics.

In August, the DVP's Gustav Stresemann had replaced the hopeless Cuno as chancellor at the head of a unity government. Despite being a nationalist in the right-wing People's Party, Stresemann recognised the impossibility of continuing passive resistance in the Ruhr, given the disastrous impact it was having on public finances and the value of the mark. On 26 September, the end of the 'battle of the Ruhr' was announced; the strikers were to return to work and negotiation with the French was to be pursued. This was the capitulation that Hitler and many others on the radical right had foreseen and, predictably, nationalist opinion exploded.[206] The Bavarian government immediately declared a state of emergency and, under the terms of the state's constitution, appointed former Prime Minister Gustav von Kahr as state commissioner general with dictatorial power to rule by decree. Alongside Bavaria's Reichswehr commander General Lossow and the Chief of the State Police Colonel Hans von Seisser, Kahr formed a power triumvirate that would rule Bavaria by force in this acute emergency, as hyperinflation reached its peak and rumour of uprisings from left and right ran wild.[207] In many ways, this move was a defensive measure to forestall a Hitler-Ludendorff putsch by bringing in the strongman of the Bavarian right, but soon the Kahr triumvirate would also be in direct conflict with Berlin as well as the Kampfbund. President Ebert declared a nationwide state of emergency on 27 September and the following day Reichswehr chief von Seeckt ordered General Lossow to shut down the Nazi newspaper *Völkischer Beobachter*. Lossow, however, refused and so General von Seeckt sacked him. But Lossow refused to relinquish his post, and Kahr reinstated him, arguing Seeckt had no right to interfere in Bavaria's affairs, effectively asserting Bavarian sovereignty. Lossow then swore an oath of allegiance to the Bavarian government, violating his oath to the Weimar Constitution and his commander-in-chief, President Ebert.

A few weeks later, the entire Bavarian Reichswehr swore the same oath.[208] Bavaria was now in a state of conflict with Berlin, the Bavarian army in a state of mutiny. Civil war seemed a real possibility and the Kahr-Lossow-Seisser triumvirate began to make plans for a march on Berlin of their own. This put Hitler, Ludendorff and the Kampfbund in a difficult political position. Ludendorff twice met with Lossow to gain assurance that the new oath was nationalist in intention, not separatist, as neither Hitler nor the Prussian general had any sympathy for Bavarian independence.[209] However, the strong stance the Bavarian leadership had taken won the approval of most of the right, and Captain Adolf Heiss, leader of the Reichsflagge, left the Kampfbund to support Kahr, leaving Röhm, who had recently been discharged from the army, to take over a splinter faction of the organisation which labelled itself the Reichskriegsflagge. By early October, Hitler was criticising the inaction of the Kahr regime while also pledging to march with him if the commissioner general were to make a move on the capital.[210] All the while, a frantic series of meetings between the Kampfbund leaders and the triumvirate, and the triumvirate and Reichswehr officers and nationalists in northern Germany, tried to build a viable coalition to overthrow the Republic. It appears that Hitler and Ludendorff particularly were more naïve than the Bavarian leaders; they seem to have believed that, given their shared aims, the triumvirate would support them come what may. Kahr, Lossow and Seisser, however, as well as the officers and nationalists they contacted in the north, all agreed that Hitler and especially Ludendorff should be excluded from their putsch plans and any future administration. This was certainly the view of the industrialist Friedrich Minoux, who was willing to back a military regime but told Seisser on 3 November that he was unenthusiastic about Hitler and Ludendorff.[211] Seisser's Bavarian State Police officers were also warned that those who were not prepared to shoot National Socialists should resign.[212] Furthermore, the triumvirate were never entirely committed to a putsch. From the capital, Seeckt continually tried to encourage Lossow and Seisser to pursue the constitutional path, while Theodore Duesterberg, leader of the nationalist veterans' association Der Stahlhelm, found Lossow decidedly noncommittal when he visited him on 28 October, despite Duesterberg's assurance that the northern Reichswehr would not impede a Bavarian advance on Berlin.[213]

The Kampfbund leaders meanwhile spent October and early November desperately trying to win support for their uprising. Ludendorff, partly through his son-in-law Heinz Pernet, had made a concerted effort to win over the officer cadets at Munich's Infantry School to the cause and cultivated this unit as a force loyal to him personally, in contrast to the disparate bands of the Kampfbund.[214] On the other hand, contacts with north German nationalists were foolishly squandered and bridges with Ehrhardt burnt.[215] On 17 October, Röhm tried to persuade Crown Prince Rupprecht to back them but instead the royal encouraged him to back Kahr.[216] Kahr was first and foremost a monarchist and therefore Rupprecht's negative opinion of Ludendorff and Hitler mattered to him, especially considering the anti-monarchist and anti-clerical leanings of Nazi politics. As a result, Hitler and Ludendorff focused their efforts on winning over Lossow and Seisser, whose armed forces were the most important factor in both Bavarian politics and any hopes of a national coup. If the Bavarian Reichswehr backed them, they reasoned, Kahr would either comply with a fait accompli or could be disposed of. During a series of meetings, Lossow was sympathetic to Hitler and Ludendorff but failed to commit. Seisser, on the other hand, gave them shorter shrift, calling their plan 'fantastic'. Hitler met the military leaders for a final time on 25 October and tried to persuade them to end their support for Kahr but once again he failed, this time differing over the role of Ludendorff – for Lossow and Seisser, the likely foreign attitude to the wartime general meant his leadership of a directorate was implausible, while Hitler insisted Ludendorff's presence was essential to win Reichswehr support.[217] On 4 November, at the laying of the cornerstone of the Munich memorial to the war dead, there was a possibility that the Kampfbund might kidnap the triumvirate (the most telling evidence being that Ludendorff stayed away from the event), but Seisser was in Berlin at the time and Hitler decided it was too risky.[218] Hitler and the paramilitary leaders had, however, by early November, decided they had to make their move. Chancellor Stresemann, acting through Admiral Scheer, had approached Ludendorff to attempt to dissuade him, but to no avail – the 'red' government in Berlin had to be destroyed.[219] The situation was boiling over, hyperinflation was reaching its zenith and inaction threatened to squander the political capital the Kampfbund had accumulated. It was time to act.

The Beer Hall Putsch

Events now moved rapidly and, as during the Kapp Putsch, the plotters were never firmly in control of them. As with Ludendorff's previous coup attempt, one is struck by the poor planning and 'staff work' made evident by the farce that was to follow, especially considering he had been the mastermind of Tannenberg less than a decade previously. Perhaps, given the serious mental health issues that affected him in 1918–19, Ludendorff's supposedly brilliant mind was in severe decline, despite the fact that he was not yet 60. On the other hand, Ludendorff's aptitude for politics was never strong and his sense of the possible had been faulty since the final year of the Great War.

The plans, such as they were, were finalised on 6–7 November, with two final meetings between the leaders of the Kampfbund on the 7th at Kriebel's Munich apartment. The putsch was scheduled for 11 November, but as with the Kapp coup, the date was brought forward due to circumstance. The plotters got word that Kahr planned to hold a rally of the patriotic associations at the Bürgerbräukeller beer hall the following evening. Hitler saw this as the perfect opportunity and convinced the conspirators to strike then.[220] Ludendorff later denied he was present at the meeting, and indeed denied that he knew any putsch was planned at all, but this is contradicted by the testimony of Oberland leader Weber (who was there) and the fact Ludendorff himself told his son-in-law that 8 November was to be an important day.[221] During the criminal investigation that followed, it was established that Ludendorff had been involved in the planning of the coup, a fact he would tacitly admit during the trial, and documents pertaining to the putsch seized by police featured marginalia in the general's own handwriting.[222] Furthermore, on 4 November he had briefed Lieutenant Gerhard Rossbach, the leader of the underground officer cadets organisation at the Munich Infantry School, on the plans for the putsch.[223] The general had also been prudent enough to withdraw all his savings, stocks and assets from the Deutsche Bank on 3 November, with a total value of 7–8 billion marks according to the Munich Police, meaning he avoided having his assets frozen should the coup attempt fail.[224] Most importantly of all, Ludendorff's actions on 8 November make little sense without his prior knowledge of the plan, therefore the classic version of the Beer Hall Putsch in which the general is caught off guard by Hitler's move (see Shirer[225] or the 2003 docu-drama *Hitler: Rise of Evil*) is not only false, but the product of Ludendorff and his circle's propaganda and truth-twisting. On the same day the putschists were finalising their plan, 7 November, General von Lossow summoned the senior officers of the Bavarian

Reichswehr to his Munich headquarters to warn them that a coup to establish a 'Hitler-Ludendorff dictatorship' was in the offing. The men were to be placed on high alert and Lossow emphasised that the military was to have nothing to do with the uprising; 'we're not going to be part of this craziness', he told them.[226] Both the putschists and anti-putschists were thrashing out their plans in the Bavarian capital that day, and given that Röhm estimated only 40–50 per cent of the Kampfbund had the training and equipment to be considered capable of taking on government forces, the odds of success were low.[227] As negotiations the previous month had revealed, support from the Bavarian army was essential to the plotters' hopes of victory.

Thursday, 8 November was to be the day of the putsch, the fifth anniversary of the overthrow of the Bavarian monarchy in the German Revolution. After a leisurely breakfast in his suburban mansion, Ludendorff's first appointment of the day was not until 4.00 pm, when – rather surprisingly, given subsequent events – he was collected by a Reichswehr staff car and taken to von Kahr's official residence on Maximillian Strasse. Here, he held a final conference with von Kahr and von Lossow, hoping to persuade them to join the uprising, while Kahr hoped to persuade Ludendorff to delay. Ludendorff had wanted Hitler to join the meeting, but Kahr had refused to see the Nazi leader. Ludendorff would later claim that in the meeting both Kahr and Lossow supported both his objective (overthrowing the government) and method (military coup) and that they merely differed over timing; Kahr believed they needed to recruit nationalists in northern Germany to the conspiracy, while Ludendorff insisted if *he* headed the march on Berlin, the army would not resist.[228] Transparently, Ludendorff enquired if Lossow would be attending Kahr's speech at the Bürgerbräukeller that evening, the second time Lossow had been asked that day by a putsch leader, for he had fielded the exact same question around noon in a phone call from Weber.[229] Ludendorff himself would not be there; he needed distance between himself and the outbreak of the putsch in order to grant himself some plausible deniability, just as he had linked up with the Kapp Putsch when 'out on a morning stroll'. The conference broke up at 5.00 pm and rather than heading straight home, Ludendorff requested the Reichswehr driver take him to visit Scheubner-Richter, the leading Nazi and chief go-between of Ludendorff and Hitler, in order to inform him of the failure of his conference.[230] Clearly, the putschists still held out hope that the Bavarian triumvirate would support their coup and despite Ludendorff's inability to win them over, Hitler and the general were determined to go ahead with their plan. The openness of Ludendorff's dealings with the men who would put down his coup is frankly extraordinary and suggests he very much saw them as allies rather than enemies. This helps explain some of his more questionable actions during the putsch and his furious reaction after its failure. Nevertheless, his inability to read Lossow and Kahr, and his over-optimistic assessment of the army's attitude towards him, were to prove fatal for the plot and further highlights the general's lack of political nous. On the other hand, Harold Gordon argues that Ludendorff and Hitler merely kept up appearances with the Bavarian leaders in order to disguise the timing of their own plan.[231] If that was the case, Ludendorff's actions that afternoon surely blew their cover, and even if the triumvirate really were in the dark, it was to make no difference to their attitude to the putsch.

Around 8.00 pm, the rally at the Bürgerbräukeller began. Many of the prominent figures (bar Ludendorff) of the Bavarian right were present in a packed beer hall to hear Kahr, supported by von Lossow and von Seisser, deliver what was by all accounts a rather dry speech on the dangers of Marxism to an audience of 3,000. Adolf Hitler and a small posse of Nazis, including Scheubner-Richter, having been met by a cheering crowd outside the hall, sat quietly in a corner sipping their beers.[232] At 8.25 pm, unbeknownst to those inside, the beer hall was surrounded by heavily armed SA stormtroopers led by Hermann Göring. Moments later, Hitler, wearing a suit and his two Iron Crosses, pistol in hand, marched forwards, steel-helmeted stormtroopers sweeping into the hall, causing panic and outrage. Upon reaching the front of the room, Hitler stood on a chair and fired a shot into the ceiling to demand silence. 'The National revolution has begun!' he declared, announcing to the stunned onlookers that the governments of Berlin and Bavaria had been overthrown. Then, he took Kahr, Lossow and Seisser into a small side room which had been booked by Rudolf Hess, an onrushing policeman being ordered to stand down by Seisser.[233]

Hitler's action was the trigger for other Kampfbund detachments to seize key objectives around the city, including the Bavarian War Ministry, the Police Headquarters and the Infantry School, with its supportive nationalist cadets. Crucially, however, the putschists assigned to secure the 19th Infantry Regiment barracks soon found themselves ejected, and the barracks was to become the headquarters for the triumvirate's efforts to quash the coup.[234] But this was in the future, and for the time being at least, the putschists had the key personnel of the state government in their hands. Rudolf Hess had arrested Bavarian Prime Minister von Knilling and several other members of the government who were in the audience, while Hitler immediately began negotiations with the triumvirate in the side room. Sweating profusely and gesturing wildly with a loaded gun in one hand and a beer in the other, he failed to win over Kahr, Lossow and Seisser to support his coup. Seisser reprimanded Hitler for breaking his promise not to launch a putsch yet, while Lossow enquired as to Ludendorff's position, given he was not present.[235] Hitler responded that the general had already been contacted and assured them that they would all receive posts in the new government; Hitler himself was to be chancellor, Ludendorff head of a new national army (presumably replacing the craven Reichswehr), Kahr regent of Bavaria, Pöhner Bavarian prime minister, Lossow defence minister and Seisser Reich police minister. The final post did not exist; police forces were regionally controlled, suggesting either Hitler and Ludendorff planned a repressive police state (Ludendorff had said the Kapp Putsch, where the plotters had not arrested or shot their enemies, was a learning experience) or maybe Hitler was making up his new cabinet on the spot and needed to invent a role for the police leader von Seisser.

Shortly after this, Hitler left the side room, according to King in order to ask Scheubner-Richter to fetch the general, although it is hard to establish exactly when Scheubner-Richter, his butler, Ludendorff's valet and his stepson, Heinz Pernet, left the beer hall in a commandeered car to fetch their figurehead.[236] Driving at 'breakneck' speeds through the foggy, snowy night, they raced the 8km from central Munich to the general's villa in Prinz-Ludwigs-Höhe. There, Ludendorff greeted them impatiently in his study, for he had been on edge since receiving a call at 8.30 pm from the Bürgerbräukeller requesting his presence. He had asked what was happening, perhaps trying to assess the state of play before committing, but the caller (Scheubner-Richter) was in a hurry and said he would soon be informed. When Pernet and Scheubner-Richter arrived at Prinz-Ludwigs-Höhe he again asked how the putsch was going, in particular enquiring of Lossow's stance. He received only a brief explanation and the putschists, wishing to avoid delay, told him there was not time for him to change into his uniform. Ludendorff was therefore bundled into the car wearing a brown tweed smoking jacket and green felt hat; once more, he could pose as the civilian who had attended a putsch by mistake.[237] On the one hand, it may have seemed rational to Ludendorff that he stay away from the proclaiming of the putsch and arrive late in casual dress in order to maintain his distance from such a risky venture. However, with hindsight it appears dangerously negligent for the general, the most respected and prominent public figure involved in the coup, to apparently be so unprepared for its outbreak as to not even have decided what he was going to wear and, more importantly, not to have been on the scene in the crucial early stages.

General Ludendorff's arrival at the Bürgerbräukeller changed the dynamic of the negotiations with the Bavarian triumvirate. Hitler had already won over the (literally) captive right-wing audience in the hall to his plan to assault Berlin, the 'Babylon of wickedness', and the arrival of the famous wartime leader only further bolstered the putschists' cause. According to a retired major general in the audience (von Kleinhenz), the general looked graver than he had ever seen him, and despite the cheers and the men standing to attention, Ludendorff entered the hall briskly and without comment.[238] He held a short conference with Hitler outside the side room in which Kahr, Lossow and Seisser were being held, presumably being brought up to speed on the situation and, one suspects, being tasked with winning the Bavarian leadership round. On entering the room, Ludendorff lied immediately, telling the trio that he had had no idea that Hitler had planned to do this. 'Gentlemen, I am just as surprised as you are,' he reportedly said, despite having encouraged Kahr and Lossow to join a coup just hours before.[239] Already, the general was building his defence should the plot fail. Despite his supposed surprise at events, Ludendorff threw himself into the task of winning over the triumvirate with alacrity, taking charge of negotiations from the ineffectual Hitler. The atmosphere now changed. Ludendorff appealed to the trio's political instincts, asking that they cooperate with *us* in the 'great national völkisch movement' and, turning first to Kahr, blackmailing his sense of honour: 'Do not refuse this call to duty. It is the most fateful hour of the German Reich. Do what we all expect of you.'[240] Kahr was not persuaded so Ludendorff left him to Hitler and the newly arrived Ernst Pöhner, one of the Bavarian premier's closest colleagues. Perhaps sensing that Kahr would not stand against the military, Ludendorff instead focused his efforts on Seisser and especially Lossow in twenty minutes of talks that were considerably more concerned with the practical details of a putsch than Hitler's rhetorical harangues had been.

Bavaria's security leaders understandably raised concerns about potential French or Czech military intervention against a dictatorship. They also pointed out that Reichswehr head General von Seeckt would immediately order a division stationed in the neighbouring state of Thuringia to put down the Bavarian revolt. Ludendorff dismissed these concerns as mere 'tactical' issues and insisted that, as during the Kapp Putsch, Reichswehr would not fire on Reichswehr, that the army would rally to a march led by him and that Germany had nothing to fear from France and Czechoslovakia. 'Besides, it is done now. There is no way to go back,' seemed to be Ludendorff's decisive argument, although his failure to plan for the military realities of an armed advance across Germany to the capital is surprising to say the least.[241] Ludendorff then forced Lossow's hand, asking him simply, 'What do you say?' Standing to attention, hand on sabre, supposedly tears in his eyes, Lossow quietly replied, 'Your Excellency's wish is my command.' Ludendorff was delighted, especially when Lossow added, 'I will organise the army as you need it, to win, Excellency.'[242] Seisser also, apparently more reluctantly, offered General Ludendorff his hand as well, before the war hero brought them both over to join the posse surrounding the intransigent Kahr. Already besieged by Hitler, Pöhner, Kriebel and Weber, Ludendorff, flanked by his new subordinates, told Kahr: 'You cannot deny yourself to the German people in this historic hour!' Kahr continued to insist the plan was doomed, that several weeks' delay was needed to link up with other nationalists. Ludendorff dismissed this line of argument; 'one or two gentlemen' in the north would make little difference to the success of the coup, he claimed.[243] Kahr's last line of defence was that as a monarchist he could not accept the Bavarian regency without the permission of the heir to the vacant thrown, Crown Prince Rupprecht. The putschists insisted they would seek out the prince in his Berchtesgaden residence and secure his assent for the cause, after which Kahr finally yielded, to the elation of Hitler and Ludendorff.[244] It appeared they now had the backing of the Bavarian state (and vitally, its army and police) in their attempt to create a nationalist dictatorship. They could add the prestigious name of von Kahr and maybe even Rupprecht to their proclamations.

It was 9.40 pm, an hour and a quarter into the coup, when the triumvirate and putsch leaders finally emerged from the side room to present themselves to the restless Bürgerbräukeller drinkers. After a short, sombre explanation from Kahr, Hitler spoke enthusiastically, announcing that General Ludendorff would be Germany's new commander-in-chief, with dictatorial powers. His insistence that this decision would 'lift the stigma of infamy and shame from the brows of German soldiers' not only harked back to the *Dolchstoss*, but also implied that the new military regime would defy the terms of Versailles and perhaps even eject the French occupiers by force.[245] Ludendorff spoke next. While predictably starting by reminding the audience of his surprise at events, he was nevertheless serious and apparently visibly emotional:

> I place myself in the service of the true nationalist government of Germany and will strive to restore to it the old black-white-and-red cockade stripped away by the infamous revolution.
>
> Everything is at stake. A German who experiences this hour cannot hesitate about giving his all to this cause, both in spirit and with a full German heart. This hour is the turning point of history. But let us look at it in full recognition of the difficulty of the task we face, convinced of and imbued with the gravity of our responsibility.
>
> Let us go to work, side by side with the entire nation. German men, I harbour no doubts about this: if we do this work with a pure heart, God's blessing will be with us. I pray for that blessing, for without God's will, nothing can be done. But I am also convinced that, when God in Heaven sees true German men are there again, He will be on our side.[246]

It was noted that the applause for Ludendorff was somewhat more muted than it had been for Hitler; his clashes with the Bavarian monarchy perhaps the cause of his divisiveness in the state. The six men, Hitler, Ludendorff, Pöhner, Kahr, Lossow and Seisser, shook hands and the crowd sang the national anthem, *Deutschland über Alles*. Next, Germany's new government, as they claimed they were, returned to the side room of the beer hall and began to act as a government; Hitler and the politicians began writing up proclamations, awarding cabinet seats and developing a programme while Ludendorff, Lossow and Kriebel (who had appointed himself Ludendorff's chief of staff) began rudimentary military planning for a march on Berlin. Ironically, it seems that the planning that had been done in advance by the putschists was concerned with the wielding of power, not how to seize it; they had for instance produced recruitment posters for Ludendorff's new National Army that was to fight a 'crusade' against the foreign invaders (presumably the French). The Kampfbund had orders to set up recruiting stations throughout the city on the morning of 9 November to begin immediately the task of expanding the German military once more after the Versailles restrictions, perhaps ready to fight a new war.[247] These preparations would prove to be premature to say the least, but surely this was the high point of the entire debacle for Hitler and Ludendorff as they prepared in earnest to assume high office. We cannot know, but the deluded general might now have begun to truly believe that he would not only command the army again, but that soon he would be dictator of Germany, with the unfettered political power he had so desired during the Great War.

The crowd was now allowed to leave, although Prime Minister von Knilling and his cabinet were held as hostages, the plotters not trusting the stolid, conservative BVP men to back their radical nationalist gamble. Hitler, however, now heard that troopers from the Bund Oberland had been captured in a botched attempt to seize the Munich Army Engineers Barracks. Believing that he now had the Bavarian authorities onside, he decided to head across town himself to negotiate with the engineers who were holding his paramilitaries. This was to be a fateful mistake, for not only did the fruitless trip waste precious time, it also left the politically inept Ludendorff in charge at the Bürgerbräukeller. Ludendorff, Kriebel, Scheubner-Richter and the Bavarian triumvirate remained in the side room off the main hall, supposedly planning the revolution. By 10.30 pm, however, Ludendorff was feeling increasingly awkward and uncomfortable, unsuited to the role of chairman. It appears he simply ran out of things to say, while the trio of Kahr, Lossow and Seisser sat quietly, looking tired and devoid of enthusiasm. Scheubner-Richter excused himself in order to telephone his wife, leaving Ludendorff even more isolated. He decided to break the silence, and suggested that the gentlemen should now return to their posts in order to put their plans into action.[248] Ludendorff himself announced he would go to the Bavarian War Ministry to take up command and suggested that the trio go home and rest. The general told Lossow, 'In the meantime, I shall go to your office [in the War Ministry] and wait for you there.'[249] This was the key moment in which the coup began to unravel, for Ludendorff totally failed to see that the triumvirate (who had consistently opposed Hitler's putsch plan right up until the coercion that evening) might actually act against the plotters once they were at liberty. By 10.40 pm, all three had left the Bürgerbräukeller. When Scheubner-Richter returned from his call, he was astounded and appalled that Ludendorff had not only released the Bavarian leaders but failed to even assign them guards. Ludendorff dismissed these concerns out of hand, insisting both that they had duties to perform and would need to be at their posts, but more importantly that they had given their word – 'I forbid you to doubt the word of a German officer,' he angrily told Scheubner-Richter.[250] Clearly Ludendorff did not regard his own word as having been violated by his truth-twisting since 1918. Hitler returned soon after, although he was apparently unconcerned about the release of Kahr and co.; like Ludendorff he believed they now supported the revolution, that the Kampfbund's fait accompli had forced their hand.[251] The two putsch leaders then reviewed a parade of the first new unit in the 'National Army', Storm Battalion Ludendorff, composed of the officer cadets that the general had helped recruit in the preceding weeks. Now, however, the war hero was restless; he was the commander-in-chief of an army again and his place was at the War Ministry, not a beer hall. With Pernet, Kriebel and a small entourage, he left the Bürgerbräukeller at 11.00 pm for the army headquarters on Schönfeld Strasse, Hitler promising to join him soon. Lossow, they both presumed, either would also be there soon, or perhaps was already in his office planning the march on Berlin.[252]

Lossow had gone straight to the 19th Infantry Regiment Barracks, which General Jakob Danner, commander of the Munich garrison, had turned into the headquarters of the counter-coup, ordering troops from across Bavaria to the state capital and informing the army that von Lossow's orders were to be ignored; he was to be regarded as a prisoner.[253] Seisser had gone to the police barracks – his 1,800 armed State Police officers were the government's largest force in the city, while Kahr had retired to his official residence to consider his next move. Arriving at 10.45 pm, Lossow first had to convince a suspicious Danner that his participation in the coup was simply a ruse, before the two generals were joined by Seisser. Practically a stone's throw from the infantry barracks, Ludendorff was at the War Ministry, in the waiting room outside General von Lossow's office, unaware both that the man he was expecting was so near at hand and that he had already betrayed the putsch. Once again, Scheubner-Richter raised concerns about Lossow's reliability and again Ludendorff dismissed any aspersions on the trustworthiness of German officers, refusing even to enter Lossow's office until the Bavarian commander arrived. However, Ludendorff was not entirely passive and serene. Although he trusted Lossow and Seisser as officers, he had doubts about von Kahr, who was after all loyal first and foremost to the Crown Prince, with whom Ludendorff had frequently quarrelled. Kahr had also been highly reluctant to join the coup. Might Kahr and Rupprecht persuade the taciturn Lossow to switch sides? In order to prevent this and secure Commissioner General Kahr, Ludendorff acted decisively and prudently. He requested of the newly arrived Hitler and his chief of staff Kriebel that Storm Battalion Ludendorff be ordered to march from the Bürgerbräukeller to occupy Kahr's official residence on Maximillian Strasse, where Ludendorff had had his audience earlier in the day.[254]

Led by Freikorps veteran Lieutenant Gerhard Rossbach, the 400 cadets of the Storm Battalion confronted the state police guarding the premier's residence and almost came to blows. Colonel Seisser, who was now at Kahr's office, appeared and assured Rossbach that their presence was unnecessary; the police had the situation under control and both Seisser and Kahr supported the new government. Confused, Rossbach dispatched a motorcyclist to the Bürgerbräukeller to request instructions. Before he could receive a reply, Rossbach received new orders in Ludendorff's name to secure the railway station. In fact, these orders were from Weber, leader of the Bund Oberland, who was supposed to have taken the station but had been unable to do so after his militiamen had been captured at the Engineer Barracks.[255] As the cadets withdrew, a police car left the residence, carrying Kahr and Seisser to the 19th Infantry Barracks. By 1.00 am, the triumvirate had reassembled at the barracks with General Danner and began a coordinated effort to stop Hitler and Ludendorff.[256] Around the same time, Franz Matt, deputy prime minister of Bavaria, had gathered what government personnel he could find and set up an administration in exile in Regensburg, some 125km north of Munich, issuing a proclamation calling for the civil service, army and police to remain loyal and refuse to obey 'the Prussian Ludendorff'.[257]

As early as midnight, a meeting in Berlin between President Ebert, the cabinet and Reichswehr chief General von Seeckt had ensured the army as a whole would not support the putsch. The steely von Seeckt had insisted the army would obey *him* (by implication not the government per se) and so he extracted from Ebert the temporary transfer of his executive powers as commander-in-chief to himself, the civilian government having been unduly alarmed by the movement of troops from across Bavaria towards Munich.[258] The mobilisation of the Bavarian Reichswehr was not troops rallying to Ludendorff's banner but General Danner's swift actions bearing fruit; troops from across the state were moving on Munich to quash the uprising. At 2.50 am, having received word that both Crown Prince Rupprecht and General von Seeckt were opposed to the Hitler-Ludendorff putsch, Kahr, Lossow and Seisser sent a declaration from the Infantry Barracks to local radio, distancing themselves from their statements in the Bürgerbräukeller. A subsequent ordinance banned the Nazi Party and Kampfbund and ordered that the putsch leaders be arrested on sight. At 3.30 am they secured the arrest of Wilhelm Frick, the Nazi-supporting former political police chief who had taken charge at the Police Headquarters earlier that night.[259] At 4.40 am, Lossow ordered General Ludendorff himself be arrested, a step that had not been taken during the Kapp Putsch out of military deference.[260] The actions of Generals Danner and von Seeckt meant that the coup never had a genuine chance of overthrowing the Republic. Ludendorff's foolish release of the triumvirate merely hastened their defection and thus brought a swifter end to the whole sorry venture.

In the War Ministry, the putschists grew increasingly agitated during the early hours of 9 November as all contact with the Bavarian leadership dried up. Ludendorff was seemingly the only one who continued to insist that von Lossow, at least, was with them and that he would surely appear soon. Considering how keen the general had been to get out of the beer hall and to his 'command post' earlier in the night, his passivity in the long hours that followed in the War Ministry is difficult to comprehend. It rather suggests that his military plans were entirely reliant on Lossow doing the heavy lifting and mobilising the Bavarian Reichswehr for the putschists. Quite simply, Hitler and Ludendorff had launched a coup that relied on the active cooperation of men who had told them just hours before they were against the plan. Such was both the trust Ludendorff placed in the army and the passivity of the plotters in the War Ministry that it was not until 1.00 am (hours after Captain Röhm's paramilitaries had seized the ministry) that the putschists arrested the staff officers who had continued to work at their desks, directing the military response to the coup and feeding information to Danner and Lossow at the Infantry Barracks.[261] Around the same time, a junior officer arrived at the ministry from the Infantry Barracks in order to recall the Reichswehr guards who were uneasily sharing their duties with the Kampfbund militiamen. Ludendorff quizzed the young lieutenant as to why they were being redeployed, the subaltern explaining they were to defend the 19th Infantry's barracks. 'Against whom?' Ludendorff demanded; nevertheless, he allowed the guards and the lieutenant to leave, merely giving them a message for Lossow, which the Bavarian commander promptly ignored.[262]

The reality was that the triumvirate's position at the Infantry Barracks was highly vulnerable – they were outnumbered and just a few streets from the putschist nerve centre at the War Ministry. However, the trusting Ludendorff failed to take decisive steps against the 19th Regiment, despite their lack of cooperation and Lossow's lack of communication. As the night wore on and more and more questions about von Lossow were raised, Ludendorff stuck to his guns: 'A German general does not break his word,' Röhm remembered him saying.[263] After an emissary sent to the 19th failed to return (he had been arrested), yet more doubts were raised, but Ludendorff could not comprehend how or why a betrayal might have occurred, telling Scheubner-Richter, 'What could they want? All three stood there and gave their word and their hand in honour, before several thousand witnesses. I just cannot conceive of their acting differently now.'[264] Immobilised by indecision, the general requested Colonel Ludwig Leupold, the deputy commander of the pro-putsch Infantry School and a Ludendorff acolyte (but also a friend of Lossow), be summoned to the War Ministry. Perhaps he might be able to shed light on the army's stance or else act as an envoy to von Lossow? Despite the attitude of his cadets, Leupold had remained neutral, awaiting official orders. He did, however, know much more about what was really going on than Ludendorff and Hitler. Arriving at the ministry around 4.00 am, Leupold was inexplicably kept waiting until 5.00 am, when he had an audience with Ludendorff, Hitler and Kriebel that clarified the situation. Ludendorff was clearly agitated by this stage, demanding, 'What is the matter with Lossow? Where is he? I have been waiting for him here since 11 o'clock – nearly seven hours. My telephone calls are not answered, my messengers do not come back. What is going on, Colonel?'[265] Leupold explained simply and calmly that Lossow's anti-putsch position had been known to him since 1.00 am, that he had been to see Lossow personally at the Infantry Barracks between 2.00 and 3.00 am to confirm this, that the triumvirate's promise of support had been extracted under duress and that the only reason Leupold had not informed Ludendorff of all this before was that he had assumed the putschists must already have been aware of it.[266] Hitler and Ludendorff were agog, and, after overcoming their initial shock, argued futilely with Leupold about the triumvirate's position – 'I cannot believe that, I just cannot believe it,' Ludendorff reportedly said.[267] Eventually, Ludendorff decided to dispatch Leupold to Lossow to try to reason with him, a venture that, as Leupold frankly told the general, was doomed to failure. With the might of the Reichswehr and Bavarian State Police about to come down on them, the putschists opted for retreat rather than capitulation. Between 6.00 and 6.30 am, Hitler, Kriebel, Scheubner-Richter, Weber and finally Ludendorff withdrew from the War Ministry for the Bürgerbräukeller on the far side of the Isar River, where over 1,000 Kampfbund fighters were still (rather inexplicably) stationed. Climbing into his car, Ludendorff still wondered aloud whether a German general could break his word in such a way. Röhm, shaking the general's hand, promised to remain at the ministry with his paramilitaries and 'do my duty'.[268]

The morning of 9 November therefore saw the increasingly tired and fractious putschists back where they had started, assembled at the Bürgerbräukeller beer hall, now without the optimism and momentum of the previous night. They still had a significant number of militiamen and 14 quadrillion confiscated marks (worth around $22,200) at their disposal but the impending arrival of military and police units to quash the coup and the lack of external support meant the situation was desperate, with Hitler now remonstrating with Ludendorff for letting the triumvirate go free, while Ludendorff insisted that had Hitler not held the Bavarian leaders at gunpoint, they would have readily cooperated.[269] Sometime after 9.00 am a coterie of foreign journalists were welcomed into the beer hall and taken to the upstairs dining room where the conspirators – or Germany's new government, as they labelled themselves – were deep in discussion as to their next move, poring over maps of the city. Ludendorff, glass of red wine in hand, told the reporters, 'my government is eager to have the approval of the United States and England', insisted a glorious future awaited the new Germany and, comically, issued press passes to the assembled newspapermen.[270] Throughout the morning, acrimonious debates raged inside the 'rebel' High Command as to their next move. Once more, military basics seem to have eluded the plotters; in a tight situation any commander's first instinct would be to call for reinforcements, yet the putsch leaders did not think to call in the various SA units of southern Bavaria to bolster their position, while Lossow and Danner had troops moving in from across the state.[271] Kampfbund commander Hermann Kriebel drew up a plan for the putschist forces to hold a line along the east bank of the Isar River from which to resist government forces and Hitler made a grand speech in favour of fighting to death, which Ludendorff cut short – the defensive plan was unrealistic.[272] Seisser's state police were now already guarding the Isar bridges, while contact with Röhm in the War Ministry had been lost (the building was now surrounded) and Ernst Pöhner, who had been sent to see what was happening at Police Headquarters, had not returned. The net was closing on the conspirators. Kriebel then suggested withdrawal: the putschists were to retreat to the town of Rosenheim in the Bavarian Alps, a nationalist hotbed that would provide both favourable terrain for a guerrilla-style defence and fresh recruits. Effectively, Kriebel was now advocating a Bavarian civil war. Ludendorff immediately dismissed the plan, saying he did not want the revolution to 'choke to death in the mud and slush of a country road'.[273] Hitler too was not keen on retreat, but he had also managed to anger Ludendorff by dispatching an envoy to Crown Prince Rupprecht to seek mediation. Around 11.00 am, the general himself made the decisive intervention. He proposed a march of the leaders and their troops through the centre of the city. There remains some confusion over the purpose of the march. Most accounts insist Ludendorff wanted to drum up popular excitement and support for the 'National Revolution' and convince the wavering triumvirate that the putsch had legs and they had erred in switching sides. However, later Ludendorff was to write that the Kampfbund advance had a more military aim: to relieve Röhm and his Reichskriegsflagge who were surrounded at the War Ministry. As Gordon has pointed out, it would make sense for the putschists to emphasise the peaceful propaganda purpose of the march and play down martial intentions after the fact, especially as the marchers themselves were heavily armed and, for the most part, in paramilitary uniform.[274] Interestingly, General Ludendorff himself, still in his tweed suit and green felt hat, was practically the only member of the procession who would be unarmed. Whatever the true intention of the demonstration, Ludendorff forcefully argued there was no point in waiting around for their situation to deteriorate further. Just five years earlier, the socialist Kurt Eisner had managed to overthrow the Bavarian monarchy with a similar march that had spontaneously attracted thousands of the city's residents to the cause of revolution. Ludendorff was also able to convince the assembled putsch leadership that the plan was relatively risk free; the day before he had said, 'the heavens will fall before the Bavarian Reichswehr turn against me' and now again he reminded the conspirators that his name would guarantee army passivity at the very least.[275] The assertion was not entirely unreasonable, given Ludendorff's experience at the Kapp Putsch where troops famously did not fire on troops, and in the early hours of 9 November, officers of 1st Battalion, 19th Infantry Regiment had agreed they would not fire on Ludendorff should they be ordered to do so.[276] Hitler, drained and despondent, was opposed to the plan, favouring further delay as they awaited a response from Rupprecht, but Ludendorff saw little point in retreat or passivity as the enemy closed in. The hero of Tannenberg, as always, saw the solution to a crisis as being offensive action. 'We march!' he declared, practically ordered, and at noon, the fateful march began.

More than 2,000 armed paramilitaries from the Kampfbund and Storm Battalion Ludendorff, having sworn an oath of allegiance to their general and been paid with stolen 50 billion mark notes, marched with the putsch leaders at their head. As well as Hitler and Ludendorff, the front rank included his stepson Pernet, Scheubner-Richter, Kriebel, Weber and leading Nazis such as Göring, Streicher and Rosenberg.[277] In front of them were four standard-bearers carrying Swastika and black-white-red Imperial German banners. Around 12.15 pm they reached the Ludwig Bridge, guarded by two squads of Colonel Seisser's armed State Police. Earlier that day the policemen had politely requested an SA unit find another route when they had attempted to cross. Despite Göring's appeals to these 'comrades', the police stood their ground and ordered the marchers to halt. In response they were charged by an SA troop with rifles and fixed bayonets. No shots were fired but the policemen were beaten with rifle butts and twenty-eight were taken prisoner. The marchers carried on, singing as they went.[278] They crossed the river and passed through the Isartor gate, then through the winding medieval streets to the city centre. The road was lined with the curious and enthusiastic, many keen to get a glimpse of the war hero Ludendorff and be part of a moment of history. The column began to swell in size as young men joined the marching stormtroopers. When they reached Marienplatz, Munich's central square, Ludendorff's optimism seemed to have borne fruit. Word was out about the new Hitler-Ludendorff government thanks to proclamations posted around the city by the putschists overnight and newspapers that had gone to press before the triumvirate's early hours' volte-face. Agitators had been spreading the word and whipping up the masses into a frenzy. As a result, the square was rammed with excited crowds who cheered the arrival of the Kampfbund and its leaders. Perhaps overwhelmed by the enthusiastic reception and the shouts of 'Heil Hitler, Heil Ludendorff', the general made another risky decision, this time gambling without consulting the other leaders.[279] Given that he appeared to have the city's populace on his side, the general seemed to regain his confidence in the chances of success and therefore led the marchers off Marienplatz and up Wein Strasse. Ludendorff was leading them in the direction of the War Ministry, where Röhm's men were besieged by Reichswehr troops. Once there, perhaps the army would flock to Ludendorff's banner as the people had, perhaps Lossow could be brought round and then the march on Berlin could finally be put in motion. Ludendorff explained his decision thus:

> There are times in life when one acts without really knowing why. I won the Battle of Tannenberg. When I ask myself how and why, I cannot really say.

The explanations are in the history books where I have tried to rationalize my decisions. Perhaps what I wanted to do that noon was to go and fetch Röhm, bring him back.[280]

As stated above, this may have been the intention all along, although the accounts of the leading putschists, and Ludendorff's own admission of spontaneity, seems to suggest the change in direction was unplanned and something of a surprise. On the other hand, it would make sense for Ludendorff and the conspirators to later deny there being a military objective to their march and emphasise spontaneity given what was about to unfold. They had certainly left the Bürgerbräukeller armed for battle. They were now headed in the direction of Odeonsplatz, where State Police under Lieutenant Michael von Godin had been deployed to seal off approaches to the War Ministry. Upon hearing of the approaching march, Colonel Seisser ordered over the telephone that Hitler and co. be stopped at all costs. There are two roads that lead onto Odeonsplatz from the south and seeing the police forming up ahead of them, Ludendorff led the demonstration right off one of them, Theatiner Strasse, and then left at the opera onto the other, the narrow Residenz Strasse. 'We shall go around them,' Ludendorff had declared, but this primitive flanking manoeuvre was hardly likely to deceive the police.[281] The putschists were now just 600m or so from the War Ministry on Schönfeld Strasse and they vastly outnumbered the Reichswehr forces under General Danner who were besieging Röhm. Residenz Strasse opens up onto Odeonsplatz square at a monument known as the Feldherrnhalle, or Field Marshal's Hall. Appropriately, this monument to martial prowess would see the undoing of Hitler and Ludendorff's poorly planned putsch. Responding to Ludendorff's minor shift in approach, Lieutenant Godin had set up a police cordon at the Feldherrnhalle, blocking the marchers from accessing the square with 130 State troopers.

The fateful confrontation took place at approximately 12.45 pm. Marching twelve to sixteen abreast, the 2,000 putschists filled the entire street and must have made an intimidating sight. Ludendorff likely believed the police would be brushed aside, as at Ludwig Bridge, and indeed a first line of police was swiftly overwhelmed by sheer weight of numbers. By the time Residenz Strasse reaches the Feldherrnhalle it is barely wider than a back alley, with high-sided buildings on either side. The noise of singing, shouting and thousands of boots marching on the cobbled road must have been immense, so both the police's shouts of 'halt' and Hitler's bodyguard's call of 'Don't shoot! Excellency Ludendorff is coming!' were unlikely to have been heard.[282] Once again, SA stormtroopers charged forward and clashed in hand-to-hand combat with the policemen, who held their ground, swinging their rifles like clubs as the huge crowd of putschists threatened to engulf them. It has never been established who fired the first shot, although both sides blamed each other. Whoever was to blame, the shot triggered a wild firefight that lasted around a minute and left fifteen marchers, four police and a bystander dead. Scheubner-Richter was shot through the heart and died almost instantly. He had linked arms with Hitler beside him and dragged the Nazi leader down, dislocating the latter's shoulder but saving him from further harm. Hitler's bodyguard, Ulrich Graf, took eleven bullets as he shielded his Führer. Ludendorff's valet, Kurt Neubauer, had half his head blown off. The military men such as Göring, Kriebel and Ludendorff himself went to ground instinctively, as their training had taught them, although Göring was hit in the thigh. In many subsequent retellings of the putsch, just as Ludendorff was incorrectly reported to be in full uniform, he also supposedly stood tall as bullets whizzed around him and simply marched forward towards the police line. This version of events is difficult to believe and is contested by many eyewitness accounts. It is highly unlikely that, had he indeed stayed on his feet and kept advancing, Ludendorff would have survived the carnage completely unscathed as every other figure in the front row was either killed, wounded, went to ground or ran.[283] Once the firing had stopped and the smoke began to clear, it seems the general promptly got to his feet and marched on, alone, into Odeonsplatz. A young police officer told him he would have to take him into custody, to which Ludendorff assented, his gamble having evidently failed. He was taken into the Residenz, the royal palace that had been the Munich home of Bavaria's kings, to await interrogation. As the uneasy officers attempted to pay him due respect, addressing him as 'Excellency', he shot back:

> Do not call me 'Excellency'. From now on I am simply Herr Ludendorff. The German officer lost his honour today. I am ashamed to have ever been a German officer. You are all revolting. I want to vomit before you. As long as you and others like you wear that uniform, I will never put mine on again.[284]

Other antics during those afternoon hours of custody included tirades of abuse against a variety of officers, refusing to allow his captors to inform his wife that he was safe and insisting that, as a prisoner, he should be escorted to the toilet.[285] The embarrassed officers refused to escort him and eventually the obstinate general was forced to concede defeat to human necessity. Ludendorff the petulant sore loser was again in evidence, and as before, his word was not to be trusted, for just a few months later at his trial he would don the uniform of a German general. Ludendorff also made sure to quickly distance himself from Röhm's claims to army negotiators that, in holding out at the War Ministry, he was acting under the orders of the new commander-in-chief, Ludendorff. The general claimed no such orders existed and, having been informed that he had given him freedom of action by his 'superior', Röhm surrendered at 1.30 pm.[286] The putsch was over.

Gordon has claimed that the general was 'quite ill' by the time of the putsch and was therefore not an 'active director' of events; rather Hitler was the leader and Ludendorff is painted as an old, sick man (he was actually only 58, with fourteen years left to live), a mere figurehead and a passenger in the coup.[287] Nevertheless, not only does Gordon concede that Hitler deferred to Ludendorff on military matters (and the coup in essence was a military plan reliant on using the Bavarian Reichswehr to seize Berlin), it can also be argued that the key decisions that shaped the putsch were almost all made by General Ludendorff. It was he who had been decisive in winning over the triumvirate where Hitler had failed, and he alone who had decided on releasing them. It was the general who had insisted on decamping to the War Ministry and that they remain there through the night to wait for Lossow. It was Ludendorff who called in Colonel Leupold to advise on Lossow's position, who scotched plans for a withdrawal to Rosenheim and not only proposed the march to the city centre but also actively directed it to its final bloody conclusion. Whatever Hitler's private views of Ludendorff by this stage (and there is evidence the outward deference was by now a front[288]), he publicly revered the general and did not dare overrule him on the night of 8/9 November. Ludendorff called the shots, with disastrous consequences. Amidst the chaos and confusion on Residenz Strasse, the body of a tall man in a dark jacket was for a time mistaken for Ludendorff. Most of the putschists who got away believed it had been the general who had fallen. In actuality, it was a judge and friend of Ernst Pöhner, Dr Theodor von der Pfordten. In his coat pocket was found the draft of a new constitution for the 'Nationalist Republic'. The regime that Ludendorff and Hitler had sought to impose would have been an authoritarian administration that would have abolished parliament, expelled all Jews, seized their property and incarcerated all political enemies in 'collection camps'.[289] In the years 1919–23, General Ludendorff truly had been one of Germany's most dangerous men. The bloody march in Munich and the coup in Berlin three years before attest to the mortal threat he posed to the young German democracy. Unlike at Kapp, he was not able to escape or evade responsibility in November 1923. Now, Erich Ludendorff would stand trial for treason.

Chapter 3

Figureheads: Hindenburg and Ludendorff as Leadership Contenders

As should have become clear, in the immediate post-war years up to 1923, far-right politics had primarily been paramilitary politics, focused on the raising of armed militias that first crushed Communist uprisings, then might provide a vehicle to overthrow the hated Republic. After the failure of the Hitler-Ludendorff putsch in Munich, the mounting evidence that the army under von Seeckt would not actively support a coup and after the rapid economic recovery brought about by Stresemann, the rebellion option was off the table for German nationalists. Far-right politics moved increasingly away from a military focus to a civilian one and Hitler's masterstroke in the mid-1920s would be to abandon the pursuit of putsches in favour of electioneering. Erich Ludendorff might have commanded respect among militias led by ex-army officers, but he was ill-equipped to succeed in the realm of civilian politics. His 'brand', discredited by the trial that followed the Beer Hall debacle, proved to be an electoral damp squib and the war hero who had once been courted by Hitler and others would find himself increasingly irrelevant in a changed political scene. Quite simply, the Nazi Party and the far right more widely no longer needed him. Instead, the other partner in the wartime 'silent dictatorship', Paul von Hindenburg, would find himself thrust to the political centre stage as a figurehead for conservative Germany.

On trial

Previous biographies of Ludendorff tend to write him off after the failure of the Munich putsch and imply that he quickly disappeared into obscurity, but the period 1923–25 was the most active of his political life.[1] A few hours after being arrested on the Odeonsplatz, the Bavarian triumvirate afforded Erich Ludendorff the privilege he had conferred on Kahr, Lossow and Seisser the night before – he was allowed to go free on his word of honour while the rest of the putsch leaders were rounded up and incarcerated.[2] He went home angry and indignant, apparently believing his imprisonment would have been beneficial for the cause.[3] Over the subsequent weeks and months, Ludendorff's thirst for intrigue showed no signs of being quenched, as he met with representatives of Bavarian separatist movements and even emissaries of Benito Mussolini.[4] Soon, the general was back in one of his periods of intense, frenetic activity, this time working on his defence and visiting Hitler in prison regularly, sometimes for four or five hours at a time, presumably to coordinate strategy for the upcoming trial.[5] According to his wife, he worked harder planning his legal defence than on planning the putsch, and practically barricaded himself in his study.[6] He talked for hours on the topic with anyone who would listen, emphasising the propaganda value of the trial, and his defence counsel even moved into the Ludendorff villa to work day and night with the general, going so far as to write to newspaper editors to try to secure positive coverage.[7] Their legal argument, predictably, was that the Bavarian triumvirate were the real villains and the next few months saw an embittered Ludendorff engage in vitriolic attacks on Kahr, Lossow, Seisser, and the State government. In letters to his friends, political pamphlets and public pronouncements, the general bitterly criticised the hypocrisy and betrayal of the Bavarian leadership; he denied the putsch was a putsch, rather a revolution; and he condemned the triumvirate as being in the service of the Jesuits and Rome (ironically, Kahr was a Protestant).[8] The authorities responded by persecuting Ludendorff, keeping him under surveillance, cutting his telephone line for a time and confiscating political donations that were directed to the war hero.[9] Ernst Röhm was outraged at the treatment of the man he called 'the saviour of the Fatherland' and recorded in his memoirs with indignation: 'He was watched when walking out; all callers were observed; his mail was intercepted and read; gifts of money meant for the bereaved of the freedom fighters were confiscated; and his phone was tapped by the Reichswehr.'[10]

It was therefore likely to have been of some satisfaction to Ludendorff that, under pressure from Berlin, the Bavarian Prime Minister von Knilling ended the regional state of emergency and dropped the mutinous Kahr and Lossow in February 1924. This was seen as a political necessity on the eve of the trial, the date of which was pushed back to allow for the removal of Kahr and Lossow, so that the State administration could avoid direct responsibility for the putsch.[11] Nevertheless, the political picture looked bleak for Hitler and Ludendorff. Not only were they and their comrades facing a serious treason trial, but the NSDAP and the Kampfbund were banned across Germany and support in the Reichswehr appeared to be evaporating. A personal dispute had arisen when Ludendorff had accused Crown Prince Rupprecht of derailing the Beer Hall Putsch by meeting with Kahr on the night of 8/9 November and, alongside a Catholic cardinal, persuading the Bavarian premier to suppress rather than join the revolt. An outraged Rupprecht demanded a retraction and apology from Ludendorff (he had not even been in Munich that night) but the obstinate general refused and he ended up losing a libel suit, which both brought the animosity between the two war leaders into the public domain and severely damaged Ludendorff's reputation in military circles.[12] Twenty-seven senior Bavarian officers declared the 'Prussian' Ludendorff an 'outlaw' and vowed to exclude the general from their 'social community', implicitly compelling officers to choose between Ludendorff or Rupprecht.[13] The prince, who held the rank of field marshal, was encouraged by the Bavarian government to make more public appearances, so that he might draw nationalist and military support in the region away from Ludendorff, and indeed four local Nazi Party branches did repudiate the general and pledged their loyalty to Rupprecht.[14] Ludendorff's standing in the region was also increasingly damaged by his stance on the Catholic Church, which his denunciation of von Kahr as a Jesuit had hinted at.

In 1923, Ludendorff had been introduced by the Nazi Party co-founder Gottfried Feder to Mathilde von Kemnitz, a doctor and psychiatrist whom the general had engaged to treat to his long-suffering wife Margarethe's morphine addiction.[15] A divorcee in her forties, Mathilde was an intelligent woman of strong character; she was one of very few women who had forced her way into pre-war German universities, studying at Freiburg, Berlin and finally Munich and engaging not just in medicine and psychology but also feminism, radical nationalism and philosophy, and living independently from her practice in the Bavarian capital.[16] Ludendorff, who was famously attracted to strong women, quickly developed a powerful emotional and intellectual bond with the visiting psychiatrist and her radical views began to influence his own. Dr Kemnitz had already begun writing far-right conspiratorial tracts in the early 1920s and her ideas were, even for völkisch nationalists, rather extreme; she believed German racial heritage necessitated the abandoning of Christian morality, every form of which was contaminated by its roots in Judaism.[17] Ludendorff adopted wholesale her analysis of Catholicism, and, in time, Christianity more widely, integrating it into his own anti-Semitic and Social Darwinist worldview set out in *Military Leadership and Politics*.[18] Years later, remembering this period, Ludendorff would write:

> Gradually I recognised the pernicious forces which had caused the collapse of the people [in 1918], and in them the real enemies of the freedom of the German race. More and more plainly I became aware of the ... secret supra-national forces, namely: the Jewish people and Rome, along with their tools, the Freemasons, the Jesuit order, occult and Satanist structures ... Moreover, I realised how the racial inheritance and national characteristics – the base for a people's life – were being systematically destroyed by these forces ...
>
> Of decisive influence on the course of my own inner struggles was my becoming acquainted with the earliest work of Dr Mathilde Kemnitz ... I adopted it as my own view that the Christian doctrine and the way of life it had given to the people was the basic cause of the whole evil, and that it served solely as a means for obtaining for the Jew the mastery of the world, which had been granted to him by Jehovah.[19]

In the eyes of the general, Christianity itself was a tool of the Jews that was undermining the German race. Now Germany's struggles, and indeed her military defeat, could be blamed on Moscow, Judah, Rome and their agents, the Freemasons and Jesuits, all part of a sinister global conspiracy inexplicably arrayed against the Reich. In many ways, one can chart a clear progression in the general's thinking, from the original *Dolchstoss* idea of 1918–19 that blamed unreliable politicians and disruptive revolutionaries, to his views after his 'research' into the Jewish question that resulted in *Military Leadership and Politics* in the early 1920s, through to his final, deluded conclusions after his contact with Kemnitz. As Chickering has argued, Mathilde 'was to provide a quasi-metaphysical framework in which Ludendorff could arrange coherently the various demons that he had identified as Germany's bane'.[20] Clearly, Ludendorff's radicalisation was a process; in his Bürgerbräukeller speech during the putsch, he had still referred to God's favour and his attacks on von Kahr et al. in 1923–24 were focused on Rome and Catholicism rather than Christianity as such. But in clerical, traditionalist Bavaria, Ludendorff's new views were unlikely to win many friends, even in nationalist circles.

On 26 February 1924, the Ludendorff-Hitler trial, as it had been widely referred to, began at a temporary courtroom that had been set up in the Munich Infantry School. For the general and the nine other defendants, the stakes were high. Not only could they face lengthy gaol terms, and in the case of Austrian-born Hitler, deportation, but a media circus of national and international journalists were in attendance; the opportunity for propaganda and political point-scoring was not lost on the accused. For Ludendorff, having avoided responsibility and accountability for defeat in 1918 and the 1920 Kapp Putsch, the threat of incarceration must have been only slightly ameliorated by the news that the prisoner governor at Landsburg was preparing a special cell for him, converting the conference room in the administration building into a generous two-room apartment complete with manservant.[21] An added element of jeopardy was that the trial was to be conducted by the Bavarian People's Court, a temporary body that had been established during the revolution which offered no right of appeal. As well as Hitler and Ludendorff, the defendants were Hermann Kriebel, Ernst Röhm, Friedrich Weber, Ernst Pöhner, Wilhelm Frick, Lieutenant Robert Wagner of the Infantry School, head of the Munich unit of the SA Wilhelm Brückner, and Ludendorff's son-in-law Heinz Pernet. SA commander Hermann Göring and the most senior figure in the Infantry School cadet ring, Gerhard Rossbach, had both fled to Austria to avoid prosecution. The defendants were to be tried for high treason under Article 80 of the Weimar Constitution and, given the People's Court's reputation for dispensing quick justice, the putschists had few reasons to be optimistic. The only positive was that Bavaria had refused to recognise the 1922 Law for the Protection of the Republic, passed after the assassination of Walther Rathenau, which would have seen the conspirators tried at the State Court in Leipzig by considerably less favourable judges.[22] As it was, the presiding judge, Georg Neithardt, was a prime example of the danger of leaving the judiciary unreformed after the fall of the monarchy; in private he had described Ludendorff as 'the only positive Germany had left', addressed the general as 'Your Excellency' and press rumours of his favourable attitude towards Hitler became so prevalent that he felt it necessary to address them during the trial.[23]

Having arrived in a chauffeur-driven car and being greeted by cheering crowds, Ludendorff (who unlike the other defendants was permitted to return home at the end of each day's proceedings) led the accused into the courtroom, cool and calm.[24] The fact he interrupted the judge to correct the spelling of his home village of Kruszewnia rather set the tone for Ludendorff's attitude to proceedings that day. In the indictment that was read by prosecutor Hans Ehard, it was emphasised that, contrary to his claims, Ludendorff was aware of the putsch before 8 November and had been spreading the word to potential supporters. A highly significant moment came at 10.20 am as the prosecution requested that the large audience of supporters and press be removed for the remainder of the trial for national security reasons. Judge Neithardt did indeed have the courtroom emptied in order for the motion to be discussed. Unsurprisingly, the defence was dead against the proposal, with Ludendorff's lawyer emphasising that his client have the right to defend himself against the 'monstrous' charges in public. As this point, the general intervened again, ranting in his shrill voice against the indictment itself, labelling it treason and telling the judge, 'If I were a prosecutor, I would take action against this prosecutor!'[25] Even the supportive Neithardt regarded this as going too far, however, and Ehard again took aim at the general, reminding him that the prosecution were merely doing their duty, something he should understand. Nevertheless, the judges eventually decided that the trial was to be public, a major victory for Hitler that set the stage for the rest of the day.

The Nazi leader was allowed by the judge to take up the remainder of the court's time on the 26th with a long, rambling but characteristically captivating oration designed for the benefit of the assembled media rather than the court. He spoke for hours on topics ranging from his upbringing in Austria, to his experience during the war, to the putsch itself and the actions of the craven Bavarian triumvirate. Hitler even painted a picture of the Germany that would have been built had the coup succeeded, with himself as the 'drummer' rallying the people to the cause and Ludendorff as a victorious general, driving the French from the Fatherland. The British *Daily Express* correspondent, sensing the deferential atmosphere, despondently wrote the trial off at the end of the first day, labelling it the 'Whitewashing of General Ludendorff'.[26] On the second day of proceedings, the prosecution attempted to get the trial back on track, interrogating the defendants in detail. Bund Oberland leader Friedrich

Weber was first to be quizzed, revealing that the putschists had believed that not only did they have the support of the Bavarian military, but that Ludendorff's leadership of the coup would have ensured the support of the entire Reichswehr, surely guaranteeing success. Prosecutor Ehard then went for the jugular, asking, almost mockingly, how Weber had not known that General Ludendorff had 'very little influence in the army, particularly in North Germany'. Unsurprisingly, Ludendorff was on his feet and complaining immediately, and members of the audience shouted 'Outrageous' and 'Disrespectful'.[27] Dispite the fact that the point was a sound one and the root cause of the failure of the putsch, Weber took the opportunity to launch into a long, sycophantic monologue in praise of General Ludendorff, the 'greatest commander in German history'. There seems to have been a concerted effort by the defendants to protect, and indeed venerate, Ludendorff's reputation, with Ernst Pöhner and Hermann Kriebel later, on days two, three and four, playing on the concept of the general's honour and comparing him favourably to Kahr, Lossow and Seisser, who had broken their word – Ludendorff, in the words of Kriebel, 'towers above this quagmire of lies, deception and broken promises. He will always stand proud. No pearls fell from his crown because he fell in with robbers [the triumvirate].'[28] The treachery of the Bavarian leaders was a central theme of the testimonies of all the putschists and the argument of the defence rested on the triumvirate's complicity in the coup; if the state authorities had supported them, how could they be tried by the state for their actions? Despite this, Ludendorff found himself subjected to scrutiny and ridicule in a manner he had never experienced before during the trial, and indeed Ludendorff's lawyers would, over the course of the proceedings, demand the judge clamp down on press lampooning of the general, railing against foreign journalists and successfully securing the ejection of a cartoonist, supposedly a Jew, who had drawn Ludendorff as a shrew.[29]

The most anticipated testimony (at least among foreign journalists who would have known little of Hitler, but perhaps too for many national newspapermen considering his wartime celebrity) was of course that of General Erich Ludendorff, and, at least in terms of providing a good story, he did not disappoint. Due to numerous delays and overrunning speeches, the general was not to give his own testimony until the afternoon of the fourth day of the trial, 29 February. Ludendorff was not a good public speaker; he lacked the charisma and voice to hold an audience, and rather pathetically opened with the statement, 'I cannot express myself as Hitler did yesterday in his marvellous speech.'[30] Instead, he spent the duration of his speech rifling through typewritten pages and notes, constantly moving his spectacles from his nose to his forehead and back again as he stumbled his way through a three-hour presentation on Germany's recent history and the failure of the putsch. Naturally, the Bavarian triumvirate were the real villains of the previous November and the general insisted the coup had not been against the Reich or Bavaria, but against its officials. Of more interest to the assembled pressmen was Ludendorff's analysis of Germany's ills. He singled out three internal enemies in a manner that revealed his political and racial prejudices and betrayed the growing influence of Dr Kemnitz on his thinking. Marxists had undermined the German war effort; Jews had defiled the German race and should be allowed no more influence on Germany's affairs than foreigners. So far so in keeping with the Nazi message. However, his final target was the pernicious influence of the Catholic Church, which he asserted had not only betrayed the Fatherland but was undermining its rebirth. This attack went down like a lead balloon in a usually raucous courtroom, and indeed it is hard to imagine how he could have alienated himself more effectively from Bavarian opinion than taking a swipe at Catholicism.[31] There was also much that was confusing and tangential about his speech, not least his quoting of Bismarck, his discussion of Rhinish separatism and his opinions on the restoration of the monarchy.[32]

Unsurprisingly, the press reaction was almost unanimously negative, with a common theme being Ludendorff's portrayal as an old, confused man, out of touch with reality. Once again, it is worth mentioning that he was still only 58 years old, but to the assembled reporters, he seemed older. 'Ludendorff seemed like a man from another planet,' declared the *New York Times*, which highlighted his political ignorance and incompetence and argued he had only succeeded in giving 'a black eye to extreme German nationalism'.[33] The SPD newspaper *Vorwärts* fired both barrels: Ludendorff was 'totally lacking in political judgement ... no better than what clear-sighted subordinates knew him to be during the war, an "insane cadet".'[34] Closer to home, the supportive nationalist paper *Deutsche Allgemeine Zeitung* called the speech 'regrettable', an Augsburg paper labelled him 'Ludendorff the Clueless' while the Bavarian press carried a detailed rebuttal of his attacks on the Catholic Church, highlighting the millions of Catholics who had fought during the war and the intervention of the Papacy, which had helped prevent the Allies trying Germany's wartime leaders, not least Ludendorff himself, for war crimes.[35]

Up to this point, although the general's reputation had been on the slide (as demonstrated by opinion in the upper echelons of the Reichswehr before the Munich Putsch), he still commanded considerable respect, especially among nationalists. His performance in the trial gave many on the right pause for thought – he had come across as an unstable conspiracy theorist, and indeed to some extent that is exactly what he was. He had divided his own base with his attacks on faith and monarchy, issues that Hitler remained shrewdly ambiguous over, and indeed the Nazi leader declared he was a Catholic later in the trial. At best, Ludendorff was considered a loose cannon, at worst a deranged liability, although supporters explained away his poor performance as a result of sheer pent-up fury at the injustice of the whole affair, rather than any nervousness on the part of the Great War hero.[36]

It took ten days to get through the defendants' statements and to begin hearing from witnesses. The second witness was Colonel Leupold, who had revealed to the putschists at 5.00 am on 9 November that Lossow was against them. During the cross-examination, Ludendorff interrupted proceedings once more, asking Leupold to confirm that the general had sent him with a message to Lossow, which had included a pledge that the putsch forces would not fire on Reichswehr and police.[37] Of course, Lossow had sent no reply and Ludendorff considered this a damning piece of evidence, although the SA certainly had attacked police during the march, both at the Ludwig Bridge and on Residenz Strasse. On the morning of 8 March, Ludendorff made a short statement that was much better received, in which he clarified his position and that of the coup as not being against the Reichswehr but in support of it. Instead, the putsch had been targeting the enemies of the army and the Reich: 'In our love of the Fatherland, in our love of the Reichswehr, in our concern for the honour and glory of the Reichswehr, we will take on every one of them!'[38] Not only was this speech very well received, but the subsequent witness, Major General Karl von Hildebrandt, vigorously defended Ludendorff, insisting he loved Bavaria and its monarchy, he had attacked the Catholic Centre Party rather than the Church per se, and that he was far from the Prussian bully that the regional press was portraying him as.[39] Over the next few days, the Bavarian triumvirate were called to the stand and Ludendorff was particularly impressive in cross-examining von Kahr, using his undoubted grasp of military detail to run rings around the former premier and prove that his administration had tripled the size of the Bavarian Reichswehr, evidently preparing for a march on Berlin.[40] The alert Seisser, meanwhile, deflected effectively questions about the triumvirate's failure to inform Hitler and Ludendorff of their change of heart, arguing that commanders never reveal their plans to their enemies and, besides, by 5.00 am the putschists knew the authorities were against them, and yet they marched to confront them – a point Ludendorff labelled 'construction after the fact'.[41] Overall, however, the triumvirate came out worst from the trial (although they were not prosecuted), as opponents of democracy decried their cowardice in failing to act the previous autumn while the proceedings made it clear to republicans the extent to which these supposed saviours of governmental authority had been planning Berlin's overthrow themselves.

On the eighteenth day of the trial, Judge Neithardt allowed Ludendorff to give testimony for a second time. The general was clearly on the defensive and attempted to not only mend fences with the right but also save himself from a guilty verdict; he was a monarchist, he claimed, and his putsch had been designed to install a mere transitional dictatorship – just like those seen in wartime Britain, France and the USA (a comment which again led to questions about the general's sanity). He claimed that he had been unaware of any plans for a putsch and that he had never even considered a march on Berlin, rather 'moral coercion' to force the government from office – a threat that he never intended to fulfil. When the judge pointed out that this contradicted his previous testimony on a number of points, Ludendorff lamely replied, 'I have heard so many things … that I really do not know the details any longer.'[42] His defence now rested on ignorance and, unsurprisingly, the press leapt on this show of confusion and cowardice, despite the fact Hitler had defended Ludendorff's new position, insisting he had only approached the general to fulfil a military role and that he had no knowledge of political objectives.[43] The image Ludendorff chose to portray in the trial – the ignorant, confused passenger of the putsch, an unimportant figure who came along for the ride – has survived to a surprising extent given it was an entirely transparent cover-up and swiftly falls apart once one examines the events of 8–9 November and, indeed, the preceding weeks. In fact, this was just the latest, least dignified move in the deceptive general's campaign to distance himself from the plots in which he was involved.

The closing arguments were heard on 21 March and, under pressure from the judge, the prosecution used Ludendorff's revised testimony as the basis of recommending a verdict of not guilty on the charge of high treason, but guilty of aiding and abetting on the basis he was unaware of the plot in advance. Prosecutors recommended a sentence of two years for the general, in comparison to eight for Hitler.[44] On 27 March, after all twelve defence lawyers had made their closing statements, the defendants were allowed to address the court a final time. Hitler was saved until last, so Ludendorff spoke second to last. In a vague statement that was nevertheless the most well-received of his performances in the trial, he focused on the plight of Germany, saying unless the völkisch movement succeeded it would disappear, before claiming that 'world history' will send servants of the Fatherland (himself and his comrades) 'to Valhalla', an assertion that once again drew press derision.[45] The verdict was to be given in five days' time, on 1 April 1924. Donning his uniform, complete with *Pickelhaube* helmet and an impressive array of medals – for the first time since his vow never again to wear it less than six months previously – Ludendorff along with the other defendants posed for photographs outside the courtroom.[46] Interestingly, Hitler was the only veteran not to attend in uniform, perhaps because the lowly lance corporal would have looked junior when flanked by seven decorated officers. The judge was famously lenient and five of the defendants, including Röhm, Frick and Pernet, were found guilty of merely aiding and abetting high treason and were handed probationary sentences – they walked free. Hitler was given five years but eventually served just eight months. Extraordinarily, Ludendorff was found not guilty on all charges. The crowded courtroom exploded in celebration at the verdict. The legal reasoning given was that, in effect, the general had not realised he was committing treason, that he had not known about the coup beforehand and was swept up in the emotion of the occasion and that he believed (despite having to persuade Kahr to participate) that he was serving the legitimate government of Bavaria in joining the putsch.[47] It was a whitewash and Judge Neithardt had bent over backwards to interpret events in the general's favour. As the judge was about to bring proceedings to a close, Ludendorff interrupted for a final time. He bizarrely denounced his own acquittal, claiming he wanted to serve punishment like his comrades and that the verdict was 'a disgrace which this uniform and these decorations do not deserve!'[48] This final intervention was met with raucous applause and shouts of 'Heil Ludendorff', but the embarrassed Neithardt eventually brought the marathon trial to an end and the general could walk free. An official tried to show Ludendorff out by a side door to avoid the melee in front of the building but he refused to leave and challenged the police present to arrest him. The judge asked that he leave, to which Ludendorff replied that he was now a free man. Instead, he furiously barged his way through to the front entrance, where a large nationalist crowd sang and chanted and applauded the defendants who had been able to walk free.

Why Ludendorff acted so petulantly at this moment is hard to explain; Gordon has suggested he may have realised how embarrassing the verdict was (by implication he was made out to be an insignificant player in the putsch) or he may have wanted to be an imprisoned martyr of the cause.[49] Both these explanations seem somewhat unlikely; given how consistently Ludendorff had worked to avoid responsibility for his actions, and given his revision of his incriminating testimony, it seems highly unlikely he wanted to go to prison. Additionally, it is hard to imagine he had the political foresight to realise the trial might render him insignificant, and indeed such a claim is contestable regardless. Perhaps the general, attempting to emulate Hitler, wanted to steal the show with a dramatic gesture. Maybe the answer is simpler; at other highly emotional moments, Ludendorff had reacted with petulant, nonsensical rage, for instance upon his arrest on the Odeonsplatz, but also dating back to the war. Clearly, there was something of a pattern emerging. Unsurprisingly, the press made a mockery of the verdict and Ludendorff's conduct, with one Munich paper pointing out that the judge's reasoning only made sense if the general was to be considered senile or feeble-minded.[50] On the other hand, nationalist organs celebrated the vindication of the putschists, pointing out their 'noble motives' and the *Deutsche Allgemeine Zeitung* in particular celebrating that Germany's 'greatest solider' had not been imprisoned.[51] There can, however, be no question that the trial damaged Ludendorff's political career. He had gone into the proceedings as the leading figure of the putsch, the hero of the far right. But while Ludendorff had shrunk from blame and responsibly as the trial had progressed, Hitler had embraced it wholeheartedly, and thereby gained kudos and political credit for launching the putsch in the first place and bravely standing by his beliefs in the face of the law. The public version of the plot now had Ludendorff playing a decidedly secondary role, unaware of the plans until the night of the coup, implying he was not consulted or involved in its preparations. In the trial itself, Hitler's monologues had drawn acclaim and he had outmanoeuvred the strongman of Bavarian politics, von Kahr, while Ludendorff's speeches had fallen flat. The general's confusing and contradictory statements, his poor performance in the witness stand and his assaults on the Catholic Church had severely diminished his standing amongst all but the most convinced disciples of the radical right.

The struggle for control

The next year or so would be the most active of Ludendorff's political career as he made, for the first time, a concerted effort to seize the leadership of the völkisch right. Following the ban of the NSDAP and the imprisonment or exile of many of its leaders, Hitler had placed *Völkischer Beobachter* editor Alfred Rosenberg in charge of a temporary successor organisation, the GVG (Grossdeutsche Volksgemeinschaft). However, the GVG never monopolised former Nazis, and some, including Gregor Strasser, a senior SA leader, aligned themselves with the German Völkisch Freedom Party (DVFP). The DVFP was a far-right splinter of the largest party of the right, the Nationalist People's Party (DNVP), and was led by the Prussian landowner and politician Albrecht von Graefe. The DVFP seemed to be a natural haven for politically homeless Nazis; the party had made a deal with the Nazis back in March 1923 which effectively divided the Reich between them – the NSDAP was to represent völkisch nationalism in south Germany while the Freedom Party would do the same in the north. Graefe was a Hitler ally, who had been in the front row of the fateful march through Munich the previous November.[52] It could therefore be argued that the DVFP was something akin to a north German sister party to the Nazis and, given it was still unmolested by the law, it could fill the void for former Nazis until the party could be rebuilt. Ludendorff was far from a passive observer in all this. The German far right had been galvanised by the Munich Putsch, but a leadership vacuum had emerged given that Hitler and many of his allies were in prison, the NSDAP was banned, and Rosenberg was walking the tightrope of leading an illegal organisation. Ludendorff believed he was the man to fill the void and unite the völkisch right, and as early as December 1923, he was envisaging a leadership triumvirate of himself, Hitler and Graefe.[53]

The Nazi movement was thus split from the off, both geographically and generationally; the older generation in the party, the pre-war anti-Semites like Rosenberg, Hermann Esser and Julius Streicher, remained loyal to the GVG, although this group had little presence outside of Bavaria. Meanwhile, the younger generation of Nazi activists, the so-called 'Front generation' who had fought in the war and included Röhm and Strasser, and especially those Nazis outside of Bavaria who often lacked a personal connection to Hitler, were drawn into the DVFP orbit.[54] Rosenberg had rejected a proposal from Graefe for a unified party organisation and leadership in January 1924 but Ludendorff had overruled Hitler's proxy and insisted it be accepted shortly before the trial, on 24 February.[55] From prison, Hitler had assented to the move although he instructed it be on a temporary basis. The following day, the eve of the trial, Ludendorff publicly endorsed Graefe as his representative in northern Germany. The general had conferred his prestige on Hitler by publicly embracing the Nazi leader during the September 1923 German Day rallies; now he was doing the same to Graefe. In so doing, he was staking a claim to the leadership of the Reich-wide völkisch radical right, for he could be the figure that united the DVFP and NSDAP and, almost like the relationship between the Pope and the Holy Roman Emperor, Ludendorff was asserting that to be legitimate, a far-right leader required his blessing.[56]

While the putsch trial was still going on, the movement was wracked by a dispute over whether to run in the forthcoming elections to both the Bavarian parliament and the Reichstag, four years on from those called in the wake of the Kapp Putsch. Hitler was dead against electoral politics, seeing it as a waste of money and voicing his opposition 'clearly and plainly' to Ludendorff.[57] But Hitler was in prison and his party was illegal, while Ludendorff was free to wheel and deal with Graefe, Strasser and other leading figures still at liberty. Just five days after the conclusion of the Ludendorff-Hitler trial, a Nazi successor organisation under Gregor Strasser labelled the Völkisch Bloc came an impressive third in the Bavarian state elections, polling 17.1 per cent of the vote (just 0.1 per cent behind the SPD), attracting one in three votes cast in Munich and winning twenty-three seats in the regional parliament.[58] The ruling BVP and the mainstream nationalists of the DNVP were the biggest losers in a result that seemed to justify Ludendorff and Graefe's stance. Although he allowed his name, alongside those of Ludendorff and Graefe, to be put to the Völkisch Bloc's Reichstag election manifesto, Hitler continued to oppose the electoral strategy. Once again, the Nazi leader was to be proved wrong. Running as the Völkisch Bloc in Bavaria, the DVFP in Graefe's north Prussian heartlands and the Völkisch-Social Bloc everywhere else, a joint ticket between the radical right parties came sixth in the national poll on 4 May 1924, winning 1.9 million votes (6.5 per cent) and thirty-two parliamentary seats. Although most of the strong results had come in DVFP areas (and twenty-two of the victorious candidates were from the party), the Bloc still polled 16 per cent in Bavaria.[59]

Among the ten Nazi candidates elected as Reichstag deputies were Ludendorff himself, Röhm and Frick. Undoubtedly, the national attention given to the putsch trial and beginning of negotiations with the Allies that would lead to the Dawes Plan, where the government agreed to a revised reparations schedule, contributed to far-right success. In the face of this achievement, Hitler finally embraced the electoral approach, admitting that the Nazis must now 'hold their noses' and participate in parliamentary politics, even if 'out-voting them [Catholics and Marxists] takes longer than shooting them'.[60] Twice in

May, Ludendorff visited Hitler in prison and attempted to win him over to the idea of the Nazi and DVFP factions in parliament merging, and even for a fully-unified party to be constructed. While not ruling out the suggestions, Hitler delayed and clearly was unenthusiastic, placing various conditions in the way of such a merger, such as the new party's headquarters having to be in Munich. However, when the newly elected Reichstag assembled on 24 May, the parliamentary deputies (which included Ludendorff and Graefe) of the Nazi and Freedom parties, agreed to sit together as the National Socialist Freedom Party (NSFP). While this may not have seemed a controversial move, given they had run on a joint ticket, it was a clear step towards a united far-right party under joint leadership, something both Hitler and the GVG old guard were highly suspicious of. Furthermore, in his press release announcing the merger of the two Reichstag factions, Ludendorff declared that Hitler supported the idea of a single party.[61]

> It is the will of the völkisch leaders, General Ludendorff, Hitler and v. Graefe that all their followers throughout the entire nation should build in the future only a single unified political organisation and cease each separate political action. ... The deputies elected by the NSDAP, the DVFP and other friendly orgainsations must build a completely unified faction under the name National Socialist Freedom Party.[62]

The general was sweeping the völkisch movement along with him, and Hitler's wishes seemed to matter little to Ludendorff, who was aghast at the crowd of 'flatterers and Byzantines' that constantly milled around the Führer's cell, both visitors and guards. Perhaps he was losing his ardour for the Nazi leader as their views increasingly diverged.[63] Meeting with a decidedly anxious group of north German Nazis, who were fearful of a DVFP power grab, Hitler insisted he had been presented with a fait accompli and that the merger was merely between the two Reichstag delegations, not the two parties as a whole. On 11 June, Ludendorff released another statement that contradicted this version of events and again insisted Hitler supported unification, causing confusion in the party and throwing Hitler into a rage.[64]

Ernst Röhm had meanwhile, since his release at the start of April, been rapidly constructing a paramilitary association encompassing all of Germany known as the Frontbann. Comprising the remnants of the SA and Kampfbund fighting leagues, he had also succeeded in recruiting northern paramilitary groups to the cause through his association with Graefe and could boast 30,000 members in just a few short months.[65] The military head of the Frontbann was to be Ludendorff, while Graefe and Hitler would share the political leadership. Hitler, however, was annoyed by the prospect of his own militia being absorbed into an umbrella organisation that was not under his personal control. In yet another conference in Landsberg prison in mid-June, Ludendorff, Graefe and Röhm tried, and failed, to persuade Hitler to support the new paramilitary organisation. He 'did not want to lose his decisive influence', in the opinion of Röhm.[66] Without having secured Hitler's blessing, Röhm simply turned to Ludendorff to serve as leader of the Frontbann, a role the paramilitary described the general as fulfilling with determination and devotion. Having been outmanoeuvred and overruled at every turn, on 7 July Hitler announced he was withdrawing from politics, resigning the leadership of the party and that he would take no further visitors as he was working on a book. As Kershaw has argued, rather than being a Machiavellian power move, Hitler's withdrawal from politics in the summer of 1924 was in fact the result of his powerlessness.[67] Indeed, Hitler had even had to defer to Ludendorff in announcing his own withdrawal from politics; he had told the general of his decision in early June but Ludendorff had insisted Hitler delay the announcement until July.[68] Since the start of the year, decisions regarding *his* movement had been taken above his head and Ludendorff had frequently ignored or even contradicted his wishes. Surprising electoral success had been achieved without his presence or consent and a Reich-wide paramilitary organisation was taking shape. The DVFP was the larger party and so any merger might become a takeover, but what could Hitler do? Ludendorff was clearly in favour of unity and he seemed to be calling the shots, with most Nazi members deferring to his leadership while the Führer was imprisoned. A related, and possibly more important concern for Hitler was that his chances for parole would be drastically increased if he distanced himself from political activity. Indeed, his negative reaction to the Frontbann may well have been related to his fear of the effect a new paramilitary body associated with his name would have on the opinion of the authorities. By publicly withdrawing from politics, Hitler made the job of the sympathetic Landsberg prisoner governor in securing his release considerably easier.[69]

The political setbacks he had suffered while incarcerated likely made Hitler more determined to secure an early release in order to end his powerlessness and prevent initiatives being made in his name but without his consent. Ludendorff and Graefe quickly pounced on Hitler's surprise statement, Ludendorff of course having enjoyed a month's notice. Although the general was pained by the strained relations between Hitler and Graefe, he had no problem taking advantage of the former's absence to the benefit of the latter. On 9 July, two days after Hitler's withdrawal, Ludendorff and Graefe issued a joint statement which declared that the Führer's decision had been intended to bring about völkisch unity, that Hitler wanted Ludendorff and Graefe to take over his office and leadership position, and that the duo would now merge the two parties and lead 'a great völkisch army reaching as far as the German language is spoken … until the day the hero of Munich is freed and can once again step into their circle as the third leader'.[70] The implication was that this new far-right triumvirate was here to stay and this was further reinforced when Gregor Strasser was brought in to join Ludendorff and Graefe in the leadership of the NSFP as placeholder for Hitler.

In response to the calls for full unification, a Nazi Party conference was called for 20 July 1924, held at the Hotel Hohenzollern in Weimar and attended by eighty leaders and delegates from across Germany.[71] Despite the fact he was late, Ludendorff, the guest of honour, was warmly received and one witness described the attendees 'internally bowing together' on the general's arrival. Diehards such as Alfred Rosenberg and Hermann Esser spoke out violently against the merger and raised the temperature with personal attacks and petty disgagreements. Ludendorff made a short speech demanding support for the merger, insisting Hitler had authorised it, but also criticising the Führer for changing his mind three times on the issue and thereby making Ludendorff 'a teller of fairy tales'.[72] The response was decidedly mixed, although Gottfried Feder told the delegates that the will of General Ludendorff should be regarded as a direct order. After the afternoon break, Ludendorff spoke again, expressing his dismay at the squabbling. He also argued that the merger was not a goal in itself but a means to an end, namely, freeing Germany. 'I am the only one of you who has made a sacrifice. I could withdraw to my well earned honour. I don't need to fight,' he told the conference angrily.[73] Finally, he concluded that he would pursue the merger with or without their support and dramatically left the hall. In so doing, Ludendorff had displayed all his weaknesses as a politician; he was vain and headstrong, intolerant of opposition and unwilling to negotiate, believing his military rank and prestige commanded obedience. By leaving in disgust, he allowed the conference to descend into further discord and end inconclusively.

Graefe and Ludendorff now plotted to seize control over the Nazi movement entirely and complete its incorporation with the Freedom Party. The plan was that a conference in the town of Weimar on 15–17 August would secure the assent of the leading Nazis still at liberty and consolidate the new triumvirate's hold over the radical right. It was to be a huge event, with thousands of supporters in attendance, over twenty speeches and six public meetings in the Weimar National Theatre, which was supposed to crown Ludendorff's achievement in finally unifying the völkisch right.[74] The general's keynote speech opened the conference. Ludendorff told delegates, 'The procession through the streets of Munich gives me the right to think of myself as part of the leadership of the National Socialist Freedom Movement,' the name of the new organisation that was to come out of the merger. The NSFB, Ludendorff continued, was a movement rather than a party, whose goal was a National Socialist revolution, akin to what was proclaimed at the Bürgerbräukeller the previous November. In order to protect the movement against 'bacteria', it would be necessary to fuse all völkisch paramilitary organisations under the Frontbann and all Reich and state völkisch political parties and parliamentary factions under the NSFB.[75] For the remainder of the day, there followed private discussion between leaders from the two parties that brought in the evening the announcement of 'the unanimous will to unite the organisations of the National Socialist German Workers' Party [NSDAP] and the German Völkisch Freedom Party [DVFP]'. It appeared that the conference had triumphed, Ludendorff's goal had been achieved and there was much rejoicing in the packed beer halls of Weimar that night. However, this was hollow unity. For one, the intransigent leaders of the northern branches of the NSDAP had refused to attend. Bavarian leaders from the GVG, although they formally joined the NSFB, also remained opposed to a full merger and the first sign of trouble occurred on the second morning with an unscheduled outburst from Julius Streicher, who demanded Hitler have the final word on unification once he was freed and declared the movement was in danger of becoming primarily concerned with party politics.[76] The Hitler question remained unresolved and cast a shadow over proceedings. Ludendorff was able to secure a telegram from Hitler greeting the delegates and read it out in his closing speech on the second day, but he got nothing more from the Führer, certainly not an endorsement of unity, and the reception the telegram's reading got suggested Hitler remained the most popular leadership figure.[77] The divisions and jealousies between, on the one hand, the National Socialist Freedom leadership – Ludendorff, Graefe and Strasser – and on the other, the official Nazi successor group GVG, now led by Julius Streicher and Hermann Esser, made agreement impossible. Ludendorff had high hopes for a second-day speech by Mathilde von Kemnitz, the intention of which was winning over the völkisch movement to anti-Christianity, but self-evidently this intiative too failed, even if the speech apparently made a deep impression on Ludendorff himself.[78] Formally, the Weimar talks resulted in the creation of the National Socialist Freedom Movement (NSFB), a unified party in name only given that a significant number of leading Nazis from the GVG (and therefore much of the Bavarian movement), as well as the North German Nazi leadership, failed to join. The GVG had refused to accept the nomination of Ludendorff as leader of a united party and the general stormed out of a meeting with the more intransigent Nazis a few days later.[79] Despite his supporters pulling out all the stops to use the general's status to overawe opposition, from an oath of loyalty given by the assembled Frontbann militia on the final day to constant references to his mythical status as the 'Victor of Tannenberg', Ludendorff had to accept the consolation prize of chairmanship of the NSFB, which really was simply a rebadged NSFP, given the GVG's obstinacy.[80] The Ludendorff, Graefe, Strasser triumvirate still could not take full control of the movement and faced particular difficulties in the south. It was clear that Hitler was not prepared to embrace the vision of a united front and a leadership triumvirate, but Graefe and Ludendorff were hamstrung, only able to act in Hitler's name. Effectively, all those who had already supported a merger celebrated the creation of the NSFB at Weimar, while all who opposed unity simply refused to subordinate themselves to the new organisation. The NSFB was also ideologically incoherent, a 'mongrel thing' straddling both a revolutionary and paramilitary vision as well as a parliamentary and electoral vision of the völkisch movement's future direction. David Jablonsky probably put it best when summarising the conference thus: 'Ludendorff wanted to head a movement and at Weimar in August 1924 he achieved his wish. But the NSFB ... was not a unified movement, and the results of the Weimar conference appeared to many to be the symptoms of weakness rather than strength in the völkisch movement.'[81]

By the end of the summer, the völkisch movement was totally divided. Many north German Nazis were opposed to Graefe and suspicious of the new National Socialist Freedom Movement, despite the fact Strasser and many former NSDAP branches participated in the NSFB. The petulant GVG had alienated everyone, including its original leader Rosenberg, and Röhm's Frontbann was seen as a hindrance due to the negative attention it could draw from the authorities. Hitler's attitude to all this remained ambiguous as the north German Nazis, desperate for a firm stance, found to their frustration when they asked their Führer for guidance.[82] The supposed unity conference at Weimar had been a mere 'political Oktoberfest' and the creation of the NSFB had achieved nothing. However, all these groups, as well as Ludendorff and Graefe, pledged their loyalty and allegiance to Hitler and claimed to have his blessing; as Ernst Röhm, despite increasingly not seeing eye to eye with the Führer, pithily commented: 'If even a General Ludendorff can place himself under the Corporal Hitler, so can everyone else accept Hitler as leader.'[83]

Many activists in the völkisch movement were understandably torn; they admired both Ludendorff and Hitler, but the open conflict between the NSFB, north German NSDAP and GVG divided loyalties; there was a north-south divide, a unification versus independence divide, a paramilitary versus parliamentary divide, Bavaria versus the rest of the Reich, and divided loyalties between Hitler and Ludendorff.[84] Ludendorff's problem was that he was no politician; he did not possess the skillset to persuade or cajole Nazi leaders to join his unification plan. He simply relied on his prestige and standing, believing, almost as if he were still in the army, that by making it clear what his wishes were, those subordinate to him would simply fall into line. From September, the Frontbann faced increasing persecution from the Bavarian government. In particular, the oath of loyalty sworn to Ludendorff was declared illegal and the general had to distance himself from the paramilitary organisation, being painted as merely a patron rather than a commander.[85]

On 1 October, Röhm met with the Völkisch Bloc's Bavarian parliamentary delegation, with Ludendorff also present, to beg for assistance for his ailing militia, but no help was forthcoming and instead far-right groups across Germany, including the Bloc and the GVG, began to cut ties and publicly repudiate the Frontbann. Given that the general both failed to intercede on Röhm's behalf in the meeting, and that he neglected to answer a desperate letter from the former captain requesting his assistance, it seems Ludendorff considered the Frontbann to be doomed.[86]

Later that month, the Völkisch Bloc formally joined the NSFB, but this only succeeded in drawing a stream of criticism from the GVG and Hitler diehards. Ludendorff oversaw the expulsion of the obstinate Esser and Streicher from the Bavarian völkisch movement, only for Esser to launch a scathing attack on the general, arguing he was out of touch with the 'true movement' and insisting that only Adolf Hitler had the right to exclude anyone from the National Socialist movement. This was a watershed moment because for the first time, Nazis (and specifically the GVG) were openly criticising Ludendorff, and Julius Streicher soon followed Esser's example in his newspaper *Der Stürmer*.[87] Furthermore, the implication from both men was that Ludendorff was in fact subordinate to Adolf Hitler.

Amidst this climate of disunity and tension, the far right now faced another electoral battle that it was in no shape to fight. The results of the first Reichstag election of the year had made coalition building impossible and so a second general election was called for 7 December 1924. The May election had seen a surge for the right generally, with the DNVP gaining twenty-four seats and coming within a whisker of displacing the Social Democrats as the largest party. However, the political temperature was significantly lower by the winter. Prosperity had largely returned, negotiation rather than confrontation with the Allies seemed to be bearing fruit and the circus of the Munich Putsch trial, so fresh in the mind when Germany had gone to the polls earlier in the year, was a fading memory, with Hitler himself now long absent from the political stage thanks to his incarceration. Even in reactionary Bavaria the political climate had cooled, as the moderate BVP conservative Heinrich Held assumed the premiership and the paramilitary groups withered, starved of Reichswehr training and arms and discredited by the failure of the Beer Hall debacle.[88] Furthermore, the NSFB Reichstag delegation had been mostly ineffectual, in no small part due to the contempt many held for parliamentary politics. Ernst Röhm had only made a single speech in the Reichstag, and that was to request the release of Kampfbund leader Hermann Kriebel.[89]

The divisions in the far right continued during the election campaign; Ludendorff ordered the Frontbann to lie low and Röhm's nominations for the party list (which included putschists Kriebel, Rossbach and Göring) were turned down.[90] Even more seriously, three leading Nazis (Julius Streicher, Herman Esser and Artur Dinter) defected from the NSFB on 24 November, with Ludendorff commenting angrily that Dinter's professions of 'loyalty unto death' at the Weimar conference of August suggested he was now living 'life after death'. Despite protestations from Graefe, Ludendorff also insisted on writing the religious aspects of the party's electoral programme, although the general at least did not fully break with Christianity in the campaign, proclaiming vaguely that the NSFB 'stood on the foundation of a Christian worldview'.[91] The campaign was also dogged by intense internecine warfare within the völkisch movement. The GVG leaders, especially Julius Streicher, launched full-blooded attacks on Ludendorff and the NSFB. While emphasising his respect for Ludendorff the commander, Streicher decried Ludendorff the politician, and the GVG and Nazi old guard in general condemned the pursuit of electoral politics as betraying the movement's roots. Hitler, meanwhile, remained noticeably silent, failing to condemn the attacks on Ludendorff or back the NSFB election effort – and without Hitler's open support, Ludendorff had no hope of uniting the far right.[92]

The National Social Freedom Movement lost a million votes compared to the joint Nazi-DVFP ticket of the spring, down to eighth place on 3 per cent of the vote, behind even the BVP, which only ran in the state of Bavaria. Only in Graefe's own constituency of Mecklenburg was the party poll higher than 10 per cent and in Bavaria it was less than 5 per cent.[93] Their parliamentary delegation was cut by eighteen, down to just fourteen deputies in total, and Röhm and the other militia figures lost their seats, although Ludendorff retained his. He was not, however, an effective parliamentarian; Ludendorff hardly ever attended the institution he so loathed and described his time in the Reichstag as a 'punishment'.[94] The new NSFB had been rendered politically insignificant just months after its conception and just as electoral success in the spring, modest but unexpected, had bolstered the position of Ludendorff, Graefe and Strasser within the völkisch right, now their standing was considerably damaged. Longing for the absent and capable Hitler to take the reins only increased and his early release just before Christmas 1924 paved the way for the Führer's political rebirth.

Upon his release, Hitler was met by Strasser and Nazi Party founder Anton Drexler who intended to take the Nazi leader straight to see General Ludendorff at Prinz-Ludwigs-Höhe, as the völkisch press had reported was his intention.[95] Hitler refused and sent them away, instead calling a non-political friend to take him home. His top priority was the re-establishment of the NSDAP under his sole leadership. Ludendorff's preference for a triumvirate with Graefe was clearly a hindrance to these plans; the NSFB potentially represented a rival party that would split the already fractured far right further. Hitler, likely angered by the general's actions during his captivity, was more than willing to put distance between Ludendorff and himself. In a series of crucial meetings with Bavarian Prime Minister Henrich Held starting on 4 January, Hitler secured the lifting of the ban on the Nazi Party in the state and permission for its newspaper to begin publication again, having promised not to launch a putsch but also criticising Ludendorff's anti-Catholic and anti-Rupprecht views.[96]

While there was an element of playing to his audience, Hitler likely now saw Ludendorff as a direct rival for leadership of the völkisch movement and therefore was unconcerned about throwing him under the bus. That same month, Graefe had written to Hitler demanding the Führer disavow the northern Nazis who remained opposed to a unified party or else the DVFP would abandon the National Socialists. This was precisely what Hitler wanted, so he did not reply, and the result was an acrimonious NSFB conference in Berlin on 17 January. Leading figures from the old DVFP, including Graefe, laid into the absent Hitler, claiming he was in the clutches of the Catholic Church, a Bavarian separatist, and a spent force politically. Understandably, the Nazis in attendance were outraged and the meeting ended in petty insults. The NSFB, and with it Ludendorff's scheme for a united far-right party and a leadership triumvirate, were dead in the water.[97] Ludendorff and Graefe resigned as leaders of the NSFB and effectively dissolved the organisation on 12 February. The north German nationalist Graefe reconstituted his Freedom Party (DVFP) and gave up on hopes of unification with the Nazis. But Hitler did not have things all his own way; one Munich branch of the NSFB backed Ludendorff over Hitler but their letter of complaint to the Führer was thrown in the bin.[98] When Hitler announced he was to refound the NSDAP, local NSFB branches and leaders across Germany pledged their allegiance to him, instantly expanding the party well beyond its Bavarian heartland. The Nazi leader's attitude towards Ludendorff remained ambiguous, but was certainly no longer deferential, and in private he was disparaging. The Nazi leader made his views on the general clear to Rudolf Hess: 'I would like his name to disappear if possible from the movement because he makes it harder for me to win the workers.'[99] He insisted that Ludendorff was only a military leader rather than a political one, that the breach with the war hero had come from others who had sought to drag the general's name through the 'swamp of the parliament' and, tellingly, Hitler revealed he wanted 'only true National Socialists' in leadership positions of the new party.[100]

The refoundation of the NSDAP, symbolically held at the Bürgerbräukeller, on 27 February 1925 was a personal triumph for Hitler that ensured his dominant position as Führer of the movement. Ludendorff was absent and Hitler failed to mention him in his speech, while in his first piece in the reconstituted *Völkischer Beobachter* published the day before, Hitler referred to the general as 'the most loyal and selfless friend' of the Nazis, but not, crucially, as a leader. Ludendorff's supporters (and there were cries of 'Heil Ludendorff' in the Bürgerbräukeller meeting) perceived all this as a slight and Hitler did face a real political headache in prising away his own members from their allegiance to the general.[101] An opportunity presented itself the very next day, however. The Social Democratic president of Germany, Friedrich Ebert, died unexpectedly, aged just 54.

The 1925 presidential election

The president of the Weimar Republic was elected in a direct, first-past-the-post format with a twist. In the first round of voting, if a candidate gained a majority of votes (50 per cent plus one), he or she would be elected president without need for further rounds. However, given that this was highly unlikely in a crowded party field, a second round had been provided for in the constitution. In the second round of voting, whichever candidate won a plurality of votes, i.e. the most, regardless of winning a majority of votes cast, would be elected Reich President. This encouraged compromise candidates and joint tickets in the second round, meaning the first was almost a litmus test of popular support in order for the list of candidates to be whittled down for the second. Given the poor showing of the NSFB in the December 1924 Reichstag elections, it was highly unlikely that the Nazis would be able to influence, never mind win, the forthcoming presidential contest. The wider right, however, was desperate to capture the presidency, and with it the considerable executive powers that could be used to bring about an end, or at least a reshaping of the Republic. To this end, a right-wing committee of the DVP, DNVP and various patriotic associations attempted to agree on a unity candidate to campaign for the entirety of the political right.[102]

The Nationalists (DNVP) proposed Defence Minister Otto Gessler, a close ally of the military, while the People's Party (DVP) suggested the sitting non-party chancellor Hans Luther. However, DVP leader and Foreign Minister Gustav Stresemann opposed a military figure for the sake of Germany's rapprochement with the Allies, while the Nationalists disliked the idea of campaigning for a technocrat when the aim was to win the presidency for the right. Hindenburg, the committee's choice in 1920 until the Kapp Putsch had put paid to hopes of an election, was mentioned but soon dismissed due to his advanced age (he was by now 77 and the president was to serve a seven-year term).[103] Eventually, the committee settled on Karl Jarres as a compromise candidate. Jarres, at 50 years old, already had a good track record in conservative politics behind him; he had been Lord Mayor of the Ruhr city of Duisburg since 1914 and had held cabinet rank as interior minister and vice chancellor of two centre-right Weimar administrations in the recent past. Optimism about the chances of a Jarres victory was raised when the so-called Weimar Coalition parties (SPD, DDP, Centre) failed to agree a joint candidate for the first round and instead each fielded their own man, Prime Minister of Prussia Otto Braun, for the Social Democrats, former Chancellor Wilhelm Marx for the Centre and Willy Hellpach for the Democrats. The Communist leader Ernst Thälmann also ran. On the other hand, his anti-clerical leanings meant Jarres was unlikely to attract Catholic support (indeed, the BVP ran Bavarian Premier Heinrich Held), the failure to attract the DDP and Centre into a unified bourgeois campaign was a severe dent to Jarres' hopes and his close ties to heavy industry in the Ruhr meant his appeal beyond the conservative middle classes was limited.[104] Campaigning as the Reich Bloc, the rightist committee was nevertheless able to enlist a broad range of conservative and nationalist opinion in support of Jarres, ranging from the largest parties of the right in the form of the DVP and DNVP to many far-right and völkisch groups, not least Albrecht von Graefe's refounded Freedom Party.[105]

However, rather than closing ranks with the rest of the German right, Hitler insisted in a short conference with the NSDAP's leaders that the Nazi Party field a candidate of their own, and that that candidate be Erich Ludendorff, despite the fact the general had no hope of winning.[106] In advocating Ludendorff's candidacy, the Nazi leader had three goals. First and foremost, Hitler used the presidential election as a test of loyalty. As we have seen, Hitler's main aim after his release from prison had been the consolidation of his personal hold over the fractured Nazi movement and its organisation. Ensuring the membership would follow him, rather than the various other leaders, movements and factions of the völkisch far right, was of vital importance to the Führer, as was moving the NSDAP decisively away from alliances and amalgamations with other organisations, which had been the norm in recent years. Chiefly, of course, he wanted to ensure a total break with Graefe and the northern DVFP, to put to bed the threat of merger once and for all.[107] This self-isolation was, on the whole, unpopular among the Nazi rank and file, so used to cooperating with the wider radical right, a policy that made sense for such a small party. Therefore, Hitler conceived the presidential election as a test of loyalty. As Orlow has argued, by breaking with the rest of the right in campaigning for Ludendorff, Hitler forced every NSDAP member to make a choice: were they loyal to the wider völkisch movement or were they loyal to Adolf Hitler?[108] Cooperation with the rest of the right would mean disobeying Hitler and disrespecting the venerated general. Supporting Ludendorff would mean cutting ties with the organisations Nazi activists had grown used to collaborating with. Second, Hitler conceived the presidential campaign from the get-go as a sure-fire method of discrediting Ludendorff as a leadership rival. Well aware of the general's political limitations, and the negligible chances of success on the basis of the 1924 results, Hitler calculated that a torrid defeat would only serve to further tarnish Ludendorff's reputation.[109] By pushing the general to stand as a token candidate, Hitler lost nothing, but a dismal electoral performance would serve to prise more Nazi supporters away from the idea that Ludendorff was suited to a leadership role in the party. Finally, as we have seen, Ludendorff still had considerable support within the Nazi movement and some party branches were highly concerned about Hitler's distancing of himself from the general. A good example of the importance of the joint appeal of the two men would be the reaction of a branch in Schleswig-Holstein to Hitler's refounding speech: 'Honouring Ludendorff as of old, we move forward in loyal comradeship in arms with Adolf Hitler.'[110]

By campaigning for Ludendorff, Hitler could ensure that these members remained loyal to his leadership and the party's new direction – Ludendorff supporters would be forced into Hitler's arms.[111] The nomination of Ludendorff was therefore a shrewd move; it prevented a split between supporters of Hitler and Ludendorff, ensured there *would* be a split with the DVFP and other völkisch movements, and would likely serve to discredit the general, whom Hitler clearly now considered an obstacle to his own total control over the party. Quite simply, it was a win-win-win for the Nazi leader and a no-win scenario for Ludendorff.

Had he been politically astute, Ludendorff may have sensed the dangers that accepting Hitler's nomination might bring. However, Ludendorff always lacked political nous and was eager to take up the Nazi leaders' proposal. After all, this was the post he had striven for in all his political schemes to date – to be Germany's head of state and supreme commander-in-chief – and his vanity would not allow him to say no.[112] Hitler visited the general's villa shortly after Ebert's death, and after he left, Margarethe Ludendorff remembered her husband excitedly informing the family that:

> I have just had an anxious discussion with Hitler as to what we can do to prevent the election of Dr Jarres. Something must be done, we are quite clear about that, and we have come to the conclusion that I should stand as the candidate of the National Socialists. Hitler is convinced that the risk must be run. Even if we do not succeed in obtaining sufficient votes, our policy will in any case split the vote and at least prevent the election of Jarres.

Ludendorff's wife and daughter expressed horror at the proposal and Margarethe demanded why, if the Nazis so needed a candidate, Hitler himself did not run. The general, after some thought, replied:

> Hitler knows perfectly well that although he has a great following in Bavaria he can count on very few votes in north Germany and east of Berlin. On the other hand the name of Ludendorff is well known and respected in the whole Reich. In particular the East Prussian and Silesians have been bound to me by gratitude and devotion ever since the war.[113]

As before, Ludendorff's sense of the possible, his grasp of his own popularity and his political wisdom were to prove deficient. He was not helped by the fact that the Nazi campaign itself was lacklustre. Hitler was banned from speaking in public in Bavaria on 9 March, and most other states swiftly followed suit, neutering the Führer's electoral impact.[114]

The NSDAP had barely any money and only the fractured remnants of an organisation following the period of prohibition known as the *Verbotzeit*. Furthermore, Nazi officials were openly dismissive of the campaign as merely a vehicle to discredit Ludendorff.[115] Apart from staging a few events and publishing some campaign materials, the party's efforts were therefore very limited, and the general himself did not campaign nor deliver any speeches.[116] Ludendorff had been haemorrhaging followers since his anti-Catholic outbursts in the Putsch trial the previous year and, as we have seen, even in the Nazi heartland of Bavaria he was widely unpopular due to the enmity between him and Crown Prince Rupprecht.[117] Despite his recent collaboration with them, Graefe and the northern völkisch organisations refused to support Ludendorff (which would have represented an implicit endorsement of Hitler) and remained loyal to Jarres, meaning Ludendorff's appeal was limited only to radical rightists who supported Hitler in the fractious splits of 1924–25. The only significant figure who did embrace the Ludendorff campaign wholeheartedly was Ernst Röhm, who saw his loyalty to the general as ranking above that to Hitler. Despite in his memoirs claiming that both he and Ludendorff believed the election was merely a litmus test of far-right support, not a realistic bid for the presidency, the paramilitary leader threw himself into political meetings and wrote several addresses to both the German people and his Frontbann members.[118] In an appeal to the nation, Röhm declared:

> Germans! On 29 March 1925 [polling day] you have to say whether you like the Ebert government or not. You have to decide if things should continue as they have during the six years of Ebert's regency since the glorious November 1918, or not. Whether you favour that the Jew orders and the German obeys; whether you accept that your savings are finally gone, or whether you look forward to a day when the fruit of your industry and labour and years of thrift will be handsomely repaid. You must choose between:
>
> The swindler Barmat republic or the Völkisch state
> Slave colony or constitutional state
> Jewry or Germany.

Meanwhile, in an address to veterans and the Frontbann, Röhm signed off: 'Every one of you who hates this parliament of whores, give your vote on 29 March to the man in whose name the strongest protest against ingratitude to the former warrior is expressed: Quartermaster-General Ludendorff!'[119]

Without a vigorous campaign, without Hitler's speeches, lacking oratory or campaigning skills of his own and without even the unanimous backing of the völkisch movement, Ludendorff's presidential campaign was never going to succeed. Hardly surprising therefore that, just as all his previous political projects had been, his run for the presidency was an abject failure. The scale of the defeat, however, must have come as a bitter disappointment. Held on 29 March 1925, of just over 27 million votes cast, the general received 285,793 – less than 1.1 per cent.[120] He came bottom of the poll, receiving more than 600,000 fewer votes than the NSFB had in their disappointing Reichstag election showing just three months previously – hardly surprising when one considers that much of the far right had backed Jarres. Even Bavarian Prime Minister Heinrich Held, representing the interests of a single state and backed only by the BVP (who had no presence outside the region) had polled nearly four times as many votes as Ludendorff. The result was not just a reverse but a humiliation and, for the most part, the general had simply been ignored by the electors. Amidst a crowded field of seven potential presidents, the lacklustre Ludendorff campaign had failed to make any impression. The Reich Bloc had topped the poll with 10.4 million votes, but at 38.8 per cent, Karl Jarres was well short of the majority he needed to win in the first round.

The first round of the presidential election destroyed any reasonable hopes Ludendorff might still have held of asserting his leadership over the German far right. His personal political 'brand' was dead. Only Röhm of the leading Nazis seems to have been dismayed by defeat, mourning in his memoirs that a Ludendorff victory would have 'brought an inglorious end to the orgy of mediocrity' that had overwhelmed Germany since 1918.[121] Hitler had continued to strengthen his hold over the Nazi movement as the election campaign had gone on, reconciling Gregor Strasser and appointing him as head of the party in northern Germany on 11 March, before taking on Röhm and his Frontbann the following month.[122] The Nazi leader ordered Röhm to take command of the reconstituted SA and to absorb the Frontbann into the Nazi stormtroopers, thereby bringing the paramilitary association under Hitler's personal authority. A chastened and humiliated Röhm, who still saw Ludendorff as his supreme leader, refused and withdrew from far-right politics for a number of years, while the Frontbann swiftly fell apart.[123]

This move away from independent paramilitary organisations weakened the army officers (not least Ludendorff and Röhm) who had played the predominant role in radical nationalist politics in the years after 1918. Now, the civilian Hitler had taken command and his deference to and reliance on military figures was over. The policy of self-isolation and a clean break with the rest of the far right also came to fruition thanks to the election. The other parties of the völkisch and nationalist right were confused and angered by the Nazi decision to field their own candidate, isolating Hitler's supporters from the rest of the movement and thereby tying them more closely to himself. A party directive of May 1925 prohibited all cooperation between the NSDAP and other völkisch organisations, the stated reason being the betrayal of Ludendorff by the other parties.[124] Ludendorff's disastrous campaign had served Hitler's political purposes nicely.

Regardless of the internal drama within the Nazi Party, the Reich remained without a president and both pro- and anti-republican parties deemed it necessary to change their strategy for the second round. Just five days after the first ballot, the Weimar coalition parties (SPD, DDP, Centre) united into the People's Bloc to run a joint candidate, settling on the Centre Party's Wilhelm Marx. Marx was unimpressive personally, but he was a compromise candidate, liberal enough for the left but still very much a figure of the Prussian establishment, surely well-suited to the non-partisan role of Reich President. An accomplished lawyer and judge in his early sixties, Marx was the chairman of the Catholic Centre with a long parliamentary career behind him. He had replaced Stresemann as chancellor in 1923 and had only recently resigned from that post, making him the most experienced statesman on the ballot as well as being widely regarded as a man of integrity.[125] He had polled 3.9 million votes in the first round, but more importantly, the candidates of the three People's Bloc parties (Marx, Braun and Hellpach) had polled a combined 13.2 million votes, or 49.4 per cent.[126] Given that the winning candidate in the second round only needed a plurality of votes, it appeared inevitable that the republican parties would win; all they needed was for their voters to turn out a second time as surely no single candidate would surpass Marx's presumed 49 per cent. Win a few extra votes and the presidency could be theirs by a majority. Even if Jarres were to win over all of the first round Nazi and BVP voters (Held and Ludendorff withdrew for the second round), he would still fall short. The right-wing Reich Bloc committee therefore began, under pressure from the DNVP, to search for a new candidate for the second ballot, to be held on 26 April. The Reich Bloc was a vehicle of the powerful rightist pressure group the Reich Citizen's Council. Despite describing itself as non-political, it was, in L.E. Jones's words, 'aggressively middle class and antisocialist', and it's primary aim was constitutional reform to replace parliamentary democracy with a more authoritarian system to solve, as they saw it, the 'tyranny of political parties' that democracy had produced.[127]

Winning the presidency was key to this radical reform programme and, against the united People's Bloc, running Jarres in the second round seemed an admission of defeat. The DNVP now revived the idea of nominating Hindenburg. The benefits were obvious: Hindenburg's mythical hero status was pervasive throughout German society. He was probably the most famous man in the country and his name alone would massively increase support for the Reich Bloc in the second round, creating a genuine prospect of victory.[128] Furthermore, it was well known that Hindenburg shared the Reich Bloc's political vision. He was a monarchist, nationalist and militarist of the finest pedigree and an opponent of the Weimar system. He had said privately that he was an unequivocal supporter of the Nationalist DNVP and was even approached to stand for the party in the 1919 elections to the constituent assembly.[129] Far from living in quiet retirement since his first presidential bid had been derailed in 1920 (as some biographers of the field marshal imply), Hindenburg had made clear his support for anti-democratic groups in the early 1920s through various controversial public appearances, such as his tour of East Prussia in 1922 (which was accompanied by severe political violence) and his presence at the highly nationalistic 1924 Tannenberg celebrations.[130] On the other hand, Hindenburg was far from the ideal candidate. As has already been mentioned, he was by anyone's estimations too old for the job at 77, and at his age, hardly suited to carry out a radical and politically challenging reform programme to remould or even bring down Weimar from the inside. Some on the right were concerned that a Hindenburg candidacy would defy the whole object of the Reich Bloc's strategy. Rather than a show of strength for the right that would demonstrate a firm rejection of the Weimar system on the part of the German people, the election would become a circus centred on a living legend; a vote for Hindenburg would be about emotionally pledging allegiance to a national hero rather than endorsing a clear political agenda. This view was expressed by Franz Seldte, leader of the nationalist veterans' association Stahlhelm, who preferred to back Jarres because:

> There is no doubt that millions of voters voting for Hindenburg on 26 April will immediately return to their traditional party and interest affiliations after the election. The election result will not be a verdict on the strength of the national movement [the nationalist right], but will only be a sign of how broad and great Hindenburg's veneration is amongst the largest sections of society.[131]

Furthermore, Hindenburg's opposition to Stresemann's foreign policy of fulfilment, working with the Allies, could be an issue.[132] And what of the field marshal himself? He had written to a friend just before the first ballot that he had no interest in taking the presidency, a position he still maintained belonged to 'my Kaiser', and he expressed displeasure at the idea of living 'under a roof decorated with the black, red and gold flag' of the Republic.[133] Despite not wishing to risk damage to his own carefully crafted myth, Hindenburg did, however, lay down in the same letter the conditions under which he would accept the office, namely, if all 'reasonable' people (read 'right-wing') backed his candidacy as the 'only way of salvaging the Fatherland' (winning the election), if the exiled Kaiser agreed, if the Allies would not interfere and 'if I could be guaranteed not to be generally embarrassed by failure in the elections'.[134] The contents of the letter were made known to the Reich Bloc committee and the DNVP decided to act. Hindenburg would be persuaded. As early as 29 March, the DNVP Reichstag deputy for Hanover, where Hindenburg lived, visited the war hero to ask him to run. The field marshal demurred, insisting he would respond to the appeal of 'all patriotic Germans' but not a single party.[135] The DNVP redoubled its efforts but a second visit in early April proved equally unsuccessful, a 'disinclined' Hindenburg insisting he required the backing of the Reich Bloc as a whole, including Jarres himself, if he were to consider running.[136]

An announcement by leading figures from the BVP proved timely at this delicate stage. A group of Bavarian deputies let it be known that they would back Hindenburg over the candidate of their sister party (and fellow Catholic) Marx should the field marshal stand for election.[137] The crucial visit came on 7 April, prompted by Hindenburg informing the committee that he had finally decided against running on account of his age and he pledged his full support to Jarres.[138] Admiral Alfred von Tirpitz, a distinguished military man of Hindenburg's generation and founder of the wartime far-right Fatherland Party, was immediately dispatched to see the field marshal alongside a DNVP representative. Hindenburg's son Oskar told them their trip was wasted; his father had decided against running for fear of the damage to his reputation and being stripped of his rank.[139] Tirpitz nevertheless persisted, insisting on seeing his old comrade and playing to the field marshal's vanity and sense of duty, and as well as making allusions to the restoration of the monarchy, he also argued persuasively about the appeal Hindenburg would hold to Catholics who would otherwise vote for Marx.[140] The gambit worked and Hindenburg was convinced to run, on the condition that the Reich Bloc withdrew their support for Jarres. However, the issue was not yet decided. Also on 7 April, a frustrated Jarres had informed the Reich Bloc committee that he would withdraw his candidacy should there be any further delay in the nomination process. In a crunch meeting on 8 April, the Nationalist (DNVP) members of the committee pushed hard for Hindenburg while the chairman dropped the bombshell that Jarres was on the brink of angry withdrawal, raising the possibility of the Reich Bloc being left without a candidate if the committee failed to come to a decision in that very meeting. After a series of telephone calls to Hindenburg to ensure he would definitely run and to Jarres to confirm the wording of the statement of his withdrawal, the meeting ended with the formal announcement of Hindenburg's candidacy.[141] Typical of his political style, the old field marshal explained his decision in a letter to one of his daughters: 'Did it reluctantly, but out of a sense of duty. May God see to it that everything from here on out is good for the Fatherland.'[142] We need not necessarily take this all at face value, however. It certainly suited Hindenburg's purposes to appear as the reluctant leader, called out of retirement to serve his nation, and indeed this harked back directly to the self-cultivated legend of his wartime service. Further, when one looks objectively at the negotiations that took place in late March and early April, it becomes clear that Hindenburg was not the unwilling statesman forced out of retirement but rather he set out clearly his terms and then accepted nomination once those terms, most importantly the unanimous backing of the right, had largely been delivered. Rather than reluctant, he appears simply inflexible on the conditions for his running.

Hopes that the Hindenburg campaign would attract broad support soon proved well-founded. Not only did he receive the backing of the Reich Bloc and its affiliates, such as the DVP and DNVP, but Hitler withdrew the defeated Ludendorff and pledged the Nazi Party's support for the war hero.[143] Further support came from the Economic Party, voice of the *mittlestand*, the lower-middle-class small business owners. While the DVP and Stresemann still held concerns about Hindenburg and resented the DNVP's highjacking of the committee, the foreign minister nevertheless fell in line and published an article on 19 April in *Die Zeit* endorsing Hindenburg wholeheartedly.[144] The stance of the BVP was crucial. Heinrich Held naturally withdrew from the second round, and rather than backing the Catholic statesman and leader of their sister party

(Marx of the Centre), and the BVP, as we have seen, threw their weight behind the Lutheran Hindenburg. The field marshal's monarchist politics and Bavaria's aversion to the Republic made the move predictable, but undoubtedly the million votes the BVP may well have brought to Hindenburg proved decisive. The war hero's chief aim of being the candidate of a unified right was entirely achieved, with practically every party and organisation on the rightist spectrum backing his candidature. On the other hand, one of Hindenburg's principle reservations about running had been the dragging of his name through the mud. For the most part, however, the People's Bloc avoided personal attacks on such a revered figure, reasoning they would be counterproductive. In particular, the bourgeois Democrat and Centre parties consciously avoided criticism of Hindenburg, expressing their respect for the field marshal himself but questioning the malevolent forces behind the Hindenburg campaign. 'We do not blame the old man,' wrote liberal newspaperman Theodor Wolff, 'He does not and cannot see that his candidacy plays into the hands of Germany's worst enemies,' while the Catholic press lamented 'Poor Hindenburg', his retirement again disturbed.[145]

A famous People's Bloc campaign poster expressed the same sentiments, portraying the war hero's famous face as a literal mask behind which marched a Nazi, a soldier, an aristocrat and a Bavarian in traditional dress. The Social Democratic press equally claimed Hindenburg was unaware of what was going on, writing that 'our fight is not against him'.[146] Wilhelm Marx himself refrained from attacking Hindenburg, instead praising his great victories in the war, while a DDP leaflet read 'For the Fatherland's sake and for Hindenburg's sake, vote Marx', expressing the opinion that the old man should be left to retire in peace.[147] This embarrassingly confused campaigning was unsurprisingly ineffective and drew the ire of the Communists, who refused to countenance withdrawal from the second round and instead targeted Hindenburg directly:

> Vote for the Mass-murderer?
> Vote for the Kaiser's henchman?
> Vote for the Profiteer's friend?
> Vote for the Hangman of Democracy?
> If you would elect all four
> VOTE FOR HINDENBURG![148]

What of the Reich Bloc campaign? Hindenburg himself made just one written pronouncement, his so-called Easter Appeal on 11 April. Entitled 'Reconcile rather than Divide', it focused on national unity, and emphasised that he spoke for all Germans and was no dictator in the making.[149]

> As a soldier I have always been concerned with the nation as a whole, not with parties ... In a parliamentary state they are needed, but the head of the state must stand above them and, independently of them, work for every

German ... No war, no internal rising can obtain freedom for a nation which is still in chains and, alas, rent by internal discord. What we must do is to work hard, quietly, peacefully ... I do not consider decisive the form of a state, but the spirit which inspires that form. I offer my hand to every German who is national-minded, maintains the dignity of the German name at home and abroad, and wants religious and social peace, and ask him to help me work for the rehabilitation of our Fatherland.[150]

For those who read between the lines, there was implicit criticism of the internationalism and supposed lack of patriotism of the left in what was meant to be a unifying and nonpartisan statement. The field marshal made just one campaign speech, suitably in his home city of Hanover (he did not go out on the 'campaign trail'). Speaking at the town hall on 19 April, he again emphasised the nonpartisan character of his candidacy and insisted he would respect 'the existing constitutional foundation and Germany's present situation in the world', as well as insisting that forms of government did not matter to him – words that likely disappointed many on the Reich Bloc committee but would undoubtedly broaden the field marshal's appeal and calm international opinion.[151] When the Reich Bloc asked him to speak in Berlin and Munich, he refused, stating (rather ominously for a future head of state), 'I do not speak and I do not travel.' As Goltz has pointed out, this was not a major disadvantage; while Marx toured the country, Hindenburg did not need to – his myth was already as widespread as could be, and there was no need to present him to the people.[152] Hindenburg also made a radio address to the nation, the first in German history, at 8.00 pm on 24 April, two days before polling day. One million Germans owned a radio and many more crowded round the sets of neighbours and friends to listen to Hindenburg promise to serve all Germans, again presenting himself as the unity candidate who would abide by the constitution.[153] His only other public appearance was a press conference of foreign journalists in Hanover, whom he told:

I am no militarist, as my opponents claim. ... Nor am I the old man in a wheelchair, as some people would like to have the country believe. ... As for the tasks of the future, I have no ready-made answers. I am not going to get involved here in any detailed questions; if I should become President, the Chancellor and my cabinet will have to govern in accordance with the laws and the Constitution.[154]

The Reich Bloc campaign for Hindenburg, in contrast, was far from passive. In order to emphasise the supposedly apolitical and unifying nature of a Hindenburg presidency, the campaign organisation ensured that wherever possible, choirs, youth clubs, sports teams, women's organisations and other similar associations fronted local events.[155] He was, according to DNVP propaganda, 'The saviour of the German people' and 'A man who leans neither left nor right, not towards the monarchy, not towards the Republic, but only knows his duty to serve the state and the people'.[156] The campaign, essentially defensive in nature, emphasised Hindenburg's nonpartisan character and 'Why Hindenburg' leaflets addressed concerns about his age and military past, for instance pointing out the advanced age of other great historical figures at moments of triumph, from Goethe to Blücher.[157] As well as emphasising tradition, duty and honour, values that the electorate likely already associated with the Hero of Tannenberg, the idea that Hindenburg was above party strife and representative of purely patriotic interests also struck home, as did attacks on Marx as an ally of socialism.[158]

The fact that Hindenburg's nomination had been brought about by and for party political ends was quietly ignored. Not voting for Hindenburg was condemned as unpatriotic and 'a miserable act' in the right-wing press, which called on Germans to thank the old man for his service to the nation by voting for him, in direct contrast to People's Bloc claims that the field marshal would rather be left in peaceful retirement.[159] Hindenburg's iconic, stolid image was also central to the Reich Bloc campaign. A huge plaster bust of the war hero was driven through Berlin, while election posters, in a deliberate echo of wartime propaganda, featured merely the field marshal's face staring back at onlookers, practically demanding loyalty.[160] New technology aside from the radio was also utilised, with Hindenburg's name being projected into the night sky in Berlin and a recent documentary film about Tannenberg being screened at various Reich Bloc events.[161] The campaign presented the already legendary figure of Hindenburg as all things to all men; to women he was presented as a family man with strong traditional values; to veterans he was their old leader to whom they still owed allegiance; to the right he was a nationalist saviour who would end the shame of Weimar; to those less politically sympathetic he was above politics and was going to respect the constitution; while to the non-political population he was a selfless servant of the nation. To practically all Germans, Hindenburg was a war hero whose reputation was beyond repute and to whom a great deal of gratitude was still felt.

There is a strong argument to be made that only Paul von Hindenburg could have defeated the People's Bloc in 1925, and indeed on 26 April, amidst a wave of political violence as rival activists clashed, the field marshal defeated the combined forces of social democracy, liberalism and political Catholicism. His celebrity status, heroic reputation and an effective campaign, as well as the failure of his opponents to go onto the offensive, all played a part. Equally, had the KPD withdrawn or the BVP backed Marx, the result would likely have been different. With 14.6 million votes, Hindenburg finished around 900,000 votes ahead of Marx and claimed a 48.3 per cent share of the poll.[162] The 1.9 million votes cast for the third-placed Communist Ernst Thälmann were entirely wasted and would have swung the result the other way. Turnout was up around

9 per cent on the first ballot and of 3.5 million new voters on 26 April, 3 million voted for Hindenburg.[163] Additionally, electoral analysis has revealed that as many 400,000 Catholic Centre voters, not to mention 500,000 BVP voters from the first ballot, switched to Hindenburg.[164] While the social democratic vote had held up well, some 100,000 Democrat voters had also switched from Hellpach to Hindenburg rather than backing the People's Bloc, which, alongside the shift of Catholic support, highlighted the weakness of the loyalty of 'moderate' centre-right bourgeois opinion to the Republic.[165]

The last few national elections had made painfully clear that supporters of the three chief democratic parties were in the minority among the electorate, even in the middle of Weimar's so-called 'Golden Years'.[166] By mobilising non-voters, especially women, as well as drawing monarchist and traditionalist Catholics away from Marx, Hindenburg had added more than more than 4.2 million votes to the Reich Bloc poll achieved by Jarres just a month beforehand, pulling off a remarkable victory. He had unified bourgeois Germany, the politically active and apathetic middle classes, conservatives and nationalists, and the radical and moderate right, in a way that no party or individual had been able to since the war. According to one newspaper that interviewed female Hindenburg voters, it was the war hero's undiminished popularity that won the day, as well as a sense that he would bring 'good times' and restore losses from hyperinflation – a pledge the campaign never made.[167]

Progressive opinion was aghast at the unexpected defeat, the so-called 'Red Count' liberal aristocrat Harry Kessler confiding in his diary that Hindenburg was 'the god of all those who long for a return to philistinism'.[168] Hindenburg was now to serve as the only elected head of state in German history, the ultimate political figurehead. Stahlhelm leader Franz Seldte had been accurate in his prediction, however: this was not a victory for the transformative rightist programme advocated by the Reich Citizen's Council and its committee – this had been the victory of one man and his legend. Was the saviour of 1914 to be the saviour of 1925?

Field Marshal Paul von Hindenburg (left) and General Erich Ludendorff (right) as Chief of the General Staff and First Quartermaster General respectively, pose with Kaiser Wilhelm II, 1917.

The making of an icon: the famous wartime 'Iron Hindenburg' statue in Berlin and one of the countless examples of Hindenburg kitsch – the field marshal decorates an ashtray.

Wartime portrait of Erich Ludendorff from 1918, when his grand plans failed, his mental health collapsed, and he devised the Stab-in-the-Back myth.

Postcard to raise money for the Ludendorff-Spende, a charity for wounded war veterans that ran from 1918 to 1923, of which the general was honorary president. The inscription reads: 'No victory without sacrifice, no peace without victory.'

One of many visualisations of the poisonous Stab-in-the-Back myth that pervaded German perceptions of the Great War thanks to Hindenburg and Ludendorff.

Two protagonists of the Kapp Putsch farce – General Walther von Lüttwitz (centre) converses with Defence Minister Gustav Noske (right).

Corvette Captain Hermann Ehrhardt (second from left), commander of the key Freikorps milita Marine Brigade Ehrhardt, during the Kapp Putsch.

Early twentieth-century postcard of Berlin. The Reichstag building dominates the Tiergarten park, with the Siegesallee running up to the Brandenburg Gate, just visible in the distance. This is where Ludendorff supposedly ran into the putschists while he was out on a morning walk through the park.

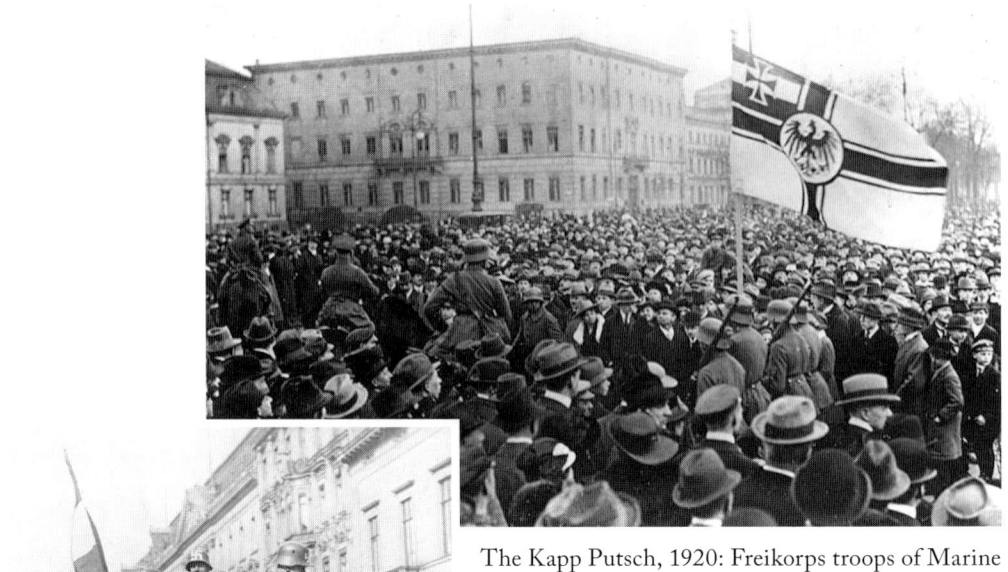

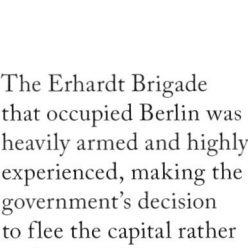

The Kapp Putsch, 1920: Freikorps troops of Marine Brigade Ehrhardt march into central Berlin. Note the swastika decal painted onto their helmets.

The Erhardt Brigade that occupied Berlin was heavily armed and highly experienced, making the government's decision to flee the capital rather understandable.

Ludendorff in Bavaria: the general (centre) with Bavarian premier Gustav von Kahr (left) and Munich Chief of Police Ernst Pöhner (right), 1921.

Ludendorff as Nazi leader, reviewing SA troopers of the newly formed *Kampfbund* at the German Day rally, 2 September 1923.

A Nazi meeting at the Munich Bürgerbräukeller, sometime in 1923. The same beer hall would play host to von Kahr's address on 8 November 1923 that Hitler hijacked to proclaim the National Revolution.

The Beer Hall Putsch: *Kampfbund* paramilitaries guarding the Bavarian War Ministry, where Ludendorff wasted the early hours of 9 November 1923, and the central Munich Marienplatz that morning, where the general made the fateful decision to march on the same ministry.

The Feldherrenhalle in 1915, a martial monument that stands on the southern edge of Munich's Odeonsplatz. The fateful march that Ludendorff and Hitler led through the city on 9 November 1923 ended bloodily when they ran into a police cordon at the end of the narrow Residenzstrasse (left).

Ludendorff is chauffeured to the final day on the putsch trial, 1 April 1924, greeted by cheering crowds.

The final day of the Beer Hall Putsch trial, 1 April 1924. Ludendorff (wearing the uniform he swore never to put on again) stands to the left of Hitler and is joined by: (from left to right) his stepson Pernet, Weber, Frick, Kriebel, Brückner, Röhm and Wagner.

The nationalist veterans' association *Der Stahlhelm* campaign for Hindenburg, April 1925. Note the Imperial colours and the distinctive posters which mirrored wartime propaganda.

A giant bust of Hindenburg is ferried around Berlin during the 1925 campaign.

The newly elected Reich President von Hindenburg (approaching the podium) is presented to the Reichstag.

The Weimar era Presidential Palace on the Wilhelmstrasse, Berlin.

Hindenburg attending the grandiose dedication of the Tannenberg Memorial, where the Nazis would eventually bury him, September 1927. This was the scene of the president's painful public break with Ludendorff.

Hindenburg's eightieth birthday celebrations – 40,000 schoolchildren watch the conclusion of the presidential motorcade at the Grunewald Stadium, 2 October 1927.

Hindenburg as father of the nation: star-struck children welcome him to a sporting event, February 1930. His son and aide-de-camp Oskar is behind him.

Postcard featuring the official portrait of Hindenburg as Reich president, late 1920s.

Last gasp of parliamentary democracy – the Grand Coalition cabinet: (front row, left to right) Economics Minister Julius Curtius, Foreign Minister Gustav Stresemann, Chancellor Hermann Müller, Defence Minister Wilhelm Groener, Minister for Occupied Territories Joseph Wirth; (back row, left to right) Postal Minister Georg Schätzel, Justice Minister Theodor von Guérard, Transport Minister Adam Stegerwald, Interior Minister Carl Severing, Agriculture Minster Hermann Dietrich and Finance Minister Rudolf Hilferding.

First experiment in presidential government – the 'Hindenburg Cabinet': (front row, left to right) Interior Minister Joseph Wirth, Finance Minister Hermann Dietrich, Chancellor Heinrich Brüning, Foreign Minister Julius Curtius, Postal Minister Georg Schätzel; (back row, left to right) Minister for Occupied Territories Gottfried Treviranus, Justice Minister Johann Viktor Bredt, Labour Minister Adam Stegerwald, Economics Minister Paul Moldenhauer, Justice Minister Theodor von Guérard.

The House of Hindenburg – State Secretary Otto Meissner (centre, on steps) watches as Oskar von Hindenburg helps his father into a car at the Neudeck estate.

Re-electing the Saviour: Berlin posters during the 1932 presidential campaign. At the famous Potsdamer Platz, voters are told to 'Vote for a man, not a party', a skyscraper tells voters, 'Against the system of eternal strife', while passers-by at the Brandenburg Gate are simply told, 'Vote Hindenburg!'

Innovative Hindenburg pamphlet for the second ballot. 'Awake', the front cover implores, in an echo of the famous Nazi slogan 'Germany awake'.

The reader is bombarded by images of British and French betrayal on disarmament and trade, while the stereotypical voter Michel sleeps, oblivious to Germany's plight. The caption informs voters that Germany will continue to be cheated so long as 'we wear ourselves out in useless, tiresome party strife' and so long as Michel sleeps.

Meanwhile, Michel is dreaming of a fantasy world in which poverty is ended by printing money, credit is available on tap, the world disarms and the French cancel reparations – an implicit criticism of the Nazi and Communist utopian visions.

But as he wakes, Michel realises both that miracles only happen in dreams and that 'If everyone pulls in the same direction, we're strong!' Therefore, in order to save the work of Bismarck and prove Germany's enemies wrong, the nation must unite behind Hindenburg.

Finally, Michel casts his vote for the president under the slogan 'Away with radicalism! Do not leave the rudder of state to the inexperienced! Only Hindenburg deserves your vote.'

Heinrich Brüning addressing a mass rally during the 1932 Hindenburg campaign.

Hindenburg election poster proclaims 'A hero's burden calls for heroes' as the 84-year-old appears as Atlas, lifting a globe emblazoned with the German imperial eagle. Hitler is protesting: 'But I'm still much stronger.'

The *Illustrated London News* reports on Hitler versus Hindenburg, the presidential second round.

Two 1932 Hindenburg pamphlets: one in the Imperial colours of black-white-red tells military veterans to stay loyal to Hindenburg as Hindenburg had stayed loyal to them, while the other tells voters, 'Hindenburg must remain Reich President' to protect Germans' freedoms.

The 'cabinet of barons', or 'my friends', as Hindenburg called them: (front row, left to right) Agriculture Minister Magnus von Braun, Interior Minister Wilhelm von Gayl, Chancellor Franz von Papen, Foreign Minister Konstantin von Neurath; (back row, left to right) Justice Minister Franz Gürtner, Economics Minister Hermann Warmbold, Defence Minister Kurt von Schleicher.

The Reichstag, 12 September 1932 – an impotent Papen (standing, centre-left) is ignored by the speaker, Hermann Göring, as he attempts to dissolve the Reichstag and avoid an embarrassing vote of no confidence. He lost the resulting vote by 512–42.

The Hitler Cabinet: (front row, left to right) Minister without Portfolio Hermann Göring, Chancellor Adolf Hitler, Vice Chancellor Franz von Papen; (back row, left to right) Labour Minister Franz Seldte, Commissioner for Works Günther Gereke, Finance Minister Lutz Schwerin von Krosigk, Interior Minister Wilhelm Frick, Defence Minister Werner von Blomberg, Economics and Agriculture Minister Alfred Hugenberg.

Goebbels's dramatic Day of Potsdam ceremony, 21 March 1933, put the president centre stage and tied Hindenburg's mythos and prestige to the new Nazi regime in a deliberate attempt to win over Hitler sceptics.

Hindenburg and Hitler, field marshal and lance corporal, *Ersatzkaiser* and heir apparent.

NSDAP election poster for the March 1933 Reichstag elections, Hitler's proclaimed 'final election', in which the Nazis won their best-ever result with Hindenburg's image at the centre of their appeal.

Above: The lavish Hindenburg funeral held at the gigantic Tannenberg Memorial, East Prussia, 7 August 1934.

Right: Ludendorff's grave, which stands to this day, in the town cemetery of Tutzing, Bavaria.

Chapter 4

Constitutionalism and Conspiracy Theories: Hindenburg Ascends, Ludendorff Fades

Although the role of Hindenburg and Ludendorff in the growth and consolidation of the Nazi Party in the second half of the 1920s was peripheral, it is nevertheless necessary to trace their contrasting political fortunes over the remainder of the decade in order to provide the context for the crucial events of the early 1930s. The period 1924–29 is often referred to as the 'Golden Age' of the Weimar Republic, a time of economic boom, artistic expression and relative political stability, at least compared to the crisis-ridden years that had come before. However, as the leading statesman of the age Gustav Stresemann famously remarked, 'The economic position is only flourishing on the surface. Germany is dancing on a volcano. If the short-term loans are called in, a large section of our economy would collapse.'[1]

Hindenburg, as the Republic's new president, helped restore a sense of unity and order and contributed to the contentment and tranquillity of the period. This did not mean that the president was universally popular and Hindenburg would soon be smarting from vicious attacks from what he considered his own supporters – the nationalist right. As Weitz has argued, the image of President Hindenburg as a bumbling old man, a passive figurehead of a president, is simply inaccurate.[2] Indeed, the Weimar Constitution did not allow for a merely symbolic head of state, as for instance presides over the modern German republic, but rather expected the president to play a key, nonpartisan role. Meanwhile, in a country largely devoid of paramilitary activity and putsch plotting, Ludendorff was forced to carve out a new niche for himself, which took him even further down the conspiratorial rabbit hole.

Hindenburg: Father of the nation

The election of Hindenburg as president was met with unbridled joy and celebration amongst German nationalists and conservatives. The diary entry of an upper-middle-class businessman, Hans Georg Klamroth, reveals the extent to which nostalgia, tradition and the myths disseminated by the field marshal since the war paved the way for a Hindenburg presidency:

> The result is greeted with jubilation by the radio audience in our living room. They applaud the victory of the past and recall earlier times when 'everything was better' and they were still unshaken by the miseries of democratic chaos. The fact that Hindenburg has stood for war gives him legendary status, and the fact that the war was lost is not a matter for reproach. Everyone knows the reason: the 'stab in the back' on the home front.[3]

The celebration of the new president's inauguration was a huge event as hundreds of thousands of conservatives and nationalists reclaimed the public spaces that the left had largely dominated since the revolution of 1918, the paramilitary Stahlhelm and Young German Order came out in force and Hindenburg supporters proudly displayed the old Imperial black-white-red colours.[4] There were, however, serious concerns about the election of Germany's former warlord to the presidency; among supporters of the Republic there were fears of a sharp swing to the right, while the news was greeted with a wholly negative reception abroad.[5] The famous liberal journalist Theodor Wolff wrote despondently:

> The republicans have lost a battle … We are ashamed of the many millions who are revealed to the world to be so politically immature. The … election was a test of intelligence before the world gallery. Before sympathetic, horrified friends and scornful enemies roughly half the German people have failed the test.[6]

There can be no doubt that Hindenburg's election was a severe defeat for the Republic – for an ardent monarchist, a manifestation of the militaristic past and a complete stranger to democratic politics had been elected to arguably the most important role in the republican system.[7] The irony was that the exact opposite was concluded at the time. Before, during and after his inauguration, Hindenburg was keen to stress his solemn commitment to the duties laid out in the constitution and there was no immediate change of government or policy. The new president was at pains to emphasise that he was not about to rip up the political system and would abide by the rules and regulations that restricted his new office.[8] The new president's unexpected constitutionalism surprised and delighted the left and centre pro-democratic parties that had been defeated in 1925 and within a year, a new strain of the Hindenburg myth was evident, with the head of state now also a symbol of democratic stability and constitutional order, as one perceptive observer noted:

> The legendary figure of the old military commander had such allure that even otherwise clearly democratically inclined people were not capable of reasoned judgement. They believed that they were dealing with a man of perhaps limited intellectual strength, but whose character … guaranteed selflessness, loyalty and honesty in simple clarity and steadfastness.[9]

This perception of Hindenburg as an honest, even-handed guardian of the nation committed to the Weimar system was reinforced by his early decision to retain Otto Meissner as State Secretary of the President's Office, the most influential civil service post in the land. A lifelong bureaucrat, Meissner was regarded as a liberal due to the fact he had been Ebert's right-hand man and was (until 1926) a member of the DDP. In fact, Meissner's liberalism was greatly overplayed by contemporary democratic opinion, for he would subordinate his own views to the new president's, move considerably to the right in the coming years, and would remain in post after the Nazi seizure of power, dutifully serving Hitler right up to the Führer's suicide in 1945.[10] The role of Meissner and his son Oskar as Hindenburg's political aides would be all the more important for the ageing Hindenburg due to the fact he had been widowed in 1921 and thus deprived of what one biographer termed his 'sounding board', a woman who knew the real Hindenburg behind the mythical reputation and provided balance and rationality in his life.[11]

There can be no doubt that many of Hindenburg's supporters were bitterly disappointed when his commitments to constitutional government transpired to be genuine. The radical rightist Stahlhelm and Pan-German League, both of whom had campaigned for the president's election, were frankly confused when he failed to dismantle democracy in his first months in office and soon the Pan-Germans would be condemning the war hero as a traitor.[12] Furthermore, Hindenburg's election was a key factor in an ongoing trend in the mid-1920s that saw many conservatives accepting the need to work within the republican system, thereby isolating the radicals who remained determined to overthrow Weimar. A leading DNVP moderate, Martin Schiele, claimed that Hindenburg's election 'offers the strongest guarantee for the strength and permanence of our state system' and the president's example of working within the constitution facilitated a wider accommodation of German conservatives with democracy, Count Kuno von Westarp being a fine example.[13] It is indeed difficult to locate Hindenburg accurately on the German right.[14] Once in office, his constitutionalism and reluctant support for a conciliatory foreign policy suggested he was a moderate conservative. Yet he had been strongly identified with the nationalist right before his election, supported the DNVP, was affiliated with the Stahlhelm and in his political style contrasted with most moderate right-wingers in his reliance on charisma and force of personality and a reputation built on the Imperial past and Prussian militarism. What cannot be doubted is that Hindenburg's vision of a unified *Volksgemeinschaft* (people's community) was a restricted one, reliant on the exclusion of the Social Democrats and trade unions from political power and societal influence; his repeated calls for national unity were implied attacks on the class politics of the left and in this sense he had more in common with the nationalist right than the moderates.[15]

Despite the disappointment of the right at Hindenburg's outward loyalty to the constitution, there can be no doubt that he interpreted his role differently to his predecessor, the Social Democrat Ebert. In the coming years, Hindenburg oversaw what Kolb calls a 'silent change in the constitution'. Effectively, with parliament often deadlocked and government's tenures being precarious to say the least, Hindenburg was able to bring his considerable personality and charisma to bear on the cabinets he presided over and in particular in the tricky negotiations over the formation of coalition governments. In this way, with one exception, Hindenburg was able to exclude the SPD from office and push for the inclusion of his favoured DNVP – therefore while it is true to say that, in his first few years as head of state, Hindenburg abided by the constitution, he certainly pushed the boundaries of interpretation and altered the norms of presidential behaviour, privately violating the nonpartisan character of his post.[16]

Already in late 1925, Hindenburg was able to bolster his power and influence beyond that which the constitution envisaged. Hindenburg had inherited a fragile coalition government of bourgeois parties labelled the *Bürgerblock*, which stretched from the political centre ground in the form of the DDP to the nationalist right with the DNVP, all under the leadership of a non-party chancellor, the technocrat Hans Luther. In October, the three Nationalist ministers resigned over the Reichstag's ratification of the Locarno Treaty, a diplomatic coup orchestrated by Gustav Stresemann that saw Germany welcomed back into the international community for accepting its Western borders under the Versailles treaty, while leaving the possibility for revisions in the east. Outraged as what was seen as a capitulation to the Allies, the Pan-German League, Stahlhelm and other nationalist paramilitary groups sent a delegation to persuade President Hindenburg not to sign the treaty into law. Hindenburg, however, saw no alternative and had realised that Stresemann's foreign policy was Germany's best hope of securing better terms, so he did the opposite of what his supporters had hoped for and signed the treaty on 28 November 1925, an act that ruined the president's reputation with the radical right.[17] Over the winter of 1925/26, the prolonged cabinet crisis only strengthened Hindenburg's hand as powerbroker and a pillar of stability, and his reluctance during negotiations to invite the Social Democrats into the coalition ensured both that a minority moderate coalition of the DDP-Centre-BVP-DVP (still under Luther) took office and that the door was kept open for the DNVP to return.[18]

Luther's second government did not last long. In May 1926, a fresh crisis emerged over an order that German consulates were to fly the old Imperial colours as well as the new republican flag. A no confidence motion tabled by the Democrats, a member of the governing coalition, toppled Luther, but Hindenburg almost provoked a constitutional crisis by backing his chancellor to the hilt over what was an emotive issue for the president.[19] One of the most glaring flaws with the Weimar Constitution was the fact that there were no provisions for when or how often the president could use his emergency powers under Article 48. In November 1926, the Interior Ministry drafted a law to limit these extensive presidential prerogatives, but this effort was scotched by Hindenburg, who wrote: 'A strictly formalistic definition of the manner of exercising the president's rights, or even a limitation of those rights, would weaken his authority and gravely endanger the security of the state.'[20] There can be no doubt also that the extent to which Hindenburg's predecessor, Ebert, had used Article 48 powers in the difficult early years of the Republic, convinced the president that emergency decrees were both legitimate and necessary.[21] Following the flag controversy, Wilhelm Marx – a moderate Catholic politician and Hindenburg's 1925 rival for the presidency – was appointed chancellor. The cabinet remained virtually the same as under Luther and, as a minority government, was viewed as a stopgap measure by all sides of the political spectrum before a more broadly based coalition could be created. However, while the DDP and Centre Party were planning a Grand Coalition with the Social Democrats, Hindenburg was in touch with the Nationalist Party leader Kuno von Westarp discussing the possibility of a right-wing administration.[22]

The government eventually fell in December 1926. The SPD had launched a series of biting parliamentary attacks on the government, most sensationally in revealing the secret – and illegal – cooperation between the Reichswehr and the Soviet Union. German military personnel were receiving training in Russia and getting access to weapons and equipment prohibited under the Treaty of Versailles. In the resulting confidence vote, the Social Democrats were supported by the DNVP, eager to get back into power and aware of Hindenburg's preference for a coalition of the bourgeois right, or *Bürgerblock*.[23] Hindenburg was outraged by what he perceived as a traitorous attack by the SPD on the nation's defence policy and he made it known that he both regarded the appointment of the defence minister as his own presidential prerogative as commander-in-chief (contrary to the constitution) and that he would not tolerate any attempt to remove the current incumbent Otto Gessler.[24] This effectively ruled out Social Democratic participation in the government as they were calling for Gessler's head over cooperation with the Soviets. It would be no exaggeration to say that in the government formation of January 1927, Hindenburg played an unprecedentedly active role, straying way beyond the bounds imagined by the constitution's writers – if not beyond the letter of the law – when it came to the influence he exerted on the leaders of the political parties. He clearly told Marx to form a new cabinet that would exclude the Social Democrats and instead build an alliance of groups who favoured the 'interests of the fatherland'; in effect, he ordered him to work with the DNVP.[25] This caused not a little difficulty, for, aware of their considerable support among working-class Catholics and Christian trade unionists, many in the Centre Party were highly reluctant to cooperate with the reactionary and anti-democratic Nationalists.[26] In a meeting with party leaders on 10 January, Hindenburg ruled out a Grand Coalition and pushed hard for a *Bürgerblock* government.[27] By the third week of January, negotiations had become bogged down, but the president intervened. He succeeded in bouncing the Centre Party into cooperation with the DNVP with an open letter of 20 January to Marx calling on him to form a coalition with the Nationalists, the first time a president had used his influence with public opinion in this manner.[28] Then, after chairing a series of meetings between the Centre and the DNVP, he compelled the Nationalists to make a series of concessions, not least accepting that Marx continue as chancellor, in return for four cabinet seats, and the new government finally took office on the 29th.[29]

Hindenburg was not the only military figure using his influence during these tense negotiations. Kurt von Schleicher confirmed his position as the political head of the Reichswehr and the president's right-hand man in assisting his efforts to bring the DNVP into government behind the scenes. During 1926 and 1927, Schleicher became Hindenburg's most trusted confidant and political advisor. The name Schleicher in English translates as sneaker or creeper and therefore the officer's name was strangely apt, for Schleicher was an irrepressible schemer, a political fixer of the first order who would become the most influential behind-the-scenes figure in the Weimar Republic. Schleicher was charming and had a natural affinity with the president as a military man. He was also personal friends with Colonel Oskar von Hindenburg, the president's son and aide-de-camp, who was literally the closest figure to his aged father as he increasingly needed help with day-to-day life, and therefore a useful 'in' for Schleicher. Schleicher was a staff officer of undoubted ambition and intelligence who believed the army's primary objective should be achieving domestic stability and persuading the Reichstag parties to back covert rearmament (a subtle contrast to the policy of his former head, Seeckt, of keeping the Reichswehr out of politics). Peter Hayes, in his unparalleled study of this unique figure writes: 'Schleicher behaved as a technician of politics. He treated all parties, save the KPD, as abstract units of power of which at any given time some combination had to be found that would advance his broad objectives for Germany.'[30]

Schleicher's role as liaison officer between the Defence Ministry and the politicians of the Reichstag gave him extensive political contacts and influence. The coming appointment of his wartime mentor Wilhelm Groener (who considered Schleicher not only his protégé but practically an adoptive son) as defence minister in January 1928 would see Schleicher's power formalised and consolidated through his unusually rapid promotion to the rank of major general and the creation of the Office for Ministerial Affairs within the Defence Ministry. This was essentially a Reichswehr political bureau, which Schleicher himself headed as a de facto permanent secretary of the Defence Ministry, giving him licence to exercise political power in the name of the army. His primary political objectives in the second half of the 1920s were to try to turn the DNVP into a reliable governing party of the right and persuade the SPD to tolerate German rearmament.[31]

In the governmental crisis of winter 1926/27, Schleicher also presented Hindenburg with a dangerous alternative should coalition talks break down. Rather than permitting a Grand Coalition with the SPD, a viable option in terms of parliamentary arithmetic, Schleicher gave the president the following advice:

> All the figures involved must be informed that, after the last two cabinet crises, there can no longer be a government without a firm majority, since the President is no longer willing to tolerate the back and forth of these constant crises. If the parliament does not succeed in forming a government with a secure majority, then it would be President's duty to appoint a government enjoying his confidence, without regard for the wishes of the parties, and to give it all constitutional powers to secure a majority in parliament.
>
> Personally, I am convinced that such action will create a government on a broad basis or at least the necessary atmosphere for new elections. The people always sympathise with a clear course and a firm will.[32]

Effectively, Schleicher was suggesting a presidential government that would rely on the person of Hindenburg and the powers invested in the office of president for its authority and legitimacy rather than a parliamentary government whose authority derived from the unstable Reichstag. Schleicher reckoned the threat of such a solution might coerce the parties into agreement. This would represent a radical departure from the intentions of the constitution, which had envisaged a parliamentary democracy in which government formation was dependent on the parties of the Reichstag and chancellors were beholden to the confidence of the lower chamber rather than being the pawns of the president. Nevertheless, under the extensive powers granted to the head of state by Article 48, combined with the president's right to hire and fire chancellors, a presidential cabinet was by no means illegal or impossible. The governmental crisis of December 1926 to January 1927 had allowed Hindenburg to force his political preferences on the nation; by laying out the parameters of negotiations and pushing the Centre Party into the arms of the DNVP, he had ensured that there would be no shift to the left with a Grand Coalition, and no continuation of moderate, centrist government, and even had his scheme for a *Bürgerblock* cabinet failed, he was contemplating a presidential cabinet that would have ignored the Reichstag.

Less than two years after his inauguration, Hindenburg was already stretching his constitutional oath to its limits. In January 1928, a year after he had strived so hard to create it and move Germany to the right, the *Bürgerblock* government hit an impasse over the Reich School Bill, the views of Catholics, National Liberals and Nationalists being too far apart to find common ground on education. Hindenburg was deeply frustrated as efforts to forge a new coalition floundered and elections had to be scheduled for the spring.[33] He did, however, succeed in persuading Marx and his cabinet to stay on in a caretaker capacity to steer the budget and various other pieces of legislation through the Reichstag until the dissolution came at the end of March and he was commended for his statesmanship in ensuring that, rather than with a dramatic collapse, the *Bürgerblock* cabinet wound down peaceably ahead of elections that would have been due that year in any case.[34] Every indication was that the coming polls would see a swing to the left with gains for the SPD and losses for the DNVP. The president's legal efforts to steer the political agenda in his preferred direction had failed, largely due to the obstinance of the parties in the Reichstag and their failure to compromise.

Unquestionably, it was the symbolic and ceremonial roles that befell Hindenburg as head of state in which he excelled and proved genuinely popular. For the bourgeoisie, deprived of their monarchical figurehead, Hindenburg became something of an *ersatzkaiser* (substitute emperor) and his age meant he was seen as a 'father of the nation', often referred to as simply 'the Old Gentleman'.[35] One of the ironies of the Hindenburg presidency was that, to the field marshal's own dismay, his role as a stand-in sovereign almost certainly contributed to the rapid fading of German monarchism and the practical disappearance of the exiled Kaiser from public consciousness.[36] Building on his pre-existing hero status, in the second half of the decade, Paul von Hindenburg became the most visible, most popular figure in Germany. Hindenburg's distinctive image could be found not only on coins, postage stamps and portraits in German homes but also on a whole host of popular products. Enterprising businessmen used Hindenburg's name or face to sell their wares, often without the president's permission. The Hindenburg brand helped sell a huge range of products, from spectacles to cars to wines, with one vineyard asserting that the Old Gentleman himself was their product tester.[37] The writers of popular fiction even sought the Presidential Palace's approval for their Great War novels, and Hindenburg and his staff took on the role of editors and curators of Germany's perception of the conflict with alacrity.[38] When the president, in his field marshal's uniform, attended army manoeuvres in September 1926, the town of Mergentheim was overrun by well-wishers: 'Hundreds of people jammed the streets in front of Hindenburg's hotel, serenading the old man with the [national anthem], weeping, holding up their infants to catch a glimpse of him.'[39]

Hindenburg's influence over the hearts and minds of the German people was not always unassailable; a 1926 referendum proposing the expropriation of the property of Germany's royal families was successful despite a letter from the supposedly neutral president expressing his desire that the scheme fail appearing in the press during the campaign, and he had to put his monarchism to one side in sacking General Hans von Seeckt for allowing the ex-Crown Prince to attend army manoeuvrers that same year.[40] Nevertheless, Hindenburg was once again centre stage at the inauguration of the Tannenberg Memorial in September

1927. At this gigantic monument, in which were interred no less than twenty unknown soldiers, the field marshal and head of state reviewed thousands of veterans from nationalist and patriotic associations (the republican and Jewish veterans' associations were not invited), before delivering a bellicose speech that insisted Germany had been 'in the right' during the First World War:

> The accusation that Germany was responsible for this greatest of all wars we hereby repudiate; Germans in every walk of life unanimously reject it. It was in no spirit of envy, hatred, or lust of conquest that we unsheathed the sword ... With clean hearts we marched out to defend our Fatherland, and with clean hands did we wield the sword. Germany is ready at any moment to prove this fact before an impartial tribunal. In many graves, the symbol of German heroism, rest men of every party without distinction ... May every discord therefore break against this monument.[41]

Such scenes pale in comparison to the nationwide celebrations that marked the president's eightieth birthday less than a month later on Sunday, 2 October 1927. The praise that was showered on the president in the press was almost hysterical, with one commentator boldly declaring: 'When the German people elected Hindenburg, it admitted the morality of its whole history,' while the former chancellor Hans Luther wrote, 'the German people has found itself again in Hindenburg's name.'[42] The public festivities were even more outlandish; in Düsseldorf, 30,000 watched fireworks draw the president's iconic head in the sky; in Rothenberg, a human pyramid hung his portrait from the top; and in Berlin, military bands played a specially composed *Hindenburg Song* as 200,000 lined the 8km route of the president's motorcade as he was ferried to the Grunewald stadium for a ceremony of songs and formation marching by 40,000 schoolchildren.[43] The birthday celebrations also included a ceremony in which representatives of German agriculture and industry presented the president with the deeds to Neudeck, the ancestral East Prussian estate of the Hindenburgs, which had been owned by his cousin. The gift was an initiative of a landowner and DNVP deputy, Elard von Oldenburg-Januschau, who also so happened to live on the neighbouring estate. Oldenburg-Januschau had at first attempted to persuade Wilhelm Marx to use donations given to the Hindenburg fund for war veterans and widows to buy the estate as a birthday gift to the president, but the chancellor had considered this inappropriate.[44] Instead, Oldenburg-Januschau had raised funds from among his fellow Junker aristocrats, from the veterans' associations such as the Stahlhelm and Kyffhäuserbund, and from big business and industry, who donated 805,000 of the 1.2 million Reichsmarks raised.[45] Clearly, this most generous of gifts, an extensive East Prussian estate, was a gift from the military, agrarian and business elite, to whom Hindenburg was not only closely tied but also now indebted to. Additionally, this literally made the president a member of the landowning nobility (and therefore more directly concerned by agricultural issues), and it also reinforced his social and emotional ties to the Junker class and ensured that during his long spells at Neudeck he socialised with reactionary Prussian aristocrats, not least his new neighbour, Oldenburg-Januschau.[46]

Hindenburg had actually asked for something quite different for his birthday – donations to the aforementioned charity fund for veterans and war widows. Meissner organised the fundraising campaign, which saw 200,000 posters plastered around the country and 160,000 copies of a special illustrated book on the president's life sold, with the proceeds going to charity. In total, the Hindenburg fund raised 7.1 million Reichsmarks, and the total would have been higher had the campaign not coincided with the Neudeck and the Tannenberg Memorial fundraisers.[47] While Hindenburg-adoration had since 1925 spread to democratic and liberal circles thanks to the president's perceived constitutionalism, there can be no doubt that above all he remained a symbol for the right. Not only did the president refuse to take part in any ceremonies celebrating the revolution that had brought the Republic he presided over into being, but his public pronouncements, as at the Tannenberg Memorial, were frequently belligerent and nationalistic, a good example being his New Year's Address of 1929:

> The entire German people greets today the beginning of the new year with deep bitterness, because a great part of our land is denied the freedom on which we have just claim – just in God's eyes and in man's eyes. We have long hoped for its attainment. And we still want to hope, despite harsh disappointment, that in the new year the German people will be given back its full right of self-determination.[48]

That year saw the release of *The Iron Hindenburg in War and Peace*, a highly popular documentary film about the president's life, which had been carefully edited by Meissner and the Old Gentleman himself before release, which hammered home all the key points of the Hindenburg myth – the epic victory at Tannenberg, the Stab in the Back, the unifying presence in the new republic. The film's key message was that Hindenburg had saved Germany both from external invaders and internal strife and the 'saviour' remained a hugely popular national figurehead throughout the 1920s.[49]

Ludendorff's withdrawal

While Paul von Hindenburg's career reached new heights in the mid-1920s following his election to the presidency, Erich Ludendorff's dismal failure to attain the same office doomed his lofty political aspirations. As we have seen, Hitler persuaded the general to run to serve his own purposes. His electoral performance, which his wife Margarethe later wrote was a 'public disgrace', resulted in him becoming 'publicly stigmatised as a disappointed man who tried to make trouble', while Hitler reportedly reacted to the inglorious 1.1 per cent his candidate had achieved with the words, 'Good – now we've taken care of him.'[50] By backing Ludendorff, Hitler had ensured that his party and its activists were isolated from the rest of the German right, thereby strengthening his singular control, and Ludendorff, as well as being discredited was now isolated, having thrown his lot in with a party that no longer had a use for him. Historians are unanimous that the 1925 presidential election destroyed Ludendorff politically, ruining any remaining chances he had of leading the völkisch far right and condemning him to political irrelevancy for the rest of his days.[51]

This is not how Ludendorff saw things at the time, of course. The Nazi Party held a torchlit parade through Munich to celebrate the general's sixtieth birthday in April 1925, although his biographer Goodspeed claims he was aware that this was political opportunism on the part of the party rather than a 'personal tribute'.[52] All was not well in the NSDAP, for there was a clear conflict that had been growing for some time over the nature of the Nazi movement; was it primarily a paramilitary or a civilian movement? The latter would allow the civilian (and lowly lance corporal) Hitler to lead, while the former implied respect for military rank, which would necessitate deference to Ludendorff. Having refounded the party in the spring, Hitler worked hard through 1925 to make the NSDAP a bureaucratic, civilian political party that was totally subordinated to his own leadership. Ludendorff's obvious political incompetence and electoral failings made it easier for Hitler to bring his followers into line, but even so, the shift away from a militaristic, Freikorps-esque movement was unpopular and cost the party in the short term; the Potsdam branch had gained 138 members following Hitler's release from prison in late 1924, but by August 1925, less than thirty of them remained active.[53]

Naturally, the essentially civilian, bureaucratic vision of the Nazi Party that Hitler was consolidating did not correspond to Ludendorff's vision for a political movement. Keen to make a political comeback, Ludendorff was excited when former military colleagues encouraged him to start a new völkisch federation at the August 1925 Tannenberg commemoration.[54] As a result, in collaboration with the conspiracy theorist Mathilde von Kemnitz, the general established the Tannenberg League in September 1925, a far-right veterans' association, headed by Ludendorff himself.[55] Ominously, Ludendorff declared at the League's founding meeting in Regensburg, Bavaria, 'Freedom cannot be achieved without a solution to the Jewish question!'[56] The organisation was to be a movement rather than a political party as such, whose stated aim was national and spiritual reawakening and the defence of Germany and Germanness against supranational, conspiratorial forces. Politically there was very little to separate the Tannenberg League from the NSDAP; they both called for a Third Reich, a Greater Germany, denounced Weimar foreign policy and warned of internal enemy (Jews, Freemasons etc.), meaning the two organisations were usually competing for the same audience.[57]

Many veterans and former Freikorps fighters who sympathised politically with the NSDAP but were dismayed by the new direction Hitler was taking the party, saw the Tannenberg League as a natural home for their paramilitary activities and it soon attracted 30,000 members.[58] Ludendorff's aim was to promote his own brand of far-right politics among Great War veterans, with the mythical victory of Tannenberg, Ludendorff's greatest achievement, as the clarion call. However, by focsuing its appeal to veterans (who were already well served with several associations, not least the nationalist Stahlhelm), Ludendorff was limiting his reach, restricting his political activities to veterans' reunions, and ultimately, the League's membership would slip as the Nazi Party gained momentum in the late 1920s.[59] Furthermore, the NSDAP did not take kindly to rival organisations. In December 1925, Hitler banned the many instances of dual membership of both the Nazi Party and the Tannenberg League, thereby preventing Ludendorff's vehicle from becoming the paramilitary arm of National Socialism and further isolating the NSDAP from the wider völkisch right that Ludendorff had been so keen to bring together.[60] Also, Ludendorff consciously refused to seek mass appeal for his movement, believing the masses to be fickle and untrustworthy.[61]

The year 1926 would see Ludendorff throw his lot in, not with Hitler, but with Dr von Kemnitz. That summer, he secured a divorce from Margarethe after seventeen years of marriage and the 61-year-old tied the knot with Mathilde von Kemnitz on 14 September, wearing the uniform he had pledged never to don again.[62] As we have seen, the general had fallen increasingly under the spell of the outlandish psychologist since 1923, his views becoming more extreme, and particularly anti-Christian, to conform with hers, and he now committed himself to a joint political and philosophical venture with his new wife. Hitler apparently joked that if the secret conspiratorial powers that Ludendorff raved about had half the power the general claimed, they could have done little better than introducing him to Kemnitz.[63] Ludendorff moved into his wife's home in Tutzing, southern Bavaria, where (in his own words), 'Hereafter [we] fought jointly against the supranational force and their tools ... mutually enriched our minds, and widened the struggle for freedom.'[64]

Margarethe's memoirs, published in 1929, do not mention Kemnitz nor her ex-husband's activities after the marriage and one gets the sense that not only must she have resented the second Mrs Ludendorff, but she was embarrassed for her husband, for whom she displays considerable affection in her book – he now lived by his lifelong motto: 'I shall go my own way.'[65]

Ultimately, the only thing surprising about Ludendorff's split with Hitler is that it came so late, for although they had many views in common, by the mid-1920s, their visions had become incompatible – Ludendorff naturally believed in soldierly supremacy and a military dictatorship under himself, while Hitler was determined to take the power away from the soldiers in the völkisch movement and create a unified party under his own sole leadership as Führer.⁶⁶ Both men saw themselves as the future leader of Germany, making cooperation nigh on impossible. By 1927, it was clear that Ludendorff had left the Nazi orbit and the two leaders were publicly attacking each other, with Hitler claiming the general was a freemason.⁶⁷ For his part, Ludendorff would claim that Hitler was an agent of the Papacy.⁶⁸ The parting was not without some pain; there was disquiet for instance in the Hanover Nazi Party, which concluded that Ludendorff was the 'greater man', but they insisted they remained loyal first and foremost to their Führer.⁶⁹

While Hitler was slowly building the NSDAP into a nationwide force, Ludendorff's Tannenberg League increasingly became a peripheral conspiratorial sect on the most extreme fringes of the far right. In July 1927, the Tannenberg League was reorganised, with strict, almost military discipline and direction from the top. Any disagreement with the Ludendorff couple's line was tantamount to betrayal and would result in expulsion, and Mathilde's influence can be seen in the admission of women into the League that year as it moved away from being a veterans' association into a quasi-religious cult.⁷⁰ The year 1928 would see the Nazi and Tannenberg movements move decisively apart; for although they essentially shared a common aim in creating a Jew and Marxist-free Germany built on racial and racist theories, by that time, the Ludendorffs' own religion, the Deutsche Gotterkenntnis (see below), came to the fore of the organisation, which increasingly became merely a haven for disgruntled Nazis and Ludendorff worshippers.⁷¹

The Ludendorff couple now cut themselves off from reality in their Tutzing home, which became a place of pilgrimage for their ever-shrinking band of devotees. As in the early 1920s at Prinz-Ludwigs-Höhe, Ludendorff could hold court over fawning followers, only now his circle was considerably smaller, if more fervent.⁷² Ludendorff, with the support of his new wife, now dedicated the remainder of his life to a confused and chaotic study of conspiratorial forces, which included the Jews, the Freemasons, Communism, and Christianity – primarily, but not exclusively, Roman Catholicism. As Chickering has commented, the study of this final phase of Ludendorff's life, the 'emotional management of humiliation', might be better left to psychoanalysts rather than historians, as the general displayed some symptoms of delusional disorder and isolated himself almost completely: 'I no longer had anything to do with [his former political allies]. I removed myself from the nationalist paramilitary groups, as well as from the associations of officers and troops. With me remained but a few Germans.'⁷³ An essentially vain man, Ludendorff was evidently afraid and consistently attempted to avoid responsibility and blame. His chastening defeat in the 1925 election was simply the latest in a procession of disastrous failures, from German defeat in 1918, to the embarrassment of the 1920 and 1923 putsches and 1924 trial.

Perhaps mentally broken, Ludendorff now retreated into a mystical world where his own failings could be attributed to dark forces, and a small circle of sycophants, not least his own wife, nursed his ego back to health. Indeed, although he was further from power and influence than he had been for decades, Ludendorff genuinely appears to have been more contented in his new world than he had ever been in his life.[74] His most recent biographer, Jay Lockenour, actually argues that Ludendorff's mental condition is largely irrelevant to historical study, and that whatever condition he may or may not have suffered from, it provided him with the energy and vision to explore his own mythical world for years to come. After all, although Adolf Hitler clearly suffered from some mental abnormality, it is in a large part irrelevant to our historical study of the man.[75] Free from the criticism, factionalism and cut and thrust of nationalist politics, he could indulge his prejudices without fear of rebuke. He and Mathilde set about writing pamphlets and books laying out their eccentric, hateful theories with volumes such as *The Secret of the Might of the Jesuits and Its Aim* or *The Destruction of Freemasonry Through Disclosure of Its Secrets*.[76] While Mathilde mostly wrote on religion and philosophy, Erich concentrated on military and political matters. His ideas about the mobilisation of society in war and peace gained some traction in right-wing intellectual discourse but when the general met nationalist writer and thinker Ernst Jünger, the latter complained that Ludendorff 'began almost immediately to talk about the Freemasons and would not drop the subject'.[77]

Nevertheless, the Ludendorffs did carve out a niche for themselves, establishing the Ludendorff Press in 1929, a publishing house in Munich which had an audience of some 100,000 that eagerly consumed the couple's prolific output.[78] Along with numerous books and pamphlets, they published several newspapers and periodicals, most notably the *Ludendorffs Volkswarte*, and owing to their sole ownership of the press and its output, made for themselves a handsome living. Indeed, the Tanneberg League was directed to become almost the marketing arm for the Ludendorff Press, with individual branches awarded commission for each new subscriber to the newspaper and members ceaselessly encouraged to strike up conversations with friends, family, colleagues and commuters about the Ludendorff cult and attempt to recruit them with free copies of pamphlets, books or papers.[79] The press's biggest success came from Mathilde Ludendorff's vision for a new Germanic, neo-pagan religion, the Deutsche Gotterkenntnis (which translates poorly but might best be framed as the worship of a German God). Essentially, Mathilde's revelation was that the German people were daily tortured by their living under a foreign religion (Christianity) and could only achieve phsycological freedom, spiritual peace and racial purity if they embraced a specifically Germanic spirituality.[80] Her pamphlet outlining her new faith, *Salvation from Jesus Christ*, sold over 400,000 copies and her husband claimed, 'on the dissemination of *Salvation from Jesus Christ* depends the liberation of every single German, of the German nation, and of all nations.'[81] The Ludendorffs henceforth became effectively leaders of a pagan cult and the general in particular began to see the new faith as the key to mobilising the nation and sustaining morale in wartime, a religion free of Christian (and thereby 'Jewish') influences.[82] He apparently described himself as 'a heathen – and proud of it'.[83] To be frank, Ludendorff had transformed himself from a figurehead to an embarrassment for the nationalist right, both because of his insane pronouncements and his frequent quarrels with other military and political figures. He had fallen out with Hitler (himself a fringe figure in the mid-1920s) and Crown Prince Rupprecht, and he soon added Admiral von Tirpitz and Field Marshal von Hindenburg to that list. The falling-out with Tirpitz came when he described the party that the admiral held a seat for, the DNVP, as 'a gang of perjured renegades'.[84] This comment illustrates how far Ludendorff had removed himself from the mainstream right, for in 1919 he had worked with the Nationalist Party's Karl Helfferich in composing Hindenburg's famous Stab-in-the-Back inquiry testimony, staying in his Berlin villa, while the 1920 Kapp Putsch had involved numerous contacts in the DNVP, not least Wolfgang Kapp himself. The split with his closest colleague and the man with whose name he was and is forever associated, Paul von Hindenburg, was even more painful. Ludendorff does not appear to have held a grudge against his former superior for beating him to the presidency; after all, they had competed in different ballots. Hindenburg was due in the summer of 1925 to make his annual visit to the Ludendorffs during his regular hunting holiday in Bavaria. However, as Margarethe reports:

> All preparations were made, but an express letter arrived which gave us the unexpected and very disappointing news that he could not come.
>
> The Field Marshal was no longer a private person able to do and say what he liked. He was President of the Reich and had to take account of public opinion both at home and abroad and to pay attention to the wishes and scruples of his Chancellor and Cabinet.
>
> The Chancellor [Luther], had at the last moment protested against Hindenburg's visit to Ludendorff at Ludwigshöhe and demanded its cancellation on political grounds.
>
> Ludendorff foamed with rage: he felt himself deeply wounded. I have seldom seen him in such a state. He had always insisted: 'Come what may, in the eyes of the world Hindenburg and I must always stand together and be and remain the pattern of German loyalty and German unity.'
>
> Now that ideal, too, was shattered.[85]

Ludendorff was totally humiliated by this snub from his closest comrade, for the field marshal's annual visit was a major event in Prinz-Ludwigs-Höhe and clearly Ludendorff felt he had lost face. The implication in Hindenburg's explanation, that Ludendorff was an embarrassment to the president, that it would be bad PR to pay him a visit, was nothing less than an act of betrayal from a man who, Ludendorff would have felt, owed him so much.

Two years later, at the official opening of the Tannenberg Memorial, Ludendorff had his revenge with a snub of his own. Ludendorff had accepted the invitation to the ceremony on the condition that he did not have to meet Hindenburg, and he refused to attend the official banquet the night before in order to avoid his old chief. On the day of the ceremony, Ludendorff refused to stand next to the president in the review of the troops, making a point of standing several metres away.[86] Margarethe called Ludendorff's calculated snub 'like a blow from a club, well-aimed and delivered with full force – brutal and with consequences which were duly taken into account'.[87] And it had the desired effect. Hindenburg was deeply upset by the incident; he left the ceremony early, missing Ludendorff's speech, and he forbade the Tannenberg League from participating in the large public celebrations of his eightieth birthday less than two months later. As a result, Ludendorff was deliberately shunned by his military colleagues, both at the ceremony and after, while the president ruminated fretfully on the incident for weeks.[88] The two were never reconciled after this incident and Ludendorff indulged in a number of attacks on Hindenburg in the following years, drawing attention to the fact the Neudeck estate had been bequeathed to his son Oskar rather than the field marshal himself (to avoid inheritance tax[89]), and writing a blistering denunciation of the president upon his signing of the Young Plan in 1930 (see below): 'Field Marshal von Hindenburg has forfeited the right to wear the field-grey uniform of the army and to be buried in it. Herr Paul von Hindenburg has destroyed the very thing he fought for as Field Marshal.'[90]

By the late 1920s, Erich Ludendorff was an isolated, irrelevant, if contented political figure on the furthest extreme fringe of far-right politics. He saw agents of or spies for conspiracies everywhere, from Hitler to his own sister.[91] He was happy but unimportant, his role in the rise of the Nazis effectively over. To most Germans, outside of his small band of diehard conspiracy theorist followers, Ludendorff the great general was now a figure of fun, as illustrated by the following poem written by the satirist Kurt Tucholsky:

> Are you anxious, Erich? Are you scared, Erich?
> Does your heart pound, Erich? Do you take flight?
> Do the Masons, Erich – and the Jesuits, Erich,
> Want to stab you, Erich, what a fright!
> These Jews are becoming ever unseemlier.
> All misfortune is the work of these … schemers.[92]

Hindenburg and the Grand Coalition

As we have seen, the rightist *Bürgerblock* coalition that Hindenburg had worked so hard to create wound down in the spring of 1928 ahead of new Reichstag elections. One issue the president did have to handle at that time was the appointment of a new defence minister, an issue he considered his personal domain as the nation's commander-in-chief and a military figure himself. Otto Gessler, whom Hindenburg had defended in 1926, was forced to resign in January 1928 in a scandal involving a profiteering naval officer. The president rejected rightist candidates put forward by the DNVP and DVP, aware that elections would likely bring a centre-left coalition to power in the near future and hoping to find an appointee who would thus be acceptable to the Social Democrats. Hindenburg apparently considered a monarchist Centre politician, Franz von Papen, who had served on the General Staff during the war, but the Defence Ministry was not keen.[93] Instead, at Schleicher's suggestion, Hindenburg plumped for Wilhelm Groener, the retired general who had replaced Ludendorff as First Quartermaster General and assisted Hindenburg in securing an armistice and then taking responsibility for accepting Versailles. Groener was a very astute appointment, for not only was he a military figure whom Hindenburg knew well and had worked with before, he was also respected by the SPD for his backing of the Republic in the 1918 Ebert-Groener Pact, and he was Schleicher's wartime mentor and a close ally of the scheming staff officer.[94] The two would dominate the German military, and to a certain extent German politics, for the next four years, and Groener soon paid his protégé back by promoting him to general and creating the Office for Ministerial Affairs within the Defence Ministry for Schleicher to head. Groener would therefore remain in situ, in a highly influential post, no matter what happened in the elections of May 1928. The Social Democrats, focusing their campaign on opposition to the costly construction of a so-called pocket battleship, scored considerable gains, upping their seats by twenty-two to 153, making them by far the largest party with eighty more seats in the Reichstag than their nearest rival, the DNVP. The election was nothing short of disastrous for Westarp's party as voters punished the Nationalists for collaboration in the two rather disappointing *Bürgerblock* governments. They lost nearly 2 million votes and thirty seats. The Nazis remained a political irrelevance with 2.6 per cent of the vote and twelve seats, down even on the disappointing December 1924 showing when the movement had been at war with itself.[95]

For the president, the most disheartening consequence of the vote was the effect the defeat had on the DNVP, the party he had strongly encouraged to enter government and where his political sympathies lay. However, the party rank and file were outraged by the leadership's compromises on foreign policy, unemployment insurance and in accepting the Weimar Constitution.[96] The conservative Westarp was soon ousted as party chairman in favour of the rabidly nationalist and anti-Semitic Alfred Hugenberg, Germany's greatest press baron, the proprietor of hundreds of newspapers and the UFA film studio. Hugenberg was an intransigent opponent of the Weimar Republic and he quickly remoulded the DNVP in his own image, renouncing any and all collaboration with the hated 'system' and instead seeking closer ties with what was soon termed the 'National

Opposition', namely the parties and movements of the far right – the Stahlhelm, the Pan-German League and, most significantly, Hitler's Nazis. The goal of the Nationalist Party, to the dismay of its more moderate parliamentarians such as Westarp, Schiele and Treviranus, was now nothing short of the overthrow of the state.[97] Hugenberg's extreme brand of politics would lead to a number of party splits over the next few years as Schiele left for the new Christian-Nationalist Peasants' and Farmers' Party (CNBL), Treviranus and later Westarp defected in 1929–30 and set up the Conservative People's Party (KVP) and other moderates would leave to found the Christian Social People's Mission (CSVD), which attempted to become a Protestant version of the Catholic Centre Party. The severe fragmentation of the DNVP over the period 1928–30 was a serious problem for Hindenburg and Schleicher, for it scuppered their hopes of transforming the party into a reliable coalition partner that would allow the SPD to be excluded from office. Nevertheless, both men took a keen interest in the new parties of the moderate right and, in particular, Treviranus and his KVP would enjoy close ties with the Presidential Palace and receive covert funding from the Defence Ministry.[98] In the short term, however, the opinion of the voters and the chaos on the right necessitated a shift to the left and the appointment of a Grand Coalition stretching from the Social Democrats to the People's Party.

As the biggest party in the Grand Coalition and the clear 'winner' of the 1928 election, the SPD would take the leading roles in the cabinet, not least the chancellorship. The Social Democrats had nominated as their candidate for the chancellor Hermann Müller. The party co-chair and former foreign minister was understated and not a talented public speaker; however, he was well-regarded across much of the political spectrum for his integrity and competence, and he could speak several languages.[99] Hindenburg once said that Müller was his best chancellor – it was just a shame he was a socialist.[100] It is also a shame that the president allowed his political biases to undermine the Grand Coalition, which in essence was the last chance for parliamentarianism in interwar Germany. During the Second Reich, the SPD had been viewed by the establishment as an enemy within – a class-based, internationalist movement that threatened the strength and unity of the nation. Naturally, this view continued to permeate the attitudes of Germany's political and business elite after 1918, and indeed the German Revolution and Stab-in-the-Back myth that came with it only bolstered the perception of the Social Democrats as an internal foe. Hindenburg, unsurprisingly given his age and background, shared this suspicion and loathing of the SPD and, although he was on reasonable terms with Müller and Prussian Premier Otto Braun, he resented overseeing a government headed by a party he disliked. Hindenburg was of course always concerned about the Reichswehr and the views of the officer corps, and senior military figures had been highly concerned by the SPD's attacks on cooperation with the Soviets and their stringently anti-rearmament election campaign. The pacifist streak within the party frustrated the Defence Ministry and, through Schleicher and Groener, the military could wield considerable influence on the president's thinking.[101] There was also a widespread perception among landowners that the Social Democrats would always protect the interests of the urban proletariat over agrarians when it came to food prices and tariffs and therefore that no succour would come the way of the Junker estates while the SPD governed the Reich and Prussia. As an East Prussian landowner himself, Hindenburg was disproportionately attentive to the opinions and concerns of the agrarian elite. All of this boded ill for the chances of the Grand Coalition and the likelihood of the president observing strict nonpartisan neutrality.

The Grand Coalition enjoyed a troubled, jaundiced existence for just under two years. From the get-go the difficulties of getting the pro-industry DVP to work with the union-affiliated SPD meant that, at least for the five months of its existence, it was a 'cabinet of personalities' from across the political spectrum, while the ministers' respective party machine hammered out a coalition deal.[102] The need to find compromises on particularly every issue created an almost permanent sense of cabinet crisis and a general precariousness that frustrated Hindenburg deeply. Now past the halfway point of his first term, it seemed like he had presided over a perpetual turnover of ministers and Gustav Stresemann was even suggesting by early 1929 that Weimar had become a 'caricature of parliamentarianism', with each party representing only the material interests of a narrow class group and therefore that the president would have to take a more prominent role in sustaining chancellors, ensuring they could legislate for the common good and acting as a 'counter-weight' to an unstable Reichstag.[103]

There can be no doubt that the presidential model that Schleicher had proposed to Hindenburg was gaining popular traction by the end of the decade. For some time, both men had been impressed by the writings of the constitutional lawyer Carl Schmitt, who had criticised what he called the 'fragile multi-party system' and highlighted how the lack of established norms or checks on the exercise of certain powers in the Weimar Constitution might facilitate a more stable, semi-authoritarian style of rule centred on a strong president that would be perfectly legal, merely violating the spirit rather than the letter of the constitution.[104] Not that Hindenburg and his circle did not get their way for much of the Grand Coalition period. Despite the great fanfare with which the SPD had promised to axe the pocket battleship programme, Müller and his social democratic colleagues assented to the will of the president and defied their own party to allow construction to go ahead, and the SPD ministers also consented to a secret Reichswehr scheme for the creation of volunteer militias and arms caches on the Polish frontier.[105] In the spring of 1929, Müller also succeeded against the odds in facilitating the passage of a compromise budget which brought the Centre Party into the fold to a greater extent, even if the obstinate right wing of the DVP was beginning to agitate for the death of parliamentarianism.[106] Nevertheless, the Grand Coalition would finally be brought down by a prolonged budget crisis in the winter and spring of 1929/30 brought on by the Wall Street Crash.

The government was weakened greatly in its final crisis by the death of Gustav Stresemann in October 1929, for not only did his own DVP rapidly shift to the political right, increasingly in the thrall of the industrial elite and desperate to terminate cooperation with the Social Democrats, but even more importantly, Weimar lost the one statesman who was capable of uniting a broad spectrum of political forces behind the Republic, from the SPD on the left to Hindenburg on the right.[107] His death came immediately after the conclusion of arguably his greatest success: the Young Plan. Over the summer of 1929, the foreign minister was able to negotiate down Germany's Versailles reparations bill from 132 to 37 billion Reichsmarks and secured a lower annual payment which more gradually paid off the debt over fifty-eight years. More importantly, Stresemann secured the withdrawal of Allied occupying troops from German soil for June 1930 (five years ahead of schedule) and the end of Allied supervision over the Reichsbank and German railways, which had been imposed by the Versailles settlement.[108] All of this was secured with no German concessions in return. The irony of the Young Plan was that Stresemann's greatest achievement – facilitating the early evacuation of Allied troops from the Rhineland, paved the way for rightist plans to dismantle the Republic, which would have been inconceivable with a strong Allied military contingent on German soil.[109] Furthermore, the Young Plan provoked yet more vitriolic outrage from the radical right. The new DNVP leader Alfred Hugenberg rallied the 'National Opposition', including the Nazi Party, into a vicious referendum campaign against acceptance of the plan centred on their proposed 'Law Against the Enslavement of the German People', Article 4 of which would make it a treasonable offence for politicians to sign or vote for the Plan.[110] Nationalist politicians such as Westarp and Oldenburg-Januschau had no success in persuading Hindenburg to oppose the Young Plan, with the president simply insisting it represented an improvement in Germany's position.[111] Thus, Hindenburg again faced a painful confrontation with the nationalist right he always wished to champion. He felt it necessary to release a detailed statement explaining his support for the agreement to the public, which vainly also implied he was sacrificing his own reputation for the good of the country, but this did not prevent a storm of abuse raining down on the Reich President from his former supporters.[112] The front page of the newspaper of the Pan-German League was adorned with a black ribbon and the editorial was written as an obituary to the field marshal, implying he was dead to the nationalist right:

> We do not think that any merit is too great to be offset by guilt. This is the case ... regarding the Reich President. The admiration, the veneration and the love that the Field Marshal had earned for his unforgettable deeds

... have been called into question through his behaviour at the head of the Reich. Today, as far as Germans with an untainted national feeling are concerned, he has completely gambled away the near-inexhaustible trust in him. We will not forget the deeds of Hindenburg, the military leader ... But we have to announce that Hindenburg, the Reich President, we recognise as our political enemy ... On this note we bid farewell to the Victor of Tannenberg.[113]

Perhaps even worse, a cartoon in the Nazi paper *Der Angriff* portrayed Hindenburg passively watching on as the German people are enslaved, under the caption 'And the Saviour watches'. In the same paper, Joseph Goebbels's editorial opened with: 'Hindenburg, are you still alive?'[114] Frustratingly for the president, the controversy would drag on until the spring of 1930 when the plan was finally ratified by the Reichstag and signed into law by the president himself. The Young Plan referendum was a dismal failure for Hugenberg, for when the vote was held on 22 December 1929, the campaign only attracted the votes of 13.8 per cent of the total eligible voters when 50 per cent was required. The significance of the Young Plan referendum lay rather in the fact that domestic politics had been stoked up and polarised by the extremist rhetoric, and that Hitler and the NSDAP were given a national platform for the first time since the Beer Hall Putsch, with the party benefitting greatly from cost-free and plentiful positive coverage and propaganda generously provided by Hugenberg's media empire.[115]

Impatient for political change throughout 1929, Hindenburg had called the moderate conservative Westarp (who remained in the DNVP at this point) to the Presidential Palace on 15 January 1930. Hindenburg had in fact been discussing ousting Müller with Westarp since as early as March 1929.[116] He told Westarp that he was looking to form a new administration reliant on the president's powers rather then the Reichstag after the ratification of the Young Plan in the spring and enquired as to the likelihood of the DNVP returning to the fold. Frustratingly for the president, the powerless Westarp informed him that under the leadership of Hugenberg, he could not see the DNVP joining any cabinet, even a presidential one – the new DNVP chairman was determined to destroy the Republic at all costs and therefore he and his party could play no part in Hindenburg and Schleicher's plans.[117] Hindenburg had intervened to save the Grand Coalition by pressuring the DVP to support Müller in a confidence vote in December 1929, but he was clearly ready for a shift back to the right.[118]

Behind the scenes, General Kurt von Schleicher was paving the way for the transition. As his preferred candidate for chancellor, Schleicher had for some time been tapping up a candidate with good contacts with both the labour movement and moderate conservatives: Heinrich Brüning. Brüning was a rising star in the Catholic Centre Party who, aged just 43, had been appointed head of the party's Reichstag delegation in April 1929. He was also clearly on the right of the party, having campaigned enthusiastically for Hindenburg's election in 1925 against the Centre's own Wilhelm Marx.[119] As a decorated machine gun officer from the Great War, a Christian trade unionist and, since first being elected in 1924, a recognised expert in fiscal and tax affairs, Brüning was well-respected across the political spectrum. He was an ardent believer in the economic orthodoxy of the day, namely that a balanced federal budget and deflationary policies would restore business confidence and competitiveness, thereby stimulating the economy. He had worked closely throughout the 1920s with those on the 'left' of the DNVP, such as Gottfried Treviranus, to try to encourage the Nationalists to enter coalitions and take part in the democratic process, and he had simultaneously tried to orientate the Centre Party towards working with the right rather than the SPD. In this, he broadly shared Schleicher's goals in desiring stable centre-right coalitions, and indeed the two had much common ground. Brüning was a dour, austere figure who lived an almost spartan existence of pious frugality, so at the very least he practised what he preached and was a man of integrity.[120] Having first met him and proposed a presidential government in spring 1929, Schleicher had sought to win Brüning round to the idea of his heading a 'Hindenburg Cabinet', telling him the president feared the country was 'sinking into the mud' and that Hindenburg desired 'to put things in order before he died, together with the Reichswehr and the younger forces in parliament [for which it would be necessary to] send parliament home'.[121]

Brüning was not won over immediately and did not see the general again until Treviranus, fresh from defecting from the DNVP in December 1929, and a close friend of Brüning's, arranged a meeting on Boxing Day between the Catholic politician and Schleicher and Meissner, representing the president. By that time, the Young Plan referendum had made it clear that the next government could not rely on the DNVP and therefore a coalition of the moderate right, headed by Brüning, was the ideal solution. However, the general's plans hit an unexpected hitch when Brüning refused to contemplate unseating Müller, whom he liked and respected, and argued that an administration reliant on Article 48 was too drastic a departure from the parliamentary democracy envisaged by the constitution.[122] Instead, they should bide their time until the DNVP came back to its senses, and besides, Brüning exclaimed, 'one thing is for certain: the Reichstag cannot be shut out.'[123] It was not until the following month that Brüning began to be persuaded of the merits of a 'Hindenburg Cabinet' on a stroll with Defence Minister Wilhelm Groener. Groener had been working on his cabinet colleagues from the DDP, Centre, BVP and DVP to lay the foundations of a moderate conservative admiration that would succeed the Grand Coalition. He reassured Brüning that they would not give up on the Reichstag, they would maintain good relations with the DNVP and that Hindenburg saw Brüning as his 'last chancellor' – he wanted to bow out with a fellow conservative at the helm. Besides, Groener reasoned, Müller's health was too poor for him to steer the country through the fiscal crisis; it was time for a change.[124]

Groener and Brüning had much in common and they quickly developed a strong working relationship. Hindenburg himself met with Brüning on 1 March 1930. The president again tried to persuade Brüning to head a new rightist government, but he failed to overcome the Centre leader's resistance – Brüning was determined to back Müller for the moment.[125] Nonetheless, the Catholic leader left the door open should Müller fail; reassuring the president that the Centre 'would not reject any appeal that his patriotic convictions might lead him to make', Brüning found a tearful Hindenburg getting to his feet and clasping his hand with the words, 'Everyone has abandoned me in my life; you must promise that your party will not leave me in the lurch at the end of my life.'[126]

Hindenburg was surrounded by influences that wanted the Social Democrats out: Groener, Schleicher and the military, the industrial and agricultural elite, delegations from the DVP and moderate conservatives in the process of extracting themselves from the DNVP. We should, however, not forget that ever since becoming president, Hindenburg had displayed his political prejudices against the SPD and the decision was hardly a painful one. The president's circle was pushing at an open door. In a crucial meeting on 11 or 12 March, Groener and Schleicher told the president that he could not risk backing the SPD over the right again, rather he should encourage the DVP to oust the government and appoint either Brüning or the DVP chairman Ernst Scholz 'as chancellor with the mission of forming a cabinet of notable individuals prepared to put our economy and finances in order without regard for the parties and state governments, without asking the party delegations or forming any coalitions'.[127]

Perhaps of even more importance, on 17 and 18 March, Schleicher arranged for delegations from German industry and agriculture, led by the DNVP's Martin Schiele, to suggest to the president a scheme for a so-called Eastern Aid Programme, a financial rescue package for the indebted landowners east of the Elbe, where agrarians had been hit hard and many old aristocratic estates were threatened with bankruptcy. Naturally, the president was told the SPD would never take the concerns of agriculture seriously. He accepted the proposals wholeheartedly and now desired a new government to implement this generous plan in his name.[128] After finally signing the Young Plan on 13 March, Hindenburg sent a strongly worded letter to Müller which implied the president had lost confidence in his government and demanded he restore a balanced budget by the end of the month, deepening the cabinet crisis and effectively putting the chancellor up against the clock.[129] Once he had decided to be rid of Müller, Hindenburg effectively gave licence to the DVP to make their move and topple the government – the party even rejected the budget plan of their own finance minister.[130] Had it not been for the president indicating his willingness to form a rightist presidential regime, Müller may well have succeeded in hammering out a compromise. A social democratic cabinet colleague had even suggested at the beginning of March that Müller ask the president for decree powers under Article 48 to pass a budget, but the chancellor rightly doubted whether Hindenburg would grant him access to his emergency powers (although famed for his use of Article 48, Hindenburg never allowed a Social Democrat to use it).[131] The end finally came on 27 March 1930, when the Social Democratic Reichstag delegation rejected a compromise agreement package proposed by Brüning, and Meissner informed a forlorn Müller that the president would not grant him emergency powers to promulgate it by decree.[132] Brüning was summoned to the Presidential Palace and accepted a commission to form a cabinet that was independent of parliament and the parties. The era of Hindenburg playing the role of constitutional president was over.

Chapter 5

The Hindenburg Republic: Hindenburg as the Arbiter of German Politics

The period 1930–33 was one of dire political and economic crisis for Germany, the severity of which cannot be overstated. Paul von Hindenburg found himself at the very centre of this maelstrom and endeavoured, with the help of a circle of advisers, most notably General Kurt von Schleicher and Chancellors Heinrich Brüning and Franz von Papen, to guide the Reich to calmer waters. Their solution lay to the political right, with the long-term aim of restructuring the Republic in a manner that would favour the military, industrial and landowning elite. From 1930 onwards, the president would experiment with a less democratic and more authoritarian style of government, using and abusing his constitutional emergency powers. As has been noted by many historians of the period, the final crisis of the Weimar Republic invested considerable and unusual historical power and agency in a few key personalities that had in their hands the fate of Germany.[1] President Hindenburg was the ultimate arbiter of German politics in this period and it was his decisions more than anyone else's that ultimately led the country down a dark path that would end with war and genocide.

Presidential government

Thanks to Schleicher's scheming and the harsh economic realities of the Depression, the Grand Coalition had collapsed and Heinrich Brüning came to power as Hindenburg's new chancellor on 30 March 1930. The Centre Party leader headed a minority administration that quite consciously was going to experiment in bending the constitution in a presidential direction, for the chancellor had the confidence of the head of state, but it was a very real possibility that Brüning would not win majority support in the Reichstag. Furthermore, Hindenburg had made it clear to Brüning when he entrusted him with forming a government that the chancellor would have access to the emergency powers the president held thanks to Article 48 of the constitution in order to solve the economic challenges Germany faced. As L.E. Jones has argued, the new government was the 'brainchild' of Schleicher but bore the 'indelible footprint' of Hindenburg, who, despite the chancellor supposedly having the prerogative to name a cabinet, had chosen some of his political favourites for key positions.² No less than six holders of the Iron Cross from the Great War were to serve under the field marshal, showing the president (and Schleicher's) preference for military men. Groener, of course, had to be retained at the Defence Ministry and there was a clear preference for the conservative rebels who were defying Hugenberg's leadership of the DNVP. The up-and-coming Gottfried Treviranus, having just turned 39, was made minister for the Occupied Territories, just a few months after breaking with the Nationalist Party. He would soon set up, with Count Kuno von Westarp, the Conservative People's Party (KVP), the latest moderate right group to leave the DNVP. Meanwhile, Martin Schiele, head of the Reich Rural League (RLB) and a stringent critic of Hugenberg, was enlisted as agriculture minister by the president before Brüning had even been appointed.³ With a mandate to save the East Elbian farmers (an objective that was close to Hindenburg's heart) Schiele was to implement an Eastern Aid programme of subsidies of 200 million Reichsmarks over five years. This flew in the face of Brüning's austerity agenda, and indeed the president intervened in the conflict between the new chancellor and Schiele in the latter's favour, promising to implement the agricultural aid programme by decree if necessary.⁴

In July, Schiele would also break with the DNVP, for whom he served as a Reichstag deputy, and join the Christian-Nationalist Peasants and Farmers' Party (CNBL), yet another breakaway group from the Nationalists. In addition, at Groener's insistence, the military was to be entirely shielded from the programme of cuts, and this policy certainly enjoyed the president's approval.⁵ With the exception of the liberal Catholic Joseph Wirth as Interior Minister, this was Hindenburg's rather than Brüning's cabinet, built around his vision of a right-wing unity government that excluded both the Social Democrats on the left and the intransigent Alfred Hugenberg on the right.⁶ It was still hoped by the president, Groener and Schleicher, and indeed Treviranus, that such a cabinet could find a right-of-centre parliamentary majority to support it, stretching from the Centre and Democrats through the moderate right to DNVP rebels and splinter groups by excluding the SPD from office and supporting agriculture.⁷ This would also serve to isolate Hugenberg and potentially result in either his removal as DNVP leader or the secession of the majority of his party to the nationalist rebel groups. There is no doubt that Hindenburg was taking a highly active political role in the fate of the Republic, despite the popular image of the Reich President as a passive and sometimes confused political actor. He was not merely using his powers of patronage, but also lending his immense prestige and constitutional power to an ambitious political project to remould the whole democratic system in a more authoritarian, or at least presidential, direction with a strong executive that would not be bound by the petty squabbling and shifting alliances of parliament. Quite deliberately, there was no coalition deal done before the cabinet took office and instead this was billed as a 'Hindenburg

Cabinet' – a new type of government based on the confidence of the president rather than the parties.[8]

Nevertheless, it would be Brüning who faced the day-to-day challenge of governing an increasingly beleaguered nation. He was well aware that the austerity programme he was determined to implement would be highly unpopular and result in material hardship for millions of Germans, but in the meantime he sought parliamentary backing for his government. Schleicher hoped that the increasing fragmentation of the DNVP would mean Hugenberg's party would be compelled to support the new cabinet in the Reichstag, thus paving the way for majority government for the time being.[9] This was essential given the cabinet had explicitly been formed to exclude the Social Democrats, meaning a majority could only be found by winning over the right. It must be said, however, that both the chancellor and the general, and indeed the president, lacked any concrete vision or programme; their aim was merely the maintenance of stability and balancing the budget. Brüning, having proclaimed himself bound by no party and answerable to the president, and all the while threatening a dissolution of the Reichstag, managed to secure the reluctant parliamentary backing of the DNVP in order to survive an early confidence vote tabled by the SPD on 3 April.[10]

The new chancellor spent the following months introducing a variety of financial measures, including an agrarian aid programme at the instance of Hindenburg, relying on dissidents in the Nationalist Party for his majority. His efforts to win the backing of Hugenberg and the whole DNVP failed quickly, not least because Hindenburg himself remained aloof and did not involve himself in his new cabinet's battle for survival. As Dorpalen has argued, although he was willing to lend his legal support to Brüning, he failed to provide the necessary political backing – he remained silent, detached and did not intervene in the tetchy negotiations with the DNVP leaders.[11] The only issue Hindenburg did publicly involve himself in at this time was a bitter dispute between the nationalist veterans' league Der Stahlhelm and the SPD-led Prussian government over paramilitary drills in the demilitarised Rhineland, an issue over which the president forced Prime Minister Braun to concede by threatening not to attend the celebrations for the Allied withdrawal. To some extent, this detachment was by mutual consent as it appears Brüning himself did not especially seek Hindenburg's intervention, and it suited the old man's passive personality.

As a result, the short phase of parliamentary government ended in July 1930. Brüning's first budget, which involved sweeping reform of the Reich's finances and a host of painful cuts, met firm opposition. Even within the coalition, the BVP objected to an increase in the beer tax, the Middle Class Party (WP) opposed an increase in the turnover tax, and most seriously, the finance minister, Paul Moldenhauer, resigned when his party (DVP) rejected what amounted to a poll tax.[12] An offer for talks from the Social Democrats was turned down, both because it would lose the cabinet backing from the right, and because its mandate from Hindenburg was specifically anti-socialist. Knowing he could not guide his budget through the Reichstag, but that he enjoyed the president's backing on the matter, Brüning instead promulgated the budget by decree using Hindenburg's Article 48 powers.[13] The Social Democrats now tabled a motion to suspend the government's emergency powers. Brüning once again looked to the right and hoped the DNVP would support him. Indeed, Hindenburg this time intervened, threatening either resignation or a dissolution of the Reichstag should the Nationalists overturn the budget.[14] Hugenberg was not cowed, asking the vote be delayed three months and demanding DNVP inclusion in both the Reich and Prussian governments in return for his support. Brüning refused – delay was unacceptable. As a result, with Hugenberg's support, the SPD motion carried by 236 votes to 221.

Incapable of getting his way, Brüning requested the president dissolve the Reichstag and thereby call new elections. While the chancellor spent the campaign portraying himself as a heroic defender of democracy and order (a tactic undermined by his own lack of charisma), the moderate right parties that formed the mainstay of his coalition wrapped themselves in Hindenburg's banner. Unsurprisingly, the three parties that had broken from the Nationalists – the CNBL, CSVD and KVP – all embraced Hindenburg and his image and myth in an attempt to win right-wing voters away from their traditional DNVP home. The Conservative People's Party (KVP) of Westarp and Treviranus was most vocal in this stance, arguing that this election was essentially a referendum on the president and his attempt to overturn 'irresponsible parliamentarianism'.[15] The People's Party also saw the election as 'For or against Hindenburg' and their campaign slogan was *Mit Hindenburg für Deutschlands Rettung* (To Germany's rescue with Hindenburg). Even the State Party, which, in their former incarnation as the Democrats, had campaigned against Hindenburg in 1925, now wrapped themselves in the Hindenburg banner.[16] There existed therefore a temporary consensus among the otherwise fractured moderate right, united behind the personality of Hindenburg and the concept of a presidential regime under the field marshal that would steer Germany through the Depression and remould, or at least reinterpret, the failing Weimar system. For ease, we shall term this broad coalition of moderate and centre-right/right parties that backed Brüning as the 'Hindenburg Bloc', for the major unifying force between this otherwise fractious group of parties was their loyalty to the president. It must be noted that no organisation or formal alliance existed with this label or any other and there was no joint ticket in the 1930 election, rather all these parties hoped to benefit through association with the Hindenburg brand. The passivity of the president himself, in both the campaign and in abortive negotiations behind the scenes to create a formal 'Hindenburg Bloc', doomed both to failure. As a result, the government platform was confused to say the least, with each coalition party offering a different message; most notably on the future of the Republic, the role of the Social Democrats and foreign policy. Brüning, the Centre Party and his DVP foreign minister Julius Curtius struck a considerably more moderate tone than the former Nationalists Schiele, Westarp and Treviranus. While Curtius advocated a cautious foreign policy, Treviranus called for a revision of the German-Polish border, and as Brüning promised to save democracy, Schiele was telling voters he hoped the Weimar system would soon collapse.[17]

Hindenburg did not make a single public statement during the election, despite his personal sympathy for the new KVP and moderate Nationalists like Schiele, allowing this confusion to spiral. The president and his circle, as well as a number of concerned political figures, were, as always, keen to keep the field marshal (and his myth) above the tawdry political fray and maintain the fiction of his nonpartisan status.[18] Unsurprisingly, therefore, the presidential cabinet failed to win the support of factions that the president himself hoped to win over, most notably the DNVP and Stahlhelm. His failure to support his own political project was to have terrible consequences. Far from a strong new executive that could tackle the crisis, the 'Hindenburg Cabinet' appeared more like the typical, indecisive and divided coalition government that Germans were growing increasingly weary of. Radical change and strong leadership were what the German people wanted, and the government did not appear to be offering it. Deprived of Hindenburg's explicit backing and undiminished aura, the president's cabinet was in for a rude awakening.

The decision to call an early election was disastrous for the Weimar Republic. Held on 14 September 1930, the results created a political earthquake and totally disrupted Brüning, Schleicher and Hindenburg's plans. After the 1928 high-water mark for the Social Democrats, the new government hoped for a right-wing recovery to alter the balance of the Reichstag and end the parliamentary stalemate that had developed in July. Instead, the major parties of the right, the crumbling DNVP and the Stresemann-less DVP, suffered serious losses, losing more than 3 million votes and forty-seven seats between them.[19] Brüning's Centre Party recovered a handful of seats and the new splinter parties of the moderate right gained small parliamentary delegations (the CNBL nineteen seats, CSVD fourteen, the KVP a disappointing four). However, the chief winners were the Communists, who gained twenty-three seats, and most of all the Nazi Party, which surged from just twelve seats to 107, becoming the second biggest party in the Reichstag behind the SPD. The Nazis' success took their rivals completely by surprise; after all, the party had been nowhere just two years before, winning just 2.6 per cent of the vote in 1928. The onset of the Great Depression had clearly had a huge impact on the political preferences of German voters, and Nazi support was strongest amongst those who had suffered the most in recent years: farmers, small business owners, craftsmen and lower civil servants who had seen their salaries slashed. Many of these voters believed a Nazi victory would deliver a better material life and revive the economy. Even more important, perhaps, what the Weimar parties could not grasp was that a huge element of the Nazis' appeal was to those disillusioned with democracy, the party system and parliament itself, and especially the lower middle-class flocked to nationalism in the face of the apparent failure of the liberal democratic order.[20] Although both Catholic and industrial working-class communities had to some extent been immune to the NSDAP's draw, the party had made very considerable gains in Protestant Germany, especially in the rural north and east, winning agricultural labourers, artisans and those employed by medium-sized businesses to their banner.[21] The Nazi Party organisation had grown considerably in size and strength over the previous few years (the party had 389,000 members by the end of the year[22]) and it had successfully appealed during the campaign both to the apathetic and non-political as the party that best represented 'Christian-German culture', the champion of ordinary people and also to the middle classes as their best hope to defend themselves against 'Marxism'.[23]

Whatever the causes, there remained the issue of what to do about the Nazi surge. For the time being, the long-term objectives of the president, his chancellor and General von Schleicher remained the same: save the economy, achieve revision of Versailles and win the support of the political right for the government. None of these tasks were easy, and the challenge facing Brüning was all the greater for the fact that although he had the backing of almost all the parties of the political centre ground and moderate right, this 'Hindenburg Bloc' commanded barely more than 200 seats in a Reichstag that required 289 for a majority. Despite having the support of the major parties of the centre/centre-right, namely the Catholic Centre, State Party and People's Party, as well as the Bavarian BVP and a host of smaller parties on the right, namely the WP, KVP, CNBL and CSVD, Brüning's was a minority government that was worryingly short of parliamentary backing. While under no illusions that he may have to govern using Article 48, the chancellor had hoped the minor moderate right parties would win a solid block of deputies in the election that would bolster his political position. In reality, they had won just sixty seats between them and it had been the Nazis who had profited from the fragmentation of the Nationalists.[24]

In October, Brüning talked to both Hitler and the Nationalist leader Hugenberg in the hope of winning their backing for his financial policies, but the meeting with the Führer only illustrated the incompatibility of the two men and Hugenberg obstinately demanded the removal of the SPD from power in the state of Prussia as the price for the DNVP's support.[25] This left Brüning totally reliant on President Hindenburg, both to maintain his position as chancellor and to pass legislation of practically any kind, and forced the administration to take on an ever more presidential style.[26] Although Hindenburg was disappointed by the failure of the talks with the Nationalists, he was less concerned about the Nazi refusal to back Brüning. Hitler had demanded the Interior and Defence ministries, a price the president was decidedly unwilling to pay, and, moreover, he had a strong dislike of both Hitler and his party as emotional rabble-rousers, the very antithesis of Prussian order.[27] Additionally, to survive votes of no confidence and to prevent Article 48 decrees being overturned, the government had to enter into a policy that was to prove highly controversial with the left, the National Opposition on the right, within the 'Hindenburg Bloc' and with Hindenburg himself – cooperation with the SPD. Brüning rejected the suggestion of a revival of the Grand Coalition from Prussian Prime Minister Otto Braun among others, fearing it would only expose the 'Hindenburg Bloc' to further attacks from the National Opposition – the Nazis and Nationalists – as proxies of Marxism. Also, it was unlikely all the rightist parties in Brüning's coalition, not least the DVP, would accept social democratic participation in the cabinet and Hindenburg himself was also determinedly opposed. Instead, in a series of informal meetings in September and October, Brüning secured the 'toleration' of the SPD.[28] What toleration meant was a policy of passive support from the Social Democrats; they would take no part in Brüning's government, or vote for their policies. But equally, fearing democracy was under threat from the Nazi surge, the SPD leadership opted to back Brüning as the 'lesser evil' until the Depression passed, and so for now they would abstain in any attempts to repeal presidential decrees or no confidence motions.[29]

With the largest party in the Reichstag effectively taken out of the equation, Brüning had some respite, although he could not count on the Social Democrats to back his legislation in parliament, so presidential decrees would have to be his primary method of governing. Furthermore, although pleased no concessions had been made to the SPD, it did irritate Hindenburg that his government of the right was reliant on the largest party of the left, on 'Marxists', to survive.[30] Political fixer General Kurt von Schleicher favoured inviting Hitler's National Socialists into the government in a junior role within the cabinet, giving them perhaps two or three ministries. Not only would this ensure that Brüning had a parliamentary majority behind him, it was part of a wider 'taming strategy' that Schleicher quickly developed and would be the foundation of his political thinking, and scheming, over the coming years. Effectively, Schleicher hoped that the Nazis' mass support could be utilised by the right-wing political and military elite that he, and indeed Hindenburg, represented. By gaining the backing of the Nazis, Schleicher reckoned that Hindenburg and Brüning's presidential administration could amass the popular legitimacy necessary for constitutional change in order to move Germany away from parliamentary democracy towards a more authoritarian system that would protect army and industrial interests.[31] Equally important, Schleicher believed that the Nazis had to be brought into government in order to temper their extremism. The burden of high office and the compromises necessary in coalitions would surely water down their political radicalism and also deny them the advantage of being in opposition and shouting from the sidelines. Just as the Social Democrats had gone from being a subversive, anti-regime party in the Kaiserreich to a pillar of the political order after the German revolution had brought them to power in 1918, so Schleicher hoped the responsibilities of government would tame Nazi fanaticism.[32] Initially, however, Brüning opposed integrating the Nazis into his cabinet and persuaded Schleicher that, for the moment, it was best to keep them as a threat to the Western Allies in negotiations over rearmament and reparations; 'give us concessions or the German people will elect a madman like Hitler'. Schleicher, for now, was convinced by this view and actually persuaded Hindenburg against inviting the Nazis to join the government.[33]

Nevertheless, Schleicher remained committed to his taming strategy, outlining it to a gathering of Reichswehr generals on 25 October 1930. Rather than a threat, he told them, the Nazis were the only party who could draw support away from the Communists and therefore suppressing them would be counterproductive. Furthermore, he argued that many Nazi supporters were patriots or those devastated by the Depression (not least the middle classes and East Elbian farmers) and the government needed to win these groups to its flag, preferably by co-opting the Nazi movement.[34] Schleicher's belief that the Nazis could, and indeed must, be tamed would shape the policies of Hindenburg's government for the next two years, with disastrous consequences.

The presidential government soon hit further problems. By the autumn, it had become clear that the situation in the agricultural sector was getting worse rather than better and the Eastern Aid rescue package introduced by Brüning and Hindenburg favourite Martin Schiele had proved totally inadequate, at least in the eyes of the landowners. The strong reactionary faction within Schiele's Reich Rural League ousted him as the organisation's leader in February 1931 and shifted the RLB into alliance with the far-right National Opposition. Nevertheless, Hindenburg remained faithful to his favourite Schiele and defended the government's agricultural policy to his friends and lobbyists.[35] The Reich Party of the Middle Class (WP), under pressure from its grassroots (who were feeling the full impact of the Depression), disappointed by Brüning's budget and opposed to cooperation with the Social Democrats, broke with the government, with their leader Johann Viktor Bredt resigning from the cabinet in December 1930.[36]

Attacks from the right on the government, and on the person of Hindenburg, were relentless, particularly on the issue of cooperation with the SPD at state and Reich level. Already in the autumn/winter of 1930, the Nationalists had begun efforts to force the president to turn rightwards. How could a 'Hindenburg Cabinet' cooperate with a Socialist government in Prussia? How could a 'Hindenburg Cabinet' include liberal-minded members such as Joseph Wirth and Julius Curtius? The Nationalist deputy and Junker landowner Elard von Oldenburg-Januschau, a personal friend of the president, informed the Reichstag that the 'Prussian government does not have the confidence of agriculture'.[37] There is some evidence that this campaign was beginning to bear fruit, for Hindenburg did indeed consider sacking Wirth and replacing Curtius with the German ambassador to Britain, the aristocratic diplomat Baron Konstantin von Neurath. Brüning, however, was able to persuade the president to stick to his guns, for now.[38] In the new year, knowing that Brüning could not be removed by a confidence vote, the Nazis and Nationalists began a campaign of disruption and obstruction to prevent the smooth functioning of the Reichstag, thereby discrediting the government and the whole Weimar system. The Nazis defied a ban on political uniforms in the chamber when all 107 NSDAP deputies appeared in their brown shirts. An anti-Semitic pogrom in Berlin soon followed, and these disruptive actions culminated in a walkout by the so-called National Opposition in February 1931.[39] The Nazis' and Hugenberg's DNVP, worryingly joined by three deputies from Schiele's CNBL, pledged to boycott the Reichstag in protest against procedural changes brought in to limit Nazi disruption. With the legislature in chaos, Brüning secured a lengthy parliamentary recess that was to last from March until October 1931.[40] During this time, Brüning would be able to promulgate decrees through Hindenburg without the danger of interference from the Reichstag, moving Germany once again in a presidential, even authoritarian, direction.

Unfortunately, the economic situation continued to deteriorate. The chancellor's economic policies were based on the notion of a balanced budget and retrenchment, both to avoid the horrors of inflation that had so recently shaken Germany, and to restore the competitiveness of the German economy (which was so reliant on exports) in the world market. Undoubtedly, however, Brüning's economic policies only served to deepen the Depression significantly. By cutting government spending, wages and unemployment benefits and hiking taxes, demand in the economy continued to dwindle and joblessness continued to skyrocket. The official figure of registered unemployed rose dramatically during Brüning's tenure, from 1.6 million in October 1929 at the beginning of the crash, to an eye-watering 6.1 million by February 1932 (40 per cent of the insured workforce).[41] Furthermore, the true unemployed figure, while unknowable, was several million higher as many women and young people not eligible for unemployment insurance were not counted in official figures. The agricultural aid programme also meant food prices remained high while the purchasing power of ordinary Germans collapsed thanks to benefit cuts.[42]

The result was deprivation and hardship on a horrifying scale. The Nazis successfully branded Brüning 'the hunger chancellor' and the presidential government's popularity melted away as the Depression continued to worsen. In March 1931, word leaked of Foreign Minister Curtius's plans for a customs union with Austria which might bolster the economy and please nationalists, but as a violation of Versailles, the union provoked an international outcry, scotching negotiations for a considerable loan from the French government.⁴³ Brüning was actually hoping that this would happen, for he wanted the fiscal situation to worsen so that he might persuade the Allied powers to suspend or even cancel war reparations. This policy bore fruit, for Brüning was able to secure the backing of first, British Prime Minister Ramsay MacDonald, and then, US President Herbert Hoover. A formal letter from Hindenburg to his counterpart in the United States secured a moritorium of the hated reparations in June 1931, and payments would never be resumed.⁴⁴ Hindenburg, despite not writing the letter, took great pride in its victory. The famous letter read:

> The misery of the German people ... compels me to take the unusual step, Mr. President, to address myself to you personally. The German people has suffered for years the greatest difficulties, they reached the limit [of the bearable] during the last winter. The economic recovery which had been expected this spring has not taken place. I have therefore taken steps, on the basis of the emergency powers which the German Constitution has given me, to assure the execution of the most urgent tasks with which the Government is faced and to provide the necessary means of subsistence for the unemployed. The measures which I have taken affect radically all economic and social conditions and demand the heaviest sacrifices from all parts of the population ... [You must take steps] by which an immediate change in the situation so threatening to both Germany and the rest of the world could be brought about.⁴⁵

However, in turning down economic aid in order to worsen the crisis and secure Allied concessions, Brüning was playing with fire. He had tolerated greater suffering for his people in exchange for a foreign policy victory, but this only played into the hands of the extremists who prayed on the people's suffering, not least the Nazis.⁴⁶ The collapse of the customs union proposal had been devastating for the banking industries of both Austria and Germany and the German central bank had lost as much as a billion Reichsmarks in gold and foreign currency as a result.⁴⁷ A surprise declaration of bankruptcy of an Austrian bank led in July to the swift collapse of the Darmstadt and National Bank and drastic emergency measures from the government designed to prevent a run on the mark, including the closing of all banks for several days.⁴⁸ Unemployment continued to rise while confidence collapsed still further.

Increasingly, the powerful interests that had supported the presidential regime had turned against it. The agrarian lobby was dissatisfied with the aid programme, despite Hindenburg and Schiele strongarming further concessions and agricultural tariffs out of a reluctant cabinet.⁴⁹ The captains of heavy industry, radicalised by the crisis, sought an end to the extensive Weimar welfare provision and to compulsory arbitration with the trade unions, both of which they saw as limits on their profits and barriers to making their businesses more competitive.⁵⁰ Neither of these measures was possible unless Brüning broke with the champions of labour, the SPD, the party whose toleration was essential to the survival of his government. The industrial lobby therefore pushed for a shift to the right and for a government reliant on the support of the National Opposition rather than the Social Democrats. Throughout the summer of 1931, Hindenburg had increasingly agitated for a shift to the political right. Before the banking crisis, he had demanded of Brüning a more 'national-minded' (read nationalistic) cabinet, including the removal of Wirth and Curtius, following the foreign minister's customs union failure.⁵¹ Brüning had managed to persuade the president that the time was not ripe while negotiations with the Allies were ongoing but it was becoming increasingly clear that the chancellor faced an uphill struggle to maintain Hindenburg's confidence. While the experiment in presidential government was supposed to provide stability, Brüning was effectively at the mercy of Hindenburg and his whims. To some extent, he was living on borrowed time. The president was not yet determined to replace his chancellor, but he was concerned about the lack of progress in tackling the economic crisis and believed that the Social Democrats and wider labour movement had to be removed from political power in order to facilitate the necessary fiscal reforms, and a rapprochement with the right. To this end, Brüning would have to end his cooperation with the SPD grounded in their toleration policy. In its stead, the president was keen for Brüning to win the parliamentary backing of the National Opposition – namely the DNVP and NSDAP. Then, a true government of the right could be formed, potentially with Nazi and Nationalist participation.⁵²

Hindenburg, despite spending the summer at his rural Neudeck estate, was feeling increasingly under pressure from the radical right. An article in the Nazi press had wondered how such a 'bumbler' could become first a war leader then a president, while hostile organised crowds of brownshirts had confronted him throughout his time in the country, including at a visit to the Tannenberg battlefield and at his annual hunt in Bavaria, where he had lost his cool and shouted at the Nazi protestors that 'Today men are governing and not rowdies!'⁵³ Despite his defiance, Hindenburg was clearly feeling the strain, and this was hardly helped by the fact his rural aristocratic friends and neighbours were unrelentingly hostile to the 'Jesuit' Brüning and his government. Desperate to move things forward, Hindenburg had met with the Nationalist leader Alfred Hugenberg, whom he had refused to see for eighteen months, and begged him to meet Brüning and join him in government, since the chancellor was 'inspired by the noblest motives ... and was altogether one of the finest men whom he had ever met in his long life'.⁵⁴ However, once again Hugenberg demanded the impossible in the form of the removal of the SPD from office in Prussia. The meeting ended without agreement, although the president did promise to try to persuade Brüning to create a new cabinet that would include the National Opposition. Taking their lead from the president, in August the Defence

Ministry under Groener and Schleicher drew up three potential routes forward. The government could ditch the Social Democrats and bring in the National Opposition parties, it could align more firmly with the SPD and disregard the National Opposition to its right, or it could simply govern without reference to the Reichstag, forgetting the need for a majority at all.[55] Although Schleicher used his influence with the president that summer to shore up Brüning's position, the general was already looking to the future and there can be no doubt he favoured the first option. Taming the Nazis was back on the agenda.

The president looks to the right

With Brüning's presidential mandate clearly in peril, the far right increasingly scented blood. It was well known Hindenburg wanted a decisively right-wing cabinet and the National Opposition parties felt their time had come to take power and dismantle democracy from within. What was holding the radical right back was endemic disunity and bickering. While the DNVP and NSDAP were keen to sweep away rival parties, the leaders of their key paramilitary ally, the Stahlhelm veterans' association with 500,000 members, wanted a broad front of all 'national-minded' parties, including the moderate right that currently backed Brüning.[56] There was also some concern among the Nationalists about the Nazis' ambitions, especially since their surprise success in the 1930 election. During the spring and summer of 1931, the Stahlhelm leaders had put their desire for rightist unity into practice by organising an alliance of the DVP, DNVP, WP, CNBL and NSDAP to campaign for the dissolution of the Prussian parliament. As we have seen, the social democratic-led government in Prussia was a particularly sore point for nationalists, agrarians and heavy industry. By forcing new elections to be called in Germany's largest state, the National Opposition hoped to break up the SPD-Centre administration of Prussian Prime Minister Otto Braun and thereby drive a wedge between Brüning and the Social Democrats at the Reich level, for the chancellor would not break with the SPD while his own party was in coalition with them in Prussia.[57]

Although the campaign would end in failure, with the combined forces of the National Opposition and Communist Party only winning the support of 38.3 per cent of the total Prussian electorate (a majority was required), the participation of the DVP and CNBL, who were members of Brüning's government, showed a worrying lack of unity in the 'Hindenburg Bloc'. Both these parties would drift into the orbit of the National Opposition and eventually call for an end to the Republic and the exclusion of the SPD from political power. At the end of August, Brüning (at Hindenburg's behest) met with DNVP leader Alfred Hugenberg to explore the president's desire for the two to collaborate, thereby bringing the National Opposition into office alongside the moderate right. The chancellor went as far as to offer to step aside if the National Opposition was ready to assume the responsibility of governing, although the DNVP did not take his words seriously and Brüning was shocked when Hugenberg refused to commit himself to supporting Hindenburg's impending re-election. The meeting ended in acrimony and harsh words, with the chancellor refusing to give any ground to Hugenberg.[58] Increasingly, the far right now saw Brüning as their enemy rather than a potential collaborator. Given Hindenburg's preference to include these elements in his government, Brüning was therefore living on borrowed time. Now Hindenburg's son, his aide-de-camp Oskar, joined the growing chorus for a nationalist government without Brüning, even if Hindenburg himself remained committed to his chancellor. In order to heighten the pressure on the Reich President, Hugenberg now devised with Hitler a National Opposition demonstration in force. The intention was to hold a rally in Bad Harzburg that would demonstrate the unity of the radical right and their preparedness and suitability to be entrusted with governmental power. If all rightist forces could show a united front, Hindenburg might finally relent in his support for Brüning and give in to his desire for a truly nationalist cabinet.

At the rally on 11 October, great parades of Stahlhelm and SA stormtroopers were reviewed and addressed by Hitler, Hugenberg, and the Stahlhelm leaders Seldte and Duesterberg, united in their attacks on the current government. Other speakers included former central bank head Hjalmar Schacht, various Great War generals (including the retired von Seeckt, representing the DVP), and the leaders of the Reich Rural League, Pan-German League and various patriotic associations. There were also representatives of the WP and rebels from the CNBL, highlighting the haemorrhaging of support from the 'Hindenburg Cabinet' of minor right parties. The declaration of a new Harzburg Front between these political and paramilitary forces promised a new broad, united front of nationalists who might cooperate in a future government.[59] However, the unity displayed at Harzburg was only skin-deep. There was growing suspicion and rivalry between Hugenberg and Hitler (both of whom saw themselves as future chancellors) and the Stahlhelm was also divided, their deputy leader Theodor Duesterberg being deeply distrustful of Hitler. At the rally itself, Hitler had behaved petulantly, receiving the march-past of the SA but leaving the stage when the Stahlhelm marched. In reality, the aims of the DNVP, NSDAP and Stahlhelm were contradictory and each saw themselves as the leading element of the rightist alliance.[60] Not only that, but the various tirades unleashed against Brüning and his supporters at the rally only served to highlight the unbridgeable gap between the moderate and extreme right. Parliamentary arithmetic dictated that the right-wing cabinet that Hindenburg sought would require the cooperation of both Harzburg and 'Hindenburg Bloc' parties, yet the rally had seemed to undermine the possibility of such an alliance.

Just three days after the Harzburg rally, the Reichstag reconvened after its lengthy recess, with the National Opposition returning for the first time since their February walkout. The radical right fully expected to be entrusted with forming a government in the near future. Hindenburg himself was at a crossroads. As we have seen, there was growing pressure from a variety of sources to move the government to the right, with the president being the most prominent and influential advocate for such a scheme. Pyta argues that Hindenburg, having tried and failed in the summer of 1931 to identify a potential successor, threw himself into the task of finally achieving German unity and stability with fresh vigour and purpose.[61] His vision of unifying the nation did not include the political left, however, and was focused on bringing the National Opposition into government and achieving the elusive goal of unity on the fractured German right. The pressure on the president to move Brüning on only grew with the final collapse in September of the aforementioned German-Austrian customs union plan, an unceasing letter-writing campaign of the Pan-German Prince Otto zu Salm-Horstmar and a sharp critique of the chancellor's economic policies published jointly by eleven leading business organisations at the end of the month.[62] An attempt by the CNBL's Hans Schlange-Schöningen to forge the gaggle of moderate-right parties (the mainstay of the 'Hindenburg Bloc') into a united front behind Brüning floundered due to the ambiguous stance of the DVP and figures within the CNBL itself towards the chancellor.[63]

On 5 October, Hindenburg met Brüning and hijacked a meeting about their latest emergency decree to again demand a shift to the right. The conference was stormy, for Brüning was not prepared to join with the National Opposition parties. He insisted that if Hindenburg wanted a government of the radical right he was well within his rights as president to appoint one, but that he (Brüning) would take no part in it, although the Centre Party would back such a cabinet in the Reichstag. Brüning also highlighted the National Opposition parties' failure to publicly endorse Hindenburg's re-election, which was due in the new year.[64] In a second meeting, on 7 October, the chancellor was even more frank. Either Hindenburg accept his chancellor's freedom of action or else he would resign. Hindenburg responded with decidedly moderate cabinet demands. He asked that Brüning replace Foreign Minister Curtius, Interior Minister Wirth and another Centre Party moderate, Transport Minister Theodor von Guérard (in order to reduce Catholic representation). Brüning accepted these proposals, but found it difficult to find replacements with suitably rightist credentials, given the stubborn refusal of the Nationalists to cooperate and the disunity among the smaller parties. Representatives of the Ruhr heavy industry and the DVP's Ernst Scholz turned down cabinet posts and, in the end, the new government unveiled on 9 October was striking only for its resemblance to the previous one.[65]

The former defence minister and Democrat Otto Gessler met Brüning and was offered the Interior Ministry, but Gessler proposed suspending parliament and launching an all-out struggle against the extremist parties. Brüning sent Gessler to Hindenburg to outline his plan but the president rejected it out of hand, not least because Schleicher believed it would result in civil war.[66] Instead, the current defence minister, Wilhelm Groener, was handed responsibility for the Interior Ministry as well while Brüning took the Foreign Ministry for himself, as he continued to strive for major revisions of the Versailles treaty. Groener extracted a promise from the chancellor to support a scheme by which all the paramilitary leagues would be amalgamated into a national, state-run militia, which would come to be known as the *Wehrsport* programme and was a vital plank of the army's taming strategy towards the Nazis.[67] An unintended consequence of the reshuffle was that with Groener stretched between two ministries, his subordinate General von Schleicher would gain increased political freedom and begin to act as de facto defence minister.[68] A technocrat from the chemical industry, Hermann Warmbold, was made economics minister, while Gottfried Treviranus was moved off Eastern Aid to the Transport Ministry, with Hans Schlange-Schöningen of the CNBL joining the cabinet to take on the agrarian challenge. All in all, this appeared as fiddling while Rome burnt, for the changes would not satisfy the National Opposition, the industrial, agricultural and military elite, or the Reich President himself.[69]

With the defection of the DVP, the cabinet was more reliant than ever on the goodwill of the president, and by extension, Schleicher. The president in particular was dissatisfied almost immediately at the new government, for it singularly failed to win the backing of industry and agriculture, the two groups that were exerting acute pressure on him. Hindenburg forced Brüning to set up an economic council to coordinate with these special interests, but it had collapsed within three weeks of its creation.[70] But what was the alternative for the president? Hindenburg had met Hitler for the first time at the Presidential Palace on 10 October, the day before the Harzburg rally. Schleicher had actually met Hitler several days beforehand and Hitler had indicated his willingness to join a Brüning cabinet.[71] Brüning, who, along with Hermann Göring, was present for the meeting between the field marshal and the lance corporal, arranged it for tactical purposes; he hoped that meeting Hitler would demonstrate to the president the unsuitability of the far right for high office.[72] The Nazi leader left a decidedly poor impression on the old man, boring him with an hour-long monologue, after which Hindenburg criticised the rowdiness of the SA brownshirts, which he had experienced first-hand that summer. After he had left, Hindenburg complained about how uncivilised Hitler had been and deemed him ill-suited to a cabinet post, exactly as Brüning had anticipated.[73] The next day, not only was the Führer petulant and unaccommodating at Harzburg, undermining the rally's purpose of radical right unity, but Hindenburg told Brüning he resented Hitler's refusal to cooperate with the government and did not wish to meet the 'Bohemian Corporal' again.[74] The most famous quote to arise from the meeting was Hindenburg's supposed jest that Hitler was suited to no higher role than postmaster general, 'so that he can lick me from behind

– on my stamps' (the Reich President's image was on the stamps of the era).[75] On the other hand, the president did write to his daughter on 14 October that although the National Opposition had missed their first chance, they may well get a second one.[76]

Attention now turned to the reconvened Reichstag, where the National Opposition were determined to table a vote of no confidence in the chancellor. The 'Hindenburg Bloc' that had backed the presidential cabinet in 1930, stretching from the Centre Party rightwards, had all but disintegrated and Brüning was in serious danger of being ousted. He knew he could count on the SPD, Centre, BVP, DStP, KVP and CSVD, but this was twenty-one short of a majority. The DVP had jumped ships and was now, under pressure from industry, determined to oust the chancellor. The agrarian CNBL, despite the presence of Schiele and Schlange-Schöningen in the cabinet, was persuaded by the Reich Rural League (and their own grassroots) to support a no confidence motion. The Reich Party of the Middle Class (WP), with a crucial twenty-three seats, was badly divided in their attitude, critical of Brüning's economic policies but uncertain about what the National Opposition were promising, and indeed, Brüning picked up on this theme of the Harzburg Front's disunity, ambiguity and lack of vision in a blistering address to the Reichstag on 16 October.[77] Following his speech, the parliament voted 295–270 against the no confidence motion, with the chancellor securing the backing of the WP and a handful of DVP rebels. The National Opposition tabled a further eight motions seeking to undermine Brüning, from revoking the government's emergency powers to dissolving the Reichstag to bring about fresh elections, but all were defeated.[78] The chancellor had survived this dramatic test of strength and he adjourned parliament until February, winning another, brief, stay of execution.

Brüning's hold on power remained weak, for not only was the president running out of patience, but his chief advisor, General Kurt von Schleicher, was beginning to consider alternatives to the man he had groomed for the chancellorship. Schleicher had hoped that the 'Hindenburg Cabinet' would rally the right behind the president and the government, thereby taking the wind out of the sails of extremists like Hitler and Hugenberg.[79] The opposite had in fact occurred; the government was more beleaguered than ever, the Harzburg parties and organisations were increasingly raucous, while the Communists also appeared to be gaining support among the legions of unemployed. Now, Schleicher feared civil war was a real possibility and he envisaged a nightmare scenario of 'red' and 'brown' risings, rendered even more dangerous due to evidence of growing Nazi sympathies within the officer corps. As a result, in the autumn of 1931, Schleicher increasingly came to believe the time to employ his taming strategy and bring the Nazis into the fold was drawing near.[80] To this end, the general persuaded Defence Minister Groener to lift the ban on Nazi members serving in the armed forces, cultivated contact with Ernst Röhm, met Hitler, as we have seen, and invested much time and effort over the next year into the aforementioned *Wehrsport* programme. The relationship between Brüning and Hindenburg had soured already in autumn 1931 with the cabinet reshuffle, after which Treviranus had conceded that the president no longer saw the chancellor as the saviour of Germany.

Brüning himself, with his cold, technical style, was increasingly alienating the old field marshal. To give just one example, when the two were riding in a train together to attend the launch of the first pocket battleship in May 1931, Hindenburg had praised his chancellor for securing parliamentary approval for the construction of a second. Instead of accepting the praise, Brüning had responded with a lengthy exposition of his government's economic and foreign policy objectives, which the chancellor later admitted had confused the president.[81] In the months following the reshuffle, there was hardly a cabinet went by without some complaint or request from Hindenburg – usually regarding agriculture or the army. It was at the president's behest that yet another tranche of aid for the eastern estates was rushed through, provoking the resignation of the agrarian representatives from the economic council due to the neglect of western and south German farmers.[82] Brüning remained hopeful that his government could survive in some form or another until elections were due in 1934. By then, the economic situation would surely have improved and, he hoped, he would have won considerable foreign policy victories in the form of revisions to Versailles.[83] There is likely no truth in the idea that at this time Brüning was planning a restoration of the monarchy; it appears that he and Treviranus only took up this cause after Hitler's seizure of power.[84]

Underpinning both Schleicher and Brüning's strategies, however, was Hindenburg's continuation in office. The president's seven-year term was due to expire next spring and furthermore, having just turned 84 and not in the best of health, the president was hardly in a fit state for a re-election campaign. The prospect of a draining campaign and the dragging of his name through the mud filled Hindenburg with dread and the issue of his re-election became yet another issue of contention with Brüning. He was also loath to run against the parties of the right, especially the Nationalists, who had persuaded him to take up the presidency in 1925. Ideally, Hindenburg's term could simply be extended. This would require a modification of the constitution and therefore the support of a two-thirds supermajority in the Reichstag. Given that the Social Democrats had indicated their willingness to tolerate another Hindenburg term (as a bulwark against fascist takeover), it would simply be a case of persuading the National Opposition to back such a motion.[85] Despite confident assurances from the chancellor, this was easier said than done, and in late 1931 and early 1932, the government was embroiled in negotiations with the Nazis and Nationalists in an attempt to secure their backing for renewing the president's mandate without the need to go to the polls. Schleicher arranged for the president to meet with Hermann Göring on 11 December to sound out the possibility of Nazi support. Göring, whom Hitler had tasked with cultivating relations with the conservative elite, struck a reassuring tone, assuring the president that the Nazis respected Brüning but could not tolerate his cooperation with the SPD and even hinting that the NSDAP would welcome the field marshal's term in office being extended.[86] Under the impression that the task would be easy, Hindenburg told Brüning on 5 January 1932 that he would only remain president if 'the office ... be laid in his hands as an accomplished fact, because he is not inclined or in a position to undertake a new election campaign'.[87] Furthermore, he stipulated that he would take no part in negotiations regarding his candidacy and, Hindenburg insisted, he would only run for re-election as a candidate of the right.[88] This meeting only added further urgency to negotiations, as it now appeared the chancellor's political future depended on him securing an extension to Hindenburg's term. On 7 January, Hitler met with Defence and Interior Minister Groener to hammer out the presidential issue, but Groener found the Nazi leader to be evasive regarding Hindenburg; the NSDAP had no intention of letting Brüning off the hook, but was not yet ready to publicly break with the president.[89] Brüning and Schleicher were brought into the talks, and although they conceded one of the Nazi conditions – Prussian elections were to be held on time that April – they refused to budge on Hitler's key demand of new Reichstag elections, which would surely only strengthen the Nazis' hand. Goebbels's diary reveals that the Nazis were in fact playing for time in these negotiations; they had no intention of permitting Hindenburg's term to be extended and merely wanted to string Brüning along so his failure would be all the more damaging.[90]

Nationalist leader Alfred Hugenberg joined the talks on 10 January and promptly torpedoed them by insisting on Brüning's sacking as chancellor as a precondition for DNVP support.[91] The fallout was public and acrimonious, and Hindenburg's secretary, Otto Meissner, now issued a threat to the cabinet, claiming the president would only run for re-election if he was only opposed by the Communists. This came after a private conference between Meissner and the National Opposition leaders, in which Hitler had demanded the sacking of Brüning, the appointment of a far-right government and fresh Reichstag elections, with a new parliament then extending Hindenburg's term.[92] It was now resoundingly clear that the Nazis and Nationalists had no intention of compromising with the presidential regime unless power was handed over entirely to them. Hindenburg deeply resented both the fact the National Opposition were placing demands and conditions on him, and that Brüning had failed to secure the extension of his term. It remained unclear whether he would be prepared to contest a presidential election.[93] Schleicher and Brüning now changed tack in their effort to secure the support of the radical right for a Hindenburg candidacy rather than an extension. They reached out to the veterans' associations, the nationalist Stahlhelm and the less ideological

Kyffhäuserbund, seeking their nomination of Hindenburg as president as a way of outflanking the National Opposition and splintering the Harzburg Front. Schleicher still hoped that Hindenburg might be re-elected as the leader of a united moderate and radical right, thereby facilitating the appointment of a rightist government that would include, but not be dominated by, the NSDAP.[94] This was, after all, a key condition that Hindenburg had set out at the beginning of January; he wanted to unequivocally be the candidate of the right. However, these negotiations also floundered, for although the leadership of both veterans' leagues were sympathetic, and Hindenburg was an honorary member of the Stahlhelm, the latter in particular refused to act without the sanction of their Harzburg allies, namely Hugenberg and Hitler.

Hitler deliberately dragged his feet over the next few weeks as he went through the process of securing German citizenship so that he would be eligible to run. Once again, the president, his circle and the government were united, this time against the devious and untrustworthy Hitler, who, it appeared, had been playing them all along.[95] Groener in particular, sensing the Führer's true intentions, abandoned the taming strategy (that his subordinate Schleicher so cherished) and told Hindenburg that it was unthinkable for a Prussian general to sack his chief of staff (meaning Brüning) on the eve of battle.[96] Brüning did indeed offer his resignation to the president on 27 January following his failure to rally the right behind Hindenburg's re-election, but the old man tearfully turned down the chancellor's offer, protesting, 'My dear, good friend, you cannot do that to me.'[97] Nevertheless, when Brüning asked him directly on 6 February, Hindenburg was still ambivalent about running, and that same day, Kurt von Schleicher tried to persuade Hugenberg to back the president in return for a change of chancellor, probably to Groener, and an offer of the vice chancellorship to the Nationalist leader. Hindenburg had ordered the general to again try to win the National Opposition's support for his presidency and he was willing to dispense with Brüning as chancellor in order to achieve this.[98] Hugenberg was keen to claim the Chancellery for himself and instead brought the Nazis back into the talks, wary that Schleicher might be trying to split the National Opposition. Inevitably, this resulted in deadlock as the Nazis demanded the chancellorship and Defence Ministry, terms that Hindenburg rejected, bringing an end to Schleicher's latest gambit to win over the far right.[99] Hindenburg himself received the Stahlhelm leaders Seldte and Duesterberg on 10 February but the meeting ended acrimoniously as they demanded concessions to the right and the president pounded his desk, insistent that great concessions had already been made and angered that the National Opposition appeared to be using him as a political bargaining chip.[100] As they left the conference, it transpired that the Stahlhelm leaders were unaware of the offer made by Schleicher to the National Opposition, and when they learnt the details, they declared themselves in favour and ready to back Hindenburg on the understanding that a Groener-led rightist government would take office in the near future.[101] With the Stahlhelm about to break ranks with the Harzburg Front, Hugenberg rushed to see the paramilitary leaders but Duesterberg insisted under no circumstances would the Stahlhelm publicly oppose Field Marshal von Hindenburg, telling the obstinate Hugenberg: 'The Stahlhelm will never stand against Hindenburg. It would be unbearable for the Stahlhelm if the Field Marshal made good on his threat to resign his honorary presidency [of the organisation].'[102]

However, Hugenberg and the DNVP were not prepared to break with their Nazi allies and the Stahlhelm was afraid to shatter the hollow unity of Harzburg, so Schleicher's offer was finally rejected. Desperate to avoid a rift with the war hero, Duesterberg wrote to Hindenburg the next day, proposing the president not run in the first round but, instead, only in the inevitable second round run-off where he might appear as a genuine national unity candidate. Hindenburg was utterly outraged, appalled at the suggestion the sitting president hang back in reserve, believing it beneath the dignity of his office.[103] Confusion and disunity continued to reign on the far right; a final attempt by Schleicher to win over the National Opposition by delaying the presidential election until after the Prussian State elections (which, it was predicted, would see the SPD lose control of the state) was rejected. Then, Göring surprised Hugenberg, Seldte and Duesterberg by demanding on 13 February that the Harzburg Front back Hitler's candidacy. Realising that the Nazis had played them all along and, having no intention of handing total power to the Führer, the DNVP and Stahlhelm agreed to nominate Theodor Duesterberg for the first round of the election. Their hope was that although Duesterberg had no chance of winning, by withdrawing in the second round, they might win concessions from Hindenburg in exchange for their support.[104]

Whatever vestiges of far-right unity the Harzburg rally had created, they were now well and truly dead, given the Nazis on the one hand and DNVP and Stahlhelm on the other were running competing candidates. Brüning had been right that the National Opposition could not be trusted and were not ready for government, while Hindenburg remained deeply frustrated at the right in general and the Stahlhelm in particular for their dithering. In contrast, even though the president remained non-committal, the campaign to re-elect Hindenburg had been gearing up since mid-January, with various parties and figures from the moderate left through to the moderate right announcing their support. Given he was not running as a candidate of a political party, Hindenburg's nomination in a presidential election required a popular petition to be signed by 20,000 voters. This effort was overseen by a cross-party committee headed by the apolitical Lord Mayor of Berlin Heinrich Sahm and their appeal was fronted by a variety of political and economic figures, including former Defence Ministers Gustav Noske and Otto Gessler, 1925 presidential candidate Karl Jarres, Bavarian militia leader Georg Escherich and several captains of industry and agrarian representatives. Launched on 1 February, in just two weeks the petition attracted over 3.6 million signatures, highlighting the latency of both Hindenburg's mythical appeal and his supposed non-partisan authority as a figure who stood above parties.[105] The KVP's Kuno von Westarp, a political friend of the president, presented him with a letter signed by 430 conservatives, landowners and old officers asking him to run again. Nevertheless, it was not until 15 February, when the leader of the Kyffhäuserbund met the president to inform him he would back his re-election, that Hindenburg finally announced his intention to run, convinced at last that he would not be perceived as the candidate of the left.[106] The supposedly non-political veterans' league told its members: 'Let us old soldiers place in our revered honorary president the trust he deserves and display the loyalty he has shown us. Let us not abandon our Hindenburg!'[107] The old field marshal fired off a series of letters to his friends among the aristocracy and officer corps, many of whom had put pressure on him to shift to the right. He cut a dejected and frustrated figure, angered both by the protracted and fruitless negotiations with the National Opposition and his portrayal as the candidate of the political left and centre, including in his letters examples of conservatives who had endorsed him.[108] In one such letter, the president summarised succinctly his deep frustration with the radical right:

> It became clear that the Harzburg Front was only a fiction – or more to the point that it never existed. To be sure, the groups that belonged to it were united in their rejection of the Brüning government, but because of their own disunity they were incapable of forming a government themselves. They weren't even capable of settling upon a single candidate for the Reich Presidential elections.
>
> I hope you can see from all of this that the assertion that it was I who resisted a government of the Right is absolutely false. It was not I – nor the Reich chancellor Brüning – who stood in the way of such a development but *solely the disunity of the Right*, its inability to come together even in the major points. It is deeply regrettable that the Right – as fragmented as it is – is led to the loss of influence and self-destruction by leaders driven by one-sided partisan ambitions.[109]

The stage was thus set for one of the most dramatic presidential elections in history, a showdown between two charismatic hero figures who projected themselves as saviours of the nation. It appeared that the fate of Germany hung in the balance, and the political schemes of Brüning and Schleicher certainly did. Would the German people opt for Nazi dictatorship or the continuation of the presidential republic?

The field marshal versus the lance corporal

In the public announcement of his candidacy on 16 February, Paul von Hindenburg told the nation it would have been irresponsible for him to 'leave his post' in a time of crisis and that running was his 'patriotic duty'.[110] The old man remained a national icon in 1932 and it could be argued that his first seven-year term, while clearly alienating many of his old supporters on the nationalist right, had added new layers to the Hindenburg myth. For Hindenburg was now not only the war hero, victor of Tannenberg, symbol of Prussian militarism and order – he was also seen as a guarantee of political stability, a guardian of the constitution, a safe pair of hands, a bipartisan father of the nation.[111] Rather comically, the frequent allusions to Tannenberg during the campaign drew a flurry of complaints from Ludendorff and his tiny circle, which were confidently ignored.[112] Different aspects of the Hindenburg myth appealed to different demographics and political factions, but interestingly, just as in 1925 when the republicans had venerated the person of Hindenburg but criticised his candidacy, so much of the right would campaign against the president while insisting they respected the field marshal and his war record. Nazi propagandist Joseph Goebbels provided a textbook demonstration of this tendency when he told local party leaders that the campaign must 'not be directed against the personality of y [Hindenburg], but rather against the system he represents. This system has to be fought most vigorously with all means available, whereas the personality of y should only be mentioned in the second instance.'[113] As Goltz had observed, the election, rather than a rational democratic process, became for many a question of loyalty or treachery towards the heroic Hindenburg, a dichotomy that suited the president's cause.[114] This would be a battle between two men who were portrayed as charismatic saviours of Germany; policy substance was light (from the Hindenburg camp non-existent), it was a pure clash of personalities.

The 1932 election was a bizarre case of inverted fronts, a 'reversal of voter coalitions'. For while Hindenburg had been the candidate of the nationalist right in 1925, in 1932 he effectively stood against the right as the candidate of the political centre ground, rallying moderates of all colours to his banner, while anti-republicans fiercely opposed him. In 1925 he had been the candidate of the nationalists; in 1932 he was opposed by the nationalists. The People's Bloc that had backed Wilhelm Marx in 1925, made up of the 'Weimar Coalition' of SPD, Centre and DDP, all now supported Hindenburg, having opposed him seven years earlier. Meanwhile, the Nazis and DNVP, Stahlhelm and Reich Rural League, who had all supported Hindenburg in 1925, all opposed him in 1932. The only parties that campaigned for Hindenburg in both elections were the DVP, WP and BVP, while conservative moderates who had defected from the DNVP in the late 1920s (the KVP, CSVD, CNBL), as well as the patriotic Young German Order, also backed the Reich President in both contests.[115] L.E. Jones has noted that German Catholics in particular, whether of the Centre

Party or BVP, were particularly vociferous in their support for and solidarity with the Hindenburg campaign, for the threat that the Nazis posed to Catholic institutions had long been recognised.[116] In summary, Hindenburg had gone from being a figurehead for anti-democratic forces to being seen as a guardian of the present order.

Despite strong ideological differences, the Social Democrats campaigned vigorously for the president, under the slogan *Smash Hitler, Vote Hindenburg*.[117] To some extent the period 1925–30 had convinced the SPD that, despite the departure from parliamentarianism since the appointment of Brüning, Hindenburg was a constitutional president whom they could trust to act as an 'imperturbable dam' against extremism. The SPD newspaper *Vorwärts* said of voting for the field marshal: 'if you don't do it out of love, do it out of hate.'[118] Otto Braun set out the social democratic case for Hindenburg in a letter to a party colleague:

> The next months will bring the decision. It must seem strange to you that I, as I indicated above, am supporting the candidacy of Hindenburg ... The presidential election, which is a crucial prelude to the Prussian elections, will decide whether Germany's future development will continue along the peaceful pathways of republican state life or if the German people will have to wade through a fascist valley of misery. With six million unemployed and countless more suffering and doubting the future, this struggle for the Republic will take place under the worst conceivable conditions, all the more so since the proletariat has been torn asunder into mass armies engaged in a fight to the finish in the truest sense of the word ... Realising that the political decisions of the next few weeks in Germany and Prussia will be decisive not just for the destiny of the German people but also for the future course of political developments in Europe, we are committed to salvaging for the Republic all we possibly can in light of the confusion that exists in the minds of all.[119]

The importance of the Social Democrats to Hindenburg's re-election cannot be overstated; the SPD held as many rallies for the president as all the other pro-Hindenburg parties combined and its Reichsbanner paramilitary organisation was the only pro-Hindenburg presence in the streets to counter the violence and intimidation of the Nazi SA and Communist Red Front.[120] The Iron Front antifascist alliance that the SPD had recently created alongside the Reichsbanner, trade unions and other affiliates was at its most active during the Hindenburg campaign, and although Iron Front and SPD rallies rarely extolled the virtues of the president, they were very clear about the threat of Nazism.[121] Heinrich Brüning campaigned tirelessly for the president, for his political survival was at stake. Addressing huge rallies across the country, the chancellor told audiences that Hindenburg was the nation's saviour and every vote against him was a vote against national unity.¹²² He had effectively fired the starting gun of the campaign in a Reichstag speech of 25 February in which he had directly attacked the supposed patriotism of the Nazis and lauded the Reich President:

> One thing alone, besides my trust in a higher Power, has sustained me during the difficult tasks of the last two years and rekindled my hopes again and again, and that is the fact that I could serve a man like President von Hindenburg ... Don't think that you can even approach the stature of a historic figure like this, and do not forget one thing: only the re-election of the President can make the world believe that the German people is still characterised by piety and by respect for its history, for tradition, and for the greatness of man.¹²³

There can be no doubt that the chancellor bore the brunt of the pro-Hindenburg campaign, speaking not just on behalf of the Catholic Centre and BVP, but also for the president's official campaign committee, and, given Hindenburg's own failure to address rallies or make speeches, it largely fell to Brüning to sell the Old Gentleman to the country.¹²⁴ The pressure that Brüning was under was highlighted when, just after announcing his decision to seek re-election, Hindenburg asked the chancellor to replace Groener as interior minister with an elderly aristocratic friend of no particular political distinction, Oskar von der Osten-Warnitz. Given that both Brüning and Osten-Warnitz's own party, the DNVP, considered this a bizarre choice, the issue was kicked into the long grass for the time being, but it was clear Hindenburg's patience was running thin.¹²⁵ Nevertheless, Brüning's campaigning showed a new, more animated and passionate side to his character and gave the impression to most observers that he retained the president's fulsome backing.¹²⁶ In particular, he kept up the political attacks on the Nazis, even accusing them of the true 'stab in the back' by sabotaging the negotiations to extend the president's term while the government was attempting to win revisions to Versailles.¹²⁷

The moderate right parties naturally also rallied around the president, with the KVP's Westarp playing a prominent role in the campaign committee, and the CSVD labelling Hindenburg a God-given leader.¹²⁸ Several parties were in the awkward position of backing Hindenburg's re-election but being opposed to his presidential government headed by Brüning – a stance that voters and many party activists found confusing. The People's Party (DVP) had, as we have seen, since late 1931 been distancing itself from Brüning's 'Hindenburg Cabinet' and voted with the National Opposition in the no confidence motion the previous autumn. However, the party backed the president in the presidential race. To do otherwise would have been embarrassing, if nothing else because their youth movement was called the Hindenburg League.¹²⁹ Nevertheless, many local parties were reluctant to support the president, knowing his victory would likely strengthen Brüning, and as a result did not campaign actively.¹³⁰ The same can be said of the CNBL; despite its cabinet presence, the party machine favoured a government of the right being formed in collaboration with the National Opposition and had voted against Brüning in the aforementioned confidence vote. Despite considerable pressure from the Reich Rural League, the CNBL leadership refused to budge and lent its weight to the Hindenburg campaign.[131] Despite their support for the president's re-election, a fresh no confidence motion in the government was tabled on the Reichstag's final day of sitting before the election, 26 February, and, as in October, the DVP and CNBL sided with the National Opposition and Communist Party, but once again, Brüning survived by twenty-four votes.[132]

It is clear that Hitler was for a time hesitant to run against a figure as popular and revered as Hindenburg, for defeat seemed almost certain. However, at the insistence of leading Nazis, not least Joseph Goebbels, the Führer was persuaded to stand. This was simply too good an opportunity to miss; not only did the extensive powers of the presidency offer the possibility of a constitutional path to dictatorship, but perhaps more pertinently, a strong showing for Hitler would cement his place as the leader of the radical right, ending his status as a mere partner of Hugenberg and the Stahlhelm. There is also considerable evidence that as the campaign wore on and mass enthusiasm for Hitler became ever more visible, senior Nazis (including Hitler) began to believe they were going to win the election. The Nazi campaign was feverish and modern; 8 million leaflets and 50,000 gramophone records were distributed, 34,000 meetings were held and Hitler addressed dozens of rallies, often two or three a day.[133] In order to counter Hindenburg's war hero status, Nazi election material emphasised Hitler's *Frontsoldat* (front soldier) background, hoping to win veterans away from loyalty to their wartime leader.[134] The Nazis were careful not to attack the venerated field marshal personally, especially on his war record, and Hitler in particular avoided criticism of Hindenburg.[135] A common charge was that while Hindenburg claimed to represent the unity of the nation, the parties and organisations supporting him were divided on practically every issue – the Nazis could sidestep criticising Hindenburg by pointing to the contradictory claims of the various parties campaigning for the president.[136] Nevertheless, Nazi propagandists were strident in their attacks on the Republic and its political class, who they claimed were hiding behind Hindenburg. Goebbels himself caused an uproar in the Reichstag and in the Hindenburg camp when on 23 February he claimed that the war leader was being praised by the 'deserters' party', meaning the Social Democrats, alluding to the Stab-in-the-Back myth.[137] He went further during his speech, claiming that Hindenburg had betrayed his supporters of seven years previous:

> I protest against the charge which has been levelled against the National Socialist movement that it has abandoned Hindenburg. No, Hindenburg has abandoned the cause of his one-time voters. We entrusted him with the

highest office of the Republic in the belief that at least in basic questions he would adopt the policies which the national[ist] Germany considered vital. He has done the very opposite. He has unequivocally sided with the middle, he has sided openly with the Social Democrats.[138]

Visual evidence of the inverted fronts from the previous presidential election was provided by a Nazi cartoon entitled *A dishonest game behind an honest mask*, which was a direct reversal of a 1925 People's Bloc poster – this time, rather than Hindenburg's distinctive face being used as a mask by militarists and brownshirts, a Nazi magazine portrayed a Jew, a Bolshevik and a capitalist playing cards behind a giant Hindenburg mask.[139] Another Nazi poster included photographs of prominent Jewish and Jewish-looking (such as the Catholic Adam Stegerwald) politicians who were backing Hindenburg and contrasted it with a selection of leading Nazis in gallant poses. The poster was completed with captions reading *We are voting Hindenburg* in Hebrew font and *We are voting Hitler* in a classical Germanic-Gothic typeface.[140] Vicious rumours were circulated about the president and his family; it was claimed that his son Oskar and State Secretary Meissner were members of the SPD, or that Oskar had become a Catholic, that his daughters (who were in their fifties and forties respectively) were in the Socialist Students' League, and yet another rumour claimed that the president had only run for re-election as his family could not afford the upkeep of his estate without his salary. In East Prussia, voters were told that if Hindenburg was re-elected, the Poles would invade the province, and, even more fantastically, it was claimed that Hindenburg was in fact dead or very ill. It was reported that the president did not rise until 11.00 am, that Brüning had Catholic chaplains guiding his hand as he wrote, and that the government was to cut pensions if the president won.

The effect and spread of these rumours was so widespread that General von Schleicher was forced to explain to Crown Prince Wilhelm, heir to the German monarchy, that Oskar von Hindenburg could not be a Social Democrat as he was a serving member of the armed forces.[141] The DNVP and Stahlhelm meanwhile were under no illusions about the slim chances of their candidate Theodor Duesterberg, despite the strength of Hugenberg's press empire. Their election appeals also walked the thin line of respect and admiration for Hindenburg (and indeed Hitler, given they hoped to maintain some semblance of unity in the National Opposition), while criticising the 'system' and calling on voters to ignore their emotional loyalty to the president.[142] The Duesterberg camp had no positive message, not least because they could not reasonably claim to have a chance of winning. Overall, the harsh criticism in the rightist press, the vicious rumours and the implication that he was a tool for the left and/or Jews that was the backbone of the Duesterberg and Hitler campaigns certainly cut close to the bone with the president, and he found the campaign a deeply unpleasant experience. Writing to a friend, Hindenburg revealed how badly the opposition of the Stahlhelm veterans' league in particular affected him:

> From a sense of loyalty which I feel towards my old comrades-in-arms I kept my hand over the Stahlhelm from the first days of my Presidency. I refused to give up my honorary membership ... after this was suggested to me by the Government for political reasons, and through the years I maintained friendly and personal relations with the Stahlhelm and its leaders. In fact, if someone else had been elected President in 1925, I feel certain after all the experiences I have had in the last seven years that the Stahlhelm would long have been dissolved ... I cannot follow the Stahlhelm leaders who maintain in their public statements that they still are loyal to me. Yet they oppose me in the election and emphasize their opposition by presenting, together with the German Nationalist People's Party [DNVP], their second-in-command as a rival candidate who claims to represent the black-white-and-red idea – against me, of all people. You can understand that I feel very bitter about the Stahlhelm's attitude towards me. This is not my idea of loyalty.[143]

As Goltz has pointed out, the Hindenburg campaign was actually more modern and sophisticated than the much-vaunted Nazi effort. The United Hindenburg Committees, a thoroughly conservative body, had supplanted the cross-party Sahm committee that had organised the petition to secure Hindenburg's nomination. The UHC steering committee was headed by a retired general, a former senior civil servant as well as Kuno von Westarp, and chaired by Günther Gereke, a young CNBL Reichstag deputy.[144] The committee made it clear to the Social Democrats that they should run their own separate pro-Hindenburg operation, or 'march separately' – the official Hindenburg campaign was to focus on patriotic and bourgeois appeals focused on the president himself rather than the Brüning government or republican unity.[145] The finance minister, State Party leader Hermann Dietrich, was even barred from speaking at an official Hindenburg event as he was considered too liberal, with one UHC official telling him that there had been 'a real palace revolution' and that most members of the committee were 'determined to overthrow Brüning's government and do not want to give any cabinet member a chance to make propaganda'.[146]

There can be no doubt that the official Hindenburg campaign was grounded almost entirely in the Hindenburg myth – that the appeal to the country was centred on the field marshal's charismatic persona as a symbol of tradition and unity in whose person stood the only chance to heal the bitter divisions of German society.[147] This was to be the third iteration of Hindenburg as saviour: in 1914 he had saved East Prussia from Russian invasion; in 1925 he was portrayed as the saviour from Weimar party chaos; and in 1932 he was the saviour who would unite a polarised nation and a bulwark against societal collapse. The campaign spent no less than 7.5 million marks, 1 million more than the Nazis. Hindenburg enjoyed the backing of key figures from the establishment elite, despite the defection of a number of prominent former generals, industrialists and landowners to the National Opposition. The majority of the official campaign's funds came from big business, with large donations coming from the Krupp and Siemens dynasties. Carl Duisburg, head of I.G. Farben and the overall chairman of the UHC, donated 1 million marks of his own money to the campaign.[148] On the other hand, many business and industrial leaders were reluctant to back Hindenburg, desiring a change in the political system, and only 269,000 marks was raised from German industry.[149] Given the disappointing fundraising results, the cabinet authorised on 1 March 1.8 million marks of government money to be essentially laundered through the Prussian Interior Ministry and distributed to the pro-Hindenburg parties in the state. A further 500,000 marks of unpaid bills left at the end of the campaign was paid by the government in July 1932. The corruption did not end there, for an additional 500,000 marks of the UHC's funds were squirreled away by the chair, Günther Gereke, for use by his own Christian-Nationalist Peasants' and Farmers' Party (CNBL) in the forthcoming Prussian State elections.[150]

Although the leaders of many special interest and patriotic groups once again rallied to the banner of Hindenburg, they often faced considerable backlash from their grassroots. In particular, the leaders of the aristocratic association and of the veterans' Kyffhäuserbund were both forced to resign after endorsing the Reich President.[151] Naturally, much of the Hindenburg Committee's campaign material relied on the image and myth of the president. Huge posters of Hindenburg's instantly recognisable face were displayed in public places with the simple slogans 'With Him', 'Vote for our best' or 'Vote for a man, not a party'. The propaganda stressed both Hindenburg's 'father of the nation', trustworthy status, and his supposed non-partisan character, and a number of posters also emphasised how the president rose above the party fray, often with literal depictions of brawling Communists and Nazis. A rather comic poster portrayed Hindenburg as a Herculean figure, lifting a giant globe and preparing to drop it on a weedy, protesting Hitler.[152] A special effort was made to retain 'old' Hindenburg voters from 1925, with pamphlets specifically targeting those who had elected the field marshal last time around and another leaflet in Imperial German colours persuading war veterans to remain loyal to their leader rather than support Duesterberg and the Stahlhelm. Far from mere posters and rallies, however, the UHC made a conscious effort to take advantage of modern technology and new campaigning techniques. A propaganda film, featuring sound, was shown in over 200 cinemas and a slide of Hindenburg's image shown in 4–5,000. Fifteen loudspeaker cars toured 1,200 towns and villages, playing a statement from the president and carrying campaign material and platform speakers to rural Germany. Reportedly, recordings of Hindenburg's voice silenced political opponents and helped to combat claims about the president's health and mental faculties.¹⁵³ Much of the media, outside the Nazi, Hugenberg-owned and Communist press, was sympathetic, and carried photos and articles about the president frequently during the election, for instance, a popular spread entitled 'Hindenburg at work', which detailed a day in the life of the president, was picked up by 1,187 local papers.¹⁵⁴ The broadsheet press was equally supportive, an editorial of the liberal *Frankfurter Zeitung* claiming that:

> Hindenburg can't tell us what he is going to do in the future, what measures he will take ... whom he is going to appoint as Chancellor if a change should become necessary. He cannot tell us, but in his case we need not know, for we have the experience of the last seven years to go by, and the pledge of the Old Gentleman that he will not deprive us of our constitutional rights.¹⁵⁵

The UHC also distributed detailed material to local offices providing direct refutations to Nazi attacks on the president's political record, emphasising, for instance, the 'freeing' of the Rhineland from Allied occupation, which played neatly into the existing Hindenburg myth as the liberator of East Prussia.

In the final week before polling day on 13 March, the UHC stepped up the campaign considerably. One hundred and thirty Hindenburg banners were hung over busy Berlin streets, including before the Brandenburg Gate, while huge placards were erected at busy road junctions such as Potsdamer Platz. Over 100,000 posters were put up in total, as well as 3 million illustrated leaflets handed out, a further 10 million dropped from aircraft on top of 21 million already distributed in the preceding weeks.¹⁵⁶ As in 1925, Hindenburg's name was projected into the night sky above the capital. An 'historians' appeal' was organised for the final few days of the election, with seventy-four prominent academics of both liberal and conservative politics signing an open letter that noted how the president transcended 'all parties, all classes, and all divisions' and appealed to the public to unite 'around his trusted and powerful personality'.¹⁵⁷

Hindenburg's only contribution to his own re-election was his radio broadcast to the nation of 10 March. As in 1925, he refused to make public appearances but was willing to use this new technology to address the nation. In order to ensure the president made no slips, the speech was pre-recorded although millions of Germans believed it to be live.¹⁵⁸ Hindenburg told listeners why he had decided to run again, rehearsing familiar sentiments about duty and honour, before calling on the German people to unite behind his candidacy. Eschewing policy detail or future plans, in the broadcast the president instead made it clear that he did not consider himself the candidate of the left, noting the first requests for him to seek re-election came from the right.¹⁵⁹ He maintained a healthy distance between himself and the Brüning government, noting that some of the recent decrees 'could be improved', but that any action was better than no action.¹⁶⁰ The speech concluded with the field marshal harking back to the war years that had made his name:

I cannot believe that Germany is to be plunged into domestic feuds and civil war. I recall to you the spirit of 1914 and the frontline attitude which was concerned with the man and not with his social status or party ... I will not give up the hope that Germany will come together again in new unity.[161]

The strength of the Hindenburg myth was such that, despite the fact he was no great public speaker, the president's words had a deep emotional impact, and over the next few days he received a flood of appreciative letters. In one such letter, a teacher described how twenty people in his village crowded round his radio set and that they had all pledged themselves to remain loyal to the field marshal, with the teacher himself writing that he was so moved by the broadcast that he cancelled his plans for the evening. A Berliner wrote in a similar vein that she sat in front of her portrait of Hindenburg while listening to the speech and felt a strong bond of loyalty; she not only pledged her allegiance in her letter to the Reich President but also condemned those who were betraying and slandering him now, writing, '2,000 years ago the saviour was also crucified, but he still succeeded.'[162]

Other than the broadcast, Hindenburg also agreed to be filmed reviewing the Berlin Guards Regiment and reading an extract from his statement accepting his nomination, but this was the limit of his campaigning.[163] Although he made no other public pronouncements, he did meet deputations of farmers, artisans and students and was rather more candid. He went so far as defending the SPD against the Goebbels charge of being a party of deserters and seemed most concerned about the extreme polarisation overwhelming the country and its damage to German foreign policy, and in particular, achieving the revisions to Versailles which Brüning was so doggedly pursuing:

The preparations for civil war are complete. The hostile fronts are in place, and they hate each other more than the Versailles Treaty. Germany's irreconcilable enemies are waiting for this civil war ... They await our fraternal struggle as a pretext to attain the final goal that they could not attain in 1919: the destruction of the Reich ... To the Germans suffering under foreign and unjust rule I cry, 'The fatherland has not abandoned you; we are merely powerless to oppose the violation of your legal rights as long as our internal feuds cripple us.'[164]

On 12 March, Hindenburg's speech was followed up by the showpiece event of the UHC, a huge rally at the Berlin Sportpalast, attended by an estimated 15,000. The nationalistic Young German Order provided paramilitary security in a highly choreographed event. Westarp, Gereke and Sahm of the campaign team and Groener, Schlange-Schöningen and Brüning from the government all addressed the crowd with an assortment of speeches on the virtues of the Reich President. Brüning was of course the star speaker, and he returned to his attacks on the Nazis, accusing them of seeking nothing but dictatorial power for themselves. The speech finished with a crescendo as Brüning called for Germans to resist the Nazi appeal and instead unite behind the man who was 'recognised throughout the world as a symbol of German strength and German unity... Hindenburg has to win because Germany has to live!'[165]

The results of the first ballot held on 13 March 1932 were a resounding win for the Reich President, but he fell agonisingly short (170,000 votes) of the majority required to forgo the need for a run-off. Hindenburg attained a 49.6 per cent vote share, winning the support of 18,651,497 Germans. Hitler was far behind with 11.3 million votes (30.1 per cent) and Duesterberg and the Communist leader Thälmann were nowhere on 6.8 per cent and 13.2 per cent respectively. There was a real sense of deflation among the Nazi leadership, who by the end of the campaign genuinely believed they had a chance of winning in the first round.[166] Equally, the result was disastrous for the Nationalists; Hitler had left them in the dust and the Duesterberg candidacy had attracted just over 2.5 million votes.[167] Given the fact the DNVP had achieved a very similar poll in their 1930 nadir, it was now obvious that all the agitation of the National Opposition had only increased the strength of the Nazis. Additionally, with a Hindenburg victory all but certain in the second ballot, given that only a plurality of votes was required, Hugenberg and the Stahlhelm leaders no longer had the strong negotiating position with the president they had anticipated; quite simply, Hindenburg did not need their support to win in the run-off. Despite his clear margin of victory, Hindenburg himself was disappointed. He had expected a first-round victory and did not look forward to further electioneering, considering his having to go to the people again for a mandate embarrassing and an unnecessary stress having come so close to winning in one round. Furthermore, he was shocked that half the country did not have confidence in him and deeply saddened that Hitler had won in his home province of East Prussia, a fact that was all the more galling as it was the site of his Tannenberg victory.[168] From the perspective of the democratic and moderate parties that had backed the president, there were also worrying electoral trends; the Hindenburg vote in 1932 was roughly 2 million down on the combined 1930 vote of all the parties who had endorsed the president. The Nazi vote, on the other hand, had almost doubled in the same space of time. Surely also, otherwise apathetic or rightist voters had backed Hindenburg in this election but would not turn out to vote for moderate parties in an ordinary party contest.

The second ballot was scheduled for 10 April, but with Easter Sunday falling on 27 March, the government announced a political truce, which banned all political meetings, and was in place between the first ballot and the beginning of April.[169] Effectively, therefore, there would only be a week of campaigning before the voters went to the polls again, playing into the president's hands. For the second round, the Nazis realised they had to draw bourgeois voters, especially women, away from Hindenburg if they wanted to win. To this end, they toned down their attacks and sought to direct their campaign in a more 'positive' direction by focusing on Hitler's so-called 'flight over Germany'.[170] Given the second-round campaign only lasted for seven days, it was decided that the Führer would fly from city to city, addressing twenty-three rallies in a week, while at the same time generating a media circus as he touched down and took off at each town.[171] The strategy of the DNVP and Stahlhelm had been to withdraw their man, Duesterberg, in the second round in return for concessions from Hindenburg. However, the plan had fallen apart. Duesterberg's suggestion to Hindenburg and Hitler that the run-off be cancelled, the president be considered re-elected and new Reichstag elections be called in their stead was contemptuously ignored by both candidates and Hugenberg was reduced to telling his supporters to vote for whomever they wished.[172]

Such was Hitler's success and his apparent national appeal that Hugenberg had lost all authority over the Harzburg Front and he found himself without any bargaining chips; his allies the Reich Rural League, Pan-German League and other leading nationalists backed Hitler for the second round after Duesterberg's defeat rather than holding out for a deal with the president.[173] The pro-Hindenburg camp cannot be said to have rested on their laurels, despite the president's huge lead. It was vital that Hindenburg voters turned out again in the second round in similar numbers to ensure the final result was not close. While the dynamism of the Nazi campaign attracts much historical attention, L.E. Jones is right to point out that the Hindenburg campaign, even in the dead rubber second round, matched the Nazi effort for creativity and intensity.[174] The United Hindenburg Committees produced a propaganda film entitled *The Life and Deeds of Our Hindenburg*, which was shown in cinemas throughout the week of campaigning, but the official campaign was, as before, essentially defensive and backward-looking, devoid of any dynamic vision for the future. The SPD, who might have been forgiven for losing its fervour, did its utmost to get the millions of Social Democrats and trade unionists who had voted Hindenburg in March back to the polls, with their Iron Front holding no less than 10,000 meetings per day in the campaign week.[175] While unable to fly their candidate around the country, the UHC did hire thirty Lufthansa aircraft to drop 20 million leaflets across Germany, although a scheme to fly the *Graf Zeppelin* airship over the nation in a campaign stunt fell through.[176]

One such pamphlet was entitled *Awake* (*see* plate section), in what was surely a deliberate play on both the Nazi slogan 'Germany Awake' and the Communist anthem *Wake up, wretched of the Earth*, called on Germans to wake up from the utopias being peddled by the far left and right. The politically naïve, easily led German stereotype in the character of Michel is shown dreaming of the fantasy future that he has been promised by political extremists; a society in which nobody goes hungry, credit is available to all, poverty has been eradicated by printing money, war reparations have been cancelled, trade barriers torn down and global disarmament has become a reality. The reader is informed coolly that miracles only happen in dreams and that only the tried and tested capabilities of an experienced leader can turn Germany around. Turning over, the reader sees that Michel has woken up to a revelation: 'If everyone pulls in the same direction, we're strong!' The reader is reminded of German innocence over the Great War, that Hindenburg stands above party, that Bismarck's work in unifying Germany is at risk and that even the literary giant Goethe would have sympathised with Hindenburg. 'The world must see even more clearly: Germany is determined to gather its strength, Germany stands behind Hindenburg, Michel is awake!' the pamphlet declares. Finally, we see Michel 'act' after being trapped in a dream world; he casts his vote for the field marshal and Reich President, as the reader is encouraged to ditch radicalism and not to trust inexperienced leaders: 'Only Hindenburg deserves your vote.'[177]

Money was a real issue in the second round for the UHC, as Duisburg's fundraising efforts only garnered 118,200 marks, 50,000 of which was from his own pocket. The situation was saved when Günther Gereke, head of the steering committee, appeared at the UHC headquarters in Berlin with a satchel containing 1 million marks. It later transpired the money had been illegally syphoned off from secret Reichswehr funds by General Kurt von Schleicher, highlighting the importance of Hindenburg's re-election to his taming strategy.[178] Schleicher wrote to a friend regarding the election:

> Hindenburg is the only candidate who is in a position to defeat Hitler. Since I am convinced that Hitler is as suited for the presidency as a hedgehog for a face towel and because I fear his presidency would lead to civil war and ultimately to Bolshevism, the decision about for whom I will vote is in this case not difficult.[179]

Unfortunately, disunity among the pro-Hindenburg parties was even worse than before as they vied for position ahead of the imminent batch of state elections, including the crucial state of Prussia, that were due on 24 April. The only event of real note in the second round was that Crown Prince Wilhelm, son of the exiled Kaiser Wilhelm II, announced on 3 April that he was voting for Hitler, as his father vainly believed the Nazi leader would restore the monarchy. The prince had considered running himself in the second round to unite the entire right, but this fanciful project was nipped in the bud by the elder Wilhelm, who still believed he could return as head of state.[180] On the day of the poll, Hindenburg issued his final written address, returning to familiar tropes:

> Forget your quarrels and close ranks! Again, as I did when I assumed office seven years ago, I am asking the entire German people to work with me. We must concentrate our strength if we are to cope with the confusion and

misery of the times. Only if we stand together, will we be strong enough to master our fate. Forward therefore in unity and with God![181]

Held on 10 April, the second ballot resulted, unsurprisingly, in Hindenburg's re-election as Reich President. The old man had achieved a remarkable result; no other party or individual in German history has won such a high proportion of votes cast in a free and fair national election. Receiving 19,359,983 votes, 53.1 per cent of those cast, was as clear a mandate as a Weimar election would produce, and the fact that the Hindenburg vote rose by 700,000 despite the result being a foregone conclusion and turnout dipping noticeably was also impressive.[182] Hitler, however, had also done well. He had gained over 2 million votes on the first round, rising to a 36.7 per cent share and cruelly highlighting to the president that the vast majority of Duesterberg supporters – Nationalists and veterans – preferred Lance Corporal Hitler to Field Marshal von Hindenburg, despite their vociferous support for him in 1925. The Communist vote actually fell by over a million also, roughly corresponding to the fall in turnout, suggesting many KPD voters did not bother going to the polls the second time around.[183] Although Westarp would claim that 5–6 million conservatives voted for Hindenburg, this is almost certainly overstating the case; the 700,000 new voters the president won in the second round were certainly almost all rightists who had initially backed Duesterberg, but overall there can be no doubt that Hindenburg was overwhelmingly re-elected in 1932 by the very voters who had opposed him in 1925, the left, liberals and Catholics, and modern historians estimate 60 per cent of those who voted Hindenburg in 1925 voted Hitler in 1932.[184]

The popular history of the rise of the Nazis often brushes over the presidential election of spring 1932 with remarkable brevity.[185] Perhaps because it ended in defeat for the Nazis, it does not easily fit into the narrative of Hitler's inexorable rise to power. However, the fact that there was a man in 1932 whom the German people trusted more than Hitler to see them through the economic and political crisis is highly significant, and more recent studies by L.E. Jones and Anna von der Goltz highlight the undoubted importance the election holds in explaining the demise of Weimar.[186] In many ways, despite the dearth of coverage, this was the pinnacle of Hindenburg's political career, even if he did not see it that way. The old man had united a majority of the nation behind him, achieving the unity he claimed he always longed for, drawing in millions of supporters from the left, right and centre, Catholics and Protestants, trade unionists and industrialists, the proletariat, bourgeoisie and aristocrats. The extremists of right and left had been comfortably defeated. In many ways, the election had given the president a mandate to build a broad-based coalition that might see off the radicals and preserve democracy, even in an amended form. Yet Hindenburg did not see things that way. He was disappointed that Brüning had not secured an extension to his presidency through the Reichstag, frustrated that the National

Opposition had failed to support his candidacy, annoyed that the election had gone to a second round, frankly embarrassed that he had been elected on the votes of Social Democrats, Catholics and republicans, and embittered by the attacks on him and his family in the right-wing press. He also felt betrayed that so many Hindenburg voters of 1925 had switched their allegiance to the upstart corporal, Hitler. He believed that 'the right people' had not voted for him this time around and he was absolutely determined to prove he was not beholden to the parties that had re-elected him, fearing it would taint his legacy.[187]

The Hindenburg that emerged from the 1932 presidential contest was thus not a triumphant or invigorated leader, as one might expect of a politician who had just won such a decisive victory. Instead, he was determined to prove to his critics and lost friends that he was a true nationalist and not a tool of those subversive forces, social democracy and Catholicism. Above all, this meant Brüning's days were numbered, not least because the chancellor's greatest ally in influencing the president, Kurt von Schleicher, had also decided the time was ripe for change. Nazi success in the presidential election convinced the wily general that the taming strategy must be put into effect sooner than anticipated, lest the Nazis seize power in an uncontrolled manner. Both Brüning and his old mentor Groener now stood in the way of Schleicher's schemes and the general had in fact been undermining the chancellor during the campaign, telling leading DVP politicians that his economic policies were not working.[188] And Hindenburg had run out of patience in his long quest for a government of the right. The leftist writer Carl von Ossietzky accurately summarised the outcome of the election at the time with an analysis that bore remarkable resemblance to the pessimistic assessment of some rightists upon Hindenburg's 1925 victory: 'Indeed, no political thesis or programme has triumphed. Only a very famous old man has ... Hindenburg has triumphed, a piece of legend, a heroic frame onto which anyone can clamp whatever colourful web of illusions he desires!'[189]

A cabinet of 'my friends'

When the social democrat and Prussian premier Otto Braun had congratulated Hindenburg on his victory, the president had replied that he did not feel bound by the policies of the parties that had supported him.[190] Essentially, despite the fact he had just been re-elected by moderates of left and right, Hindenburg had every intention of forming a government of the nationalist right, made up of the very parties that had campaigned against him – primarily the DNVP and Nazis. Attention swiftly turned to the major state elections scheduled for just a fortnight after the presidential second round. The state legislatures of Prussia, Bavaria, Württemberg, Hamburg and Anhalt were holding their first parliamentary elections since 1928. Prussia was of course highly significant, not just for its size, but because while Bavaria and Württemberg were ruled by conservatives, the red-black (SPD-Centre) government of Prussia had long been a target for industrial, agrarian and rightist ire, as we have seen.[191] The fact that the presidential campaigning now merged seamlessly into campaigns for regional elections promised to keep the country in a state of high political tensions, with the consequent street violence, for an extended period. This was a matter of some concern for both state administrations and the Reich government, especially Interior Minister Wilhelm Groener. While Schleicher and Hindenburg now had serious doubts about Brüning, Groener remained a firm ally of the chancellor.[192]

In early April, the state governments of Prussia and Bavaria, controlled by the moderate left and right respectively, had come to the interior minister asking for something to be done about the extreme violence of the Nazis, which had been exacerbated by the presidential election campaign. Further cause for concern had been found in a March Prussian police raid that had revealed secret SA orders to seize power on election day if Hitler had won.[193] They effectively served Groener an ultimatum: either the Reich government take immediate action, or the states would take measures of their own.[194] The influential General von Schleicher was, however, opposed to such a move, not least because it would undermine his attempts both to co-opt the Nazi Party and incorporate its paramilitary wing into his *Wehrsport* scheme, effectively bringing the brownshirts under army control. To Schleicher, it made little sense to suppress the SA when it represented a ready source of manpower to expand the military when rearmament came.[195] He wrote to Groener, his superior in the Defence Ministry, at the end of March (when the ban was first being considered), making clear his contempt for the Social Democrats running Prussia:

> Your excellency is supposed to be won over for a struggle against the right in the Prussian elections, to be stamped as a loyal ally of the socialists ... I am really looking forward to 11 April [the day after the presidential election], when we can speak plain German to this pack of liars ... I am very glad that we have a counterweight [to the SPD] in the form of the Nazis, even though they are of course not our brothers and must be treated with the greatest of care. If they did not exist, it would be necessary to invent them.[196]

For Schleicher, far from a threat, the Nazis were an essential piece in the political game he was playing to reforge the Republic in a rightist direction. Even when the government became aware in early April that the SA were under orders *not* to resist a Polish invasion, Schleicher was not convinced.[197] There is some evidence that Groener was persuaded by his protégé's thinking, at least at first, for he defended the Schleicher position in a 5 April conference with police chiefs from across the country. However, the police representatives were so forceful in their denunciation of the Nazi stormtroopers that the interior minister felt compelled to act.[198] Shelving the *Wehrsport* programme for the time being, Groener quickly sought and received Brüning's approval for a ban. Although he would later claim that he had opposed the prohibition decree as premature, Brüning was ready to go on the offensive against the Nazis in April 1932, as shown by his fiery election speeches. Brüning was also reassured that he could afford to suppress the Nazis by the failure of the Communists to make substantial ground despite the seriousness of the Depression.[199]

Hindenburg was extremely reluctant to sign the decree presented to him on 13 April. His son and aide-de-camp Oskar advised (perhaps under Schleicher's influence) that his father should refuse as he believed it would only make the president more unpopular with the right.[200] Oskar was becoming ever more influential within the president's inner circle, not just due to his close friendship with Schleicher (who was the same age), but also perhaps because his father's growing physical decline made him ever more reliant on his son.[201] Oskar was now firmly in Schleicher's camp and against Brüning. The elder Hindenburg had seen Brüning the previous day, when, as was form, the chancellor offered the government's resignation should the newly elected president desire it. The chancellor could be forgiven for being surprised when the president he had campaigned so hard for only turned down the offer 'for now' and demanded that after the Prussian elections, a break with the SPD be brought about.[202] Being presented with the SA ban plans the following day hardly served to improve the president's mood. The prohibition of the SA would trash Hindenburg's hopes of shifting to the right, for it drove a clear wedge between his government and the radical right. Even worse from the president's perspective, it appeared, coming just three days after polling day, as a clear concession to the left and moderates who had re-elected him. He only acceded when Brüning and Groener threatened to resign if he did not comply.[203] This merely served to weaken the relationship between the president and the men who had been his favourites in the cabinet, whom he had defended for a long time. In the wake of the disappointing election, this latest blow only further undermined his confidence in his chancellor. Even worse, General von Schleicher now used his contacts and influence to undermine the ban. Although local police forces enforced the ban effectively, the general had forewarned the Nazis, meaning few weapons or incriminating material were discovered in police searches.[204] Schleicher also asked the head of the navy, Admiral Raeder, to see the president and protest against the decree, but the admiral declined. The same cannot be said for Schleicher's closest ally, Chief of the Army Command General Kurt von Hammerstein, who alongside another senior officer went to see the president to counsel how unwise a decision it was.[205] Nevertheless, the ban was highly effective and was utterly humiliating for Hitler and the Nazi leaders, who exploded with rage, threatening the government with a putsch, only to be immobilised by the seizure of their cars, driven by uniformed chauffeurs.[206]

In a further attempt to sabotage the ban, Schleicher's department, acting on the president's orders, compiled a dossier of evidence against the social democratic paramilitary organisation, the Reichsbanner, attempting to prove that they should be banned as well. The dossier was a hatchet job, designed for political purposes to show the president as even-handed and not in favour of the left, and was composed mainly of clippings from right-wing newspapers.[207] It formed the basis for a testy letter sent on 16 April by Hindenburg to Groener calling for the Reichsbanner to be added to the ban. The letter, clearly with the president's knowledge, was leaked to the press, harming the credibility of both the decree and Hindenburg's old comrade Groener.[208] The defence minister could have sacked both Schleicher and Hammerstein for insubordination, but he knew this would only further harm his relationship with the president, upon whom his post depended. Groener stood firm on the Reichsbanner issue, and Brüning backed him. In a private conversation a few days later that is reported in Brüning's autobiography, the chancellor gave his interior and defence minister his full support. However, he also asked Groener for the truth about the war and Hindenburg's role. Groener explained the field marshal's weakness, both in November 1918 and over the Versailles ultimatum in June 1919, and how, with tears in his eyes, Hindenburg had placed the full burden of responsibility on Groener's shoulders on both occasions. Brüning, at least according to his memoirs, was shocked and told Groener:

> 'Your Excellency, I understand the tragedy of your life. I do not want to sound bitter, but if you had told me any of these things in February 1930 [before he became chancellor], then I would not have succumbed to the same appeal and the same tears of the Reich President against my better judgement. My instincts were against him when he made his first appeal to me. Only your guarantee that you would see to it that the president stood behind me until success had been achieved persuaded me to accept the assignment …'
>
> I now knew that a policy based on a personality like Hindenburg's must inevitably fail. The only thing that could still save us was a decisive success in Geneva.[209]

Schleicher, Groener, Brüning and Hindenburg had been largely united in their aims and strategy when presidential government had been introduced in 1930. It now appeared that there was a clear rift between the four most important men in government and this situation could not be maintained for long.

The state elections of 24 April were another triumph for the Nazis as they surged across the country. In their home state of Bavaria, the Nazis were held off remarkably well by the ruling BVP, who narrowly beat the Nazis and retained the support of the regional parliament.[210] The real prize for the NSDAP was Prussia. Far and away Germany's largest state with 57 per cent of the Reich's population, Prussia, as we have seen, had been ruled by the 'Weimar Coalition' pro-democracy parties since the creation of the Republic and was a social democratic bulwark. Here, the Nazis came very close to the 37 per cent achieved in the presidential second round and exploded from the six seats won there in 1928 to 162, making them by some distance the largest party in the Prussian Parliament. However, Nazi success had drained support from the other rightist parties, especially the DNVP and DVP, who lost eighty-six seats between them, meaning that the right as a whole was just short of the 212 seats needed for a majority in the state legislature. Any Nazi-Nationalist coalition would therefore be immediately removed by a vote of no confidence from the Communists and pro-democracy parties. Equally, the SPD-Centre-State Party coalition currently in office had decisively lost its working majority.[211] The 'Hindenburg Bloc' parties of the moderate right faced a near total wipeout, failing to build any momentum from the presidential election. Abortive attempts to form an electoral alliance between the DStP, DVP, CNBL, WP, CSVD and KVP came to nothing when the DVP and CSVD both insisted on running alone. The CNBL, WP and KVP, hoping to cement cooperation from the Hindenburg campaign, did run a joint ticket as the National Front of German Estates, fronted by Westarp, but they polled a dismal 1.64 per cent and failed to win a single seat. The CSVD also won a pathetic 1.16 per cent and the DVP, once the great party of Stresemann, hardly did better with 1.7 per cent.[212] As in 1930 (and despite the clear victory for the Hindenburg myth in 1932), it appears that parties that attempted to wrap themselves in the Hindenburg banner were not overly successful. Perhaps the German people's loyalty was to the person of the president rather than the brand of conservative politics most closely associated with him. Prussia was therefore in a state of unresolvable deadlock, with the social democratic Prime Minister Otto Braun and his cabinet remaining in office as a caretaker administration for the time being.

The only workable coalition combination was an alliance between the Nazis and Catholic Centre, and negotiations to that end began in earnest. Brüning, the most prominent figure from the Centre Party, suggested a Nazi-Centre administration headed by a trusted conservative with the police under Reich control.[213] The Nazis were definitely tempted by the offer, with party number two Gregor Strasser arguing for acceptance and Goebbels also considering it, but these efforts were sabotaged by General von Schleicher, who had decided a Prussian coalition would ruin his strategy of taming the Nazis. Schleicher believed the NSDAP should only be given executive power in particular circumstances that would facilitate his own control and manipulation of them, and crucially this could only happen once the Nazis had been shorn of the SA. Therefore, handing Hitler control of Prussia and its large and powerful police force would jeopardise the general's efforts to use the Nazis for his own purposes.[214] To this end, the general undermined the talks with the Centre Party behind the scenes, persuading Hitler to refuse a coalition in Prussia unless the Nazis could enter coalition at the Reich level. At Schleicher's behest, Hitler terminated the talks on 28 April.[215] This only served to further undermine Brüning, for Hindenburg had been waiting for a new rightist government in Prussia and it appeared as if his chancellor had failed him again.

Another hammer blow fell on the cabinet when the Reichstag reconvened. Brüning started the parliamentary session in fine form and easily saw off yet another confidence motion, this time after Nationalist leader Alfred Hugenberg failed in a bid to bribe the Middle Class Party (WP) to vote against the government in return for 200,000 marks.[216] With the betrayal of Schleicher, a man he considered his 'protégé, friend and adoptive son', Groener was disorientated and politically isolated.[217] His relationship with both Hindenburg and the army was now in serious jeopardy. Even worse, Schleicher now considered Groener and Brüning, and their SA ban, as the greatest obstacle to his taming strategy.[218] A meeting between Brüning and Schleicher on 2 May that had been intended to clear the air ended acrimoniously when Brüning the frontline soldier derided the staff officer Schleicher as lacking nerve at a vital moment for the country; only men who had been in the trenches had the courage to hold fire until the enemy came so close one could not miss.[219] The rupture was complete. The general, who unquestionably saw politics as a game, was now preparing to remove both the defence minister and the chancellor from the board. On 6 May, the economics minister, the technocrat Hermann Warmbold, resigned in a move that may have been instigated by Schleicher, but doubtless signified widespread industrial dissatisfaction with government policy.[220] On 10 May, Groener, who appeared ill or confused, attempted to defend the SA ban to a hostile Reichstag. In an embarrassing episode, the minister got bogged down by the constant Nazi interruptions, getting drawn into shouting contests with the heckling deputies.[221] The speech was widely regarded as a disaster that totally discredited the under-pressure minister and even Westarp told Brüning that it would be best to cut Groener loose in order to avoid the government being dragged down with him.[222] The army had also lost confidence in their head, or at least Schleicher decided they had. He informed the government on 11 May that unless Groener was removed, he and other senior army leaders would resign. In demanding a minister's resignation, Schleicher had usurped Hindenburg's constitutional role, but the president approved of the action and objected to neither the intention nor the methods of the general.[223] Groener did indeed resign as defence minister on 12 May but clung on to the Interior Ministry, still enjoying the full support of Brüning. Groener did, however, tell the chancellor not to intercede with Hindenburg on his behalf, lest it bring down the government itself.[224] Hindenburg accepted this compromise for now, but insisted his decision to retain Groener in the cabinet was not final and that he would think about it during a spell away from Berlin at his Neudeck estate.[225]

Groener's departure from the Defence Ministry was a serious blow for the government, even if he did remain as interior minister; not only did it weaken Brüning's most powerful ally, but it also removed the last vestiges of restraint and accountability from the scheming von Schleicher, who was, to all intents and purposes, no longer answerable to anyone. The general had been conducting a series of secret meetings with Hitler in late April and early May in which they had been conspiring to bring Brüning down. These meetings concluded with a gentleman's agreement on 8 May that if the Nazis backed a new presidential government of the right, the government would lift the SA ban and call new Reichstag elections, which the Nazis desired.[226] Schleicher now had the green light to make his move, and with Groener politically finished, Brüning could not last much longer. The chancellor offered the Defence Ministry to Schleicher, seeking to bring him inside the tent, but Schleicher demurred in a move interpreted by the press as the beginning of the end.[227] For the time being, the crucial Economic and Defence ministries stood vacant as Brüning cast about for replacements for his sinking ship.[228]

Sensing the government's weakness, the National Opposition went back on the offensive. The Reich Rural League, as well as aristocratic landowners from the DNVP, including Hindenburg's friend von Oldenburg-Januschau, launched a savage attack on a leaked government decree (which had actually been rejected by the cabinet) to resettle unemployed workers on foreclosed estates. They labelled it 'agrarian Bolshevism', a 'descent into state socialism' and, as a landowning aristocrat himself, the president was particularly receptive to the accusations levelled against Brüning and his ministers. Furthermore, Hindenburg's secretary Meissner colluded with Schleicher to ensure that the president was bombarded with petitions, letters and newspaper articles about the scandal.[229] The extent to which the outrage was deliberately whipped up in order to influence the president is demonstrated by the fact that Hindenburg must have been already aware of the plans due to the regular reports he received from Meissner on cabinet business, and he had not raised any concerns before. Now he was being told that the government was going to socialise Prussian agriculture, strip the great families of their holdings and, as Baron von Gayl warned Hindenburg, the German people would be less likely to defend their soil against foreign invasion should they be deprived of its ownership.[230] Relations between president and chancellor had already hit rock bottom after the Groener affair, and after going to his Neudeck estate on 12 May, Hindenburg did not see Brüning until the 29th. All the while, Schleicher regularly telephoned the president or talked to Oskar, who acted as a conduit between the two.[231] On 26 May, Meissner came to Berlin and told the press that the president sought revisions to the government's latest decree. In private, he told Brüning that Hindenburg's price for signing the decree was the dropping of Groener and the formation of a more right-wing cabinet, as well as the formation of a Nazi-Centre coalition in Prussia.²³² With the government teetering, the Christian-Nationalist Farmers' and Peasants' Party ministers, Schiele and Schlange-Schöningen, did their utmost to persuade Hindenburg to keep faith with the cabinet and its agricultural programme, although the latter's letter was so forthright in tone it made the president consider asking for Schlange-Schöningen's resignation.²³³ Finally, on the morning of 29 May, Brüning had his audience with Hindenburg. The chancellor demanded an end to the 'shadow government' of the president's inner circle (by implication Schleicher, Meissner and Oskar) and said he should rely on the advice of his ministers instead. He reassured the president that he would continue to negotiate towards a rightist coalition in Prussia but ignored the other demands laid out by Meissner on the 26th. Brüning clearly felt he needed to go on the offensive to survive and he gave full vent to his frustration with plotters and schemers, especially in the army.²³⁴ Hindenburg then read from a prepared statement. He made it clear that this 'unpopular cabinet' would not be allowed to issue any more presidential decrees and Brüning would not be permitted to carry out a reshuffle. Brüning drew the obvious conclusion and observed that the president must wish him to resign. Supposedly with tears in his eyes, Hindenburg told his chancellor, 'I must turn to the right at long last, the newspapers and the whole nation demand it. But you have always refused to do so.' Brüning protested this point but the president insisted 'the others' told him this was the case. Hindenburg did insist that he still had faith in Brüning (but not the cabinet) and suggested at the end of the discussion that Brüning stay on as foreign minister, but the chancellor rejected this suggestion, not least because Hindenburg could give no direction as to the composition of the next cabinet and its policy but also because it was irreconcilable with the concept of loyalty to the president's voters. It was agreed that the conversation could be concluded the following day, and Hindenburg asked that Brüning bring the cabinet's resignation with him.²³⁵

Brüning summoned the cabinet the next morning and informed them of the dramatic meeting. There was much anger around the table about the way they had been treated and Groener in particular apparently exploded with rage, threatening to go to the press to reveal the whole sordid affair. Brüning persuaded him not to, echoing Groener's own comments about 1918–19 in telling his colleague, 'I beg you, don't. In spite of all, Hindenburg is the only rallying point the country still has.'²³⁶ After the cabinet, Brüning saw a rather apologetic Hindenburg and submitted the government's resignation at noon on 30 May. He suggested as his successor Carl Goerdeler, the government's price commissioner and Brüning's candidate for the Prussian premiership, and Hindenburg promised to meet him. That afternoon, the president had the cheek to ask Brüning to see through his final emergency decree, which entailed more painful cuts, but the outgoing chancellor refused to accept the odium and thereby shield his replacement. As he left for the final time, Brüning claimed that Hindenburg said, 'Now I can have a cabinet of my friends.'[237]

The positive relationship between the president and Brüning had been the bedrock of the German governmental system since 1930. Undoubtedly, that relationship had begun to fray in the second half of 1931 as Hindenburg agitated for a shift to the right. It had been severely damaged by the failure to secure a parliamentary extension to his presidential term and, to an even greater extent, by the outcome of the ensuing election. Nevertheless, Hindenburg was probably willing to give Brüning the month of June to see if he could win concessions at the forthcoming Lausanne Conference – it had been Schleicher, Meissner and his own son Oskar who had worked in the background to ensure Brüning's dismissal happened sooner rather than later.[238] L.E. Jones argues that once he had secured Hindenburg's re-election, Brüning became disposable to Schleicher and the Reichswehr.[239] His continued suspicion of the Nazis and willingness to cooperate with the SPD only further alienated the chancellor from the president, the right and the army. It also cannot be ruled out that Schleicher feared Brüning was close to pulling off a great diplomatic triumph that would restore his prestige and Hindenburg's confidence, and indeed war reparations were finally cancelled just over a month later at the Lausanne Conference.[240] Furthermore, throughout May, the cabinet had met almost daily, working feverishly on a public works programme to tackle unemployment that might be instituted if reparations debts were annulled.[241] The news of the sacking was a shock to both the German public and foreign leaders, both of whom had assumed the presidential election had bought Brüning a stay of execution. Just six weeks later his government had been forced from office. Now Germany faced a further period of political uncertainty.

Given the crisis situation Germany was in, and the impending Lausanne Conference, the president made it clear to Schleicher that a new chancellor had to be appointed quickly. Brüning's recommendation – Carl Goerdeler – was a non-starter for the general due to economic reforms he had proposed in April.[242] On 30 May, the day Brüning handed in his resignation, Hindenburg had an audience with the archconservative Count Kuno von Westarp, leader of the KVP and a key figure in the presidential election campaign team. The president begged Westarp to take the chancellorship, being (as was so often the case) reduced to tears, but the count refused, instead telling Hindenburg he should stick with Brüning and not to call elections that would wipe out the moderate right.[243] The choice of the next chancellor had already been made by Kurt von Schleicher rather than the president, however – the Catholic conservative Franz von Papen. On the afternoon of the 30th, Papen had met with Ludwig Kaas, chair of the Centre Party, and was ordered not to take the post. Just hours later, Papen went back on his word. Once again turning to the tearful, emotional plea, President Hindenburg persuaded Papen in a private audience not to listen to his party leader:

Well, my dear Papen, are you going to help me out in this difficult situation? [Papen explains why he must decline the chancellorship.] How can you desert an old man who once more has taken on the responsibility for the Reich despite the weight of his years – now that he asks you to take on a task on which depends the Reich's future? I expect of your sense of duty that you will not decline my call. [Hindenburg explained that the Centre's objections did not matter to him, he wanted a government free of party influence.] You have been a soldier and did your duty in the war. In Prussia we know only obedience when the Fatherland calls![244]

If Papen had ever intended to decline the Reich Chancellery, his resistance now crumbled. He had never been a loyal party man, having endorsed Hindenburg over the Centre Party's own Wilhelm Marx in the 1925 presidential election. The idea that Papen was surprised by his appointment is built on his unreliable, post-Second World War memoirs, and is somewhat undermined by the fact Goebbels recorded in his diary on 25 May that Schleicher had informed him Brüning was to be sacked and replaced by Papen. Schleicher had also firmly offered the aristocrat the chancellorship on 28 May (before Brüning had even been told his fate) although Papen had decided to consult Centre Party chair Ludwig Kaas before accepting the appointment.[245] At the very least, von Papen had several days' notice and probably more due to the fact he had met with Schleicher near the start of the month, presumably to be sounded out for the top job.[246]

Franz von Papen was the very antithesis of Heinrich Brüning. True, both were members of the Catholic Centre Party, but that is where the similarities ended. Brüning, while conservative, was a political moderate. Although he had certainly made mistakes, there can be no doubt he was a skilled and serious politician. Papen on other hand was a reactionary nationalist, belonging to the far right of the party, and his political achievements amounted to nothing more than a few years on the backbenches of the Prussian parliament; he had never made a single speech in the chamber and had lost his seat in April's state elections. Whereas Brüning was cold, austere and frugal, Papen was a wealthy aristocrat, a raconteur and a charmer, always jovial but lacking in substance. The French ambassador to Berlin famously wrote:

> The President's choice met with incredulity. No one but smiled or tittered or laughed because Papen enjoyed the peculiarity of being taken seriously by neither his friends nor his enemies ... He was reputed to be superficial, blundering, untrue, ambitious, vain, crafty and an intriguer ... He is one of those persons who shouldn't be dared to undertake a dangerous enterprise because they accept all dares, take all bets. If he succeeds, he bursts with pleasure; if he fails, he exits with a pirouette.[247]

Even their military careers could not have been more different – Brüning the dogged machine gun commander, Papen the dashing cavalry officer. Papen became internationally notorious in 1915 when he was expelled as German military attaché to the United States for attempting to sabotage the American arms industry and then allowed confidential documents revealing a network of German agents to fall into Allied hands.[248]

Schleicher believed that, as a Centre Party member but of clear nationalist leanings, von Papen would enjoy the backing of a broad parliamentary coalition, stretching from the Nazis to the Catholic Centre. In this, he clearly failed to predict the rather predictable reaction of the Centre to their leader Brüning's unceremonious sacking. He had also promised Hitler fresh Reichstag elections should he support the new cabinet, thus rendering all Schleicher's calculations about parliamentary arithmetic moribund given the current Reichstag was about to be dissolved. The general had engineered Brüning's appointment, but as we have seen, Brüning was very much his own man. On the other hand, Schleicher's choice of Papen as chancellor only really makes sense as a puppet, or even a useful idiot, for his own schemes.[249] The general supposedly told a friend who had questioned the wisdom of appointing a man who did not have much of a head and Schleicher replied, 'He need not have, but he'll make a fine hat!' The composition of the new cabinet, had, after all, already been all but finalised by Schleicher before Hindenburg even offered von Papen the chancellorship.[250] The general had usurped not only the president's constitutional role in selecting a head of government, but also the chancellor's in selecting a team of ministers. Schleicher himself now took the job he had turned down barely a fortnight before when offered it by Brüning, resigning his army commission to become defence minister. A few of the cabinet were Hindenburg's personal picks, such as von Neurath, whom he asked for the previous October, and von Gayl, who had helped turn the president against 'agrarian Bolshevism'.

There can be no doubt that Hindenburg was absolutely delighted with the composition of the new cabinet, made up almost exclusively of conservative and nationalist aristocrats and landowners, many of whom had served in the military and had little or no party affiliation.[251] It must be said, however, that for all his cunning in ousting Brüning, appointing Papen and composing a cabinet designed to please the president, Schleicher underestimated the new chancellor, for he had not counted on the influence the Prussian nobleman might have on the president. Hindenburg and Papen quickly struck up a warm and genuinely close friendship, and for the old man, used to Brüning's detached and matter-of-fact style, dealing with the irrepressibly blithe Papen must have been a welcome relief. Undoubtedly, Papen, despite his lack of political qualities or qualifications, quickly became Hindenburg's favourite chancellor and he started to refer to him by the affectionate nickname Fränzchen, or little Franz.[252] As a result, Schleicher would come to be displaced in the president's confidence by the new man Papen, with disastrous consequences for both the scheming general and Germany.

Most parties were aghast at Hindenburg's decisions, as evidenced when the various parliamentary leaders had audiences with the president on 30–31 May following the opening of the latest session of the Reichstag. Incidentally, Hindenburg did not mention Papen's name to any of them.[253] He received a chorus of disapproval from the party heads, which was hardly surprising considering he had sacked a chancellor who had won a confidence vote just a fortnight before for no clear reason in the midst of complex international negotiations. The Centre Party reacted with a ferocity to Papen's appointment that caught both the new chancellor and the kingmaker Schleicher off guard.[254] It was clear this government would therefore not be able to attract a Reichstag majority. Furthermore, the parties, on the whole, opposed new elections and even Hugenberg warned Hindenburg not to trust the Nazis. Westarp told the president that Brüning had been doing all he could to move the government to the right without losing the toleration of the SPD. Only the DVP actually endorsed the change of government and the Nazis refused to offer any support in writing, despite reassuring Schleicher that they would abide by their gentleman's agreement of 8 May.[255] Within a few days, it became clear that the Nazis would not honour the deal and were opposing the Papen cabinet.[256] Even more worrying perhaps was that, although he would not have recognised it, Schleicher was entering the crucial phase of his taming strategy, i.e. direct negotiation with the NSDAP, politically weakened by the fact he had just lost his two most powerful assets other than the president – Brüning and Groener.[257]

Then, in quick succession, came a raft of policies designed to appease both the Nazis and the president; the Reichstag was dissolved pending fresh elections, the SA ban was lifted, an emergency decree was promulgated ending help for East Elbian peasants, and a means test for unemployment insurance was introduced (the last measure in particular ensured an end to support for the government from the SPD and Centre, tied as they were to the social democratic and Christian trade unions). A scathing attack from Papen on his predecessor (which included the allegation that no true Christian would cooperate with Social Democrats) burnt any remaining bridges with moderate forces.[258] Given that the country had just gone through a two-round presidential contest then a bitterly contested batch of state elections, a fresh national poll was hardly what the nation needed, nor what most of the parties wanted, especially as the current Reichstag still had over two years left to run. Not only that, but the parliament had been in session for less than a month when the dissolution was announced on 4 June. An election only suited the Nazis and Communists, desperate to further destabilise the system and sure of massive gains on their 1930 results. Desperately concerned about the rise in political violence, the premiers of the south German states of Bavaria, Baden and Württemberg met with the Reich

President, protesting the rescinding the of SA ban. Hindenburg, who had Papen by his side to answer most of their questions, only fobbed off these state leaders, assuring them that the brownshirts 'are inspired by strong national[ist] feelings' and reassuring them with an empty promise that should widespread political violence resume, the SA would once again be prohibited.[259]

Within a few weeks, Papen and Schleicher had succeeded in alienating practically the entire political spectrum. The new government was quickly dubbed with a nickname that stuck – the 'cabinet of barons'. Not that Reich President Hindenburg was concerned. After all, these were his 'friends' and he had finally achieved the goal he had sought for many months, the formation of a government of the nationalist right. However, his new cabinet was in an even more precarious position than Brüning's. For while Brüning could count on not just the Reich President's authority, but also the support, or at least toleration, in parliament and the country of a wide spectrum of parties, the Papen cabinet had no popular base whatsoever. It was a true presidential cabinet in the sense it was founded entirely on Hindenburg's power and prestige. The paradox was that, as before, Hindenburg did his best to remain above the political fray and avoid becoming involved in the day-to-day business of government and politics, thereby depriving his government of its only source of authority.[260]

For the fourth time already that year, attention now turned to polling day on 31 July. Exacerbated by the lifting of the SA ban, the election campaign was again marred by violence and disorder. Eighty-six people were killed in political violence in the month of July, including thirty-eight Nazis and thirty Communists, only further adding to the atmosphere of chaos.[261]

Just as in the 1930 election when the president had failed to make any positive statement in favour of his 'Hindenburg cabinet' and its parties, so too in July 1932 did he remain silent, failing to endorse the Papen government.[262] While Hindenburg was undoubtedly motivated in this by the public non-partisanship of his office, his actions, especially in the last weeks and months, had made a mockery of any vestige of neutrality that he might still hold, and he failed to draw the obvious conclusion that by moving towards a presidential system of political legitimisation, the president would have to involve himself in politics. Not that it was especially clear who voters sympathetic to the new chancellor should vote for, given the vociferous opposition of the political parties (including both the Nazis, and Papen's former home, the Catholic Centre) to the cabinet, and Papen's equally vociferous opposition to 'party politics'. Abortive attempts to found a Hindenburg party by those on the moderate right predictably fell apart, not least because Hindenburg had nothing to do with them. Thus voters could only back the government indirectly by supporting the two parties most associated with the landowning and industrial elite – the DNVP and DVP, despite the fact Hugenberg was not close to Papen and the DVP appeared to be rapidly disappearing as a political force.[263]

Lacking any sort of prestige or kudos, the Papen government cast around for good publicity. It plumped for Prussia, where the removal of the SPD-Centre coalition of Otto Braun had long been near the top of right-wingers' wish lists. On 17 July, a convenient *casus belli* presented itself when fifteen people were killed in a bloody clash between Nazis and Communists in Altona in northern Prussia.[264] On 20 July, the Reich government carried out what amounted to a coup against the Prussian government. Using a presidential decree signed by Hindenburg, Papen proclaimed himself Reich-Commissioner for Prussia, ousting the Braun cabinet and replacing them with his own appointees. Reichswehr troops seized the Prussian government buildings in Berlin and arrested police officials. Any civil servants with social democratic leanings were purged and martial law was enforced in the capital. Three leading Prussian police officials were arrested, and the social democratic interior minister was removed from his office by force. The flimsy pretext for this blatant disregard of the rule of law was to blame the Prussian administration for failing to deal with political violence, despite the primary cause of such violence being the lifting of the SA ban by Papen himself. The chancellor in an address to the nation threw in baseless accusations of collaboration with the Communists. Demoralised, powerless and committed to legality, the SPD failed to mount armed resistance or call a general strike, doubting the defence of a caretaker administration would be a sufficiently emotive rallying cry.[265]

In reality, it was probably the last opportunity the labour movement had to forestall dictatorship. For Schleicher, the Prussian coup had two main advantages. First, there remained the possibility that the Nazis would conclude a coalition deal and come to power in Prussia. By gaining control of Germany's largest state, without his oversight, Schleicher believed the Nazis might yet circumvent his taming strategy. Second, given the strong possibility of a Nazi surge in the imminent elections, the general hoped that strong action by the Papen cabinet – in particular removing the Red-Black Braun administration so hated by the German right – might swing rightist voters back towards the non-Nazi right, essentially to the old Hindenburg Bloc parties.[266] This strategy was fatally flawed in that it both massively underestimated the Nazi appeal and ensured the Social Democrats and Centre were now irrevocably lost to the presidents' circle as potential political allies. Hindenburg himself was entirely complicit and indeed pleased with this blatant assault on his own voters; he had long agitated for regime change in Prussia, feeling like many Prussian nationalists that it was a national embarrassment to have Marxists and Catholics running the great state of Bismarck. He had signed Papen's decree and appointed him Reich-Commissioner without what Dorpalen labels 'any twinges of conscience'.[267]

Predictably, with the Great Depression at its height and Nazi terror on the streets, the NSDAP surged dramatically in the election, although it only matched rather than surpassing the 37 per cent achieved by Hitler in the presidential second ballot. This meant the SPD (which had fallen to 21.6 per cent) was for the first time displaced as Germany's largest party, as a brown wave of 230 Nazi deputies entered the Reichstag. The Communist Party also made modest gains of twelve seats, and ten more seats went to the Catholic parties, their voters likely outraged by the sacking of Brüning and the Prussian coup. However, July 1932 saw the annihilation of the moderate parties, especially of the centre-right parties, who had once been the backbone of Hindenburg's political vision and had most closely and loyally associated themselves with the president's brand. The DVP collapsed to 1.2 per cent of the vote, losing all but seven of their seats, while the State Party was reduced to a rump of four deputies. The Christian-Nationalist Farmers' and Peasants' Party (CNBL), whose leaders Schiele and Schlange-Schöningen had been responsible for the failed Eastern Aid programme, was all but wiped out, reduced from nineteen deputies to just a solitary seat as rural areas across the country turned brown. The CSVD and WP became tiny factions of just three and two deputies each. The KVP did not even run and Westarp and Treviranus disappeared from the political stage.[268]

Far and away the most devastating effect of the election was one of simple parliamentary arithmetic. A Nazi-Centre Party coalition would command a majority, and Brüning did explore this option, to no avail.[269] More importantly, the Nazis and Communists combined now held 319 seats, a majority of thirty. While the two parties were extremists on the opposite end of the spectrum who would never cooperate to form a government, and while Communists and brownshirts murdered each other in the streets on a daily basis, in the Reichstag they had a common aim – prevent the proper functioning of parliament in order to cause deadlock and instability that would discredit the democratic system. Since 1930, we have seen various disruptions and no confidence motions tabled by the extremists, but the Reichstag of 1930 had a narrow majority that tolerated the Brüning government, rendering the obstructive tactics of the far left and right largely ineffective. Now, the 'negative majority' of Nazis and Communists could vote down any law, overturn any presidential decree and unseat chancellors to their hearts' content. Papen's government was surely doomed as soon as the Reichstag reconvened, while the whole model of governance used by Hindenburg and his circle since 1930, i.e., rule by presidential decree, had now been taken off the table.

Even more seriously, under Article 43 of the constitution, the president could be impeached with a two-thirds Reichstag majority. A similar majority could uphold an Article 53 motion indicting the president for illegal activities in office. The Prussian coup might provide ample ammunition for either charge, especially as the SPD could provide the votes needed to carry such motions.[270] With an NSDAP-KPD majority, the president would have to change tack. The people had rejected the 'cabinet of barons', which better than any other symbolised his personal political vision, and it now no longer seemed feasible to keep the Nazis out of office any longer, at least not without substantial constitutional changes to take power away from the Reichstag. Papen now started to consider dissolving the Reichstag without calling fresh elections, a move that would essentially move Germany into a dictatorship under Hindenburg. The president and chancellor attended the formal Constitution Day celebrations on 11 August, in which the address delivered by Interior Minister von Gayl promised that the government would defile the very constitution they were celebrating by curtailing universal suffrage, placing limits on the number of permissible parties, removing Article 58 (which dictated that the cabinet was answerable to the Reichstag), creating a stronger upper chamber and making permanent the Reich government's control over Prussia.[271]

Following the election results, and faced with such an apocalyptic outlook, Defence Minister von Schleicher had changed tack, for the scheme of constitutional reform filled him with dread. Whereas before, he had envisaged the taming strategy as incorporating the Nazis as a junior coalition partner, now it seemed the NSDAP had a legitimate claim to the leading role. Schleicher was prepared to countenance such a move, perhaps because he considered Hitler to be under his influence. Historian Peter Hayes argues the most important factor for the general was the fact he believed a Papen government that excluded the Nazis and tried to rip up the constitution would provoke civil war, with one ally admitting, 'Schleicher prefers a Hitler chancellorship because he does not want to allow it to come to a test of the Army.'[272] Thus, in a meeting with the Nazi leader on 5 August, Schleicher gave the impression that Hitler's demands for the chancellorship for himself and the Interior Ministry for his number two, Gregor Strasser, would likely be accepted by the president.[273] The Nazis also demanded the ministries of Justice, Agriculture, and Air, and the Prussian Interior Ministry (with its control over the country's largest police force), but Schleicher believed such a strong Nazi presence had to be risked if civil war was to be avoided and also felt that Hitler would concede control over the SA to the army in the form of the *Wehrsport* programme if he was made chancellor.[274] In contrast, President Hindenburg contemptuously ignored the results of the July election. He had no intention whatsoever of removing Papen, his new favourite, as chancellor, whatever the will of the country.[275] Convinced that the cabinet pleased the people that mattered to him, he saw no need to change anything. Given the seemingly positive outcome of his meeting with Schleicher, however, Hitler went into his famous audience with Hindenburg on 13 August 1932 with a degree of confidence that he was to be awarded the chancellorship. The president, meanwhile, had no intention of doing so and therefore took offence to the Nazi leader's presumptuousness, not forgetting that in his previous meeting with Hitler in October 1931, he had been decidedly unimpressed by the Führer. On 10 August, in a meeting with Schleicher and Papen the president had firmly rejected the prospect of making Hitler chancellor, and this may be the origin of his famous 'Bohemian Corporal' remark regarding the Führer.[276] Hindenburg was also deeply concerned by the dramatic uptick in Nazi violence and their ardent opposition to the Papen government. The election results had been greeted with a fresh orgy of SA violence, with triumphant stormtroopers targeting political opponents and racial enemies, culminating in the brutal murder of a Polish immigrant in his home on the night of 9/10 August in Silesia that shocked civil society.[277] On the morning of 13 August, Hitler met with Schleicher and Papen seperately ahead of his audience with the president. To his surprise, and outrage, they both offered him merely the vice chancellorship. When Hitler arrived at the Presidential Palace at 4.15 pm, a large crowd had gathered, assuming they were catching a glimpse of the new chancellor. Instead, as Hitler now knew, Hindenburg was cool and detached rather than forthcoming.[278] Hitler was joined by Wilhelm Frick and Ernst Röhm, while the field marshal had his secretary Meissner and his chancellor by his side. Hindenburg started by asking directly if Hitler would serve in Papen's government, saying he would welcome the Nazis' cooperation. Hitler repeated the refusal he had given the chancellor that morning – the Nazi movement was so large and powerful that he demanded 'the leadership of the state to its full extent for himself and his party'.[279] Hindenburg showed nothing but contempt for this suggestion, unsurprising given his aversion to the concept of party. He was not prepared, 'before God, his conscience and the Fatherland', to hand total power to a single party, especially one so intolerant of others as the Nazis. He asked Hitler directly whether the Nazis would be in opposition to the government, to which Hitler replied in the affirmative, protesting he had no choice but to do so.[280] The tone of the conversation now changed, in Dorpalen's phrase, to one between field marshal and corporal. Hindenburg expressed bitter disappointment that Hitler had gone back on his earlier pledge to support the government and he also reprimanded Hitler for not conducting himself and his party in a gentlemanly manner, and finally demanded an end to political terror. The president drew the meeting to a close in a manner that revealed he still hoped to cooperate with the Nazis, albeit in a subordinate role, telling Hitler, 'We two are old comrades and want to remain so. The road ahead may bring us together again. So I extend my hand as a comrade.'[281]

Although within the twenty-minute meeting Hitler was composed, afterwards he exploded with rage; there can be no doubt this was a huge setback and appeared to leave the Nazi leader with little option other than armed insurrection. Hitler railed against those present, not least Papen, asking him how he intended to govern without the Reichstag. The chancellor replied nonchalantly, 'The Reichstag? I'm surprised that you of all people think the Reichstag is important.'[282] All the votes and seats Hitler had amassed counted for nothing if Hindenburg refused to make him chancellor. Hindenburg too had showed self-restraint in the meeting, filled as he was by now with not a little contempt for Hitler and particularly unhappy at having to shake the hand of Röhm, who was widely (and correctly) rumoured to be a homosexual.[283] The fact that Papen leaked to the press a sensationalised version of the meeting which overplayed the dressing-down Hitler had received was the first indication that the monster Schleicher had created was starting to develop a mind of its own; Papen, rather than a puppet or useful idiot, was scotching Schleicher's hopes of coming to terms with the Nazis by antagonising Hitler. Clearly, Papen had ambitions of his own and, now that he had the president's confidence, wished to consolidate his hold on power. The only problem was that, without Nazi support, Papen had no solution to Germany's political deadlock.[284]

The president did not see any issue, however, blithely departing for his Neudeck estate that very evening, content his work was done. Doubtless he appreciated the chorus of positive headlines the next morning as Papen's leak ensured the Old Gentleman was once more hailed as a national hero, the defender of order against chaos and the 'guardian of the constitution' against Nazi dictatorship.[285] All the while, Hindenburg and his government discussed the legality of violating the constitution. In a conference at his Neudeck estate on 30 August, Papen and von Gayl persuaded the president that after dissolving the Reichstag, the government should consider decreeing that elections be delayed longer than the statutory sixty days. Both argued that Germany was in a crisis and the precepts of the constitution could be legitimately ignored – both because public opinion would understand and because it was the president's constitutional duty to protect the well-being of the people. His emergency powers under Article 48 allowed for virtually any measure conceivable to defend the state and Gayl also hinted at the possibility of restoring the monarchy in the long term. As Papen argued, 'If Field Marshal and Reich President von Hindenburg who has upheld the constitution so conscientiously decides in the case of a special emergency to deviate just once from the constitution, the German people will surely accept this.'[286] Hindenburg was all too ready to accept this logic and signed a decree dissolving the Reichstag with the date blank, ready for Papen to use at his leisure.

The deficiency of Papen and Hindenburg's strategy was cruelly demonstrated when the Reichstag reconvened after the election and summer recess. First, a new Reichstag presidium was elected, consisting of the parliament's speaker and various other official roles. Nazi predominance ensured Hermann Göring was chosen as the Reichstag's new speaker. He and his fellow presidium members had their customary audience with the president in early September. Göring was keen to insist that there was no need to dissolve the Reichstag; it was not deadlocked but could function as a legislature, as demonstrated by the presidium elections. On the other hand, a DNVP deputy elected to the presidium contradicted the other delegates, telling Hindenburg that he and his party, as well as the German people, supported the cabinet's efforts to create a governmental system immune from party politics. Hindenburg responded that he saw no reason to dismiss his government just because it was the will of some parties, that its policies were inspired by patriotism and that he would retain it even in the event of a no confidence vote.[287] The president had abandoned all pretence of democratic respectability.

On 12 September, knowing full well that the opposition would wish at the earliest opportunity to carry out a no confidence vote that he had no chance of winning, Papen attended the Reichstag expecting to make his first speech to the new parliament. However, events took an unexpected turn when a KPD deputy demanded the order of business be amended and a no confidence motion be held first. Just a single Reichstag deputy had to object to overrule this suggestion, but no one spoke out.[288] A half-hour adjournment allowed Papen to have his pre-signed dissolution decree hurriedly fetched from his office in the Reich Chancellery. He effectively hoped to dissolve the newly elected assembly before it had the chance to do anything at all, highlighting how far democracy in Germany had sunk. Papen then attempted to rise to speak in order to announce the dissolution of the Reichstag, but Speaker Göring simply ignored him, deliberately looking the other way. Papen waved his folder and eventually threw it (complete with the signed presidential order dissolving the parliament) onto Göring's podium and walked out with his ministers. The Nazi aviator disregarded the chancellor entirely (despite the fact the assembly was now legally dissolved) and informed the Reichstag that instead of hearing from Papen they would vote on a no confidence motion tabled by the Communist Party. In the resulting vote, Hindenburg's cabinet of his 'friends' received a mere forty-two votes of confidence (mainly from the DNVP and DVP) and 512 votes against (from virtually all other parties).[289] It was a complete humiliation, the worst parliamentary defeat any German government has ever suffered. Papen decided to not yet play his final card of suspending elections but sought to punish the parties who had so embarrassed him by subjecting them to yet another election campaign, with polling day scheduled for 6 November 1932. A heated meeting between Hindenburg, Papen and Göring followed in which the president stood by his chancellor, insisting the vote was not binding because the Reichstag had already been dissolved when it was held and therefore Papen would remain.[290] While Hindenburg and Papen got their way, the case for impeachment was growing against the president, for the dissolution was constitutionally highly questionable. Not only that, but while the no confidence vote did not stand, its effect in totally discrediting Papen and his cabinet cannot be denied. And as a result of the wranglings in Berlin, most of the country was to go to the polls for the fifth time that year.

Hindenburg digs Weimar's grave

As we have seen, Hindenburg was now contemplating amending the constitution and was determined to retain Papen as his chancellor regardless of the democratic will of the Reichstag and the electorate, let alone taking into account the preferences of his own voters in the spring. He was now behaving more like a replacement Kaiser than a constitutional president; unaccountable and delegating power to a narrow circle of favourites rather than acquiescing to the will of the parliament. Hindenburg's plans for the future, such as they were, were outlined by Chancellor von Papen's most significant speech of the election campaign. On 12 October 1932, Papen spoke to an audience of Bavarian businessmen and outlined the government's intentions regarding constitutional reform and a more authoritarian future:

> We want to create a powerful and nonpartisan state authority which will not become a plaything to be tossed about by political and social forces, but will stand above them unshakable as a *'rocher de bronce'* [an allusion to a phrase used by a Prussian king to describe the statuelike nature of his soldiers]. The reform of the constitution must ensure that such a powerful and authoritarian government has the right relationship to the people.
>
> The great basic laws contained in Part II of the Weimar Constitution are not to be undermined, but it is time to revitalize the forms of political life. The Reich government must gain more independence from the parties. Its existence must not be at the mercy of chance majorities. The relationship between government and the popular legislature must be regulated in such a way that the government rather than the parliament controls the authority of the state.
>
> To counterbalance one-sided decisions by the Reichstag based on party interests, Germany needs a special First Chamber with clearly defined authority and strong legislative powers. Today the Reich President's power of decree, based on Article 48 of the Reich constitution, is the only remedy for the extreme parliamentary system and for the failure of the Reichstag. But as soon as normal, stable conditions prevail once again, there will no longer be any reason to apply Article 48 in its present form.
>
> The Reich government will complete the draft of the constitution so that it will be ready when the new Reichstag convenes.[291]

Papen also addressed the Nazi question, which remained at the forefront of German politics, including Hindenburg's role in Hitler's grasp for power:

> The current claim that I, the chancellor, prevented National Socialism from taking governmental responsibility is a falsification of history. Herr Hitler did not accept the offer of 13 August of a share of power in the Reich and in Prussia, which would have assured the NSDAP decisive influence in

the government, because he believed, as the leader of a movement with 230 seats in parliament, that he had to lay claim to the position of chancellor. He made this claim based on his party's principle of 'totality' and 'exclusivity'. The insistence of the NSDAP that they had not demanded full power, but had been ready to give other men outside of the movement a role in the government, is therefore another false representation of the facts which it is my duty to correct. Would such a concession have changed anything in their claim to exclusive leadership? It is well known that the Reich President, who alone has the right to appoint the chancellor, rejected this claim to totality. There cannot be any doubt why he rejected it. It certainly is not a question of personal aversion to the movement's leader, because the Reich President stands head and shoulders above such considerations. The motives shaping the decision of the head of state were solely based on principle.

The essential element of every conservative worldview is that it is anchored in the divine order of things. That is also its fundamental difference from the doctrine followed by the NSDAP. Their principle of 'exclusivity', of the political 'all or nothing', and their mystical messianic belief in their powerfully eloquent Führer as the only one called to preside over our destiny gives the party the character of a political religion. And it is precisely here that I see the insurmountable difference between a conservative politics based on religion and a National Socialist religion based on politics.[292]

Despite his name being increasingly dragged into the campaign, as per usual, Hindenburg himself remained above the political fray. The president's eighty-fifth birthday, on 2 October, also attracted much comment in the press. The running theme of most editorials was praise for the Old Gentleman, and in particular his political wisdom at such a turbulent time, with even the Nazi press taking a deferential tone. In light of the fall of Brüning and more pertinently the Prussian coup, the Social Democratic *Vorwärts* struck a more sombre tone:

> Half a year ago the German Social Democrats cast their ballot for him to ward off grave political dangers. If they cannot wholeheartedly join in [today's] celebrations, their aloofness is due to the many events which have taken place between that election and this anniversary. ... This may be hard, but for the sake of truth it must be said that our political opposition which we have never concealed and which we have carried on in chivalrous form against our aged head of state has been reenforced by many human disappointments. These disappointments keep us from entering the circle of the celebrants.[293]

Despite the authoritarian turn that the presidential regime appeared to have taken in recent months, the liberal *Frankfurter Zeitung* noted that most democrats continued to revere Hindenburg: 'The same people who reject Papen do not feel hindered in believing in Hindenburg, in spite of everything that has happened. The people view Hindenburg as the representative of their best virtues.'[294] Naturally, Papen's statement on the president's birthday was positively messianic: 'I believe that Providence has sent us a man in Hindenburg as we need him in this most difficult emergency. Miracles do still occur in the history of our people.'[295] The Hindenburg myth, in all its various forms, remained alive and kicking, despite the controversies of the summer.

As in July, however, supporters of the president's government could only back it indirectly by voting DVP or DNVP, the two once-dominant parties of the German right who had been reduced to small factions by the Nazi surge. The DVP at least could claim to be 'the only party which has stood by Hindenburg through all the political shifts and changes'.[296] The campaign itself was lacklustre and uninspired, as might be expected as election fatigue set in after so many polls in quick succession. Activists were exhausted, voters apathetic and party coffers empty. This latest election seemed to offer little hope of resolution.[297] The only thing the Nazis' latest efforts achieved was to alienate a section of their own supporters, who were confused by Hitler's refusal to work with Hindenburg and Papen and put off by the party's vociferous attacks on what was essentially a right-wing authoritarian regime. Middle-class voters, the backbone of the Nazi electorate, might also have been frightened off by the outbreak of a public transport strike in Berlin on 2 November, just four days before polling day, which was a joint action by the Nazi and Communist trade unions.[298]

The election of 6 November 1932 was a severe setback for the NSDAP, but it did little to change the political landscape. It had been little more than three months since the last Reichstag election on 31 July 1932, and in that short time, the Nazis had haemorrhaged 2 million votes. The 37 per cent achieved in July, in the Prussian elections and in the presidential second round, now seemed like a peak that had passed rather than a base camp on the way to a Nazi majority. A slight bump in support for the DNVP and DVP suggested that some right-wing, middle-class voters were beginning to slip away from the Nazis back to their traditional allegiances, perhaps frustrated with voting for Hitler four times already that year without him gaining any sort of power. If the Nazis were unwilling to cooperate with Hindenburg and his allies, there was little point in voting for them, for they would remain locked out of power. Still, the two grand old parties of the right only achieved 10 per cent of the vote and sixty-three seats between them.[299]

Nevertheless, the November elections had resolved nothing. The Nazi-KPD 'negative majority' remained (thirty-four Nazi seats lost were to some extent compensated by eleven Communist gains) making a resumption of rule by presidential decree impossible. There also remained the possibility that a two-thirds majority might be found to prosecute or impeach the president should the Nazis, Communists and Social Democrats all desire to do so. The only thing the election had changed was that a Nazi-Centre Party coalition was no longer viable at the Reich level, not that it was ever a realistic prospect. For Hindenburg and his circle, the only two options left on the table were stark, and they remained the same as in August: either secure Nazi support so that the government would again enjoy a majority or suspend the Reichstag and move towards army-backed presidential authoritarianism, at least on a temporary basis. Naturally, the government thought it best to pursue all legal avenues first and invited the parties of the Reichstag to talks. The response was almost wholly negative, unsurprising given the results of the confidence vote just two months before, with the SPD, Centre and BVP all advising Papen to resign, and the Nazis refusing to even attend negotiations.[300] The Nazis were at their lowest ebb for some time. Nazi propagandist and Berlin regional leader Joseph Goebbels admitted to some of the issues facing the party in his diary entries of early November:

> 6 November 1932: We now face difficult struggles that will require sacrifices. The main thing is to maintain the Party. The organization must be reinforced and its spirit must be raised. The series of mistakes and shortcomings that have crept in must be stopped. But we must not lose sight of the fact that hardly ten percent of the people stand behind the present government. It therefore cannot hold up. Change of some kind will have to occur. ... What is unpopular today will be popular tomorrow. We must only stand fast, not give in, and insist that we are right. ...

> 11 November 1932: I accept a report about the financial state of the Berlin organization. It is quite desperate. Only low tide, debts, and obligations, along with the complete impossibility of coming up with funds in larger amounts after this defeat ... We are advised to remain hard and not to initiate any negotiations. This is superfluous advice as we didn't think otherwise even for a second. We must now launch our attacks on the Communists more scathingly. During the strike we came into unpleasant but unavoidable contact with them. Now we have to again keep our distance. It is also important that we don't give way to illusions and stumble into a second August 13th [Hitler's fateful meeting with Hindenburg]. We must not get drawn into any more verbal negotiations at all.[301]

Goebbels was in many ways putting a brave face on things. The party had lost votes in every region of the country; there was a noticeable flight of members, and severe depression and despondency amongst those who remained.[302] At every level, the party was bankrupt, with huge debts, and a 'hopeless' financial outlook and local elections in Saxony and Thuringia only added to the woe; the Nazi vote was down on the 6 November result by more than 30,000 in the city of Dresden when residents returned to the polls on 14 November and in

Thuringia on 3 December, the vote in the Weimar district was down 9,000 on the previous month.[303] Despite the bleak outlook, Hitler refused to give up on his 'all-or-nothing' negotiation strategy – either the chancellorship or no Nazi participation. Having failed to attract a parliamentary majority, the cabinet met on 17 November and Papen convinced colleagues to submit their resignation to Hindenburg. They would continue to serve in office while the president carried out his constitutional duty of attempting to find a chancellor that could command a Reichstag majority. When he inevitably failed and asked Papen to continue in office, the cabinet would agree on the principle of having extended powers, due to the fact that it would have been demonstrated by the failed negotiations that parliamentary governance was impossible.[304] As leader of the largest party in the Reichstag, Papen was cleverly placing the onus on Hitler to resolve the deadlock.

A wary Hitler was summoned to the Presidential Palace on 19 November for a private audience of around half an hour, which Goebbels described as a 'chess match for power' between the president and Führer.[305] Once more, large crowds gathered, anticipating the announcement of a Hitler government. Predictably, Hindenburg appealed to the Nazis' patriotism and nationalism, again asking them to participate in the government: 'The times are too serious for everyone to follow his own personal interests and go his own way. We have to put our differences behind us and come together in an emergency community.'[306] However, the president did deviate into grumbling, complaining about Nazi participation in the transport strike and about the SA shouting 'Awake' at him (from the popular Nazi slogan 'Germany, awake!') during the annual Tannenberg commemoration: 'Well, I am not asleep!' the Old Gentleman muttered.[307] Again, predictably, Hitler was deferential but repeated his demand for the leadership in the form of the Chancellery. Hindenburg now moved to – as historian Henry A. Turner Jr puts it – call Hitler's bluff, requesting the Nazi leader report within three days as to whether he could form a cabinet with majority support and informing the Führer that while he would be permitted the chancellorship, the president would select the foreign and defence ministers in such an administration.[308] Hitler, however, had no intention of forming a parliamentary government or negotiating with other parties; he wanted and needed the access to Hindenburg's emergency Article 48 decree powers that Papen and Brüning had enjoyed. His counteroffer of forming a presidential rather than parliamentary cabinet that would retain Neurath and Schleicher as foreign and defence ministers was simply ignored by the president, for it had not met the requirements the latter had set out, namely a Reichstag majority. Hindenburg turned down both Hitler's verbal request in the meeting for decree powers and an open letter two days later asking for the same thing.[309] Quite simply, the president did not trust Hitler as he had Brüning and as he continued to trust Papen, although he had appeared to budge from his August position by accepting in theory a Hitler chancellorship should the Führer be able to assemble a parliamentary majority. In reality, this was something of an empty promise given the impossibility of the Nazis cobbling together a majority in the Reichstag and the party leadership rightly suspected the presidential circle of trying to 'screw us'.[310]

Hitler and Meissner now exchanged a series of letters in which the president's secretary insisted a party leader could not head a presidential cabinet, while Hitler questioned the constitutionality of Hindenburg's conditions, such as usurping the chancellor's right to select cabinet ministers, and continued to demand the powers his predecessors had enjoyed.[311] Hitler also complained that Brüning had been a party leader but entrusted with presidential powers, but Meissner deflected, claiming that Brüning's administration had started life as a parliamentary one and only evolved into a presidential cabinet when the chancellor had gained the full confidence of the Reich President.[312] The sterile negotiations were brought to an end on 24 November by an open letter from Hindenburg's office to Hitler, which stated:

> [The president] believes he cannot answer to the German people for giving presidential powers to the leader of a party that has over and over emphasised its exclusivity and has opposed him personally and the political and economic measures he has regarded as necessary. The president must under these circumstances fear that a presidential cabinet led by you would inevitably develop into a party dictatorship with all of its consequences for a heightening of the contradictions in the German nation, something he could never reconcile with his oath and his conscience.[313]

At the same time, Hindenburg also met with the leaders of the DVP, DNVP, BVP and Centre. The SPD were not even extended the curtsey of an invitation. The rightist parties endorsed Hindenburg's authoritarian direction, although Hugenberg, embittered by the failures of the Harzburg Front, warned the president not to trust Hitler. Only Ludwig Kaas, chairman of the Centre Party, struck a more alarmist note, epitomising the fear of Germany's political and economic elite in warning that another bleak winter combined with Nazi failure would only help the growing Communists.[314] It must be said that Hindenburg was only going through the motions with these audiences; he simply read out questions prepared by his secretary Meissner and ended each meeting by telling his visitor:

> At this time I limit myself to the statement that I shall under no circumstances turn over the government to the parties again, nor am I willing to appoint a government formed by the parties and dominated by them. I also am very anxious to keep intact the union of Reich and Prussia.[315]

Clearly, the president was set on both Papen and the extra-constitutional route, yet paradoxically, Hindenburg's democratic credentials remained strong. After the now-famous episode of 13 August, the president's latest rebuff of Hitler produced a second wave of the newest strain of the Hindenburg myth – that of Hindenburg as guardian of the Republic and defender of constitutional order.³¹⁶

While Papen appeared to have indirectly triumphed from the abortive negotiations and was all set to suspend parliament and rule by decree undisturbed, the man who had made him chancellor was growing increasingly worried. The Nazi-Communist Berlin transport strike of early November had put the frighteners up Defence Minister Kurt von Schleicher and many establishment figures. The prospect of united action by the NSDAP and KPD and their considerable union and paramilitary arms might be enough to overwhelm the forces of order and played into Schleicher's pre-existing fears about revolutionary elements within the Nazi movement that needed to be tamed. In reality, he and the army had little to fear; Hitler was highly embarrassed by the strike action but could not condemn it on the eve of an election.³¹⁷ The actual likelihood of Nazi-Communist cooperation in a general strike or revolutionary uprising or putsch was practically nil, not least due to rabid anti-Bolshevism of the Nazis and in particular the SA. However, in the second half of November, Schleicher's fears crystallised into opposition to Franz von Papen, the man he alone had crowbarred into the Reich Chancellery just six months before. Schleicher earnestly believed that should Papen get his way and attempt to suspend the Reichstag, declare a state of emergency and overturn the constitution, it would provoke a civil war or general strike. It would be a civil conflict in which, Schleicher believed, the army and establishment would be in a perilous position – for the November elections demonstrated that Papen's scheme would have just 10 per cent of the populace behind it and it would face the opposition of the Nazis and Communists, as well as the SPD and organised labour. Communists, as well as the SPD and organised labour. Together, these forces could paralyse the country, and in this context the transport strike of early November, which had brought Berlin to a standstill, might be an early portent of the chaos to come.³¹⁸ Papen, though, was absolutely determined to remain in power despite his decisive rejection by both the electorate and the Reichstag in recent months. Equally, Hindenburg was totally committed to Papen, both because his cabinet was an embodiment of the president's political vision by this stage and perhaps even more importantly because Hindenburg had struck up a genuine friendship with the charming cavalry officer. He liked and trusted him more than any of his previous chancellors and rejected all advice in late November from Meissner, Brüning, Kaas and others that he should contemplate an alternative chancellor, angrily telling Kaas, 'I am getting into an ever more difficult position, they want to take away the man in whom I have confidence and force another chancellor upon me.'³¹⁹

Sticking with Papen, however, meant drastic action. Presidential rule by Article 48 was not sustainable as the continued Nazi-Communist negative majority meant decrees could be overturned and a vote of no confidence could be tabled at any time. The Reichstag therefore would have to be dissolved and fresh elections delayed to prevent the cabinet being overthrown or rendered impotent. The likely violent opposition to this from the KPD and NSDAP would have to be defeated by the forces of order, meaning the Nazis and Communists may well have to be suppressed. To facilitate this, President Hindenburg would have to call a state of emergency, thereby suspending the civil liberties guaranteed by the constitution. As Papen had made clear, significant constitutional revision would follow. This was a path that naturally came with great risks. Papen made the case for this presidential-military dictatorship to Hindenburg and Schleicher in a crunch meeting on the evening of 1 December in the Presidential Palace. He reassured Hindenburg that although he was right to take his oath to the constitution seriously, the extraordinary circumstances demanded flexibility and that there was historical precedent in the actions of Bismarck and Wilhelm I. Additionally, he promised not to revise the constitution without a referendum or the approval of a new national assembly. In effect, the dictatorship would be a temporary one, at least for the foreseeable.[320] What the chancellor did not realise was that General von Schleicher was actually opposed to such a scheme. Crushing the Nazis was risky, would fly in the face his long-term 'taming strategy' and wreck the *Wehrsport* programme. Furthermore, while a move against the Nazis was conceivable in the spring, when Schleicher had powerful allies in Brüning and Groener, and also could have counted on the backing of the SPD, Centre and the south German states, all these forces had been alienated by Papen and would never support a power grab by the cabinet of barons.[321]

More than anything else, Schleicher feared a repeat of 1923: uprisings from the extreme left and right, the danger of civil war, and the loyalty of the officer corps torn by nationalist sympathies. He wrote at this time: 'prospects for the army in this extremely unhappy: concern that we would stand in a few days in the streets against nine-tenths of the people.'[322] He clearly believed the Reichswehr could not risk backing a Papen dictatorship, if nothing else due to the chancellor's own unpopularity. The general also was reassured by communication from Hermann Göring that Hitler's latest rejection of cabinet participation was not final.[323] In order to remove Papen, Schleicher knew he would not be able to turn the president against the chancellor (as he had done with Brüning), for Hindenburg was clinging to Papen despite his numerous failures and obvious failings. Instead, it was necessary to undermine the case Papen would make for suspending the Reichstag and declaring a state of emergency. To this end, Schleicher had his adjutant, Lieutenant Colonel Eugen Ott, organise a Reichswehr war game for 24–25 November.[324] The war game simulated a worst-case scenario of a joint Nazi-Communist uprising coinciding with a Polish invasion of East Prussia. The conclusion was that the army would be defeated. It should be noted that Poland had no military plans whatsoever against Germany's frontiers (at this time they were fully focused on the Soviet threat) and the Defence Ministry was aware of this – Ott's war game was therefore a political ploy to strengthen the hand of his master.[325] Schleicher had sat on this information over the last few days, suggesting he intended to use it for maximum political effect. At this point, as the three men who would decide the fate of Germany discussed the 'nuclear option' of a state of emergency, Schleicher interrupted Papen and offered a more palatable solution. He continued to hold his tongue about the Reichswehr war game, offering a positive rather than an apocalyptic case for a change of chancellor. The general claimed he could form a government with majority support in the Reichstag, removing the necessity for such drastic steps as a state of emergency or violation of the constitution.

Many histories of the period, even those published in the last few years, claim that Schleicher proposed to form a government with the backing of a broad front, an alliance stretching from the labour movement and Social Democrats through to the moderate wing of the Nazi Party and their union syndicate.[326] This 'union front' would be united in their support for job creation schemes and measures to alleviate the suffering of the working class. Crucial to this scheme would be splitting the Nazi Party by inviting Hitler's number two – Gregor Strasser – to join the government, bringing with him about sixty Nazi Reichstag deputies. In all likelihood, the broad alliance strategy is a myth that has become accepted fact simply because it was heavily rumoured at the time, repeated in the memoirs of politicians who were not privy to Schleicher's thinking and has subsequently been repeated by historians ever since. In reality, the leading studies of Schleicher's political career conclude that there is no firm evidence he ever intended to split the Nazis and form a broad alliance, and there is considerable evidence to the contrary.[327] Before, during and after his chancellorship, Schleicher insisted in both public and private that he had no intention of splitting the Nazi Party, and that such a split would only benefit the Communists, telling fellow officers and the British ambassador that December that a Nazi split was not in Germany's interests and instead it was necessary to 'harness the movement in service to the state'.[328] The general also had an article planted in the press on 14 December insisting that the Nazi Party could only achieve its goals by cooperation with 'those forces which have always formed the core of the Prussian-German state [the military and conservative elite]', effectively an appeal for full cooperation.[329] Around the same time he also told his military colleagues that there was no way any Nazis, even Strasser, would participate in his government without the 'Messiah's blessing' (i.e. Hitler's approval), but that this was something he hoped to win.[330] Furthermore, Gregor Strasser had no intention of defecting and he remained totally loyal to the Führer – his clash with Hitler was over strategy rather than ideology or vision. Strasser, as head of the party machine and organisation, was desperately worried by the apparent Nazi decline in late 1932 and was painfully aware that the coffers were empty. With the situation only likely to deteriorate as time went on, Strasser considered Hitler's all-or-nothing strategy of holding out for the chancellorship and accepting no other government role as sabotaging the party's chances of gaining power. Strasser believed that even with a junior role in a coalition, the Nazis would be able to seize control of the state and create a dictatorship, and indeed was preparing the party machine for exactly this scenario.[331] Therefore, Strasser emphatically did not represent the 'moderate' wing of the Nazis, nor an anti-Hitler faction, he merely disagreed with his leader's negotiating tactics in the second half of 1932.

Both Schleicher and Strasser therefore saw their talks in December as a way of persuading an obstinate Hitler to relent; for the cunning general, Gregor Strasser, was a reliable partner within the upper echelons of the Nazi leadership who would be key in persuading the Führer to come round – not a potential Nazi defector. Indeed, when Strasser was pushed out of the party on 8 December, Schleicher was devastated and in denial; he did not want Strasser and his supporters to cede from the NSDAP, he wanted Strasser to use his influence to bring the whole NSDAP behind his regime.[332] What of the idea that Schleicher planned to enlist the support of the labour movement? Although Schleicher did make contact with the social democratic unions (ADGB) in the autumn/winter of 1932, and they made positive noises about his job creation scheme announced in December, this should not be seen as part of his effort to build a parliamentary majority; indeed, the general had told the French ambassador a few days before his appointment as chancellor that the SPD would undoubtedly oppose his cabinet.[333] The ADGB leaders did not control the political policy of the SPD, and there had been a growing rift between the two over the course of the year. Quite simply, the unions would not be able to compel the Social Democratic parliamentary party to back the general's government even if they had wanted to.

The SPD meanwhile condemned the union leaders' flirtation with the new chancellor, and parliamentary support or even toleration of Schleicher was a political impossibility for the Social Democrats due to their worrying losses to the Communists in recent elections (largely interpreted as a consequence of their toleration of Brüning) and the defence minister's recent role in the Prussian coup.[334] Schleicher's aim in charming the unions was to ensure both popular support for his economic proposals and, more importantly, an attempt to forestall a general strike or other worker unrest should he be made chancellor or even achieve his goal of bringing the Nazis into government – after all, the great fear that had prompted him to oust Papen was that the latter's government had been opposed by the Nazis, Communists *and* organised labour.[335]

However, the most damning argument against the notion Schleicher was seeking a broad alliance by splitting the Nazis is simple parliamentary arithmetic. Even if the general believed he could win the support, or at least toleration, of sixty Nazi defectors, the SPD, Centre, BVP and all the minor splinter parties of the centre-right and right, he would still fall short of the 293 votes he needed in the Reichstag.[336] The only way a workable majority could be formed in this scenario would be if Schleicher could add either the DVP or DNVP to this rainbow coalition, yet both of these parties were totally opposed to administrations that were even tolerated by the SPD and were determined to exclude the labour movement from political power. As we have seen, the Nationalist leader Hugenberg's obstinate opposition to the Brüning government was grounded in the fact the chancellor was tolerated by, and therefore had to keep happy, the Social Democrats. In the meantime, the DVP had broken with Brüning in 1931 and aligned itself with the National Opposition in supporting the formation of an entirely right-wing government.[337] Neither party would have backed a 'union front' government; both had leant their parliamentary backing to Papen's cabinet of barons precisely because it had excluded the SPD and removed them from power in Prussia. The reality since 1930 had been that a government could either have the backing of the Social Democrats and the labour movement, or the business and landowner-orientated DVP and DNVP, not both. A 'union front' of both moderate Nazis and their NSBO syndicate and the Catholic and social democratic unions and parties was therefore not a basis for a majority Reichstag government due to simple arithmetic. And without the 121 seats the SPD commanded, Schleicher had no hope of building a non-Nazi majority; even if he had enlisted the DVP, DNVP and indeed all parties rightwards of the SPD, plus his sixty Strasser Nazis, he would have fallen even further short of the 293 target. Thus, the theory that Schleicher convinced Hindenburg that the president could avoid extra-constitutional measures by entrusting the defence minister with forming a majority government based on splitting the Nazis relies on the supposition that both men did not grasp basic addition, without even getting into the political realities such a coalition evidently defied. Schleicher promised to build a Reichstag majority, but this was literally only possible if he enlisted the support or toleration of the entire Nazi Party. He was well aware this meant convincing Hitler, but he believed he could succeed where Papen had failed, not least by using Strasser to influence the Führer. Therefore, the motives of both Hindenburg and Schleicher in the winter of 1932 have been looked on with more generosity than is actually due, for the president made Schleicher chancellor in December not in the hope of fatally dividing the Nazis and breaking Hitler's power, but instead believing the general might finally be able to win Nazi support for or participation in a right-wing government. Schleicher, as he told the cabinet the next morning, was seeking to build a parliamentary majority of 306 with the backing of the NSDAP, Centre, BVP and splinter parties, and this was a scheme he would vainly pursue until mid-January.[338]

However, to return to the conference of 1 December, Schleicher's proposal was, at first, rejected. A tired and agitated Hindenburg was unconvinced by the defence minister's arguments, doubted the Nazis could be won over and instead asked Papen to form a government and prepare for a state of emergency.[339]

Schleicher was stunned and silent; his scheme had unexpectedly fallen at the first hurdle and the president no longer appeared to take his advice at face value. Hindenburg now seemed to trust Papen more than him. Schleicher soon sprang into action, however, telephoning the seven army district commanders to canvass their opinion on a state of emergency, and all advised against it, warning of the inadequacy of their forces.[340] Papen also hoped to shore up his support and to that end called a cabinet meeting for the next morning, 2 December 1932. With the ministers assembled and running out of time and options, Schleicher now chose to play his ace card – Wargame Ott, as it was codenamed. Lieutenant Colonel Ott was summoned and he, alongside his superior, presented the findings of their doomsday scenario. Despite the fact that this was a rather fanciful scenario, the cabinet was duly shaken and Papen reportedly wept at the news the army might fail.[341] Ott certainly laid it on thick, pointing out that sabotage and passive resistance would undermine the forces of order and that in the event of a general strike, the continuity of essential services and the food supply could not be guaranteed. Historian F.L. Carsten points out that the scenario failed to mention at all the considerable forces, likely numbering in the millions, that would have assisted the Reichswehr and police, namely the Reichsbanner, social democratic and Christian trade unions, which combined had considerably more influence within the industrial workforce than the Nazis and Communists, making the general strike predicted in the war game a red herring.[342] Schleicher did concede that this was a worst-case rather than a likely scenario but none of the ministers questioned the Reichswehr's findings, perhaps, as Dorpalen suggests, because most of them had already decided they did not wish to back Papen any longer.[343] Schleicher told his frightened audience (the finance minister wrote that the report left a 'devasting impression' on the cabinet[344]) that he was not willing to risk the Reichswehr to save a government that was opposed by 'nine-tenths of the German people'.[345] While the army's report was almost certainly overly pessimistic, and probably had been designed deliberately for this political end, it had had the desired effect.[346] The cabinet were convinced that a state of emergency was no longer an option, essentially leaving the chancellor high and dry. Papen immediately went to the president and relayed what had happened in cabinet. He asked whether Hindenburg wished him to continue, as he had done the previous night, arguing that Schleicher was exaggerating and saying that if he, Papen, were to remain as chancellor, a new defence minister would have to be found. The only alternative, Papen stated, was for Hindenburg to make Schleicher chancellor.[347] As seems to have been typical in moments of crisis, the supposedly stoical Hindenburg both spoke with a shaky, emotional voice, tears running down his cheeks, and abandoned the man closest to him: 'You will think me a scoundrel, my dear Papen, if I change my mind now. But I am too old to take on the responsibility for a civil war at the end of my life. So in God's name we must let Herr von Schleicher try his luck.'[348]

Ultimately, the chance to avoid taking such a serious gamble with his presidency, and more importantly with his reputation and legacy, proved too tempting for Hindenburg to turn down. The promise of a return to constitutional normality was too alluring and, as the above quote betrays, Hindenburg seems to have been thinking as much about himself and his mythical standing as anything else.

Thus, on 3 December 1932, Kurt von Schleicher was sworn in as the third chancellor of the year. Just as after his presidential election victory, Hindenburg was cantankerous and resentful. In particular, he was angry with Schliecher for ousting his favourite *Fränzchen*, who had left the Presidential Palace with a parting gift, a signed photo of the president bearing the inscription 'I had a comrade'. Hindenbug was outraged when he heard that Schleicher had sounded out the district generals on the night of 1 December – for the president had decided at the meeting of that evening that Papen and Schleicher should prepare for a state of emergency and it appeared that the army, and Schleicher in particular, had undermined his wishes and, ultimately, disobeyed orders.[349] It must be said that Schleicher took on the chancellorship reluctantly; he had enjoyed wielding power without responsibility in the background and was neither charismatic nor well known outside of the political elite, but he felt compelled by military duty to accept Hindenburg's order to assume high office.[350] Schleicher also entered the Chancellery in a badly exposed political position – he had secretly sounded out Hitler as to whether the Führer would support a Schleicher cabinet and received a negative reply, and the general was without the strong political allies he had enjoyed in the past such as Brüning and Groener. Most worryingly, his relationship with the president was on the wane, as we have seen. The deterioration had begun when Hindenburg had responded adversely to Schleicher's suggestion that he make Hitler chancellor in early August and his friendship with the president's son and aide-de-camp Oskar had been terminated when a caustic remark made by Schleicher about Oskar had found its way back to the younger Hindenburg. As a result, Papen had come to replace Schleicher as the president's closest confidant and advisor, and the general had now been responsible for Papen's removal.[351] Schleicher was thus forming a presidential government despite enjoying little confidence from the president. To make matters worse, Papen (supposedly temporarily) remained in situ in the apartment in the Reich Chancellery as Hindenburg had asked him to stay on as a personal advisor. Papen was therefore living in the same building as Hindenburg, for the Presidential Palace on the Wilhelmstrasse was being renovated and he was staying in the Chancellery just a few doors down, while Schleicher continued to reside in his apartment in the Defence Ministry some streets away (for he remained defence minister as well as chancellor), meaning that Papen was both literally and figuratively closer to the president.[352]

Schleicher's political ascension brought little concrete change, for the cabinet of barons had been his creation. Von Gayl was dropped as interior minister as he was most tarnished by the Prussian coup, and Günther Gereke, who had chaired the Hindenburg presidential campaign, was made commissioner of works to oversee a job creation scheme. Another move designed to distance the new administration from the worst excesses of Papen's regime was that Schleicher dropped his predecessor's plan for authoritarian constitutional reform and the most unpopular measures from the latest round of budget cuts.[353] The chancellor informed his cabinet that his intention was to create a Reichstag majority of 306 seats on the basis of the NSDAP (196 seats), Centre (70), BVP (20), and the smaller rightist parties (a further 20).[354] It was now therefore time for Schleicher to try his Strasser gambit. In fact, he had been working for some time on a solution that would involve Nazi participation in his cabinet with two or three seats including Strasser as vice chancellor and prime minister of Prussia. Such terms had been all but agreed in late November between Schleicher and Strasser (who had Hitler's blessing in the negotiations), until the Führer unexpectedly, and without explanation, changed his mind on 30 November.[355] Strasser was humiliated and aghast at this last-minute change of strategy, for he was convinced that continued refusal to take a share in power would be disastrous for the party. It was too late, however, for Schleicher to change course (even though his strategy had rested on Hitler approving Nazi participation in the cabinet) for he was already in the process of ousting Papen.

On 4 December, the new chancellor met with Gregor Strasser and Wilhelm Frick and it is likely he repeated his willingness to hand over the vice chancellorship and premiership of Prussia in exchange for Nazi Reichstag toleration or even support; with the party's number two running Germany's largest state, the Nazis would surely find it impossible to oppose the government. The posts offered to Strasser should be interpreted as an attempt by Schleicher to strengthen the former's hand in negotiations with Hitler and the Nazi leadership rather than an effort to split the party, as has been discussed.[356] The only new development from the meeting was that Schleicher told Strasser that he would dissolve parliament if the Nazis refused to tolerate his cabinet.[357] This revelation was the final straw for Strasser, for it could mean one of only two things. Either Schleicher would proceed to carry out the Papen plan of a state of emergency and authoritarianism, thereby locking the Nazis out of power. Or else, Schleicher planned to hold yet another election, one in which all the indications were the NSDAP would suffer additional demoralising reverses that would only weaken their negotiating position further. Strasser therefore believed that, for the Nazis, it was now or never – join Schleicher or face oblivion. This was exactly the case Strasser made to a conference of the Nazi leaders on 5 December, but to his horror, Hitler took the opposite view, unmoved by Strasser's appeals – there was to be no compromise.[358] Hitler repeated this line in a speech to the NSDAP Reichstag delegation just hours later, confirming his opposition to the Schleicher cabinet. These dramatic events were recorded in Goebbels's diary:

> In the Kaiserhof [hotel] we have an extensive conference with the Führer. We confer about our attitude toward the Schleicher cabinet. Strasser takes the position that Schleicher has to be tolerated. The Führer has fierce clashes with him. Strasser as always in recent times portrays the situation of the Party in the blackest colours. But even if that were the case, one must not surrender to the resignation of the masses ... Strasser tries everything to draw those present at the Führer conference over to his side. All, however, stand so firmly on the side of the Führer that there can be no question of this. Finally he delivers to the Führer Schleicher's threat: If we don't tolerate his cabinet, he would again dissolve the Reichstag. Once again we formulate the conditions under which there is a possibility of giving [Schleicher] an extension of time: Amnesty, social improvements, the right to self-defence, and the freedom to demonstrate, along with a total adjournment of the Reichstag. Meeting of our parliamentary fraction: The Führer speaks very sharply on the spreading addiction to compromise. There can be no question of giving in. It is not about his person, but about the honour and prestige of the Party. Whoever now acts treacherously only proves thereby that he hasn't understood the greatness of our movement. Strasser's features grow visibly more rigid. The fraction itself is of course unanimously in favour of a consistent continuation of the struggle. Only for the time being dissolution of the Reichstag is to be avoided, if possible, as we do not now have good prospects [in a new election].[359]

All the while Göring and particularly Goebbels were working on Hitler, strengthening his resolve against Strasser's scheme, largely for personal reasons of ambition and petty rivalry.[360] Matters were made worse when a British journalist asked the party leadership about the rumoured Schleicher-Strasser conspiracy, which appears to have convinced Hitler and Goebbels that the Reich Organisation Leader was out to split the NSDAP.[361] Gregor Strasser now gave up. Exasperated at his Führer's seemingly suicidal strategy, Strasser took the only option he believed was open to him, resigning his party offices on 8 December. He told his staff that the total breakdown of the relationship between himself and Hitler over strategy made his remaining in post impossible. In a letter to the Führer explaining his resignation, he made similar points and condemned tactics that 'depended solely upon the hopes of chaos as wrong, dangerous, and not in Germany's national interest'. Strasser also, however, put paid to the rumours (and subsequent histories) that he was trying to split the party by promising to leave the country for a while to avoid becoming 'the centre of oppositional efforts or of discussions thereof'.[362]

After briefly succumbing to panic upon receiving Strasser's letter, Hitler recovered his composure and ensured the loyalty of both the party organisation and the Reichstag delegation with emotional speeches, thus preventing Strasser's resignation from triggering wider doubt in the Führer's all-or-nothing strategy.³⁶³ In many ways, the Strasser resignation marked the death of Schleicher's taming strategy, for he had lost his key ally within the Nazi Party leadership and Hitler was firmly resolved to oppose the cabinet come what may. Unfortunately, despite Strasser's departure from the political scene being made manifest by his immediately leaving for a holiday in Italy, Schleicher continued to regard Strasser as his best hope for coming to an accommodation with the NSDAP and seemingly refused to recognise the reality of the situation; that two years of work were on the scrapheap.³⁶⁴ Instead, Schleicher was operating in mid-December under the illusion that he was enjoying a political honeymoon, perhaps believing Strasser's resignation was simply a ploy to force the Führer's hand. The reopening of the Reichstag on 6 December had passed off with relative tranquillity compared to the Papen farce of September as the parties had no interest in supporting a confidence motion that would only bring fresh elections. Thus, an early communist attempt to unseat the new chancellor was rejected, even by the Nazis.³⁶⁵ The only parliamentary event of note was a blistering attack by Nazi deputy Karl Litzmann, a former general, on Hindenburg's failure to appoint Hitler chancellor, which strayed into questioning the field marshal's war record. The fact that no one rose to speak in defence of the president, as would surely have happened in happier times, suggests that the political class's usual admiration for the Old Gentleman was at a low ebb.³⁶⁶ The following day, Schleicher made his aforementioned prediction to the cabinet that he would secure the toleration of 306 deputies, including, crucially, all 196 Nazis. Further positives for the chancellor came in the successful passage of several bills, including one that made the head of the supreme court the official deputy head of state, an emergency winter relief programme, and a motion to adjourn the Reichstag after just three days to enter an extended Christmas recess, handing the new chancellor precious breathing space.³⁶⁷ In a radio speech on 15 December, Schleicher reached out for majority support, which appeared to be within his grasp:

> I am a follower of neither capitalism nor socialism ... for me concepts like 'private' or 'planned economy' have lost their terror. ... one should do in economic matters that which is reasonable in the given moment and most likely to lead to the best results for country and people, not bash in each others' heads for the sake of a dogma.³⁶⁸

His programme of job creation, land resettlement and *Wehrsport* was designed to appeal across the political spectrum and make Reichstag toleration more likely, and Schleicher heard positive noises from the Centre and trade union leaders after the speech, even if ADGB head Theodor Leipart remained ambivalent about accepting a cabinet post.³⁶⁹ However, the very same speech was rejected out of hand by the two biggest parties in parliament, the Nazis and Social Democrats, and was seriously concerning for the industrial and agrarian elite who had the president's ear.³⁷⁰

The reality was that Schleicher's scheme was dead and buried, but he appears to have remained optimistic until mid-January that a parliamentary majority could be found. In fact, not only had any hope for this dried up with Strasser's 8 December resignation, but by mid-December, Franz von Papen was already plotting his revenge. Papen had on 16 December given a speech to the Lords' Club, an influential private members' club for the aristocratic elite, in which he implicitly criticised Schleicher and reached out to the Nazis.[371] After the speech, he had met the banker Kurt von Schröder, a Nazi sympathiser, to whom Papen revealed how displeased Hindenburg was with his new chancellor Schleicher and thus how fragile the latter's position truly was – a fact that was not public knowledge.[372] This was information of vital importance for it suggested that Schleicher's ace card – the threat of dissolving the Reichstag – may be off the table, for he would need the president's backing to carry out such an action. Schröder rapidly communicated this vital intelligence to the NSDAP and set up a meeting between Hitler and Papen, which took place in Cologne on 4 January 1933. The reason Papen agreed to such an audience was a mixture of spite and ambition; he was determined to get back at the back-stabbing Schleicher and he was equally resolved on becoming chancellor again.[373] All the while, Papen retained friendly relations with the Presidential Palace, frequently visiting Hindenburg and his son over the Christmas period and continuing to use his wit and charm to exert his influence over the head of state.

The extent to which Papen's advances saved Hitler and the Nazis cannot be overexaggerated. The resignation of Strasser, who was generally popular within the movement and seen as Hitler's right-hand man, had rocked party morale. Combined with the electoral reverses of the autumn and winter and Hindenburg's multiple rejections of a Hitler chancellorship, both within and without the party the outlook for the Nazis was interpreted as bleak. This helps explain Schleicher's passive attitude for much of December and January, for the vast majority of political commentators now wrote the NSDAP off as a major force. Schleicher was not totally inactive in this time; he was aware that his hopes of being tolerated by a Reichstag majority may fall through, in which case reverting to the Papen plan of dissolving parliament was his only option. He let it be known in the officer corps that he and the president had made every effort to accommodate the Nazis but that it was Hitler who was being unreasonable, thereby pre-empting any potential Nazi sympathies within the High Command. Furthermore, he had street fighting equipment issued to the Prussian police, ordered the Defence Ministry to plan for military operations within the Reich and circulated these plans to senior officers on 27 January, and also made tentative contact with the SPD and ADGB with an offer for cabinet seats in exchange for a dissolution of the Reichstag and the suppression of the NSDAP.[374] However, these preparations were not sufficiently vigorous as the chancellor still believed he could win the Nazis round. Furthermore, the 400,000-strong SA remained too great a temptation to Schleicher; this paramilitary force was the fast track to rapid German rearmament, therefore, if at all possible, the Reichswehr must not be brought into conflict with the Nazis.[375] Furthermore, 1932 appeared to be closing on an optimistic note for the chancellor and for Germany. President Hindenburg had been largely passive in December after the lengthy negotiations of November, save an audience with Göring on 12 December on the possibility of the Nazi aviator becoming Prussian Prime Minister, a door that was closed to Göring by the Reich President when he demanded the Interior Ministry also.[376] Hindenburg did, however, warmly congratulate Schleicher on the Christmas political truce which had accompanied the adjourning of the Reichstag, telling the chancellor, 'Christmas was never so peaceful before.'[377] More than just the president's praise, Schleicher could also bask in positive news regarding the economic and political outlook; the Depression appeared to have bottomed out as the stock market had risen 30 per cent since the spring, while there were further reports of the Nazis' inevitable demise.[378]

Despite November and December 1932 being nothing short of disastrous for the NSDAP, January would see Hitler's appointment as chancellor. The wheels were set in motion by the aforementioned meeting between Hitler and Papen on 4 January, and although the two disagreed over which of them was to hold the chancellorship in a future coalition, they agreed that Schleicher had to be removed, after which a coalition of Nazis, Nationalists and conservatives could take office and would dismantle the KPD, SPD and trade unions and remove Jews from public life.[379] Papen also provided Hitler with some vital intelligence. He cast doubt on Schleicher's claim that Hindenburg was willing to dissolve the Reichstag at a moment's notice, thereby removing the threat the chancellor had used to frighten Strasser.[380] Furthermore, and perhaps most importantly, the Nazis in Papen now finally had an advocate in the Presidential Palace and a channel through which they could influence Hindenburg, albeit one who only promoted Hitler's cause in the hopes of returning to power himself; Hindenburg was given the impression by his favourite that the 4 January meeting paved the way to a government headed by Papen with Hitler as vice chancellor.[381]

On 9 January, Papen gave his personal report on the meeting to Hindenburg. Papen insisted that Hitler had given up on his aspirations for total power and was willing to work with the wider right. This was enough to persuade the president and he tasked Papen with negotiating with Hitler 'on a personal and strictly confidential basis', which nevertheless was in effect undermining his own chancellor.[382] That same day, Joseph Goebbels confided in his diary: 'Papen dead set against Schleicher. Wants to topple and eradicate him entirely. Has the old man's ear [Hindenburg]. Even stays with him. Arrangement with us prepared. Either the chancellorship or the ministries of power: Defence and Interior. Worth listening to.'[383]

State elections in Lippe on 15 January, a tiny state of 173,000, also boosted Nazi morale and allowed Hitler to negotiate from a position of apparent strength. By investing all their funds and energy into the campaign, the NSDAP was able to increase their vote to nearly 39.5 per cent, reversing the depressing trend of late 1932.[384] But the chancellor continued with his scheme to secure a parliamentary majority that would include the toleration of the Nazis. The meeting between Hitler and Papen had been widely reported but, for the time being, Schleicher did not see the danger, believing that Papen was working in the interests of the government.[385] Astonishingly, his plan continued to revolve around Gregor Strasser. Strasser had returned to Berlin and met secretly with the chancellor on 3 January. The former general had said he would have offered Strasser the chancellorship but Hindenburg would never accept this so he would become vice chancellor and Reich commissioner for Prussia instead.[386] Schleicher introduced Strasser to the Reich President on 6 January as a first step towards his appointment in the cabinet. The disgraced Nazi left a decidedly good impression, and Hindenburg was sufficiently affected that he agreed to Strasser's appointment as vice chancellor and assured Schleicher that he would then dissolve the Reichstag if need be. This was, however, contrary to Schleicher's own plan; his intention after all had been to bring Strasser into the fold in order to win Nazi Reichstag toleration. Even though Hindenburg had now offered him a way out of the trap he was about to fall into, Schleicher delayed, hoping the Nazis would become more desperate as time went on – after all, he had little desire to follow the Papen plan of dispensing with parliament and crushing the Nazis by force.[387]

Strasser met with Hindenburg again on 11 January and the president apparently said Schleicher would be his last chancellor – but the Schleicher chancellorship was unravelling quickly.[388] He still hopelessly believed that Strasser's impending appointment could ensure Nazi toleration of the cabinet. Now Hugenberg and the agrarians intervened to further isolate the Reich chancellor. The Reich Rural League, having met with Hindenburg to air their grievances two days earlier, published a bitter attack on Schleicher's agricultural policy (which ironically bore resemblance to the 'agrarian Bolshevism' that had cost Brüning his post) on 13 January, which was followed up by a similar DNVP assault on 21 January, both undermining the chancellor's hopes of a majority and damaging his standing with the president, who, ever sensitive to landowners' concerns, had actually chaired an emergency conference between the RLB and government himself and was therefore deeply disappointed by the negative outcome.[389] Nevertheless, an upbeat Schleicher told a group of journalists on 14 January that his priority was to persuade the NSDAP to abandon their 'messianic beliefs' and join his 'extra-parliamentary front in support of an authoritarian regime', a statement that reveals just how little the former general understood about a party he had been trying to 'tame' for more than two years.[390]

The cabinet met on 16 January to consider Strasser's admission into their ranks, but the assembled ministers were operating under the illusion that Hitler's former number two would secure Nazi toleration and a Reichstag majority, and indeed the chancellor told his colleagues this was his intention; over the next few days it would become clear to Schleicher that his plan had failed miserably.[391] The Lippe victory of 15 January was transformed by the Nazi press into a grand triumph, showing that Schleicher's plan to wait things out until the NSDAP saw sense had failed. Hitler refused to see Strasser, negating any possible influence Schleicher's ally could have and the Centre and SPD turned their back on what they saw as a lame duck chancellor – not that they had ever actively supported him.[392]

There were now swirling rumours about a new government of 'national concentration', effectively bringing together the parties and organisations of the National Opposition, most notably the NSDAP and DNVP, who had fallen out so acrimoniously after supposedly achieving unity at Harzberg. It appears that the president himself was laying the groundwork for such a government. On 21 January, his secretary Meissner met with Nationalist leader Alfred Hugenberg and insisted that although Hindenburg would appoint the defence and foreign ministers (as he effectively had been doing for some time), he wanted the DNVP to take part in the next administration. 'Hindenburg', Meissner told the Nationalist Party chairman, 'attaches great importance to the participation of the German Nationalists.'[393] Around a similar time, Papen had met with President Hindenburg in the presence of both Oskar von Hindenburg and Meissner. Papen had tried in vain to persuade Hindenburg to accept a Hitler chancellorship, insisiting there were various safeguards against the party dictatorship the president had repeatedly warned against – the army, the Reichstag, a conservative cabinet majority, Hitler's own assurances and, of course, the powers of the president himself.[394] Hindenburg again demurred, probably on more emotional than rational grounds in that he disliked and distrusted Hitler, but if he had cared to consider it, the president would have realised that the safeguards Papen spoke of were decidedly weak – the army, as we have seen, was fearful of a clash with the SA, the Reichstag could be ignored (as the presidential cabinets had proved), Papen and his barons lacked any sort of popular support, Hitler had broken his word numerous times and Hindenburg himself was very old and reliant on advisers.[395] The president remained unmoved, for now. The detente between Hitler and what many have called the 'House of Hindenburg' began on 22 January 1933 when the president's son Oskar and secretary Meissner joined von Papen to meet with the Nazi Führer in the Berlin villa of Joachim von Ribbentrop, the future Nazi foreign minister. For two hours, Oskar and Hitler talked privately. What was discussed is not known. It is possible Hitler promised to cancel the considerable debts the Hindenburg Neudeck estate had racked up, but it is unlikely, as is sometimes claimed, that Hitler threatened to expose irregularities with the estate or revive impeachment proceedings; this was too delicate a moment to make an enemy of the president and his family. Most likely, however, Hitler gave his usual pitch about defeating Communism and saving Germany. Whatever was said, it went a long way in persuading Oskar to support a Hitler government.[396]

It was also that night that Papen suggested he might be amenable to Hitler taking the Chancellery and settling for the post of vice chancellor himself. Papen does not seem to have seen the irony (or indeed the implicit danger) that he was now subjecting himself to the subordinate, controllable position that he had offered Hitler the previous August. Nevertheless, for now the scheme went nowhere when, the following morning, Papen broached the idea of a Hitler-Papen government to the president and he was firmly rebuffed – Hindenburg continued to oppose a Hitler chancellorship.[397] The Hitler-Oskar meeting was followed up on the 25th when Oskar met Ribbentrop and told him that a 'new national front [with Hitler as chancellor] was not entirely hopeless', suggesting he had used his influence with his father to soften his attitude towards Hitler.[398]

Over the next few days, Papen and the Nazis worked hard to enlist other parts of the National Opposition, most notably Hugenberg's Nationalists and the paramilitary veterans' association, the Stahlhelm, in order to overcome Hindenburg's opposition to Hitler by presenting a broad nationalist coalition.[399] Schleicher's plans meanwhile had fallen apart. He now realised that the hopes he had held since being appointed of building a Reichstag majority now stood in ruins – he was out of options. In an audience with the president on 23 January, he therefore repeated almost exactly the request made by Papen at the start of the previous December which had ultimately cost him his job: to dissolve the Reichstag, forgo new elections and instead repress the Nazis and Communists by force. Naturally, Hindenburg brought up the grave concerns that Schleicher himself had raised about such a possibility – had Schleicher's own department not shown in their war game that such a scenario would result in an unwinnable civil war?[400] In response Schleicher claimed that the situation was actually much improved; the chances of a general strike were negligible, the SPD and trade unions would support a state of emergency and provide thousands of volunteers to assist the Reichswehr in defeating the NSDAP. As Carsten has pointed out, while these conclusions were probably justified, they had also been true in December, when Schleicher had conveniently ignored them for his own ends.[401]

Having been persuaded once that a state of emergency would lead to collapse, Hindenburg stuck to his guns – he refused Schleicher's request. In a bitter blow to the Reich chancellor, the president conceded that he would dissolve the Reichstag if necessary, but that he would not delay elections as this would be contrary to the constitution.[402] Perhaps Oskar's influence and certainly the impending possibility of a Papen-Hitler government coloured the president's decision; why take such a gamble when he was well aware that negotiations to form a new cabinet were well under way? Ullirch also notes that in the last few days the so-called Eastern Aid scandal began to unravel as it emerged that landed aristocrats had been misusing public funds. Several of Hindenburg's landowning friends were implicated and it was a scheme he had championed; perhaps it was best to turn a new leaf, especially as the president held Schleicher responsible for allowing his name to be dragged through the mud.[403]

Further evidence against Schleicher arrived when Hindenburg received General Werner von Blomberg, commander of Reichswehr forces in East Prussia. Blomberg was actually far more pro-Nazi than most senior army officers and was persuaded by his chief of staff, Colonel Walter von Reichenau (a NSDAP sympathiser), to advocate a Hitler government. Blomberg told the president that the army did not support Schleicher's scheme for a showdown with the Nazis, that the army would disintegrate if asked to fight the SA due to significant political support for the NSDAP amongst younger officers, and that the military would welcome a 'National Front' administration led by the Führer.[404] Blomberg's intervention was crucial; Hindenburg had always been influenced by 'army opinion' and, up to this point, it had been Schleicher who had wielded it as a political weapon, acting as a spokesperson for the officer corps within the Presidential Palace, often just to get his own way. Now, he had (unbeknownst to him) been usurped, and Blomberg's testimony fatally undermined Schleicher's own claims about the viablility of a temporary dictatorship, for the chancellor had by the 26th realised that he had little chance of persuading the president to grant him emergency powers, rendering his position all but untenable.[405]

That same day (or possibly on the 27th, historians are divided and there may even have been two meetings), Hindenburg received General Kurt von Hammerstein, Chief of the Army Command and a staunch Schleicher ally, who attempted to rescue his friend from his inevitable fate.[406] Hindenburg was in a foul mood, declaring when Hammerstein entered that 'if the generals do not obey orders I shall dismiss the whole lot'.[407] Hammerstein could not resist straying into politics, despite the routine purpose of the meeting; he expressed military disquiet about Schleicher's impending removal and spoke out against his replacement with Papen, using the same arguments as Schleicher had about the unsustainability of a chancellor opposed by more than 90 per cent of the population. Hammerstein also spoke against a Hitler chancellorship, claiming the army would come under the influence of the Nazi Party and might be forced to defend a NSDAP government against popular revolt.[408] Hindenburg was outraged at Hammerstein's attempts, as a military subordinate, to influence the commander-in-chief's political decision-making, despite the fact Schleicher and, more recently, Blomberg had done so before. According to Hammerstein's own account, the president did attempt to placate him, claiming angrily he had 'no intention whatsoever of making the Austrian lance corporal defence minister or Reich Chancellor'.[409] This guarantee was soon voided.

Only the final act remained to be played out. Schleicher asked one more time for emergency powers on 28 January. By now, Hindenburg was open to a Hitler chancellorship, although he did not reveal this to Schleicher. Turned down once again, the irrepressible schemer had finally run out of cards to play, and he tendered his resignation.[410] Schleicher recommended that Hitler be appointed to succeed him, so long as he could cobble together a Reichstag majority.[411] Hindenburg had been gradually coming to this conclusion himself over the last few days and 28 January is likely the day he decided to finally give way to the prospect of Hitler as chancellor. His recent assurance to Hammerstein that he would never appoint Hitler may have simply been an effort to pacify the agitated general, or it may have been genuine, as Hindenburg probably did not change his mind until the 28th.[412] He had been told repeatedly for the best part of a week by all the men he trusted that Hitler was the man for the job – by Papen (who had taken himself out of consideration in order to force the president's hand), by his son Oskar, by Meissner, by his friend Oldenburg-Januschau, by Blomberg, by Hermann Göring in a message that insisted the Nazis would respect the president's authority, and now by Schleicher.[413] Schleicher complained of the brief twenty-minute audience he had with Hindenburg that it had been like 'talking to a wall' and that the president had merely recited prepared words rather than responded to his arguments, but Hindenburg had already settled on a new course, so debate was futile.[414] The president dismissed Schleicher rigidly and without emotion, rightly pointing out that he had failed to secure the majority he had promised and insisting he needed a new government to carry out his ideas.[415] Schleicher claimed that Hindenburg had said, 'Whether what I am going to do now is right, my dear Schleicher, I don't know; but I shall know it soon when I am up there,' pointing to the ceiling.[416] Schleicher had now suffered the same fate that he had bestowed on Müller, Brüning and Papen; he had persuaded the president to dispose of these chancellors in favour of a new political scheme, and Papen had pulled the same trick. Hindenburg, as was observed by diarist Harry Kessler, was acting now, as he had been for some time, more like a replacement monarch than a constitutional president, ignoring elections and parliament and instead relying on favourites, relatives and civil servants to conduct the politics of the Reich.[417]

The president gathered Papen, Meissner and Oskar around him and, after a half-hearted attempt to persuade Papen to return to the Chancellery, conceded that the three of them were right in pushing for Hitler, with the words, 'It is my unpleasant duty then to appoint this fellow Hitler as chancellor?'[418] Papen went immediately to the Nazi leader, who demanded the chancellorship and the Prussian and Reich Interior ministries, allowing the other posts to go to non-Nazis and insisting that the cabinet be a presidential one with decree powers rather than one that sought a parliamentary majority.[419]

Ironically, as this was happening, Hindenburg's earlier comment to Hammerstein about not appointing Hitler panicked Schleicher and his Defence Ministry circle, for they earnestly believed that the president was about to reappoint Papen. When Hindenburg had looked to the heavens, questioning whether what he was doing was right, Schleicher had thought he was talking about bringing back Papen! On the morning of 29 January, Schleicher, Hammerstein and their confidents discussed how to ensure Hitler be appointed to ensure Papen be kept out and civil unrest be avoided. The possibility of a coup against Hindenburg to ensure he did not appoint Papen was even discussed and dismissed. Hammerstein met with Hitler that same day, assured him of the cooperation of the senior Reichswehr figures and requested that Schleicher remain as defence minister in the coming administration.[420] General von Hammerstein made a brief record of the crucial, if ill-informed, army conferences that day:

> On 29 January there took place in my office a discussion between von Schleicher, who had resigned but was still acting as Reich Chancellor, and myself. It was clear to both of us that only Hitler was possible as future Reich Chancellor. Any other choice must inevitably lead to a general strike if not to civil war and so to the extremely undesirable internal development of the army against two sides, against the National Socialists and against the Left. We both considered whether we knew any means to influence the situation and avoid such a misfortune. The result of our reflections was negative. We saw no possibilities of still exercising any kind of influence on the Reich President. Finally, I resolved in an agreement with Schleicher to seek an exchange of views with Hitler. This took place on Sunday [29 January] between 3 and 4pm.[421]

In fact, the negotiations on 28–29 January between conservatives, Nationalists and Nazis had gone off surprisingly well, and Hindenburg was well pleased with both Hitler's 'moderation' in only demanding three cabinet seats, and the fact that many of his 'friends' who had made up the cabinet of barons were to be retained.[422] Furthermore, Hitler had agreed to Hindenburg's demand that Papen hold the office of Reich commissioner of Prussia, even though the chancellor had held the post since the Prussian coup.[423] By the night of 28 January, Hindenburg had secured his own choices for the Foreign and Defence ministries in the form of Neurath and Blomberg, who was ordered in the morning to return from the Disarmament Conference in Geneva.[424] The president, in overruling Papen's suggestion of General von Fritsch, was completely oblivious to Blomberg's Nazi sympathies and, especially after their earlier audience, believed him to be a perfect candidate for the Defence Ministry as, unlike Schleicher, Hindenburg believed Blomberg was a non-political professional officer with 'pleasant manners'.[425] Despite the fact Papen supposedly cherished his 'safeguards' on a

Hitler chancellorship, he allowed the president to select a man he (Papen) hardly knew for the vital Defence Ministry. Hindenburg did insist Papen hold the office of vice chancellor and the latter put in place yet another safeguard in that it was agreed he should always be present when Hitler met with the president.[426]

A final concession to the president was that the new cabinet was to be announced as a parliamentary rather than a presidential one; the post of justice minister was left vacant ahead of negotiations with the Catholic parties. This was actually a ruse by Papen, who still doubted whether Hindenburg would appoint Hitler at the head of a presidential cabinet but had no intention of actually entering serious negotiations with the Centre and BVP.[427] Talks continued on the 29th that secured the Stahlhelm's participation, and Hindenburg also gave his assent to the dissolution of the Reichstag and the holding of new elections after the cabinet had taken office – a key Nazi demand that was opposed by Hugenberg.[428]

An off-hand comment by a military go-between, however, sparked chaos in Berlin on the night of 29/30 January and sowed doubts about what seemed to be a done deal. The Schleicher-Hammerstein entourage were now operating under the outrageous misconception that they would have to persuade Hindenburg to overcome his misgivings and make Hitler chancellor rather than opting for his favourite, Papen. The go-between told Hitler in an off-the-cuff manner that if the Presidential Palace did not see sense, the Defence Ministry ought to mobilise the Potsdam Garrison and seize the Wilhelmstrasse (home to the Presidential Palace, Reich Chancellery and other key government buildings).[429] Rumours of an impending military coup to seize Hindenburg swept through political circles and created some panic, although the only tangible effect was in hurrying along the finalising of the Hitler cabinet.[430] Early on the morning of 30 January, General von Blomberg arrived in Berlin and was met at the railway station by two rival dignitaries – Hammerstein's adjutant ordered him to report to the Defence Ministry, while Oskar von Hindenburg ordered him to an audience with the president. Unsurprisingly, Blomberg opted to see the commander-in-chief. At the Reich Chancellery, the final details of the new government were hammered out between Hitler, Papen, Meissner and Hugenberg.[431]

Hindenburg's haste in summoning Blomberg and swearing in the Hitler cabinet that morning may well have been the result of the dark rumours of the previous night. The general later reported that the crucial sticking point in the January negotiations had been over the Defence Ministry, as Hindenburg would not accept a Nazi in the Bendlerstrasse, but Papen and Hitler were determined to evict Schleicher. Blomberg provided the perfect solution for the president and he was sworn in as defence minister some time before Hitler and the other ministers were, at 11.30 am on 30 January 1933.[432] After late cold feet from Hugenberg about the prospect of fresh Reichstag elections had been overcome by Papen warning of a Schleicher-Hammerstein coup, the assembled ministers were ushered into the president's office, although not before he had been forced to express his displeasure at being kept waiting.[433] Hindenburg commended his audience on the fact that 'the nationalist right has finally been unified' and, according to Goebbels, by the end of the ceremony the president was 'quite moved'.[434] The Führer was now Reich chancellor. Hindenburg's time as the arbiter of German politics was over. He finished the formalities with the remark: 'And now, gentlemen, forwards with God.'[435]

Epilogue

The One-Man Show: Hindenburg and Ludendorff in Eclipse

Hindenburg: Willing collaborator

At the time it was widely rumoured that Hindenburg was showing increasingly signs of senility when he appointed Hitler chancellor and thereby did not fully understand what he was doing, or else was duped into the decision by his inner circle. This version of events, augmented by the apocryphal story of the president believing the SA torchlit parade he reviewed on the evening of 30 January 1933 was a procession of Russian prisoners of war, has leaked into contemporary popular history.[1] Goltz has argued persuasively that republican admirers of Hindenburg convinced themselves after Hitler's appointment that Hindenburg was not of sound mind; effectively, they were so taken in by the latest iteration of the Hindenburg myth – Hindenburg as the guardian of Weimar and the constitution – that they came up with a more convenient explanation for the president's actions.[2] While it is true that Hindenburg was old and tired, there is no evidence that he had gone senile in January 1933. In fact, although increasingly physically frail, all the indications are that Hindenburg remained mentally alert until his final illness in the summer of 1934.[3] The jokes, rumours and aspersions about the health and state of mind of the Old Gentleman, or the idea that he was an honourable man being used as a puppet, were as old as his first election campaign of 1925; they had been resurrected by the Nazis in the 1932 campaign and again became popular in 1933, showing the extent to which Germans, and later historians, were willing to believe that *their* version of Hindenburg would never willingly do something they disagreed with.

The breakdown of Hindenburg's resistance to a Hitler chancellorship is not as dramatic as is usually portrayed and was certainly not the result of ill health, for he had been willing to make Hitler chancellor in November 1932, so long as it had not been at the head of a presidential cabinet with emergency powers, and he maintained the same line in January; as we have seen, Papen deceived the president about the chances of obtaining a majority to support the Hitler administration. Moreover, Hindenburg had been hoping for a right-wing government that would bring together all the forces of so-called National Opposition since at least 1931. In many ways, the Hitler-Papen-Hugenberg-Stahlhelm cabinet was the realisation of a long-held dream for Hindenburg rather than an aberration. It is true that the president had to be persuaded by his inner circle to accept Hitler for the top job and only did so with some reluctance, but, again, this was not an especially unusual development in the context of Hindenburg's career, for at various crucial moments he had allowed the key decisions to be taken by subordinates as he did not especially want to make them himself, such as in November 1918 or June 1919, when the Versailles Treaty ultimatum expired. It is true he leant on his circle in January 1933 and allowed them to push him into a decision, but he had done the same for many years, such as in the sacking of Brüning or the signing of the Young Plan. The fact that intensive efforts had to be made to persuade Hindenburg to appoint Hitler in January does not suggest he was not of sound mind and easily led, but the complete opposite. What is true, however, is that once Hitler was made chancellor, Hindenburg was relieved to take a step back from frontline politics, and he never returned to the active political role he had been forced into taking since 1930.[4] Hindenburg's personality and leadership style, both in the Great War and in his presidency, had always been passive, docile and delegatory, and in the final twilight of his life, he reverted to type.

An emergency, authoritarian government under either Papen or Schleicher and resting on the power of the president and the Reichswehr was the only viable alternative to a Nazi-led administration in late 1932 and early 1933. Such a regime would likely have received the tacit support of the pro-democracy parties, paramilitaries and trade unions had it moved against the Nazis and Communists, and as Turner has pointed out, would have been infinitely preferable to the Third Reich.[5] Paul von Hindenburg had been willing to take this path in December 1932, but Schleicher had baulked at the prospect of deploying the army to defend Papen. Equally short-sightedly, when Schleicher opted for the state of emergency route in late January, Hindenburg refused to contemplate what he had agreed to in December due to his growing distrust of Schleicher and continued resentment about the ousting of his friend Papen. The stark choice between military dictatorship or Hitler, however, was a trap of Hindenburg and Schleicher's own making. Had Brüning (or a comparable figure) remained as chancellor until the worst of the Depression was over, supported by the broad front of moderate left and right that had also re-elected Hindenburg in spring 1932, a democracy, even a presidential one, might have been salvaged from the wreck of Weimar. Hindenburg's sacking of Brüning, and then his agreement to bringing forward Reichstag elections to July 1932 that were not required until September 1934 (by which point the Nazi nimbus would almost certainly have waned), manufactured the final crisis of the Republic; the Nazi and Communist surges of that summer produced a negative majority in the Reichstag that prevented the presidential style of government that had been in place since 1930 from functioning any longer. As a result, from 31 July 1932, Hindenburg was faced with a choice of either Hitler or a state of emergency and military-backed dictatorship. He vacillated for six months as first Papen and then Schleicher tried and failed to dig themselves out of the hole they had created before the president finally opted for what he saw as the safer option of a constitutionally legal Hitler coalition.

The sad truth also is that Hindenburg had been agitating for a government that excluded the 'Marxists' (the Social Democrats and the trade unions) from political life for some time by 1933, for he saw them as internal enemies. His vision of German society and politics was an exclusive rather than an inclusive one, based on the Kaiser's Second Reich where certain classes and groups had been totally excluded from the corridors of power. He had repeatedly worked to persuade the DNVP and later the NSDAP to enter government as he believed 'national-minded' men should rule Germany. Hindenburg ultimately was no democrat and had little interest in preserving the Republic, so it is unsurprising he did not fight to defend it. The cabinet appointed on 30 January 1933 was, more so than any of the other governments of his long presidency, the fulfilment of Hindenburg's political vision of a united German right under his own leadership that excluded liberals, democrats, trade unions and the left.[6]

Hindenburg was to have two highly significant effects on the rise of the Nazis. Firstly, the shift to a semi-authoritarian, presidential system of government with a strong executive and a limited role for parliament from 1930 would have been improbable had Wilhelm Marx have been president. A president as moderate as Marx would have been unlikely to seek to remould the system in such a way and someone as experienced and competent in the exercise of executive power would not have been under the influence of a circle of advisers in the same way. As a result, some sort of centrist coalition, quite possibly a remodelled Grand Coalition, would have been in power through the worst of the Depression. The impact this would have had on the fate of the Weimar Republic is unknowable and speculation is rather pointless, but certainly Germany would have been very different without Hindenburg, Groener, Schleicher, Brüning et al. running the show and the army would likely have had less influence over politics. The second point of significance is that it seems unlikely any individual in Germany other than Hindenburg could have defeated Hitler in the presidential election of spring 1932. Hindenburg, as we have seen, was a unique figure, a true national icon, and he certainly would not have run if he had not been the incumbent. Only Hindenburg could compare to Hitler as a personality in German politics and only the Old Gentleman could appeal across left and right to win a majority in the face of the Nazi electoral surge. Given that in the second round, candidates only required a plurality of votes, it seems hard to imagine that any single candidate could have bettered Hitler's 37 per cent and therefore denied the Nazi leader the presidency. Furthermore, without the heroic Hindenburg's latent appeal to conservatives and nationalists, and the strongly patriotic tone of his official campaign, Hitler would almost certainly have bettered his 37 per cent had the field marshal not been on the ballot. It would seem therefore that the second point precludes the first; although a Marx presidency would have likely not seen a drift away from parliamentary democracy, a Hitler presidency would almost certainly have followed in 1932, two and half years before he gained presidential powers in reality. Whether a more democratic government would have better battled the Depression and thereby prevented the dramatic growth in Nazi support is unknowable, but the fact that governments the world over seemed impotent in the face of the global crash suggests an answer in the negative. Hindenburg, we might therefore conclude, was both the man who kept Hitler out in 1932 and the man who paved the way for authoritarian rule from 1930 and brought Hitler into this scheme in 1933.

In many ways, despite it coinciding with his political eclipse, the appointment of Hitler as chancellor marked the completion of Schleicher's long-term taming strategy. For the 'National' coalition Hitler headed was designed by Papen and sold to Hindenburg as serving the same purpose Schleicher's strategy had entailed: taming Nazi radicalism through the responsibilities and compromises of coalition government, winning the support of a significant portion of the masses to a right-wing establishment dictatorship and controlling Hitler through the checks and balances of the cabinet, the army and the Presidential Palace. However, as L.E. Jones has pointed out, the taming strategy without Schleicher, but instead the weak Papen in the cabinet and the crypto-Nazi Blomberg in the Defence Ministry, was doomed to fail as it lacked the strong containment measures that Schleicher himself had believed he could provide.[7] For one thing, the army under Blomberg, far from restraining the Nazis, totally subordinated itself to them. An early indication of this came on 3 February 1933 when Blomberg invited senior Reichswehr officers to a dinner party with Hitler. The generals were impressed by Hitler's outline of his objectives and Blomberg told them that the new government was an 'expression of the broad national will'.[8] A gathering of officers on 1 March that year confirmed Blomberg's subordination to the NSDAP and that of Colonel Reichenau, his former chief of staff who was now in Schleicher's old job as head of the Office for Ministerial Affairs. Blomberg told the generals that there was:

> one party on the march. Consequently, the attitude of remaining 'above party' loses its meaning and there remains only one course: support without any reservation!
>
> [Reichenau added the following] It is essential to recognise that we stand in the midst of a revolution. What is decayed in the state must fall, and this can only be done by using terror. The party wants to proceed mercilessly against Marxism. The task of the Wehrmacht is to stand at attention.[9]

Hammerstein meanwhile retired quietly as Chief of the Army Command at the end of the year.[10] Thus, one of Hindenburg's last decisive political interventions, in pushing for Blomberg rather than Papen's choice of Fritsch, had been to hand the Defence Ministry, and thus the Germany Army, to the Nazis on a plate, completely negating a vital aspect of the taming strategy. Hindenburg himself was supposed to be a key 'safeguard' against Nazi dictatorship. Over the course of 1933, the year he turned 86, his health faded further and he increasingly retreated to a semi-retirement on his estate at Neudeck. However, the president was by no means unimportant to the rapid and remarkably successful Nazi consolidation of power. Any illusions that Hindenburg might have been under that Hitler's was a parliamentary rather than a presidential cabinet soon disappeared, without the president expressing concern. Rather, he acceded to Nazi demands remarkably readily considering his previously ambiguous attitude. On 1 February, the president agreed to dissolve the Reichstag, with fresh elections (openly labelled the 'last election' by Hitler) to be held on 5 March. Furthermore, negotiations with the Catholic parties were swiftly terminated and the sitting justice minister was confirmed in his post.[11] Even more startling, the power of rule by decree, which Hindenburg had so vigorously denied Hitler in November, was granted almost immediately, with the Decree for the Protection of the German People, which limited press freedoms and gave the police power over political rallies and meetings, being signed by the president on 4 February. A further decree enhancing the cabinet's power in Prussia was also promulgated on 6 February.[12]

From a very early stage, Hindenburg was also reconciled with Hitler and abandoned his previous concerns about the 'Bohemian Lance Corporal'. This process was brought about by both Hitler's efforts to ingratiate himself with his new superior and the fact that Oskar von Hindenburg, Meissner and the new Nazi press officer in the Presidential Palace, Walter Funk – a friend of the family – both filtered out complaints and appeals from Hindenburg supporters of 1932 that reached the president's office and also provided Hindenburg with daily press briefings that were highly positive about the new government and its work.[13] Therefore, the extent of presidential interference in Hitler's early work was a gentle rebuke about the slander of Hindenburg's predecessor, Friedrich Ebert, in one of the chancellor's speeches.

The election campaign was fought in a highly charged atmosphere. Nazi terror, intimidation and harassment, and now, with Göring as Prussian interior minister and Frick holding the same post at Reich level, with police assistance, was turned against the Communists, Social Democrats and Centre Party as never before. The former Minister of Labour Adam Stegerwald was severely beaten by brownshirts, 120 Centre-affiliated newspapers were shut down, and the police broke up social democratic rallies and barred some SPD politicians from speaking. These abuses were given a veneer of legality when Göring enrolled the SA and SS as 'auxiliary police' on 22 February, allowing the Nazi thugs to bully, harass and arrest their opponents with relative impunity.[14]

Worse was to come. On the night of 27/28 February 1933, the Reichstag was set alight and suffered major damage. A Dutch Communist dissident was arrested at the scene but there was a major controversy at the time, and ever since, as to whether the Nazis were the true perpetrators. Benjamin Carter Hett has made a convincing case for wider involvement, but whatever the truth, the Reichstag fire gave the Nazis the perfect excuse for a wider crackdown.[15] On 28 February, the cabinet approved, and Hindenburg (without the slightest objection) signed the Decree for the Protection of the People and State, which soon became known as the Reichstag Fire Decree.[16] The civil liberties guaranteed by the constitution were 'temporarily' suspended (in fact the decree remained in place until 1945), the communist and social democratic press was completely shut down and 4,000 Communists were rapidly arrested, including the party's entire leadership, and interred in makeshift concentration camps, whose names would become infamous.[17] In the final days of the election campaign, conducted in a crisis atmosphere, the SA acted with total impunity.

What of the campaign itself? Hindenburg, or at least his image, was central once again. The DVP emphasised that they were the only party that had supported the president throughout and an electoral alliance of the DNVP, Stahlhelm and the partyless Papen labelled itself the Kampffront and tried to associate itself closely with Hindenburg and the non-Nazi aspect of the government.[18] The Nazis, however, were the latest party to adopt the Hindenburg legend and use the president's mythical reputation for their own ends. His distinctive image was found on NSDAP posters, and Nazi propaganda and press organs emphasised the close 'personal bond' between the field marshal and the lance corporal, with many posters portraying both men, Hindenburg's head above Hitler's – the old Germany and the new – hand in hand. The voters were asked to do what the president had done: put their faith in Adolf Hitler.[19] Despite the Communists being effectively banned, and most other parties operating under varying degrees of intimidation, the NSDAP was not able to attain the majority it hoped for, gaining 43.9 per cent of the vote. The SPD and Catholic parties remained steady and the KPD actually held on to eighty-one seats despite its leaders being interned, and merely the act of handing out Communist leaflets liable to get one arrested. Nevertheless, the cabinet, in the form of the combined NSDAP and DNVP vote, had won a majority.[20] While the Hindenburg brand did not especially help the DVP nor the DNVP's Kampffront, the Nazis' greatest electoral triumph was achieved with the field marshal front and centre of their appeal.

Hindenburg's enabling of the Nazis' rapid consolidation of power continued unabated as spring came. On 9 March, he approved the appointment of a Reich commissioner to oust the conservative state government of Bavaria (in a mirror image of the 'Prussian Coup'), just a day after assuring the Bavarians that he was not contemplating such a move and chastising them for doubting his word.[21] Hindenburg then played the lead role in one of Goebbels's propaganda masterpieces, the so-called Day of Potsdam, on 21 March. With the Reichstag in ruins, the official opening of parliament had to be conducted in another venue. Goebbels, newly appointed minister of propaganda, orchestrated an elaborate ceremony to be held in the Garrison Church in Potsdam, burial place of Frederick the Great and other kings of Prussia. The ceremony was designed to appeal to voters who had not backed Hitler in the recent elections and to visualise for the populace the melding of tradition and modernity that the Nazi regime wished to symbolise.[22] The virtues that Hindenburg, and the Garrison Church, embodied – the Prussian traditions of austere Lutheran Christianity and proud militarism – were to be associated, even conferred, onto Chancellor Hitler. Hundreds of thousands gathered to watch the president's motorcade tour the city in a scene vividly captured by one newspaper reporter:

> The cars are not yet in sight, but the thunderous reception is getting closer, it is becoming stronger, louder. 'Hindenburg is coming, Hindenburg is coming!' Necks are craned, nervous twitching among the masses of people. The first flags are waved, people are breathing more quickly. Then the tension is relieved like an electric shock … Boundless jubilations begin: 'Cheers for Hindenburg! Cheers for Hindenburg!' Again and again it resounds.[23]

In the uniform of a field marshal, Hindenburg arrived at the Garrison Church to an SA honour guard and met Hitler, in civilian dress, for a famous, deferential handshake. Inside the church, the newly elected Reichstag deputies, save the uninvited SPD and KPD members (Hindenburg's vision of unity excluded even the moderate left), heard a speech from the president and chancellor. First, Hindenburg told the politicians:

> In the Reichstag elections of March 5 our people has backed with a clear majority the Government called into office by my confidence and has provided it with the constitutional basis for its work … [Prussia] in awe of God became great through dutiful labour, unshakable courage, and dedicated patriotism … May the old spirit of this celebrated site inspire our present-day generation, may it deliver us from selfishness and party quarrels and rally us in national self-realization and spiritual revival for the benefit of a united, free, and proud Germany!

Unsurprisingly, Hitler followed this brief address with a speech full of lavish praise for the president and laced with the values he represented:

> In a unique rising the German people has restored its national honour in just a few weeks, and thanks to your understanding, *Herr Reichspräsident*, it has joined together the symbols of old greatness and youthful vigour … In our midst we see an aged head. We rise before you, *Herr Generalfeldmarschall*.

> Three times you fought on the field of honour for the existence and future of our people. As a lieutenant in the armies of the King [of Prussia] for German unity, in the armies of the old Emperor for the glorious establishment of the Reich, in the greatest war of all times as our Field Marshal for the survival of our Reich and for the freedom of our people. You witnessed the creation of the Reich, you saw yourself the achievements of the great Chancellor, the wondrous rise of our people, and led us in those great times which fate allowed us to witness and fight through. Today, *Herr Generalfeldmarschall*, Providence lets you be the custodian of the new rise of our people. Your astounding life symbolizes to all of us the indestructible vigour of the German nation. Germany's youth thanks you today, and so do we all. We consider it a blessing to have your consent to the work of the German rising. May this vigour inspire also this newly inaugurated representation of our people. May Providence give us the courage and perseverance which we sense in this place so sacred to every German, as we strive for the freedom and greatness of our people, at the grave of its greatest king.[24]

The ceremony then concluded with the president proceeding alone into the crypt to lay a wreath on the tomb of the Prussian kings. Hindenburg, his myth, his reputation and the values he stood for had now been co-opted for the Nazi regime-building project. Far from the Nazis being a tool to enable Hindenburg and his circle to construct a new polity, the president had become an instrument for legitimising Adolf Hitler. There can be no doubt that the Day of Potsdam was a huge propaganda success that succeeded in convincing many wavering Germans, especially the politically moderate and the bourgeoisie, to get behind the Nazi regime and support the consolidation of a dictatorship.[25] The effectiveness of the occasion is attested to in a revealing diary entry by the liberal writer and Hitler-sceptic Erich Ebermayer:

> A sea of flags in the street. All cleverly done, impressive, spell-binding even, at any rate for the masses. We must not shut our eyes in the face of what is going on. Today and here, the marriage took place between the masses led by Hitler and the 'Spirit of Potsdam', the Prussian values, represented by Hindenburg. How marvellously it has been staged by that master producer Goebbels. The procession of Hindenburg and the Government goes from Berlin to Potsdam past a line of cheering millions. The whole of Berlin seems to be on the streets. The radio announcer almost weeps with emotion. Hitler speaks. A true stateman appears to be developing. Not a word of hatred, not a word of racial ideology, no threat aimed at home or abroad. Hindenburg lays wreaths on the graves of Prussian kings and shakes hands with Hitler, who bows deeply. Cannons thunder over Potsdam, over Germany! No one can escape the emotion of the moment. Mother has tears in her eyes.[26]

Not that Hindenburg in any way resented the role he was playing or was an unwilling accomplice. There was a contemporary joke that the smallest concentration camp in Germany was Neudeck, again implying Hindenburg was a puppet being controlled and exploited, but this could hardly be further from the truth.[27]

The president was, by and large, very pleased with the government's work and was quickly taken in by Hitler. He had always preferred delegating power to others and had often been won over by his chancellors to a variety of political paths. When the Enabling Act – which handed the chancellor the power to rule by decree, thereby cutting the president out of the legislative process and allowing Hitler to become a dictator – was passed by the required two-thirds supermajority on 23 March, Hindenburg was positively delighted as he believed it would lighten his workload and because he had resented signing unpopular decrees over the last three years; he was glad Hitler would now take responsibility for the government's actions. The taming strategy had largely relied on the fact that, at the end of the day, the president held ultimate power in the form of his Article 48 decrees, but Hindenburg happily gave away his monopoly on executive power, and largely made himself politically redundant, as it meant he was, in his own words, no longer a 'signature machine'.[28] The president actually wrote to the chair of the Centre Party in an attempt to sooth his misgivings about the Enabling Act:

> I wish to assure you that the Chancellor has expressed his willingness, even without formal constitutional obligations, to take measures based on the Enabling Act only after consultations with me. I shall always try to remain in close touch with him and, faithful to my oath, 'do justice to all men'.[29]

Franz von Papen, meanwhile, rapidly became a political irrelevance. He was not a skilled politician and he had no party, movement or popular support behind him. His post of vice chancellor held no official powers and his safeguard of agreeing to always be present when Hitler consulted with Hindenburg was rendered irrelevant with the passage of the Enabling Act, and by April, Hindenburg had asked him to stop attending his audiences with the chancellor anyway.[30] Papen's power had rested on his access to Hindenburg, but once the president's influence and importance receded, so did Papen's. With the safeguards gone, the Nazis were free to consolidate their power and establish a dictatorship with cabinet decrees and state terror. Hindenburg, even taking into account the rose-tinted view of the regime he received from his inner circle, was highly supportive of his government's actions, pulling them up on just a few minor quibbles during 1933 and 1934, such as securing an exemption for Jewish war veterans from the Civil Service laws of April 1933, which banned Jews and political opponents of the Nazis from holding civil service posts (notably, Hindenburg clearly did not oppose the substance of the law, merely the inclusion of Jewish veterans, insisting that the law was fair, especially as the Nazis had been the victims of injustice from 'Jewish and Jewish-Marxist quarters'[31]), or insisting on Werner von Fritsch being appointed as Hammerstein's successor at the turn of the year. He was entirely unconcerned by the dissolution of the political parties, even the party he had once claimed to support, and which had persuaded him to run for president, the DNVP.[32] In the meantime, Hindenburg was happy to lend his weight to Nazi propaganda events, speaking at the 1 May celebrations, the August Tannenberg commemoration (where he was presented with new lands to extend the Neudeck estate) and broadcasting to the nation once again, this time the day before the 12 November plebiscite on withdrawing from the League of Nations, where he assured Germans of the wisdom of the government's decision.[33]

In 1934 he took an ever smaller role in public life. In the spring, he and Papen did have discussions with Hitler about the restoration of the monarchy and he took the chancellor's word that it would happen in time.[34] On 4 June 1934, the president retired to Neudeck for the final time. Berlin was alive with rumours of a military coup as tension between the army and the SA reached fever pitch and Papen delivered a provocative speech on Nazi excesses. However, Hindenburg, in his final illness, was persuaded to accept the NSDAP line by his inner circle and they denied Papen access to the president. The vice chancellor's critical speech made no impression on Hindenburg whatever, with Hitler reporting after a 21 June visit that 'never had the old man been as friendly'.[35] General Fritsch did see Hindenburg in late June and found him in a bad way, reminiscing about the wars of his youth but taking in little else. We should therefore be more sympathetic in our reading of the president's positive reception to the news of the bloody 30 June Night of the Long Knives, in which Hitler purged the SA and had Ernst Röhm killed as well as settling old scores with Schleicher, Strasser and Gustav von Kahr, who had scotched the 1923 Beer Hall Putsch. Hindenburg was upset by the murder of Schleicher and his wife but accepted the Nazi explanation that they resisted arrest and were involved in a coup conspiracy when the story was confirmed by General Blomberg.[36] Like many Germans, Hindenburg believed the shocking brutality of the Night of the Long Knives had to have been conducted without Hitler's knowledge, but that ultimately it had saved the country from instability.

Paul von Hindenburg died of lung cancer around 9.00 am on 2 August 1934. The cabinet had already prepared a decree merging the offices of president and chancellor and thereby conferring Hindenburg's powers to Hitler, and it was promulgated before the president had breathed his last. Hitler took the title Führer rather than the democratic-sounding president, but his position was now unassailable. Blomberg, of his own volition, had the army swear an oath of allegiance to Adolf Hitler that morning, following the death of their commander-in-chief. The diarist Victor Klemperer called it a coup d'état 'drowned out by hymns to the dead Hindenburg'.³⁷ Huge commemorations for the field marshal and statesman followed in two weeks of official mourning as the Nazis again deployed the Hindenburg nimbus for their own purposes. No music was to be played in public places, church bells were to toll for an hour each day, and civil servants had to wear a black ribbon.³⁸ The president had asked to be buried at Neudeck beside his wife, but instead his wife was exhumed, and the couple were buried at the Tannenberg Memorial in a lavish ceremony and propaganda set piece. Hitler delivered the main address at the funeral on 7 August, attended by almost 125,000 people, even using this solemn moment for political gain with words that would have made the proudly partyless and earnestly Lutheran Hindenburg recoil:

> It is one of the wondrous turns of an unfathomable wise fate that under the Presidency of this first soldier and servant of our people we could work for the rise of our German people until he himself finally opened the door to Germany's rejuvenation. In his name the alliance was concluded which merged the dynamic power of this rising with the finest minds of the past. As Reich President the Field Marshal became the Lord Protector of the National Socialist revolution and of the rebirth of our people... The German people will come to their dead hero in times of need to gain strength for their lives. And even when the last trace of his life has gone with the wind, the name will be immortal. Deceased Field Marshal, now enter Valhalla!"³⁹

At the moment of burial, the whole country observed a minute's silence and traffic was halted. There remained a final footnote to Hindenburg's career: his political testament and a referendum on the unification of presidency with chancellorship. Hindenburg himself, when writing it in the spring, had decided to split his 'political will' into two parts, one for publication, and the other only for the eyes of his designated successor, Hitler. The portion of the testament for public consumption was a parting propaganda gift for the NSDAP and was published on 15 August. It praised 'My Chancellor' Hitler and his movement for starting Germany back on the road to greatness. The second part was entirely concerned with the restoration of the monarchy, but Hindenburg left it up to Hitler as to when the time would be right to do so.⁴⁰ On the eve of the succession plebiscite, Oskar von Hindenburg addressed the nation in a radio broadcast, calling on Germans to vote yes:

> The late Reich President and Field Marshal ... having concluded his compact with Adolf Hitler on 30 January of last year and having confirmed it during that sacred hour in the Garrison Church at Potsdam on 21 March, always supported Adolf Hitler and approved all important decisions of [Hitler's] government ... My father himself saw in Adolf Hitler his direct

successor as head of the German state, and I am acting in accordance with my father's wishes when I call on all German men and women to vote for the transfer of my father's office to the Führer and Chancellor.⁴¹

There can be little doubt that Oskar's words were true; his father truly had believed in Hitler's government and, although he hoped for a monarchical restoration in the long run, he had left this decision up to Hitler. The German people obliged the twin call of the House of Hindenburg and the NSDAP, voting 89.9 per cent in favour of Hitler's merger. Thus, the final act of the president had been to complete the Nazi consolidation of power and ensure the Hitler dictatorship would survive until the total destruction of the Third Reich in 1945. As the Soviets advanced in January that year, the remains of Hindenburg and his wife were exhumed and the Tannenberg Memorial demolished to prevent them falling into enemy hands. The bodies were evacuated by the German Navy, first to the Garrison Church in Potsdam, and then alongside two Prussian kings, to a salt mine in Thuringia, where they were discovered alongside other Nazi treasures by US troops. Moved again to the American zone of occupation, the Old Gentleman and his wife were finally laid to rest for good in a secret ceremony at the quiet Elizabeth Church in Marburg. The grave of one of Germany's most famous generals and statesmen, nothing short of a living legend during the Weimar era, bears merely the inscription of his name and lifespan, with a panel added in the 1960s commemorating 'victims of war and violence'.⁴²

Ludendorff's final retreat

In the 1930s, Erich Ludendorff sank ever further into his isolated, mystical world of supranational conspiracy theories and paganism. In 1931, in a book entitled *People's War on German Soil*, he forecast that a world war between France, Italy and the USSR would be fought in German territory in 1932, with each nation the pawn of a global conspiratorial power. This publication was also the first instance of Ludendorff publicly attacking Hitler, although in private he had accused him of being an agent of the Papacy since 1926. The general's foresight derived from the fact the digits 1932 supposedly had a mystic, cabalistic significance.⁴³ This title was soon followed up with Ludendorff's *Hitler's Verrat der Deutschen an den römischen Papst* (*Hitler's betrayal of the German people to the Roman pope*), which attributed the removal of the Lutheran Kaiser in 1918, the subsequent political dominance of the Catholic Centre Party, and now the ascent of the NSDAP to the machinations of the Papacy. These were attacks, along with Ludendorff's accusation that Hitler was 'soft' on Jews, the Nazis took seriously and felt compelled to refute extensively.⁴⁴ Satirical cartoons in the *Ludendorffs Valkswarte* showed priests twisting the swastika into a cross and Jews signing up as enthusiastic Nazis. Thus, Ludendorff spent the crisis years of the Weimar

Republic, when Hitler was rising to national prominence and Hindenburg's whims were steering the fate of the nation, dedicated to the wildest conspiracy theories and totally detached from reality. The British historian John Wheeler-Bennett visited Ludendorff in the mid-thirties during his research for a book on the Treaty of Brest-Litovsk and was distinctly unimpressed:

> Ludendorff… was completely irrational. He had made a second marriage to a lady whom local Munich gossip believed to be a practising witch. Certainly he had an altar to Thor in the back garden on which he was said to sacrifice a horse from time to time. He was utterly unreasonable, and our conversation – or should I say, his monologue – consisted of a diatribe against a great international conspiracy in which the unlikely alliance of the Roman Catholic Church, World Jewry and the Grand Orient were combining to destroy civilisation.[45]

With Hitler's appointment as chancellor in January 1933, Ludendorff supposedly had a genuine moment of great prescience. Many histories of the period refer to a letter or telegram that Ludendorff sent to his old partner Hindenburg upon hearing the news:

> You have delivered up our holy German Fatherland to one of the greatest demagogues of all time. I solemnly prophesise that this accursed man will cast our Reich into the abyss and bring our nation to inconceivable misery. Future generations will damn you in your grave for what you have done.[46]

In fact, the letter is a fake and the story a fantasy, and it has been comprehensively debunked by German historians.[47]

Although Ludendorff's Tannenberg League was proscribed, in practice it largely continued to operate in all but name and the Nazi regime actually permitted their former comrade in arms considerable freedom in the Third Reich. His esoteric publishing house was allowed to continue printing its deranged volumes, save for the banning of its weekly newspaper, *Ludendorffs Volkswarte*, and the regime even tolerated, owing to the general's prestige and prior association with the NSDAP, mild criticism to emanate from the Ludendorff Press, although much of the criticism that was levelled at Hitler was reproaching the government's timidity and sluggishness in persecuting Jews and Catholics.[48] Indeed, a monthly Ludendorff paper, more focused on the Ludendorffs' religious cult, was switched to biweekly publication after 1933 and had a not unimpressive circulation of 66,572 in 1935.[49] On the other hand, some of Ludendorff's followers did face mild persecution (in comparison to the Nazis' other opponents), such as the disruption of lectures, denying of promotion and even gaol spells, and a rumoured reconciliation between the Führer and his former mentor in 1933 came to nothing when Ludendorff refused to attend the annual Tannenberg commemoration.[50]

As well as this criticism of the NSDAP from the right, so to speak, Ludendorff continued to lace his writings with conspiracy theories and promote his and Mathilde's unique pagan religion, Deutsche Gotterkenntnis, or the worship of a German God. His 1933 memoir of his early life and career noted how he was held back by the machinations of supranational forces and his 1934 study of the 1914 Battle of the Marne blamed Germany's fatal defeat on the fact that a theosophist – a member of an American occultist sect – had infiltrated German High Command.[51] Ludendorff also refused to play any part in the Hindenburg funeral, or offer condolences of any kind on his wartime partner's death, not even hanging the flag at his home at half-mast.[52] Both Heinrich Himmler and General Ludwig Beck had some sympathy for Ludendorff and his followers (Himmler for spiritual and Beck for military-historical reasons), and both sought in 1934–35 to bring about détente between the Ludendorff faction and the regime, with Beck visiting Ludendorff twice in early 1935.[53] Beck's overtures included an offer of promotion to field marshal, as the new Chief of the General Staff sought to recover Ludendorff as a hero of the Great War and a symbol for the army now Hindenburg had passed, but Ludendorff contemptuously refused the promotion, believing the rank beneath him as he already considered himself a Feldherr on a par with Napoleon (field lord, akin to supreme commander), although stories of Hitler turning up at the general's Tutzing home to offer him the baton and being swiftly shown the door are sadly false, despite being repeated by twentieth-century biographers.[54] The reconciliation was, however, sufficient to see Ludendorff praised by Defence Minister Blomberg in the public announcement of rearmament in March 1935 and for the general's seventieth birthday be publicly celebrated at the Führer's orders the following month.[55]

The year 1935 also saw Ludendorff write the most commented upon book of his long retirement. With the public announcement of German rearmament and the reintroduction of conscription that year, it appeared that the next war was on the horizon. Ludendorff wrote *Der Totale Krieg* (*Total War*) to lay out his vision for how that war should be conducted, adopting the role he had played before of a soldier attempting to learn the lessons of the previous conflict to help win the next.[56] The book was read by the Chief of the General Staff Ludwig Beck and other officers, and recently Jay Lockenour, while conceding Beck and his colleagues rejected most of Ludendorff's conclusions, argues *Der totale Krieg* had a significant impact. On the other hand, many historians have argued the book was dismissed by the German military and Nazi Party leadership, both of whom had moved beyond Ludendorff's ideas, which were essentially stuck in a First World War mindset – Hans Speier calls the prophecies he makes in the book about the next war 'history projected into the future'.[57] Chickering points out that one of the reasons that Ludendorff's ideas seemed so unoriginal and passé by 1935 was the fact that his analysis of the First World War (and in particular the causes of German defeat) had largely been adopted by both Germany's military leaders and the Nazi Party by this time.[58] He also remarks that in returning to the same subject and themes, the book was Ludendorff's final attempt to deal with the daemon that had tormented him since 1918 – the German collapse and his own responsibility for it. Of more interest, or at least more unique, were the ideas that the general put across about national morale, or psychological warfare, and about leadership. Much of the writing on the 'moral' or spiritual aspects of total war is conspiratorial nonsense which represents the Stab-in-the-Back myth in final form; Ludendorff describes how:

> In Germany, the Jews and the Roman Church, with their accomplices, availed themselves of the social and economic abuses to destroy the unity of the people ...
> In their lust for power, Judah and Rome, controlling the world finances, had, by a purely capitalistic organization of the economic life on the one hand, and by Socialist, Communist and Collectivist doctrines on the other, introduced these abuses among the nations of Europe, and thus also, among the German nation.[59]

Ludendorff censures nationalists and military figures for using the word 'fatherland' as Jehovah promised the whole world as the fatherland of the Jews, and in even stronger terms condemns Christianity as an 'alien creed' that is killing Germany's 'racial inheritance' and is the prime cause of breakdown in total war.[60] However, interestingly, in making the case for his own German religion, he asserts that coercion and force alone cannot maintain a populace's morale and will to fight – rather a society must be bound by a common belief and spirituality. Ludendorff argued that his own religion would provide such a national spirit, both as a barrier against the pernicious external influences of 'Judah and Rome' and a German variant of the contemporary Japanese Shinto culture of sacrifice and duty.[61] As far as leadership went, Ludendorff declared that in a total war, the supreme military commander (or Supreme Warlord) must take on total dictatorial powers over all aspects of the war effort and national life. Foreign, economic and industrial policy must be subordinated to him, as well as control over society in the form of propaganda and war mobilisation. He wrote:

> The man who has to carry on with head, will, and heart the totalitarian war for preserving the life of the nation, is the Commander-in-Chief. Nobody can relieve him from the responsibility which is his. This position postulates the most intensive personal work, personal achievement, and the strongest will-power.
> The man who is Commander-in-Chief must hold first place. Anything else is unsound and dangerous. Only with complete power can the

Commander-in-Chief maintain unity and force in his actions … This activity is all-embracing, as the totalitarian war embraces the entire national life.[62]

One cannot help but sense that Ludendorff was envisaging himself in such a role, for the supreme warlord would have to be, in his own words, a lonely and detached figure, and the author actually slips into the first-person present tense in this passage of the book.[63] Ludendorff here was once again grabbling with the last war and writing a playbook for how he might have delivered ultimate victory if he had been handed supreme power. Adolf Hitler of course would never contemplate fulfilling Ludendorff's wish of subordinating civilian authority to total military power, quite the opposite. As Speier wrote in the 1940s, Ludendorff's vision of the general as supreme warlord was buried with him.[64]

Undoubtedly, *Total War* was Ludendorff's magnus opus. It was the product of more than fifteen years of deranged meditation on the Great War and his bestselling work (more than 100,000 copies had been sold by 1939), which was translated into English, unlike the vast majority of his writings. The book was widely reviewed and translated and although there is no historical consensus about its intellectual impact, it did at least popularise the phrase 'total war' in the German language.[65] However, the Nazi war of annihilation that was to come was a further radicalisation of Ludendorff's vision, envisaging perpetual aggressive conflict and something the old general did not discuss – the liquidation of occupied peoples.[66]

In the last year of his life, Ludendorff was finally reconciled with Hitler and the NSDAP. On 30 March 1937, the general granted the Führer a much-publicised private audience, the result of which was both an 'official reconciliation' celebrated in the press and an announcement from Ludendorff praising Hitler and welcoming the regime's formal recognition of his Deutsche Gotterkenntnis faith.[67] That December, Ludendorff was hospitalised (ironically in a Catholic Church-run institution in Munich) by a bladder complaint and he died of liver cancer on the 20th.[68] Ludendorff's final statement was framed as a deliberate echo of his hero Siegfried's dying words; just as Siegfried had beseeched his murderer to look after his widow, so Ludendorff called on his followers to rally round his wife Mathilde as the sole leader of their movement.[69]

A lavish state funeral was laid on by the Nazis just two days later. Hitler and other party and military dignitaries marched behind the coffin, which was draped in a swastika flag, as it processed through Munich, before the body was left to lie in state at the Feldherrnhalle, the martial monument at which, largely thanks to Ludendorff, the 1923 Beer Hall Putsch had come to its bloody conclusion.[70] Blomberg, rather than Hitler, gave the oration – perhaps Hitler wished to retain a healthy distance from a highly controversial figure – although supposedly the Führer was heard to utter the words: 'Now you can go to Valhalla, great commander.'[71]

Compared to the national event the Hindenburg funeral had been, Ludendorff's passing was relatively low-key, the only significant political outcome of the ceremony being Blomberg used it as an opportunity to secure Hitler's permission to marry his lover (a former prostitute), a scandal that resulted in the war minister's resignation the following month.[72] Unlike with the icon Hindenburg, Hitler respected Ludendorff's wish to be buried in Tutzing – he had expressly forbidden in his will that he be interred at the Tannenberg Memorial.[73] A small monument featuring a bust of the general and his name above a sword was built to serve as Ludendorff's grave, and it still stands in the city's cemetery. The Ludendorff publishing house continued to operate under the direction of Mathilde even after 1945, promoting the general's legacy and his religion. Amazingly, their Gotterkenntnis creed survives to this day, with their website reassuring visitors that they are not a cult and promoting not only the Ludendorff conception of God but also COVID conspiracy theories.[74] In a complete role reversal, it appears that in the Germany of today, Ludendorff has more devotees than the long-forgotten Hindenburg.

Hindenburg, Ludendorff and German history

How should Hindenburg and Ludendorff, and their role in the Nazi rise to power, be judged by history? As Turner and Astore and Showalter have pointed out, Paul von Hindenburg was the single most significant political actor in the process of levering Hitler into power; the president's decisions in 1932 and 1933 bear the most historical responsibility for the Nazi seizure of power.[75] Far from the wise, honourable old man that he was portrayed as in the Weimar era (an image that continues to seep into popular history), Hindenburg always desired a government of the combined right and far right and he was pleased when his goal was achieved in January 1933. This is also to ignore the decisive role he played in the propagation of the toxic Stab-in-the-Back myth in the volatile post-war years, which in many ways paved the way for Nazi success a decade later and Nazi crimes against humanity in the years after his death. If one must find an historical 'what if' as to how the Nazi rise to power might have been averted, then the presidential election for spring 1932 stands out. With a resounding mandate, a clear majority of the country behind him, encompassing the Social Democrats and labour movement, Catholics, liberals and moderate conservatives, Hindenburg could easily have preserved the presidential cabinet under Brüning or a similar figure for some time to come. The actions of Groener showed that effective suppression of the more militant aspects of the Nazi Party was possible, and the government could have counted on the firm backing of the vast majority of state administrations and their police forces. The military, while tempted by Nazi promises of rearmament, especially in the junior ranks, would certainly have remained overwhelmingly loyal to the field marshal of Tannenberg over Lance Corporal Hitler had it come down to it. Reichstag elections were not due until September 1934, when the Depression had eased considerably, and further Versailles concessions were certain to have come. Hindenburg himself would not pass away until August 1934, meaning a fresh presidential election would not have presaged the Reichstag contest. Therefore, while certainly difficult, it is not inconceivable that the government, and indeed the Weimar Republic, could have weathered the Nazi storm had the president held fast after his re-election and respected the views of his own voters.

As it was, this 'what if' scenario is entirely irrelevant because Hindenburg had no interest in this option – no interest in preserving the Republic, no interest in continued cooperation with a broad political front and ultimately, no interest in maintaining Brüning in office once it became clear he was a barrier to the president's objective to form a cabinet of the nationalist right. The president's, and his inner circle's, clear desire from autumn 1931 onwards to create a rightist regime necessitated collaboration in some form with the NSDAP. This desire essentially brought about the Hitler chancellorship, with all its devastating consequences for Germany and the continent of Europe. Thus, far from the last hurdle to Hitler or the bulwark of democracy which he is sometimes portrayed as, Hindenburg should instead bear a heavy historical causal burden for the Nazi rise to power.

Erich Ludendorff bears less direct causal responsibility for the Nazi regime; he did not appoint Hitler chancellor, nor designate him as his successor as head of state. However, the eccentric general's feud with the Führer and political ineptitude should not blind us to the dire consequences of his actions. For Ludendorff was a peddler of hatred and lies without parrel in the polarised world of Weimar politics. His calculated, pernicious and self-serving construction and promotion of the Stab-in-the-Back myth from September 1918 went a long way towards convincing a generation of right-wing Germans to hate democrats, leftists and Jews and, most damagingly, to see them as a traitorous enemy within. The Stab-in-the-Back myth also normalised and popularised a conspiratorial and racist worldview that would pervade the German far right in the interwar era. Hitler and Ludendorff were kindred spirits in this sense and there can be no doubt that the general's interpretation of the First World War and German defeat rubbed off on the Nazi leader, paving the way for genocide in the second.

Ludendorff aided and abetted the most radical and violent opponents of the Republic in Weimar's early years, and by patronising putsches and assassination plots, he ensured that the German people got the worst possible first impression of democracy. By throwing his weight behind multiple coup attempts, Ludendorff helped make the period 1919–23 a dangerous and chaotic time that would colour Germans' perception of democratic government until the second half of the century. Most famously, of course, he patronised the embryonic Nazi movement, securing for them funds, connections, covert military assistance and a certain degree of respectability and notoriety. The Beer Hall Putsch is inconceivable without Ludendorff; without his army contacts and prestige in nationalist circles, Hitler and his cronies would never have believed they could win power. Ludendorff's decisions also ensured that the putsch ended with a heroic massacre rather than fading with a whimper, passing into party folklore. Without his presence at the subsequent trial, Hitler's lectures to the courtroom would not have attracted so many column inches, thereby bringing the Führer's ideas to a wider audience. In this way, the general did much to ensure the NSDAP emerged by the mid-1920s as *the* party of the extreme right. While they parted ways soon after, it was largely because there was no room for two leaders of the Nazi movement rather than because of ideological differences, and as we have seen, Ludendorff was eventually reconciled with Hitler. Had they been able to see the future, see the merciless, brutal and genocidal war machine that Hitler's Third Reich would become, Hindenburg would most likely have recoiled, while Ludendorff might largely have approved.

As politicians, Hindenburg was clearly superior. Ludendorff not only lacked the widespread popular appeal (and indeed did not seek to court the 'fickle' masses) enjoyed by his wartime chief but lacked the judgement and, to be frank, mental stability to succeed in Weimar politics. The plots in which he became involved are remarkable for their poor planning and execution and the hands-off approach Ludendorff himself adopted in order to protect himself from repercussions weakened the conspiracies he supposedly led and speak to a craven element of his character. His abrasive personality, desire to lead and extremist views meant that he was never able to build alliances and instead alienated his colleagues in both the military and political sphere. Hindenburg, on the other hand, thanks to his unparalleled hero status, was – electorally speaking – the most successful politician of the Weimar era. In all three presidential ballots in which he stood, he achieved greater support (48.3%, 49.6%, 53.1%) than any other party or individual in national elections across the entire fourteen-year history of the Republic. The Hindenburg brand was clearly an extremely potent electoral weapon and many parties sought to harness it, for the Old Gentleman's name undoubtedly attracted voters from across the political spectrum and even the apolitical.

While unquestionably an election-winner, Hindenburg was not a skilled politician, lacking energy, drive and direction, naturally on account of his age, but he was also inconsistent and unreliable, obstinate on some issues, easily led on others. Despite his popular image as the embodiment of Prussian duty and honour, he was not a dependable partner for many a chancellor; from Müller to Brüning, Papen to Schleicher, he abandoned his closest collaborators at crucial moments. He was also vain and always anxious to protect his standing with 'his people', i.e., the nationalist right, and in particular, the officer corps and the aristocratic Junker landowning class. The role of president was supposedly a nonpartisan one and although Hindenburg undoubtedly took his oath to the constitution seriously, he did little to hide his political preferences. He frequently intervened on behalf of right-wing causes and after 1930, and especially after the 1932 presidential election, he was determined to create a rightist government that would incorporate the far-right National Opposition parties, regardless of the will of the people or even his own electors. The appointment of the Hitler cabinet marked the realisation of this goal and, after January 1933, Hindenburg largely acted as if the mission he had been elected for had been accomplished. Both men must bear considerable responsibility for the Nazi dictatorship they unwittingly helped create with dire consequences for Germany, Europe and the world. Ludendorff, both through his creation and propagation of the Stab-in-the-Back myth and with his direct support and patronage gave vital oxygen to Hitler and the early Nazi movement. His backing of the Beer Hall Putsch and appearance at the subsequent trial transformed Hitler from a local agitator into a national figure, while the *Dolchstoss* helped create the atmosphere of resentment that would eventually lead to Nazi triumph. Hindenburg may have shared less of Hitler's worldview but he held executive power in the early 1930s and entrusted it to Hitler, despite everything the Nazi leader had said, done and written; one can hardly say his evil aims were hidden following the publication of *Mein Kampf* in 1925. Following the 1932 presidential election, Hindenburg betrayed the moderate parties of left and right who had re-elected him and instead openly sought an authoritarian, nationalist regime to replace or at least modify Weimar democracy. Such a solution inevitably had to include the Nazis as the most powerful party of the nationalist right and, although much is made of Hindenburg's reluctance to hand Hitler the chancellorship, the field marshal had wanted Hitler and the Nazis to join the cabinet since 1930. He was a statesman who willingly handed power to criminals, demagogues and thugs. Ultimately, the two generals played an essential role in Hitler's rise to power, which would, of course, bring in a few short years continental-scale genocide and global war and result in suffering and tragedy for hundreds of millions. The world paid a heavy price for Ludendorff's insanity and Hindenburg's inanity.

Appendix I

Elections in the Weimar Republic

Reichstag Elections 1919–1933

Party	1919 % of vote	1919 Seats won	1920 % of vote	1920 Seats won	May 1924 % of vote	May 1924 Seats won	Dec 1924 % of vote	Dec 1924 Seats won	1928 % of vote	1928 Seats won	1930 % of vote	1930 Seats won	July 1932 % of vote	July 1932 Seats won	Nov 1932 % of vote	Nov 1932 Seats won	1933 % of vote	1933 Seats won
KPD	–	–	2.09	4	12.61	62	8.94	45	10.62	54	13.13	77	14.32	89	16.86	100	12.32	81
USPD	7.62	22	17.63	83	–	–	–	–	–	–	–	–	–	–	–	–	–	–
SPD	37.86	163	21.92	103	20.52	100	26.02	131	29.76	153	24.53	143	21.58	133	20.43	121	18.25	120
DDP/DStP	18.56	75	8.28	39	5.65	28	6.34	32	4.81	25	3.78	20	1.01	4	0.95	2	0.85	5
Centre	19.67	91	13.64	64	13.37	65	13.60	69	12.07	61	11.81	68	12.44	75	11.93	70	11.25	73
BVP	–	–	4.16	20	3.23	16	3.74	19	3.07	17	3.03	19	3.23	22	3.09	20	2.73	19
DVP	4.43	19	13.90	65	9.20	45	10.07	51	8.71	45	4.51	30	1.18	7	1.86	11	1.10	2
WP	–	–	–	–	1.71	7	2.29	12	4.51	23	3.90	23	0.40	2	0.31	1	–	–
KVP	–	–	–	–	–	–	–	–	–	–	0.83	4	–	–	–	–	–	–
CSVD	–	–	–	–	–	–	–	–	–	–	2.48	14	0.99	3	1.14	5	0.98	4
CNBL	–	–	–	–	–	–	–	–	1.86	9	3.17	19	0.25	1	0.13	0	–	–
RLB	–	–	–	–	1.96	10	1.65	8	0.65	3	0.55	3	0.26	2	0.30	2	0.21	1
DNVP	10.27	44	15.07	71	19.45	95	20.49	103	14.25	73	7.03	41	5.91	37	8.34	51	7.97	52
VB/NSFB	–	–	–	–	6.55	32	3.00	14	–	–	–	–	–	–	–	–	–	–
NSDAP	–	–	–	–	–	–	–	–	2.63	12	18.25	107	37.27	230	33.09	196	43.91	288
Others	1.59	7	3.31	10	5.75	12	3.86	9	7.06	16	3.00	9	1.16	3	1.57	5	0.43	2

Presidential Election 1925

First Round, March 1925

Candidate	Party	Supported by	Votes	%
Karl Jarres	DVP	DNVP and other rightist organisations in the 'Reich Bloc'	10,416,658	38.8
Otto Braun	SPD		7,802,497	29.0
Wilhelm Marx	Centre		3,887,734	14.5
Ernst Thälmann	KPD		1,871,815	7.0
Willy Hellpach	DDP		1,568,398	5.8
Heinrich Held	BVP		1,007,450	3.7
Erich Ludendorff	NSDAP		285,793	1.1
Other Candidates			25,761	0.1

Second Round, April 1925

Candidate	Party	Supported by	Votes	%
Paul von Hindenburg	Independent	DVP, DNVP, BVP, NSDAP and other rightist organisations in the 'Reich Bloc'	14,655,641	48.3
Wilhelm Marx	Centre	SPD, DDP in a 'People's Bloc'	13,751,605	45.3
Ernst Thälmann	KPD		1,931,151	6.4
Other Candidates			13,416	0.0

Presidential Election 1932

First Round, March 1932

Candidate	Party	Supported by	Votes	%
Paul von Hindenburg	Independent	SPD, DStP, Centre, DVP, BVP, CNBL, CSVD, KVP	18,651,497	49.6
Adolf Hitler	NSDAP		11,339,446	30.1
Ernst Thälmann	KPD		4,938,341	13.2
Theodor Duesterberg	Der Stahlhelm	DNVP	2,557,729	6.8
Other Candidates			116,304	0.3

Second Round, April 1932

Candidate	Party	Supported by	Votes	%
Paul von Hindenburg	Independent	SPD, DStP, Centre, DVP, BVP, CNBL, CSVD, KVP	19,359,983	53.1
Adolf Hitler	NSDAP		13,418,547	36.8
Ernst Thälmann	KPD		3,706,759	10.2
Other Candidates			5,474	0.0

Appendix II

Governments of Hindenburg's Presidency

Date	Chancellor (party)	Participating Cabinet Parties	Cause of fall
January–December 1925	Hans Luther (Independent)	*Bürgerblock* coalition of DNVP, DVP, BVP, Centre, DDP	DNVP objections to the Locarno Treaty
January–May 1926	Hans Luther (Independent)	Centre-right minority coalition of DVP, BVP, Centre, DDP	The Imperial Flag Controversy
May–December 1926	Wilhelm Marx (Centre)	Centre-right minority coalition of DVP, BVP, Centre, DDP	The Soviet Military aid scandal
January 1927–June 1928	Wilhelm Marx (Centre)	*Bürgerblock* coalition of DNVP, DVP, BVP, Centre	Disagreements over Reich School Bill and elections of May 1928
June 1928–March 1930	Hermann Müller (SPD)	Grand Coalition of SPD, DDP, Centre, BVP, DVP	SPD & DVP objections to financial package and Hindenburg's desire for a government of the right
March 1930–May 1932	Heinrich Brüning (Centre)	'Hindenburg Cabinet' of DDP/DStP, Centre, BVP, DVP, KVP, CNBL, WP	Hindenburg's desire for a government of the right
June–December 1932	Franz von Papen (Independent*)	Independent 'Cabinet of Barons', included some figures associated with DNVP	Reichswehr opposition to Papen's demand for a state of emergency
December 1932–January 1933	Kurt von Schleicher (Independent)	Independent 'Cabinet of Barons', included some figures associated with DNVP	Schleicher's failure to find a parliamentary majority
January 1933–August 1934	Adolf Hitler (NSDAP)	Government of 'National Concentration', including figures from NSDAP, DNVP, Der Stahlhelm and independents	N/A

* Papen was expelled by the Centre Party upon assuming office.

Appendix III

Hindenburg's Cabinets

First Luther Cabinet – January–December 1925
Participating parties: DNVP, Centre, DVP, DDP, BVP (*Bürgerblock*)
Reichstag support: 274/493

Reich Chancellor: Hans Luther (Independent)
Minister of Foreign Affairs: Gustav Stresemann (DVP)
Minister of the Interior: Martin Schiele (DNVP)
Minister of Finance: Otto von Schlieben (DNVP)
Minister of Economics: Albert Neuhaus (DNVP)
Minister of Labour: Heinrich Brauns (Centre)
Minister of Defence: Otto Gessler (DDP)
Minister of Justice & Occupied Territories: Josef Frenken (Centre)
Minister of Agriculture: Gerhard von Kanitz (Independent)
Minister of Post: Karl Stingl (BVP)
Minister of Transport: Rudolf Krohne (DVP)

Changes:
- On 29 October 1925 the DNVP ministers resigned over the Locarno Treaty and were replaced by the following appointees from within the cabinet: Gessler (Interior as well as Defence), Luther (Finance as well as Chancellor), Krohne (Economics as well as Transport)
- Josef Frenken resigned on 21 November 1925, also over Locarno, and his briefs were administered by Luther (Justice) and Brauns (Occupied Territories)

Second Luther Cabinet – January–May 1926
Participating parties: Centre, DVP, DDP, BVP
Reichstag support: 171/493

Reich Chancellor: Hans Luther (Independent)
Minister of Foreign Affairs: Gustav Stresemann (DVP)
Minister of the Interior: Wilhelm Külz (DDP)
Minister of Finance: Peter Reinhold (DDP)
Minister of Economics: Julius Curtius (DVP)
Minister of Labour: Heinrich Brauns (Centre)

Minister of Defence: Otto Gessler (DDP)
Minister of Justice & Occupied Territories: Wilhelm Marx (Centre)
Minister of Agriculture: Heinrich Haslinde (Centre)
Minister of Post: Karl Stingl (BVP)
Minister of Transport: Rudolf Krohne (DVP)

Third* Marx Cabinet – May–December 1926
Participating parties: Centre, DVP, DDP, BVP
Reichstag support: 171/493

Reich Chancellor & Minister of Justice & Occupied Territories: Wilhelm Marx (Centre)
Minister of Foreign Affairs: Gustav Stresemann (DVP)
Minister of the Interior: Wilhelm Külz (DDP)
Minister of Finance: Peter Reinhold (DDP)
Minister of Economics: Julius Curtius (DVP)
Minister of Labour: Heinrich Brauns (Centre)
Minister of Defence: Otto Gessler (DDP)
Minister of Agriculture: Heinrich Haslinde (Centre)
Minister of Post: Karl Stingl (BVP)
Minister of Transport: Rudolf Krohne (DVP)

Changes:
- On 17 July 1926 Johannes Bell (Centre) succeeded Marx as Minister of Justice & Occupied Territories

Fourth Marx Cabinet – January 1927–June 1928
Participating parties: DNVP, Centre, DVP, BVP (*Bürgerblock*)
Reichstag support: 242/493

Reich Chancellor & Minister of Occupied Territories: Wilhelm Marx (Centre)
Vice-Chancellor & Minister of Justice: Oskar Hergt (DNVP)
Minister of Foreign Affairs: Gustav Stresemann (DVP)
Minister of the Interior: Walter von Keudell (DNVP)
Minister of Finance: Heinrich Köhler (Centre)
Minister of Economics: Julius Curtius (DVP)
Minister of Labour: Heinrich Brauns (Centre)
Minister of Defence: Otto Gessler (Independent – had resigned from the DDP)
Minister of Agriculture: Martin Schiele (DNVP)

---

* Marx had presided over two cabinets during the period November 1923–January 1925.

Minister of Post: Georg Schätzel (BVP)
Minister of Transport: Wilhelm Koch (DNVP)

Changes:
- On 20 January 1928 Wilhelm Groener (Independent) succeeded Gessler as Minister of Defence following the latter's resignation over the Lohmann Affair

Second* Müller Cabinet – June 1928–March 1930
Participating parties: SPD, Centre, DVP, DDP, BVP (Grand Coalition)
Reichstag support: 301/491

Reich Chancellor: Hermann Müller (SPD)
Minister of Foreign Affairs: Gustav Stresemann (DVP)
Minister of the Interior: Carl Severing (SPD)
Minister of Finance: Rudolf Hilferding (SPD)
Minister of Economics: Julius Curtius (DVP)
Minister of Labour: Rudolf Wissell (SPD)
Minister of Defence: Wilhelm Groener (Independent)
Minister of Justice: Erich Koch-Wesser (DDP)
Minister of Agriculture: Hermann Dietrich (DDP)
Minister of Post: Georg Schätzel (BVP)
Minister of Transport & Occupied Territories: Theodor von Guérard (Centre)

Changes:
- On 7 February 1929, Theodor von Guérard left the cabinet after the Centre Party's failure to agree a deal with the other coalition parties, with his roles being assumed by Severing (Occupied Territories) and Schätzel (Transport)
- On 13 April 1929, the Centre Party formally joined the government and Theodor von Guérard took the Justice Ministry, Adam Stegerwald the Transport Ministry and Joseph Wirth became Minister for Occupied Territories
- Gustav Stresemann died on 2 October 1929, his post as Foreign Minister being assumed by Julius Curtius
- Now Foreign Minister, Curtius was replaced as Economics Minister on 11 November 1929 by Paul Moldenhauer (DVP)
- Rudolf Hilferding resigned as Finance Minister on 21 December 1929 amidst the growing fiscal crisis and was replaced by Moldenhauer on the 23rd. The Economics Ministry went to Robert Schmidt (SPD)

---

* Müller had presided over a short-lived cabinet in 1920.

Brüning Cabinet – March 1930–May 1932

Participating parties: Centre, DVP, DStP, WP, CNBL, BVP, KVP ('Hindenburg Cabinet', i.e., a presidential government without a formal coalition deal between participating parties)

Reichstag support: 183/577 (after the September 1930 election, NB the cabinet was 'tolerated' by a number of parties outside the cabinet, most notably the SPD)

Reich Chancellor: Heinrich Brüning (Centre)
Vice-Chancellor & Minister of Economics: Hermann Dietrich (DStP)
Minister of Foreign Affairs: Julius Curtius (DVP)
Minister of the Interior: Joseph Wirth (Centre)
Minister of Finance: Paul Moldenhauer (DVP)
Minister of Labour: Adam Stegerwald (Centre)
Minister of Defence: Wilhelm Groener (Independent)
Minister of Justice: Johann Viktor Bredt (WP)
Minister of Agriculture: Martin Schiele (DNVP until July 1930, then CNBL)
Minister of Post: Georg Schätzel (BVP)
Minister of Transport: Theodor von Guérard (Centre)
Minister of Occupied Territories: Gottfried Treviranus (KVP)

Changes:
- On 18 June 1930, Paul Moldenhauer's party (DVP) demanded he resign as Finance Minister after they rejected his budget and he complied a few days later. He was replaced by Dietrich, whose Economics Ministry post was assumed by the permanent secretary of the department, civil servant Ernst Trendelenburg (who happened to be a DStP member)
- The Allies had withdrawn from the Rhineland by the end of September 1930, bringing to a close the occupation. Treviranus thus became Minister without Portfolio and Reich Commissioner for Eastern Aid
- On 5 December 1930, Bredt resigned as Justice Minister after his Reich Party of the Middle Class (WP) withdrew their support from the government. The ministry was passed to the permanent secretary, civil servant Curt Joël
- A cabinet reshuffle completed on 10 October 1931 resulted in; Curtius being dismissed and Brüning assuming the Foreign Ministry himself, Groener adding the Interior Ministry to his Defence brief after Wirth's dismissal, Hermann Warmbold (Independent) taking the Economics Ministry from the civil servant Trendelenburg, Treviranus replacing von Guérard as Transport Minister
- On 5 November 1931, Hans Schlange-Schöningen (CNBL) joined the cabinet as Minister without Portfolio and Reich Commissioner for Eastern Aid
- Hermann Warmbold resigned as Economics Minister on 5 May 1932 in protest against Brüning's policies. He was not replaced before the cabinet fell although Trendelenburg once again took over the department

- Wilhelm Groener was forced out as defence minister on 13 May 1932, although he retained the Interior Ministry. He was not replaced before the cabinet fell

Papen Cabinet – June–December 1932
Participating parties: N/A ('Cabinet of Barons' with no formal party participation)
Reichstag support: 44/608 (after the July 1932 election, NB the DNVP and DVP supported the cabinet but were not part of the government)

Reich Chancellor: Franz von Papen (Independent*)
Minister of Foreign Affairs: Konstantin von Neurath (Independent)
Minister of the Interior: Wilhelm von Gayl (DNVP)
Minister of Finance: Lutz Schwerin von Krosigk (Independent)
Minister of Economics: Hermann Warmbold (Independent)
Minister of Labour: Hugo Schäffer (Independent)
Minister of Defence: Kurt von Schleicher (Independent)
Minister of Justice: Franz Gürtner (DNVP)
Minister of Agriculture & Reich Commissioner for Eastern Aid: Magnus von Braun (DNVP)
Minister of Post & Transport: Paul von Eltz-Rübenach (Independent)

Changes:
- On 20 July 1920, Franz von Papen was appointed Reich-Commissioner for Prussia as part of the so-called Prussian Coup, displacing the sitting Prussian Prime Minister Otto Braun
- On 29 October 1932, Franz Bracht and Johannes Popitz (both independent civil servants) were added to the cabinet as Ministers without Portfolio. At the time Bracht was Deputy-Commissioner for Prussia and Prussian Interior Minister, while Popitz was heading the Prussian Finance Ministry

Schleicher Cabinet – December 1932–January 1933
Participating parties: N/A (effectively a continuation of the 'Cabinet of Barons' with no formal party participation)
Reichstag support: 62/584 (NB the DNVP and DVP supported the cabinet but were not part of the government)

Reich Chancellor, Reich-Commissioner for Prussia & Minister of Defence: Kurt von Schleicher (Independent)
Minister of Foreign Affairs: Konstantin von Neurath (Independent)
Minister of the Interior: Franz Bracht (Independent)

---

* Papen was expelled from the Centre Party upon assuming office.

Minister of Finance: Lutz Schwerin von Krosigk (Independent)
Minister of Economics: Hermann Warmbold (Independent)
Minister of Labour: Friedrich Syrup (Independent)
Minister of Justice: Franz Gürtner (DNVP)
Minister of Agriculture & Reich Commissioner for Eastern Aid: Magnus von Braun (DNVP)
Minister of Post & Transport: Paul von Eltz-Rübenach (Independent)
Minister without Portfolio: Johannes Popitz (Independent)
Reich Commissioner for Employment: Günther Gereke (CNBL)

Hitler Cabinet – January 1933
Participating parties: NSDAP, DNVP, *Stahlhelm*
Reichstag support: 247/584, then 340/647 (after March 1933 election)

Reich Chancellor: Adolf Hitler (NSDAP)
Vice-Chancellor* & Reich-Commissioner for Prussia: Franz von Papen (Independent)
Minister of Foreign Affairs: Konstantin von Neurath (Independent)
Minister of the Interior: Wilhelm Frick (NSDAP)
Minister of Finance: Lutz Schwerin von Krosigk (Independent)
Minister of Economics & Agriculture: Alfred Hugenberg (DNVP)
Minister of Labour: Franz Seldte (*Stahlhelm*)
Minister of Defence: Werner von Blomberg (Independent)
Minister of Justice: Franz Gürtner (Independent – had left the DNVP)
Minister of Post & Transport: Paul von Eltz-Rübenach (Independent)
Minister without Portfolio & Prussian Interior Minister: Hermann Göring (NSDAP)
Reich Commissioner for Employment: Günther Gereke (CNBL)

NB the composition of the Hitler cabinet rapidly changed as all parties bar the NSDAP were suppressed in the spring and summer of 1933, but the survivors from the 'cabinet of barons' (Neurath, Krosigk, Gürtner and Eltz-Rübenach) would continue to serve in Hitler's cabinet until the late thirties or early forties and in Krosigk's case, until 1945.

---

* Papen's formal title was in fact Deputy Chancellor, a post that existed neither before nor since.

Notes

Prologue
1. Norman Stone, 'Paul von Hindenburg', Michael Carver (ed.), *The War Lords*, (Pen & Sword: 2005), p. 54.
2. Holger H. Herwig, 'Of Men and Myths: The Use and Abuse of History and the Great War', Winter, Parker, Habeck (eds.), *The Great War and the Twentieth Century*, (Yale University Press: 2000).
3. Eric D. Weitz, *Weimar Germany: Promise and Tragedy*, (Princeton University Press: 2007), pp. 91, 101, Richard J. Evans, *The Coming of the Third Reich*, (Penguin: 2004), pp. 97–8.
4. Robert Whitfield, *Democracy and Nazism: Germany 1918–1945*, (Oxford University Press: 2015), p. 29.
5. *See* chapters 6 through 8 of Ian Kershaw, *Hitler, 1889–1936: Hubris*, (Penguin: 1999), where Ludendorff is a frequent and significant figure, while David King, *The Trial of Adolf Hitler*, (Pan: 2018) paints a clear picture of Ludendorff's centrality to the Munich putsch.
6. William J. Astore, Dennis E. Showalter, *Hindenburg: Icon of German Militarism*, (Potomac: 2005), pp. 77ff.
7. https://www.h-net.org/reviews/showrev.php?id=50802 (accessed 26/10/20), my own review of *The First Nazi* can be found here: https://www.amazon.co.uk/gp/customer-reviews/R2GPE2SKITKV55/ref=cm_cr_dp_d_rvw_btm?ie=UTF8&ASIN=0715652184#wasThisHelpful
8. Astore, Showalter, pp. 6–8.
9. More detailed accounts of Hindenburg's first career can be found in his opening chapters of biographies, e.g. Astore, Showalter, John Wheeler-Bennett, *Wooden Titan: Hindenburg in Twenty Years of German History, 1914–1934*, (William Morrow: 1936), Andreas Dorpalen, *Hindenburg and the Weimar Republic*, (Princeton University Press: 1964).
10. Astore, Showalter, p. 17.
11. For full accounts of Ludendorff's pre-war career, *see* early chapters of Roger Parkinson, *Tormented Warrior: Ludendorff and the Supreme Command*, (Hodder & Stoughton: 1978) and D. J. Goodspeed, *Ludendorff: Solider, Dictator, Revolutionary*, (Rupert Hart-Davies: 1966).
12. Parkinson, pp. 36–8, 49.
13. John Lee, *The Warlords: Hindenburg and Ludendorff*, (Weidenfeld & Nicolson: 2005), pp. 53–4.
14. Astore, Showalter, pp. 17–18.
15. Paul von Hindenburg, Charles Messenger (ed.), *The Great War*, (Frontline Books: 2013), pp. 58–9, Dorpalen, p. 9.
16. Lee, p. 58.
17. Ibid., pp. 61–4.
18. Wheeler-Bennett, *Wooden Titan*, p. 14, for a discussion of who was responsible for naming the battle, *see* Anna von der Goltz, *Hindenburg: Power, Myth and the Rise of the Nazis*, (Oxford University Press: 2011), pp. 18–20, who concludes it was probably Hindenburg.

19. Goltz, pp. 27–31.
20. Ibid., pp. 25–7.
21. George S. Vascik, Mark R. Sadler, *The Stab-in-the-Back Myth and the Fall of the Weimar Republic, A History in Documents and Visual Sources*, (Bloomsbury: 2016), p. 109.
22. Astore, Showalter, pp. 34–5, Christopher Clark, *Kaiser Wilhelm II*, (Longman: 2000), pp. 229–30.
23. Wheeler-Bennett, *Wooden Titan*, pp. 70–3.
24. Alexander Watson, *Ring of Steel: Germany and Austria-Hungary at War, 1914–1918*, (Penguin: 2015), pp. 328–9.
25. Ibid., p. 378ff.
26. Goltz, pp. 39–41.
27. Watson, p. 457.
28. Lee, p. 129.
29. Watson, p. 259ff., 460–2.
30. John Terraine, *To Win a War, 1918: The Year of Victory*, (Cassell: 2000), p. 36.
31. Ibid.
32. Lee, pp. 150–1.
33. Astore, Showalter, pp. 53–4.
34. Terraine, pp. 38–40, 65–6, Watson, pp. 520–3.
35. Tim Travers, *How the War was Won: Factors that led to victory in World War One*, (Pen & Sword, 2005), pp. 154–5, Watson, p. 522.
36. Gary Sheffield, *Forgotten Victory, The First World War: Myths and Realities*, (Review: 2002), p. 239.
37. Terraine, pp. 100, 103.
38. Astore, Showalter, p. 68, Terraine, pp. 122–3, Parkinson, pp. 172–4.
39. Goodspeed, p. 208.
40. Parkinson, pp. 176–8, Watson, p. 533.
41. Roger Chickering, 'The Sore Loser: Ludendorff's Total War', Chickering, Förster (eds.), *The Shadows of Total War: Europe, East Asia and the United States, 1919–1939*, (Cambridge University Press: 2008), p. 158, Terraine, pp. 161–2, Goodspeed, p. 211.
42. Watson, pp. 534–5.
43. Ibid., pp. 548–50, Lee, pp. 178–9.
44. Goodspeed, p. 215, Parkinson, pp. 181–2, Lee, pp, 180–1.
45. Terraine, pp. 221–2.
46. Watson, pp. 553–4, *see also* William A. Pelz, *A People's History of the German Revolution*, (Pluto Press: 2018).
47. For a detailed account of these discussions, *see* Wheeler-Bennett, *Wooden Titan*, pp. 194–205.
48. Dorpalen, pp. 20–1.
49. Evans, pp. 78–9.
50. Weitz, pp. 31–2.
51. Evans, p. 80.
52. Ibid., p. 88.
53. John Hite, Chris Hinton, *Weimar and Nazi Germany*, (Hodder: 2000), pp. 30–1.
54. Evans, pp. 14–16, 84. *See* Paul Bookbinder, *Weimar Germany: The Republic of the Reasonable*, (Manchester University Press: 1996), pp. 44–50 for a breakdown of parties, although most histories of Weimar have something similar.

Chapter 1

1. Easton, L., 'Review of Boris Barth, *Dolchstoßlegenden und politische Desintegration: Das Trauma der deutschen Niederlage im Ersten Weltkrieg, 1914–1933*', *Journal of Modern History*, 77 (2005), 1145–1147, p. 1147.

2. Benjamin Carter Hett, *The Death of Democracy: Hitler's Rise to Power*, (Windmill Books: 2019), pp. 29–33 provides a good introduction to the myth and its significance.
3. Quoted in Easton, p. 1145.
4. Vascik, Sadler, p. 1.
5. All modern military histories of the war are clear about this; *see*, for instance, Sheffield, pp. 256–7.
6. W. Deist, 'The Military Collapse of the German Empire: The Reality Behind the Stab-in-the-Back Myth', trans. E. Feuchtwanger, *War in* History, 3, 2 (1996), 186–207, pp. 192–4.
7. Easton review of Barth, p. 1146, Terraine, p. 160.
8. Deist, p. 195.
9. Travers, pp. 155–6.
10. Ibid., pp. 175, 179.
11. Deist, pp. 188, 201, 202, 206.
12. Vascik, p. 75–6, Geyer, M., 'Insurructionary Warfare: The German Debate about a Levée en Masse in October 1918', *Journal of Modern History*, 73 (2001), 459–527, pp. 506–507.
13. Wolfram Pyta, *Hindenburg: Herrschaft zwischen Hohenzollern und Hitler*, (Pantheon: 2009), pp. 259–63.
14. Quoted in Astore, Showalter, p. 58.
15. Deist, pp. 199–200.
16. Quoted in Chickering, p. 153.
17. Evans, p. 61.
18. Lee, pp. 177–8.
19. Quoted in Deist, p. 207.
20. Goltz, p. 56.
21. Vascik, pp. 1–2.
22. Evans p. 75.
23. Geyer, p. 470.
24. Wheeler-Bennett, *Wooden Titan*, pp. 166–7.
25. Quoted in Lee, p. 179.
26. Quoted in Deist, p. 207.
27. Quoted in Harold Marcuse, http://marcuse.faculty.history.ucsb.edu/publications/reviews/BarthRev069.htm (accessed 15/8/20).
28. Quoted in Astore, Showalter, p. 72.
29. Quoted in Hite, Hinton, p. 24.
30. Goltz, p. 59.
31. Ibid.
32. Ibid., p. 66.
33. Document 6.7, Vascik, p. 89.
34. Vascik, p. 88.
35. Astore, Showalter, p. 79.
36. Goltz, pp. 55, 62–4.
37. Chickering, p. 151.
38. Margarethe Ludendorff, trans. Raglan Somerset, *My Married Life with Ludendorff*, (Hutchinson: 1929), p. 176, Goodspeed, p. 219.
39. Goltz, pp. 54–6.
40. Ibid.
41. Parkinson, p. 185.
42. Ibid., p. 187.
43. Goodspeed, pp. 221–2.
44. Ibid., p. 221.

45. M Ludendorff, pp. 204–205.
46. Ibid., p. 199.
47. This is a central argument of Jay Lockenour's recent biography of Ludendorff, *Dragonslayer: The Legend of Erich Ludendorff in the Weimar Republic and Third Reich*, (Cornell University Press: 2021), pp. 10ff.
48. Geyer, pp. 518–19.
49. Vascik, Sadler, pp. 96–9.
50. Document 7.1, Vascik, Sadler, p. 95.
51. Vascik, Sadler, p. 102.
52. Chickering, p. 152.
53. Quoted in Hett, p. 31.
54. Quoted in Chickering, p. 154.
55. Parkinson, p. 193.
56. Matthias A. Fahrenwaldt, 'The Knives Are Out: The Reception of Erich Ludendorff's Memoirs in the Context of the Dolchstoß Myth, 1919–1925', Portal Militärgeschichte, 2021, p. 3 (http://portal-militaergeschichte.de/sites/default/files/pdf/fahrenwaldt_ludendorff_0.pdf) accessed 15/3/21).
57. Ibid., pp. 4–7.
58. Erich Ludendorff, *Ludendorff's Own Story: August 1914–November 1918, The Great War, Volume II, From the Siege of Liege to the Signing of the Armistice as viewed from the Grand Headquarters of the Germany Army*, (Lucknow Books: 2012), location 5416–5446.
59. Ibid., location 5468–5482.
60. Ibid., locations 5441, 759.
61. Chickering, p. 156.
62. Ludendorff, *Own Story*, location 1917.
63. Ibid., location 4426.
64. Deist, pp. 188–9.
65. Quoted in Lee, p. 178.
66. Quoted in Chickering, p. 157.
67. John Wheeler-Bennett, 'Ludendorff: The Soldier and the Politician', *VQR*, Spring 1938, (https://www.vqronline.org/essay/ludendorff-soldier-and-politician, accessed 19/10/20).
68. Chickering, p. 157.
69. Ibid., p. 158.
70. *See* Dorpalen, chapter one, for a full account of this period.
71. Astore, Showalter, p. 78.
72. E. J. Feuchtwanger, *From Weimar to Hitler, Germany 1918–33*, (MacMillan: 1993), pp. 47–8.
73. Eberhard Kolb, trans. P. S. Falla, *The Weimar Republic*, (Routledge: 1992), pp. 30–1.
74. Evans, pp. 63–5.
75. Kolb, pp. 31–2.
76. Quoted in Wheeler-Bennett, *Wooden Titan*, pp. 217–18.
77. Kolb, pp. 31–2.
78. Wheeler-Bennett, *Wooden Titan*, p. 217, Dorpalen, pp. 40–1.
79. John Wheeler-Bennett, *The Nemesis of Power: The German Army in Politics, 1918–1945*, (MacMillan: 1980), pp. 55–7.
80. Wheeler-Bennett, *Wooden Titan*, pp. 219–20.
81. Ibid., p. 220.
82. Dorpalen, p. 41.
83. Ibid.
84. Ibid., p. 42.
85. Ibid.
86. Astore, Showalter, pp. 78–9.

87. Goltz, pp. 63–5.
88. Vascik, Sadler, p. 111.
89. Ibid.
90. Wheeler-Bennett, pp. 66–7.
91. A full account of Hindenburg's appearance can be found in Pyta, *Hindenburg*, p. 470ff.
92. Dorpalen, p. 48.
93. Goltz, pp. 69–70.
94. Goltz, pp. 70–1, Wheeler-Bennett, *Nemesis of Power*, pp. 67–8, Vascik, Sadler, pp. 116–17.
95. Goltz, p. 70.
96. For preparations for the testimony, *see* Vascik, Sadler, p. 121, Wheeler-Bennett, *Nemesis of Power*, p. 67, Dorpalen, pp. 49–50.
97. Pyta, *Hindenburg*, pp. 443–5.
98. *See* Wheeler-Bennett, *Wooden Titan*, p. 233, *Nemesis of Power*, p. 67. Pyta, *Hindenburg*, p. 407ff. leaves no doubt as to what Hindenburg's intentions were.
99. Dorpalen, p. 49.
100. Goltz, p. 69.
101. Wheeler-Bennet, *Wooden Titan*, pp. 237–8.
102. Dorpalen, p. 50.
103. Ibid.
104. Ibid., *see also* Wheeler-Bennett, *Wooden Titan*, p. 234.
105. Wheeler-Bennett, *Wooden Titan*, pp. 234–5.
106. Ibid., pp. 235–6.
107. Ibid., pp. 236–7.
108. Document 8.13, Vascik, Sadler, p. 122.
109. Document 8.14, Vascik, Sadler, p. 125.
110. Wheeler-Bennett, *Wooden Titan*, p. 237.
111. Vascik, Sadler, p. 117.
112. Telford Taylor, *Sword and Swastika: Generals and Nazis in the Third Reich*, (Barnes & Noble: 1995), p. 33.
113. Goltz, p. 68.
114. Wheeler-Bennett, *Wooden Titan*, p. 238.
115. Dorpalen, pp. 52–3.
116. Goltz, p. 68.
117. Chickering, pp. 158–9.
118. Farhrenwaldt, pp. 7–12.
119. Goltz, p. 76, Dorpalen, pp. 46–7, Wheeler-Bennet, *Wooden Titan*, p. 226.
120. Goltz, p. 76.
121. Dorpalen, pp. 45–6.
122. Document 8.12, Vascik, Sadler, p. 122.
123. Hindenburg, p. 220.
124. Ibid., p. 223.
125. Dorpalen, p. 47.
126. Larry Eugene Jones, 'Conservative Anti-Semitism in the Weimar Republic: A Case Study of the German National People's Party', Jones (ed.), *The German Right in the Weimar Republic: Studies in the History of Conservatism, Nationalism, and Anti-Semitism*, (Berghahn: 2016), 79–107, pp. 80–1.
127. Viscik, Sadler, p. 205.
128. Herwig, 'Of Men and Myths', *see* prologue note 2.

Chapter 2
1. John Dornberg, *The Putsch That Failed, Munich 1923: Hitler's Rehearsal for Power*, (Weidenfeld & Nicolson: 1982), p. 316.

2. Karen Schaefer, *Germany Military and the Weimar Republic: General Hans von Seekt, General Erich Ludendorff and the Rise of Hitler*, (Pen & Sword: 2020), p. 113.
3. David Jablonsky, *The Nazi Party in Dissolution: Hitler and the Verbotzeit, 1923–25*, (Frank Cass: 1989), pp. 2–4.
4. *See* Nigel Jones's seminal work on the Freikorps for detail on their origins and background, *The Birth of the Nazis: How the Freikorps Blazed a Trail for Hitler*, (Robinson: 2004).
5. Dietrich Orlow, *The History of the Nazi Party Volume 1, 1919–1933*, (David & Charles: 1971), p. 56.
6. Ernst Röhm, trans. Geoffrey Brooks, *The Memoirs of Ernst Röhm*, (Frontline Books: 2012), pp. 16–17.
7. Mark Jones, 'Political Violence in Italy and Germany after the First World War', Millington, Passmore (eds.), *Political Violence and Democracy in Western Europe, 1918–1940*, (Palgrave MacMillan: 2015), p. 16.
8. Geyer, p. 94, Matthew N. Bucholtz, '*Kamerad* or *Genosse*? The Contested Frontkämpfer Identity in Weimar Revolutionary Politics', Millington, Passmore (eds.), *Political Violence and Democracy in Western Europe, 1918–1940*, (Palgrave MacMillan: 2015), p. 59.
9. Bucholtz, p. 56.
10. Mark Jones, *Founding Weimar: Violence and the German Revolution, 1918–1919*, (Cambridge University Press: 2018) pp. 235–7.
11. Mark Jones, 'Political Violence in Italy and Germany', p. 16.
12. Evans, p. 160.
13. Mark Jones, 'Political Violence in Italy and Germany', p. 17.
14. Nigel Jones, p. 124.
15. Marianne Weber, trans. Harry Zohn, *Max Weber: A Biography*, (Transaction Books: 1988), pp. 651, 707.
16. Weber, p. 653.
17. *See* Schaefer's chapter on Ludendorff's post-war strategy of mass mobilisation, pp. 30–42.
18. Weber, p. 654.
19. M Ludendorff, pp. 226–7.
20. Parkinson, pp. 195–6, Goodspeed, p. 224.
21. M. Ludendorff, pp. 227–8.
22. *See* Chickering, p. 159.
23. Margarethe Ludendorff, p. 177.
24. Chickering, p. 159.
25. Eric D. Weitz, 'Erwin Könnemann and Gehard Schulze, eds., Der Kapp-Lüttwitz-Ludendorff Putsch: Dokumente', *Central European History*, 38, 3 (2005), p. 494.
26. Lockenour, p. 88.
27. Goodspeed, pp. 224–6, Nigel Jones, p. 172.
28. M. Ludendorff, p. 231.
29. Goodspeed, p. 226.
30. Ibid.
31. Margarethe Ludendorff, p. 231, for an example of Ludendorff's role being omitted, *see* Carsten's study of the Reichswehr in politics *The Reichswehr and Politics, 1918–1933*, (Oxford University Press: 1966) – his detailed account of the putsch does not even mention Ludendorff.
32. Feuchtwanger, p. 73.
33. Weitz, *Central European History*, p. 495, for an example of Ludendorff being omitted from the putsch, *see* Evans, pp. 97–8.
34. Erich Ludendorff, *Vom Feldherrn zum Weltrevolutionär und Wegbereiter Deutsche Volksschöpfung: Meine Lebenserinnerungen*, (Ludendorff Verlag: 1940), p. 99.
35. Nigel Jones, p. 173.
36. Feuchtwanger, p. 72, Kolb, p. 36.

37. Nigel Jones, pp. 173–4.
38. Carsten, p. 76.
39. Nigel Jones, pp. 175–6, Feuchtwanger, p. 72.
40. Carsten, p. 76, Nigel Jones, pp. 176–7.
41. Carsten, pp. 76–7.
42. Carsten, p. 77, Nigel Jones, pp. 177–8.
43. Carsten, p. 78.
44. Nigel Jones, p. 179.
45. Carsten, p. 79, Nigel Jones, p. 180.
46. Nigel Jones, p. 180.
47. Kolb, p. 37, Feuchtwanger, pp. 74–5.
48. Feuchtwanger, p. 74.
49. Nigel Jones, p. 181.
50. Goodspeed, p. 227, Parkinson, p. 199, Nigel Jones, pp. 181–2.
51. Goodspeed, pp. 227–8, Nigel Jones, p. 182.
52. Carsten, p. 81.
53. *See* Nigel Jones, p. 190, for Seeckt's views on the putsch.
54. Pelz, p. 120.
55. Schaefer, pp. 199–200.
56. Evans, p. 100, Nigel Jones, p. 182.
57. Goodspeed, p. 228.
58. Roderick Stackelberg, Sally A. Winkle (eds.), *The Nazi Germany Sourcebook, an anthology of texts*, (Routledge: 2002), p. 67.
59. Stackelberg & Winkle (eds.), p. 68.
60. Ibid.
61. Goodspeed, p. 228.
62. Parkinson, p. 199.
63. Goodspeed, p. 228.
64. Carsten, p. 80.
65. Nigel Jones, pp. 172, 182.
66. Carsten, p. 84.
67. Carsten, pp. 84–5.
68. Kolb, p. 38, Carsten, p. 87.
69. Nigel Jones, p. 186.
70. Röhm, pp. 31–2.
71. Nigel Jones, pp. 186–7.
72. Carsten, p. 87.
73. Carsten, p. 83.
74. Pelz, pp. 121–2, Feuchtwanger, pp. 75–6.
75. Evans, p. 148.
76. Hans Mommsen, 'The Failure of the Weimar Republic and the Rise of Hitler', Michael Laffen (ed.), *The Burden of German History, 1919–1945, Essays for the Goethe Insititute*, (Metheun: 1988), p. 120.
77. Pelz, pp. 121–2, Nigel Jones, pp. 183–4.
78. Lockenour, p. 90.
79. Pelz, p. 122.
80. Goodspeed, p. 228, Nigel Jones, p. 184, Pelz, p. 122.
81. Carsten, p. 82.
82. Lockenour, pp. 90–2.
83. Ibid., pp. 82–3.
84. Pelz, p. 122.
85. Nigel Jones, p. 185.

86. Goodspeed, p. 229, Carsten, p. 88, Parkinson, p. 199.
87. Nigel Jones, p. 188.
88. Goodspeed, p. 229.
89. Parkinson, p. 200.
90. Goodspeed, p. 229.
91. Ibid., Carsten, pp. 89–90.
92. Nigel Jones, p. 188.
93. Ibid., p. 189.
94. Carsten, p. 89.
95. Ibid., Nigel Jones, p. 189.
96. Carsten, p. 89.
97. Goodspeed, p. 231, Nigel Jones, p. 189.
98. Goodspeed, p. 231.
99. Nigel Jones, p. 190.
100. Goodspeed, p. 231.
101. Weber, p. 688.
102. Robert Gerwarth, *The Vanquished, Why the First World War Failed to End, 1917–1923*, (Penguin: 2017), p. 166.
103. Nigel Jones, pp. 193–4.
104. Feuchtwanger, pp. 78–9.
105. Nigel Jones, p. 199.
106. Feuchtwanger, p. 80.
107. Nigel Jones, pp. 199–200.
108. Feuchtwanger, p. 75.
109. Carsten, p. 98.
110. Nigel Jones, p. 202.
111. Kolb, p. 39, Feuchtwanger, pp. 81–2.
112. Carsten, pp. 91–2.
113. Ibid., p. 97.
114. Anthony McElligott, *Weimar Germany*, (Oxford University Press: 2009), p. 86.
115. Kolb, p. 38, Evans, pp. 98–9, Carsten, pp. 103–104.
116. Carsten, pp. 97–9, Feuchtwanger, p. 77.
117. Dorpalen, p. 57.
118. Dorpalen, p. 56, for a more modern interpretation of Hindenburg's ambivalent position, *see* Pyta, *Hindenburg*, pp. 450ff.
119. Nigel Jones, p. 186, Dorpalen, p. 58.
120. For Hindenburg's first candidacy for the presidency, *see* Pyta, *Hindenburg*, pp. 443–51.
121. Wheeler-Bennett, *Wooden Titan*, p. 255.
122. Goltz, pp. 73–4.
123. Wheeler-Bennett, p. 255, Dorpalen, p. 58.
124. For an accessible account of the Bavarian revolution and the events that followed, *see* Cory Taylor, *How Hitler Was Made: Germany and the Rise of the Perfect Nazi*, (Prometheus: 2018). For an equally readable and scholarly assessment, *see* Kershaw, *Hitler*, pp. 110–16, Evans, pp. 156–61.
125. Taylor, pp. 73–4.
126. Kershaw, p. 116.
127. Röhm, pp. 29–30.
128. Taylor, p. 102.
129. Röhm, pp. 48, Kershaw, p. 171.
130. Taylor, p. 138, Röhm pp. 33–4.
131. A visit to the permanent exhibition NS-Dokuzentrum in Munich provides a clear insight into Bavarian political life in the Weimar era. *See also* Kershaw, p. 159, Winfried

Nerdinger (ed.), trans. Jefferson Chase et al, *Munich and National Socialism: Catalogue of the Munich Documentation Centre for the History of National Socialism*, (C.H. Beck: 2015), pp. 28–31.
132. Nerdinger (ed.). pp. 30–1.
133. King, p. 14.
134. Röhm, pp. 25–6.
135. Nerdinger (ed.), pp. 28, 34–5, 46–7.
136. Ibid., pp. 48–9.
137. Ibid., pp. 42–5.
138. Ibid., p. 31.
139. Röhm, pp. 44–6, Kershaw, p. 174.
140. Kershaw, p. 115, Taylor, p. 141.
141. Evans, pp. 160–1.
142. Nigel Jones, p. 210.
143. Ibid., p. 211.
144. Lockenour, p. 94.
145. Parkinson, pp. 201–202.
146. Ibid., pp. 203–204.
147. Röhm, p. 61.
148. Röhm, pp. 60–1.
149. Chickering, p. 164.
150. Erich Ludendorff (ed.), trans. F.A. Holt, *The General Staff and its Problems: The History of the relations between the High Command and German Imperial Government as revealed by official documents*, Vols I & II, (E.P. Dutton: 1920).
151. Chickering, p. 160.
152. Ludendorff (ed.), Vol. I, p. vi.
153. Chickering, p. 161.
154. Quoted in Parkinson, p. 205.
155. Ibid., p. 203.
156. Wolfram Wette, trans. Deborah Lucas Schneider, *The Wehrmacht: History, Myth, Reality*, (Harvard University Press: 2009), p. 41.
157. Schaefer, p. 38.
158. Quoted in Chickering, p. 163.
159. Nigel Jones, p. 212.
160. Goodspeed, p. 232.
161. Wette, pp. 57–8.
162. Parkinson, p. 204.
163. Erich Ludendorff, *Auf dem Weg zur Feldherrnhalle*, (Ludendorff Verlag: 1937), pp. 22–3.
164. Nigel Jones, p. 216.
165. Röhm, p. 47.
166. Nigel Jones, p. 228.
167. Kershaw, pp. 174–5.
168. Nigel Jones, p. 228.
169. Nerdinger (ed.), pp. 52–4.
170. Röhm, p. 89.
171. For a discussion of the ideology and roots of National Socialism, *see* Kershaw, pp. 134–9.
172. Kershaw, p. 147.
173. Nigel Jones, pp. 238–40.
174. Nerdinger (ed.), pp. 51–4, Kershaw, p. 149.
175. Nigel Jones, p. 238, Kershaw, p. 153.
176. King, p. 27, Kershaw states in fact it was Hess who made the introduction in May 1921, p. 195. Either way, it was that spring.

177. King, p. 27.
178. Kershaw, pp. 189–90.
179. Ibid., pp. 186, 194.
180. Chickering, p. 165.
181. Ibid., p. 165, Kershaw, pp. 199–200.
182. Kolb, p. 46.
183. Ibid., pp. 46–7.
184. Evans, p. 106.
185. Nerdinger (ed.), pp. 55, 66.
186. Röhm, p. 86.
187. Nigel Jones, p. 248.
188. Ibid., p. 247.
189. Kershaw, pp. 192–3.
190. Harold J. Gordon, *Hitler and the Beer Hall Putsch*, (Princeton University Press: 1972), pp. 89–92.
191. Kershaw, pp. 193–4.
192. Schaefer, p. 113.
193. Ibid., p. 164.
194. Röhm, p. 96.
195. Ibid., p. 122.
196. Parkinson, p. 206.
197. Röhm, p. 99.
198. Gordon, p. 32.
199. Röhm, pp. 107–108.
200. Kershaw, pp. 196–7.
201. Gordon, p. 58.
202. Margarethe Ludendorff, p. 245.
203. Lockenour, p. 98.
204. Kershaw, p. 199.
205. Ibid., pp. 199–200.
206. Milan Hauner, *Hitler: A Chronology of his Life and Time, Second Edition*, (Palgrave MacMillan: 2008), p. 42.
207. Kershaw, pp. 202–203.
208. Peter Ross Range, *1924, The Year that made Hitler*, (Little, Brown & Company: 2016), pp. 57–8.
209. Gordon, pp. 230, 252.
210. Hauner, p. 43.
211. Gordon, p. 248. Interestingly, Hitler and Ludendorff had contacted Minoux in late October but failed to find common ground.
212. Ibid., p. 132.
213. Gordon, pp. 248–50, Röhm, pp. 139–40.
214. Gordon, pp. 299–300.
215. Ibid., pp. 385–6. One such contact, Heydebreck, claimed that although he received a courteous reception from Ludendorff, Hitler would not see him and Göring dismissed his help.
216. Röhm, p. 135.
217. Gordon, pp. 252–4.
218. Hauner, p. 44, Gordon, p. 259, Röhm, p. 141.
219. Gordon, p. 258.
220. Hauner, p. 45.
221. Dornberg, pp. 2, 12, Gordon, pp. 259–60.

222. Gordon, p. 260.
223. Ibid., p. 300.
224. Jablonsky, pp. 31, 184.
225. William L. Shirer, *The Rise and Fall of the Third Reich*, (Pan: 1964), p. 95.
226. Ross Range, p. 68.
227. Röhm, pp. 126–7.
228. Dornberg, p. 31.
229. Gordon, p. 275.
230. Dornberg, p. 32.
231. Gordon, p. 275.
232. King, pp. 5–6.
233. Ibid., pp. 9–10.
234. Ibid., p. 76, Dornberg, pp. 86–7.
235. Dornberg, pp. 88–91.
236. King, p. 21.
237. Dornberg, p. 88, King, p. 27. Gordon incorrectly states Ludendorff arrived in full uniform, p. 288.
238. King, pp. 28–9.
239. Gordon, pp. 288–9, King, p. 29.
240. King, p. 30, Dornberg, p. 99.
241. Dornberg, p. 100.
242. Ibid., p. 102.
243. Ibid., p. 103.
244. Ibid., pp. 103–104.
245. Ibid., p. 106.
246. Quoted in Dornberg, p. 107.
247. Gordon, p. 310.
248. Dornberg, p. 133.
249. Ibid.
250. Ibid.
251. King, p. 55.
252. Dornberg, pp. 137–8.
253. King, pp. 59–60.
254. Dornberg, pp. 164–5, Gordon, p. 306.
255. Dornberg, pp. 169–71.
256. King, p. 75.
257. Dornberg, pp. 148–9.
258. Ibid., pp. 191–3.
259. King, pp. 76–9.
260. Gordon, p. 337.
261. Ibid., p. 325.
262. Ibid.
263. Röhm, p. 146.
264. Quoted in Dornberg, p. 217.
265. Ibid., p. 227.
266. Gordon, pp. 326–7.
267. Dornberg, p. 228.
268. Röhm, p. 148, King, pp. 82–3.
269. Dornberg, pp. 232–5.
270. Ibid., p. 266, King, p. 84.
271. Gordon, p. 332.

272. Ibid., pp. 330–1.
273. Ibid.
274. Gordon, p. 352, Dornberg, p. 272, King, p. 88.
275. Gordon, p. 351, King, p. 88.
276. Gordon, p. 340.
277. Dornberg, pp. 281–2.
278. King, p. 96, Dornberg, pp. 284–6.
279. King, p. 90.
280. Quoted in Dornberg, p. 290.
281. Dornberg, pp. 292–3.
282. Ibid., p. 292.
283. King, pp. 100–103, *see also* discussion in notes p. 361, 375, Dornberg, pp. 294–9. Examples of the doubtful version of Ludendorff marching on include Gordon's otherwise excellent account of the putsch, Kershaw's acclaimed biography of Hitler and in Goodspeed and Parkinson's biographies of Ludendorff.
284. Quoted in Dornberg, p. 299.
285. Gordon, pp. 469–70.
286. Röhm, p. 154, Dornberg, pp. 303–304, Gordon, p. 470.
287. Gordon, pp. 401–402.
288. Ibid., Chickering, p. 165.
289. King, p. 104, Dornberg, p. 296.

Chapter 3
1. Parkinson, pp. 220–4, and especially Goodspeed, pp. 243–9.
2. Gordon, pp. 470–1.
3. Margarethe Ludendorff, p. 252.
4. Lockenour, p. 106.
5. Ross Range, p. 112.
6. King, p. 133.
7. M. Ludendorff, pp. 260, 264–5.
8. Gordon, p. 471, Parkinson, pp. 218–19.
9. Gordon, p. 471, Röhm, p. 161.
10. Röhm, p. 161.
11. King, pp. 141–2.
12. M. Ludendorff, pp. 270–3.
13. Röhm, pp. 166–7.
14. Gordon, pp. 550, 564.
15. Lockenour, p. 111.
16. Chickering, pp. 166–7.
17. Ibid.
18. Parkinson, p. 203.
19. Quoted in Goodspeed, p. 235.
20. Chickering, p. 167.
21. Ross Range, p. 118.
22. King, pp. 138–41. I am indebted to David King's fantastic account of the Hitler trial for my own narrative of Ludendorff's role in it here.
23. Ibid., p. 150.
24. Ross Range, pp. 128–9.
25. King, pp. 151–3.
26. Ibid., pp. 157–62, 166.
27. Ibid., pp. 167–8.
28. Ibid., pp. 170, 179.

29. Ross Range, p. 156, King, p. 180.
30. Quoted in King, p. 185.
31. Ibid.
32. Ross Range, pp. 153–4.
33. Ross Range, p. 154, King, p. 197.
34. Quoted in Ross Range, p. 154, *see also* King, p. 185, which mentions one positive report in a Rosenheim paper.
35. King, pp. 197–9, p. 261.
36. Ibid., p. 185.
37. Ibid., p. 206.
38. Quoted in King, p. 220.
39. King, pp. 220–1.
40. Ibid., pp. 232–3.
41. Ibid., pp. 239–40.
42. Ibid., pp. 261–2.
43. Ibid.
44. Ibid., pp. 268–9.
45. Ross Range, p. 174, King, p. 277.
46. Ross Range, p. 178.
47. King, pp. 293–4.
48. Ibid., p. 298.
49. Gordon, pp. 482–3.
50. King, p. 296.
51. Ibid., p. 295.
52. Kershaw, pp. 226–7.
53. Jablonsky, pp. 52–3.
54. Orlow, pp. 49–50.
55. Jablonsky, pp. 62–3.
56. Kershaw, p. 228.
57. Ibid.
58. King, p. 304.
59. Kershaw, p. 229.
60. Quoted in Hauner, p. 48.
61. Kerhsaw, p. 229.
62. Quoted in Jablonsky, pp. 87–8.
63. King, p. 311, Jablonsky, p. 88. However, despite their disagreements, in a letter of 24 June 1924, Ludendorff insisted to a friend that his relationship with Hitler remained 'completely untroubled', *see* Jablonsky, p. 204.
64. Kershaw, pp. 229–30.
65. King, pp. 318–19.
66. Röhm, pp. 210–11.
67. Kershaw, pp. 230–1.
68. Jablonsky, p. 96.
69. Hauner, p. 49.
70. Jabolonsky, pp. 98–9.
71. The account of this conference and the quotes are all taken from Jablonsky, pp. 103–108.
72. Ibid., p. 104.
73. Ibid., p. 106.
74. Jablonsky, p. 118.
75. Ibid., pp. 118–19.
76. Ibid., p. 120.
77. Kershaw, p. 233.

78. Lockenour, p. 107, Jablonsky, p. 210.
79. Orlow, p. 50, Röhm, p. 214.
80. Röhm, pp. 212–14.
81. Jablonsky, pp. 122–3.
82. Kershaw, p. 233.
83. Quoted in Gordon, p. 574.
84. Orlow, pp. 45, 51.
85. Röhm, pp. 217–18.
86. Ibid., pp. 219–24.
87. Jablonsky, pp. 140–1.
88. Kershaw, pp. 212–13.
89. Röhm, p. 207.
90. Ibid., p. 225.
91. Lockenour, p. 108.
92. Jablonsky, pp. 142–5.
93. http://www.gonschior.de/weimar/index.htm (accessed 15/5/2020).
94. Goodspeed, p. 243, Lockenour, p. 107.
95. Ross Range, p. 249, Hauner, p. 50.
96. Kershaw, p. 262.
97. Kershaw, p. 263.
98. Ibid., p. 264.
99. Ross Range, p. 249.
100. Kershaw, pp. 264–5.
101. Kershaw, p. 267.
102. Larry Eugene Jones, *Hitler versus Hindenburg, The 1932 Presidential Elections and the End of the Weimar Republic*, (Cambridge University Press: 2015), pp. 22–3.
103. Dorpalen, pp. 66–7.
104. Goltz, p. 85, L.E. Jones, *Hitler versus Hindenburg*, p. 24.
105. Orlow, p. 61.
106. Kershaw, p. 268.
107. Orlow, p. 60.
108. Ibid., p. 61, Geoffrey Pridham, *Hitler's Rise to Power: The Nazi Movement in Bavaria, 1923–33*, (Hart-Davies: 1973), p. 44.
109. Kershaw, p. 268.
110. Orlow, p. 57, note 35.
111. Pridham, p. 44.
112. Chickering, p. 166.
113. Margarethe Ludendorff, pp. 227–8.
114. Hauner, p. 51.
115. Kershaw, p. 268.
116. Lockenour, p. 109.
117. Pridham, pp. 43–4.
118. Röhm, p. 227.
119. Ibid., pp. 227–8.
120. http://www.gonschior.de/weimar/Deutschland/Praesidenten.html (accessed 16/5/2020).
121. Röhm, p. 228.
122. Hauner, p. 51.
123. Röhm, p. 232.
124. Orlow, pp. 61–2.
125. Dorpalen, pp. 67–8.
126. http://www.gonschior.de/weimar/Deutschland/Praesidenten.html (accessed 16/5/2020).
127. L.E. Jones, *Hitler versus Hindenburg*, pp. 22–3.

128. Goltz, p. 87.
129. Wolfram Pyta, 'Hindenburg and the German Right', in L.E. Jones (ed.), *The German Right in the Weimar Republic, Studies in the History of Conservatism, Nationalism, and Anti-Semitism*, (Berghahn: 2016), p. 26.
130. *See* Goltz, chapter 3, for a good summary of Hindenburg's political activities up to 1925.
131. Quoted in Goltz, p. 87.
132. L.E. Jones, *Hitler versus Hindenburg*, pp. 25–6.
133. Goltz, pp. 85–6.
134. Quoted in Goltz, p. 86.
135. For a full account of the complex negotiations that followed, *see* Pyta, *Hindenburg*, pp. 461–78. For a briefer retelling, L.E. Jones, *Hitler versus Hindenburg*, pp. 26–7.
136. Pyta, pp. 464ff.
137. L.E. Jones, *Hitler versus Hindenburg*, p. 27.
138. Ibid., p. 28.
139. Goltz, p. 86.
140. Astore, Showalter, pp. 83–4, L.E. Jones, *Hitler versus Hindenburg*, p. 28.
141. L.E. Jones, *Hitler versus Hindenburg*, pp. 28–9.
142. Quoted in Pyta, 'Hindenburg and the Right', pp. 28–9.
143. Orlow, p. 61.
144. L.E. Jones, *Hitler versus Hindenburg*, p. 31.
145. Goltz, pp. 93–4.
146. Ibid., p. 94.
147. Ibid.
148. Astore, Showalter, p. 84.
149. Quoted in Pyta, 'Hindenburg and Right', pp. 39–40.
150. Quoted in Dorpalen, p. 77.
151. L.E. Jones, *Hitler versus Hindenburg*, pp. 29–30.
152. Goltz, p. 90.
153. Dorpalen, pp. 77–8, Goltz, pp. 90–1.
154. Dorpalen, p. 78.
155. Goltz, p. 88.
156. L.E. Jones, *Hitler versus Hindenburg*, p. 31, Goltz, p. 89.
157. Goltz, p. 89.
158. Dorpalen, pp. 75–6.
159. Gotlz, p. 89.
160. Ibid., p. 91.
161. Ibid.
162. http://www.gonschior.de/weimar/Deutschland/Praesidenten.html (accessed 17/5/2020).
163. Goltz, p. 97.
164. Ibid., pp. 96–7.
165. Dorpalen, pp. 82–3.
166. Ibid., p. 86.
167. Goltz, pp. 97–8.
168. Quoted in Astore, Showalter, p. 84.

Chapter 4

1. Quoted in Whitfield, p. 38.
2. Weitz, p. 118.
3. Quoted in Whitfield, p. 52, from Bruhns, *My Father's Country*.
4. Fritzsche, 'Presidential Victory and Popular Festivity in Weimar Germany: Hindenburg's 1925 Election', *Central European History*, 23 (1990), 205-24.
5. Weitz, p. 118.

6. Ibid.
7. Feuchtwanger, p. 169.
8. L.E. Jones, *Hitler versus Hindenburg*, p. 32.
9. Goltz, p. 128.
10. Ibid., p. 125.
11. Astore, Showalter, p. 82.
12. L.E. Jones, *Hitler versus Hindenburg*, p. 34.
13. Ibid., p. 33.
14. *See* Pyta, 'Hindenburg and the Right', pp. 25–47.
15. Ibid., pp. 40–3.
16. Kolb, p. 74.
17. L.E. Jones, *Hitler versus Hindenburg*, pp. 35–6.
18. Feuchtwanger, pp. 173–4.
19. Ibid., p. 178.
20. Quoted in Kolb, p. 75.
21. Evans, p. 82.
22. Kolb, p. 75.
23. Ibid.
24. William L. Patch, *Heinrich Brüning and the Dissolution of the Weimar Republic*, (Cambridge University Press: 1998), p. 42.
25. Weitz, p. 120.
26. Kolb, p. 76.
27. L.E. Jones, *Hitler versus Hindenburg*, p. 36.
28. Patch, pp. 42–3.
29. L.E. Jones, *Hitler versus Hindenburg*, pp. 36–7.
30. *See* Peter Hayes, 'A Question Mark with Epaulettes? Kurt von Schleicher and Weimar Politics', *Journal of Modern History*, 52 (1980), 35–65, for the finest assessment of Schleicher and his political career, quote on p. 40.
31. Ibid., pp. 41–2.
32. Patch, p. 42.
33. L.E. Jones, *Hitler versus Hindenburg*, p. 40.
34. Dorpalen, pp. 138–9.
35. Astore, Showalter, p. 86.
36. L.E. Jones, *Hitler versus Hindenburg*, p. 34.
37. Goltz, pp. 116–19.
38. Ibid., pp. 112–13.
39. Quoted in Astore, Showalter, p. 86.
40. Dorpalen, pp. 108–109, 111–12.
41. Wheeler-Bennett, *Wooden Titan*, pp. 315–17.
42. First quote from Astore, Showalter, p. 88, second from Goltz, p. 128.
43. Goltz, pp. 128–30.
44. L.E. Jones, *Hitler versus Hindenburg*, pp. 37–8.
45. Ibid.
46. Wheeler-Bennett, *Wooden Titan*, pp. 313–14.
47. Goltz, pp. 133–4.
48. Quoted in Weitz, pp. 120–1.
49. Goltz, pp. 104–107.
50. M. Ludendorff, p. 278, Ullrich, p. 190.
51. *See* Kershaw, p. 269, Ullrich, pp. 190–1.
52. Goodspeed, p. 244.
53. Orlow, pp. 61–3.

54. Steven Naftzger, '"Heil Ludendorff": Erich Ludendorff and Nazism, 1925–1937', unpublished PhD thesis (2002), pp. 16–17.
55. Volker Ullrich, trans. Jefferson Chase, *Hitler: A Biography, Volume I. Ascent*, (Vintage: 2017), p. 191.
56. Naftzger, p. 16.
57. Lockenour, pp. 114–15.
58. Orlow, p. 63, Chickering, p. 170.
59. Louis Leo Synder, *Encyclopedia of the Third Reich*, (Wordsworth: 1998), pp. 341–2.
60. Orlow, p. 68.
61. Naftzger, p. 6.
62. Parkinson, p. 223.
63. Chickering, p. 170.
64. Quoted in Goodspeed, p. 245.
65. M. Ludendorff, p. 284.
66. Chickering, p. 165.
67. Kershaw, p. 269.
68. Goodspeed, p. 245.
69. Kershaw, p. 296.
70. Lockenour, pp. 114–16.
71. Naftzger, p. 18.
72. Parkinson, p. 223, Goodspeed, p. 245.
73. Chickering, p. 166.
74. Ibid.
75. Lockenour, pp. 6–7, also conversations between the author and Jay Lockenour, *see* episode 34 of *History's Most* podcast.
76. Goodspeed, p. 245.
77. Chickering, pp. 171–2.
78. Ibid., p. 170, Lockenour, p. 5.
79. Lockenour, pp. 122–4, 129–31.
80. Ibid., p. 118ff.
81. Goodspeed, pp. 245–6.
82. *See* discussion of Ludendorff's *Total War* in Epilogue.
83. Wheeler-Bennett, 'Ludendorff: The Soldier and the Politician'.
84. Goodspeed, p. 245.
85. M. Ludendorff, p. 283.
86. Dorpalen, p. 132.
87. M. Ludendorff, p. 284.
88. Dorpalen, pp. 132–3, Parkinson, p. 224.
89. Dorpalen, pp. 136–7.
90. Quoted in Wheeler-Bennett, *Wooden Titan*, p. 334. For an in-depth discussion of Ludendorff's repeated attacks on Hindenburg, *see* Lockenour, p. 141ff.
91. Chickering, p. 169.
92. Quoted in Chickering, p. 170.
93. Dorpalen, pp. 137–8.
94. Ibid.
95. http://www.gonschior.de/weimar/Deutschland/RT4.html (accessed 5/1/20).
96. Patch, p. 43.
97. *See* Daniela Gasteiger, 'From Friends to Foes: Count Kuno von Westarp and the Transformation of the German Right', in L.E. Jones (ed.), *The German Right in the Weimar Republic, Studies in Conservatism, Nationalism and Anti-Semitism*, (Berghahn: 2016), pp. 48–78.

98. Patch, pp. 55–6, *see* Larry Eugene Jones, *The German Right, 1918–1930: Political Parties, Organized Interests, and Patriotic Associations in the Struggle against Weimar Democracy*, (Cambridge University Press: 2020), for an in-depth account of the disintegration of the DNVP in the late 1920s.
99. Donna Harsch, *German Social Democracy and the Rise of Nazism*, (The University of North Carolina Press: 1993), p. 44.
100. Feuchtwanger, pp. 217–18.
101. Ibid., p. 205.
102. Patch, pp. 46–7.
103. Ibid., pp. 47–8.
104. Feuchtwanger, p. 218.
105. Patch, p. 50.
106. Ibid., p. 48.
107. L.E. Jones, *Hitler versus Hindenburg*, pp. 55–6.
108. Hite & Hinton, p. 82.
109. L.E. Jones, *Hitler versus Hindenburg*, pp. 55–6.
110. Dorpalen, pp. 156–7.
111. Ibid., pp. 155–6.
112. Goltz, pp. 138–9.
113. Ibid., p. 139.
114. Ibid., pp. 140–1.
115. Kolb, pp. 103–105.
116. Patch, p. 54.
117. L.E. Jones, *Hitler versus Hindenburg*, pp. 60–1.
118. Patch, p. 57.
119. Ibid., pp. 38–41.
120. On Brüning, Patch is unparalleled, *see* early chapters for his background and early career. See also L.E. Jones, *Hitler versus Hindenburg*, especially the pen portrait, pp. 61–4.
121. Patch, p. 51.
122. L.E. Jones, *Hitler versus Hindenburg*, p. 64.
123. Patch, p. 60.
124. Ibid., p. 61.
125. L.E. Jones, *Hitler versus Hindenburg*, p. 65.
126. Patch, p. 64.
127. Quoted in Patch, p. 66.
128. Ibid., pp. 66–7.
129. L.E. Jones, *Hitler versus Hindenburg*, p. 65.
130. Harsch, p. 57.
131. Ibid.
132. Dorpalen, p. 176.

Chapter 5
1. The classic account of this development is provided by Theodor Eschenburg, 'The Role of Personality in the Crisis of the Weimar Republic', in Holborn (ed.), *Republic to Reich: The Making of the Nazi Revolution*, (Vintage: 1973), pp, 3–50. See also Hermann Beck, Larry Eugene Jones, 'The Nazi Seizure of Power in Historical and Historiographical Perspective', in Beck, Jones (eds.) *From Weimar to Hitler: Studies in the Dissolution of the Weimar Republic and the Establishment of the Third Reich, 1932–1934*, (Berghahn: 2020).
2. Larry Eugene Jones, *Hitler versus Hindenburg*, pp. 66–8.
3. Dorpalen, p. 177.
4. L.E. Jones, *Hitler versus Hindenburg*, pp. 66–7, Dorpalen, p. 177.
5. Patch, p. 78.

6. Ibid., p. 68.
7. Patch, p. 73.
8. Pyta, *Hindenburg*, pp. 578–9, Dorpalen, p. 178.
9. Dorpalen, p. 177.
10. Patch, p. 80.
11. Dorpalen, p. 181.
12. Ibid., p. 183.
13. L.E. Jones, *Hitler versus Hindenburg*, pp. 69–70.
14. Dorpalen, p. 189.
15. Ibid., pp. 190–1.
16. L.E. Jones, *Hitler versus Hindenburg*, p. 71.
17. Dorpalen, p. 196.
18. Ibid., pp. 191–4.
19. http://www.gonschior.de/weimar/Deutschland/RT5.html (accessed 2/11/20).
20. Orlow, pp. 185–7.
21. Ullrich, pp. 232–3.
22. Ibid., p. 247.
23. Orlow, pp. 182–3.
24. L.E. Jones, *Hitler versus Hindenburg*, p. 72.
25. Ibid., p. 73.
26. Ibid.
27. Dorpalen, p. 206.
28. Patch, pp. 112–15, Harsch, pp. 87–9, Dorpalen, p. 207.
29. Harsch, pp. 89–91.
30. Dorpalen, p. 208.
31. Larry Eugene Jones, 'Taming the Nazi Beast: Kurt von Schleicher and the End of the Weimar Republic', in Beck, Jones (eds.) *From Weimar to Hitler: Studies in the Dissolution of the Weimar Republic and the Establishment of the Third Reich, 1932–1934*, (Berghahn: 2020), pp. 24–5.
32. Ibid., *see also* Hayes, p. 38.
33. Hayes, p. 44.
34. Ibid., p. 43.
35. Dorpalen, pp. 210–11.
36. L.E. Jones, *Hitler versus Hindenburg*, pp. 73–5.
37. Dorpalen, pp. 209–10.
38. Ibid.
39. Ullrich, pp. 242–4.
40. Ibid., p. 244.
41. L.E. Jones, *Hitler versus Hindenburg*, p. 76.
42. Dorpalen, p. 214.
43. Hett, pp. 120–1.
44. Ibid., pp. 122–3.
45. Quoted in Dorpalen, pp. 223–4.
46. Ullrich, p. 255.
47. Dorpalen, p. 221.
48. L.E. Jones, *Hitler versus Hindenburg*, p. 76.
49. Dorpalen, pp. 220–1.
50. L.E. Jones, *Hitler versus Hindenburg*, pp. 77–80.
51. Dorpalen, p. 222.
52. L.E. Jones, *Hitler versus Hindenburg*, p. 86.
53. Dorpaeln, pp. 226–7.
54. Ibid., p. 228.

55. L.E. Jones, *Hitler versus Hindenburg*, pp. 83–4.
56. Ibid., pp. 87–8.
57. For an analysis of the Prussian referendum, *see* L.E. Jones, *Hitler versus Hindenburg*, pp. 96–103.
58. L.E. Jones, *Hitler versus Hindenburg*, pp. 105, 121–2.
59. L.E. Jones, *Hitler versus Hindenburg*, pp. 114–17.
60. Ibid., pp. 107, 117–18, 129–30.
61. Pyta, *Hindenburg*, pp. 613ff.
62. L.E. Jones, *Hitler versus Hindenburg*, pp. 122–3.
63. Ibid., pp. 124–6.
64. Patch, p. 194, Dorpalen, p. 234, L.E. Jones, *Hitler versus Hindenburg*, p. 127.
65. L.E. Jones, *Hitler versus Hindenburg*, pp. 127–8.
66. Patch, pp. 195–6, Dorpalen, p. 236.
67. Hayes, p. 45, Patch, p. 196.
68. Eschenburg, p. 37.
69. L.E. Jones, *Hitler versus Hindenburg*, pp. 128–9.
70. Dorpalen, pp. 238–9.
71. Ullrich, p. 258.
72. Patch, p. 194.
73. Ibid.
74. Dorpalen, p. 241.
75. Ullrich, p. 258.
76. Ibid.
77. L.E. Jones, *Hitler versus Hindenburg*, pp. 132–3.
78. Ibid., p. 134.
79. Dorpalen, p. 240.
80. Hayes, pp. 45–6.
81. Patch, pp. 198–200.
82. Dorpalen, pp. 248–9.
83. Patch, p. 232.
84. Ibid., pp. 7–9, 304.
85. Patch, p. 231.
86. L.E. Jones, *Hitler versus Hindenburg*, p. 140.
87. Patch, p. 231.
88. L.E. Jones, *Hitler versus Hindenburg*, pp. 150–1.
89. Kershaw, p. 361, L.E. Jones, *Hitler versus Hindenburg*, pp. 141–2.
90. L.E. Jones, *Hitler versus Hindenburg*, pp. 143–4.
91. Patch, pp. 232–3.
92. L.E. Jones, *Hitler versus Hindenburg*, p. 145.
93. Ibid., pp. 145, 148.
94. Ibid., p. 157.
95. Kerhsaw, pp. 361–2, Ullrich, pp. 294–5, Patch, p. 234.
96. Patch, p. 234.
97. Ibid.
98. L.E. Jones, *Hitler versus Hindenburg*, pp. 160–1.
99. Patch, p. 236, L.E. Jones, *Hitler versus Hindenburg*, pp. 161.
100. L.E. Jones, *Hitler versus Hindenburg*, pp. 164–5.
101. Patch, p. 236.
102. L.E. Jones, *Hitler versus Hindenburg*, pp. 165–6.
103. Ibid., pp. 166–7.
104. Patch, pp. 236–7.
105. L.E. Jones, *Hitler versus Hindenburg*, pp. 159–60.

106. Patch, pp. 237–8.
107. Goltz, p. 149.
108. Pyta, *Hindenburg*, pp. 665–6.
109. L.E. Jones, *Hitler versus Hindenburg*, pp. 174–5.
110. Goltz, *Hindenburg*, p. 148. This account of the campaign is especially indebted to L.E. Jones's excellent monograph on the election, *Hitler versus Hindenburg*.
111. Goltz, pp. 143.
112. Dorpalen, p. 285.
113. Quoted in Goltz, *Hindenburg*, p. 153.
114. Goltz, p. 151.
115. Patch, p. 237.
116. L.E. Jones, *Hitler versus Hindenburg*, p. 210.
117. Harsch, p. 179.
118. Goltz, *Hindenburg*, pp. 142–3, 162.
119. Quoted in L.E. Jones, *Hitler versus Hindenburg*, pp. 189–90.
120. Patch, p. 240.
121. William Sheridan Allen, *The Nazi Seizure of Power: The Experience of a Single German Town, 1930–1935* (Quadrangle Books: 1965), p. 87.
122. Goltz, *Hindenburg*, p. 162.
123. Quoted in Patch, p. 243.
124. L.E. Jones, *Hitler versus Hindenburg*, pp. 206–208.
125. Patch, p. 238.
126. Ibid., p. 244.
127. L.E. Jones, *Hitler versus Hindenburg*, p. 207.
128. Goltz, *Hindenburg*, p. 162.
129. Larry Eugene Jones, 'Generational Conflict and the Problem of Political Mobilization in the Weimar Republic' in L.E. Jones, James Retallack (eds.), *Elections, Mass Politics and Social Change in Modern Germany: New Perspectives*, (Cambridge University Press: 1992), p. 363.
130. Allen, p. 87.
131. For the decisions of the DVP and CNBL, see L.E. Jones, *Hitler versus Hindenburg*, pp. 183–5.
132. Dorpalen, p. 281.
133. L.E. Jones, *Hitler versus Hindenburg*, p. 250.
134. Goltz, *Hindenburg*, pp. 153–6, Dorpalen, p. 287.
135. L.E. Jones, *Hitler versus Hindenburg*, p. 247.
136. Dorpalen, p. 283.
137. Goltz, *Hindenburg*, p. 154.
138. Quoted in Dorpalen, p. 278.
139. Goltz, *Hindenburg*, pp. 154–5.
140. Dorpalen, p. 286.
141. Dorpalen, pp. 282, 288, 297.
142. Goltz, *Hindenburg*, p. 152.
143. Quoted in Dorpalen, pp. 276–7.
144. Goltz, *Hindenburg*, p. 157.
145. L.E. Jones, *Hitler versus Hindenburg*, pp. 178–82, Patch, p. 241.
146. Dorpalen, p. 283.
147. L.E. Jones, *Hitler versus Hindenburg*, p. 238.
148. Goltz, p. 158, and note 94, p. 268.
149. L.E. Jones, *Hitler versus Hindenburg*, p. 227.
150. L.E. Jones, *Hitler versus Hindenburg*, pp. 229–30, Patch, p. 242.
151. Goltz, p. 149.

152. L.E. Jones, *Hitler versus Hindenburg*, p. 252.
153. Goltz, *Hindenburg*, pp. 158–9.
154. L.E. Jones, *Hitler versus Hindenburg*, pp. 230–2, Goltz, *Hindenburg*, pp. 159–61.
155. Quoted in Dorpalen, p. 291.
156. Goltz, *Hindenburg*, pp. 158.
157. L.E. Jones, *Hitler versus Hindenburg*, pp. 237–8.
158. Goltz, *Hindenburg*, p. 159.
159. Dorpalen, p. 284.
160. Patch, p. 245.
161. Quoted in Dorpalen, p. 284.
162. Goltz, *Hindenburg*, p. 151.
163. Dorpalen, p. 284.
164. Quoted in Patch, p. 246.
165. L.E. Jones, *Hitler versus Hindenburg*, pp. 207–208.
166. Ibid., pp. 274–80.
167. Full election results can be found at http://www.gonschior.de/weimar/Deutschland/Praesidenten.html (accessed 18/11/20).
168. Dorpalen, p. 292, L.E. Jones, *Hitler versus Hindenburg*, p. 274.
169. Dorpalen, p. 294.
170. L.E. Jones, *Hitler versus Hindenburg*, pp. 291–3.
171. Goltz, *Hindenburg*, pp. 156–7.
172. Dorpalen, p. 295.
173. Patch, pp. 244–5.
174. L.E. Jones, *Hitler versus Hindenburg*, p. 295.
175. Dorpalen, pp. 294–6.
176. L.E. Jones, *Hitler versus Hindenburg*, p. 295.
177. This particular pamphlet is in the author's collection. I am indebted to Jack Arscott, Institute for Modern Languages Research, for his help in translating and interpreting the pamphlet, and his enlightening me on the common German trope of Michel.
178. Goltz, p. 158, and note 94, p. 268, L.E. Jones, *Hitler versus Hindenburg*, pp. 305–306.
179. Quoted in L.E. Jones, *Hitler versus Hindenburg*, p. 307.
180. Patch, p. 245.
181. Quoted in Dorpalen, p. 299.
182. L.E. Jones, *Hitler versus Hindenburg*, p. 308.
183. Full election results can be found at http://www.gonschior.de/weimar/Deutschland/Praesidenten.html (accessed 18/11/20).
184. L.E. Jones, *Hitler versus Hindenburg*, pp. 312–13.
185. *See* Evans, pp. 279–82, Kershaw, pp. 360–3. Even Pyta's biography is remarkably brief, pp. 679–83.
186. L.E. Jones, *Hitler versus Hindenburg*, Goltz, *Hindenburg: Power, Myth and the Rise of the Nazis*.
187. Eschenburg, p. 33.
188. Patch, p. 246.
189. Quoted in Goltz, *Hindenburg*, p. 166.
190. Patch, p. 247.
191. L.E. Jones, *Hitler versus Hindenburg*, pp. 314–15.
192. Eschenburg, p. 29.
193. L.E. Jones, *Hitler versus Hindenburg*, pp. 316–17.
194. Eschenburg, p. 34.
195. Mommsen, p. 125.
196. Quoted in Patch, p. 248.
197. Hayes, pp. 47–8.

198. Patch, p. 248.
199. Ibid., pp. 248–9.
200. Eschenburg, p. 35.
201. Dorpalen, p. 302.
202. Patch, p. 250.
203. Eschenburg, p. 34.
204. Patch, pp. 250–1.
205. Eschenburg, p. 35.
206. Patch, p. 251.
207. Pyta, *Hindenburg*, pp. 685–9.
208. Eschenburg, p. 35.
209. Quoted in Patch, pp. 252–3.
210. Pridham, pp. 275–6.
211. http://www.gonschior.de/weimar/Preussen/Uebersicht_LTW.html (accessed 2/11/20).
212. For an in-depth discussion of the Prussian election, *see* chapter ten of L.E. Jones, *Hitler versus Hindenburg*, and for the moderate right in particular, *see* pp. 331–7.
213. Patch, p. 253.
214. Hayes, p. 46.
215. Patch, p. 254.
216. Ibid., pp. 254–5.
217. L.E. Jones, *Hitler versus Hindenburg*, p. 341.
218. Hayes, pp. 46–7, L.E. Jones, 'Taming the Nazi beast', p. 27.
219. Patch, p. 254.
220. Ibid., p. 263
221. Dorpalen, pp. 313–14.
222. Patch, p. 255.
223. Eschenburg, p. 42.
224. L.E. Jones, *Hitler versus Hindenburg*, pp. 341–2.
225. Dorpalen, p. 314.
226. Hauner, p. 81.
227. Patch, pp. 255–6.
228. Dorpalen, pp. 314–15.
229. Patch, pp. 265–7.
230. Dorpalen, p. 316.
231. Eschenburg, p. 43.
232. Patch, p. 267.
233. Ibid., p. 268.
234. Dorpalen, p. 320, Patch, p. 269.
235. The account of this meeting is based on Dorpalen, pp. 320–1, Patch, p. 269.
236. Dorpalen, p. 321.
237. Wheeler-Bennett, *Wooden Titan*, p. 394.
238. Patch, p. 266.
239. L.E. Jones, *Hitler versus Hindenburg*, p. 344.
240. Ibid., p. 345.
241. Dorpalen, p. 315.
242. L.E. Jones, *Hitler versus Hindenburg*, p. 350.
243. Ibid., pp. 350–1.
244. Dorpalen, pp. 333–4.
245. Patch, pp. 267, 269.
246. L.E. Jones, *Hitler versus Hindenburg*, p. 351.
247. Quoted in Shirer, p. 207 and Henry Ashby Turner Jr., *Hitler's Thirty Days to Power: January 1933*, (Bloomsbury: 1996), p. 40. Most histories of the period provide a colourful

pen portrait of Papen's character, *see*, for example, Dorpalen, pp. 328, 332, Eschenburg, pp. 44–5, Turner, *Hitler's Thirty Days to* Power, pp. 7–8, Hett, pp. 144–6.
248. Hett, p. 145.
249. L.E. Jones, 'Taming the Nazi beast', p. 27.
250. Dorpalen, pp. 332–3.
251. Ibid., pp. 334–5.
252. Wheeler-Bennett, *Wooden Titan*, p. 397.
253. Dorpalen, p. 331.
254. L.E. Jones, 'Taming the Nazi beast', p. 27.
255. For reactions to Brüning's sacking, *see* Patch, pp. 269–71.
256. Hayes, p. 48.
257. L.E. Jones, 'Taming the Nazi beast', p. 27.
258. L.E. Jones, *Hitler versus Hindenburg*, pp. 352–3, Patch, pp. 273–6, Ullrich, p. 311.
259. Dorpalen, pp. 338–41.
260. Ibid., p. 336.
261. Hauner, p. 83.
262. *See* the complete absence of any mention of Hindenburg being involved in the campaign in Pyta, *Hindenburg*, pp. 712–14, Dorpalen, pp. 346–8, Wheeler-Bennett, *Wooden Titan*, pp. 405–407.
263. Dorpalen, pp. 347–8.
264. Hett, p. 149.
265. For the Prussian Coup, *see* Harsch, pp. 191–4, Patch, p. 278, Erich Matthias, 'The Downfall of the Old Social Democratic Party in 1933', in Hajo Holborn (ed.), *Republic to Reich: The Making of the Nazi Revolution*, (Vintage: 1973), pp. 54–63, Hett, pp. 149–50.
266. Hayes, p. 48.
267. Pyta, *Hindenburg*, pp. 712–13, Dorpalen, p. 344.
268. http://www.gonschior.de/weimar/Deutschland/RT6.html (accessed 30/11/20).
269. Patch, pp. 279–82.
270. Hett, pp. 151–2.
271. Patch, p. 284, Dorpalen, p. 357.
272. Hayes, p. 49.
273. L.E. Jones, 'Taming the Nazi beast', p. 28.
274. Hayes, pp. 49–50.
275. Dorpalen, p. 348.
276. Kershaw, p. 371.
277. Hett, pp. 150–1.
278. Fine accounts of this meeting can be found in Pyta, *Hindenburg*, pp. 719–25, Kershaw, pp. 373–4, Ullrich, p. 320, Dorpalen, pp. 352–5, Hett, pp. 155–6.
279. Quoted in Kershaw, p. 373.
280. Dorpalen, p. 354.
281. Dorpalen, pp. 354–5, quoted in Ullrich, p. 320.
282. Kershaw, p. 374, Ullrich, p. 320.
283. Hett, p. 156.
284. Patch, p. 280.
285. Dorpalen, pp. 356–7.
286. Ullrich, p. 325, Patch, p. 284, Dorpalen, p. 360.
287. Dorpalen, p. 362.
288. Ullrich, p. 327.
289. Hett, p. 157, Kershaw, pp. 385–6.
290. Dorpalen, p. 363, Turner, *Hitler's Thirty Days to Power*, p. 14.
291. Document 2.21 in Stackelburg, Winkle, p. 115.
292. Ibid., pp. 115–16.

293. Quoted in Dorpalen, p. 367.
294. Goltz, *Hindenburg*, p. 168.
295. Quoted in Dorpalen, p. 367.
296. Ibid., p. 371.
297. A fine account of the November election campaign and the popular mood can be found in chapter 3 of Paul Jankowski, *All Against All: The Long Winter of 1933 and the Origins of the Second World War*, (Profile Books: 2020).
298. Hauner, p. 85.
299. For full results, *see* http://www.gonschior.de/weimar/Deutschland/RT7.html (accessed 7/12/20).
300. Dorpalen, p. 374.
301. Document 2.23, in Stackelburg, Winkle. pp. 119–21.
302. Orlow, p. 286.
303. Ibid., pp. 287–9.
304. Dorpalen, p. 375.
305. Kershaw, pp. 392–3.
306. Quoted in Ullrich, p. 334.
307. Dorpalen, p. 380.
308. Turner, *Hitler's Thirty Days to Power*, p. 16.
309. Kershaw, p. 393.
310. Ullrich, pp. 334–5.
311. Kershaw, p. 394.
312. Dorpalen, p. 383.
313. Quoted in Turner, *Hitler's Thirty Days to Power*, p. 17.
314. Dorpalen, pp. 376–7.
315. Ibid.
316. Turner, *Hitler's Thirty Days to Power*, p. 17.
317. Hauner, p. 85.
318. Turner, *Hitler's Thirty Days to Power*, p. 19.
319. Dorpalen, p. 387.
320. Ibid., p. 389.
321. Hayes, p. 56.
322. Ibid., pp. 56–7.
323. Ibid., p. 57.
324. Dorpalen, p. 390.
325. Carsten, pp. 381–2.
326. The idea that Schleicher sought a broad alliance, 'union front' or *Querfront* still dominates mainstream history, for instance the narrative of the 2019 *The Gravediggers: The Last Winter of the Weimar Republic* is largely built around this scheme, and it is also repeated by respected historians such as Hett in *The Death of Democracy* and in Kershaw's biography of Hitler.
327. The above theory has been comprehensively dismantled by Hayes, 'A Question Mark with Epaulettes', by Turner's 'The Myth of Chancellor von Schleicher's *Querfront* Strategy' and *Hitler's Thirty Days to Power*, and the leading expert on the non-Nazi right, Larry Eugene Jones, supports this view in 'Taming the Nazi Beast: Kurt von Schleicher and the End of the Weimar Republic'.
328. Hayes, p. 60, Henry Ashby Turner Jr., 'The Myth of Chancellor von Schleicher's *Querfront* Strategy', *Central European History*, 41, 4, 2008, 673-681, p. 677.
329. Turner, 'The Myth of Chancellor von Schleicher's *Querfront* Strategy', p. 679.
330. Ibid., p. 677.
331. Hayes, pp. 55–6, Turner, 'The Myth of Chancellor von Schleicher's *Querfront* Strategy', p. 675.

332. Hayes, pp. 58–60.
333. Turner, 'The Myth of Chancellor von Schleicher's *Querfront* Strategy', p. 674.
334. For the impossibility of SPD support for Schleicher, *see* Harsch, *German Social Democracy and the Rise of Nazism*, pp. 221–2.
335. Turner, 'The Myth of Chancellor von Schleicher's *Querfront* Strategy', p. 674.
336. Ibid., pp. 676–7.
337. For the realignment of the DVP, *see* L.E. Jones, *Hitler versus Hindenburg*, pp. 117–18, 125, 128, 132–4 ,184.
338. Turner, 'The Myth of Chancellor von Schleicher's *Querfront* Strategy', pp. 677–8.
339. Dorpalen, p. 392.
340. Ibid., p. 393.
341. Pyta, *Hindenburg*, pp. 764–5, Hett, pp. 160–1.
342. Carsten, p. 380.
343. Dorpalen, p. 394.
344. Ullrich, p. 339.
345. L.E. Jones, 'Taming the Nazi Beast', p. 32.
346. Kershaw, p. 396.
347. Hett, p. 161, Dorpalen, pp. 394–5.
348. Quoted in Hett, p. 161.
349. Dorpalen, p. 396.
350. L.E. Jones, 'Taming the Nazi Beast', p. 32, Wheeler-Bennett, *Wooden Titan*, p. 419.
351. Dorpalen, pp. 384–5.
352. Ullrich, pp. 339, 369.
353. Hayes, p. 60.
354. Turner, 'The Myth of Chancellor von Schleicher's Querfront', p. 677.
355. L.E. Jones, 'Taming the Nazi Beast', p. 33.
356. Hayes, p. 58.
357. L.E. Jones, 'Taming the Nazi Beast', p. 34.
358. Hauner, p. 87.
359. Document 2.23 in Stackelburg, Winkle, pp. 121–2.
360. Hayes, pp. 58–9.
361. L.E. Jones, 'Taming the Nazi Beast', p. 35.
362. Ibid.
363. Turner, *Hitler's Thirty Days to Power*, p. 28.
364. Turner, 'The Myth of Chancellor von Schleicher's Querfront', p. 677.
365. Turner, *Hitler's Thirty Days to Power*, pp. 26–7.
366. Dorpalen, p. 400.
367. Ibid., pp. 401–402.
368. Quoted in Hayes, p. 61.
369. Ibid., pp. 61–2.
370. Ibid., p. 61, Dorpalen, p. 404.
371. Kershaw, p. 413.
372. Turner, *Hitler's Thirty Days to Power*, pp. 42–3.
373. Ibid., 42.
374. Hayes, pp. 60–1.
375. Turner, 'The Myth of Chancellor von Schleicher's Querfront', p. 678.
376. Dorpalen, p. 403.
377. Ibid., p. 408.
378. Turner, *Hitler's Thirty Days to Power*, pp. 28–9, Ullrich, pp. 346–7.
379. Hauner, p. 88.
380. Turner, *Hitler's Thirty Days to Power*, p. 46.
381. Orlow, p. 297.

382. Ullrich, pp. 352–3.
383. Ibid.
384. Orlow, pp. 297–8, *see also* http://www.gonschior.de/weimar/Lippe/Uebersicht_LTW.html (accessed 22/12/20).
385. L.E. Jones, 'Taming the Nazi Beast', p. 37.
386. Ibid., p. 36.
387. Hayes, p. 62.
388. L.E. Jones, 'Taming the Nazi Beast', p. 37.
389. Ibid., Ullrich, pp. 354–5, Dorpalen, pp. 413–15.
390. Turner, 'The Myth of Chancellor von Schleicher's Querfront', p. 679.
391. Hayes, pp. 62–3, Tuner, 'The Myth of Chancellor von Schleicher's Querfront', pp. 677–8.
392. Hayes, p. 63.
393. Ullrich, pp. 361–2.
394. Dorpalen, p. 422.
395. Ibid., pp. 422–3.
396. Ullrich, p. 361, Kershaw, pp. 417–18, Dorpalen, pp. 423–4, Turner, *Hitler's Thirty Days to Power*, p. 115.
397. Ullrich, p. 361.
398. Carsten, p. 388.
399. Turner, *Hitler's Thirty Days to Power*, pp. 136–7.
400. Dorpalen, pp. 425–6.
401. Carsten, p. 389.
402. L.E. Jones, 'Taming the Nazi Beast', p. 38.
403. Ullrich, p. 363, Kershaw, pp. 416–17.
404. Carsten, p. 390.
405. Turner, *Hitler's Thirty Days to Power*, p. 128.
406. L.E. Jones, 'Taming the Nazi Beast', p. 39. *See* note 89 of Jones's essay for a discussion for the date of this meeting, which is frequently given as either the 26th or 27th. Jones suggests Hammerstein may in fact have seen Hindenbueg on both days.
407. Quoted in Carsten, p. 391.
408. Ibid.
409. Hans Magnus Enzensberger, trans. Chalmers, *The Silences of Hammerstein*, (Seagull Books: 2017), pp. 104–105.
410. L.E. Jones, 'Taming the Nazi Beast', p. 39.
411. Turner, 'The Myth of Chancellor von Schleicher's Querfront', p. 680.
412. Email exchange between the author and Larry Eugene Jones.
413. Turner, *Hitler's Thirty Days to Power*, pp. 143–5.
414. Ullrich, pp. 363–4.
415. Dorpalen, p. 433.
416. Ibid.
417. Ullrich, p. 364.
418. Dorpalen, p. 433.
419. Hauner, p. 88.
420. Carsten, pp. 392–3.
421. Quoted in Enzensberger, pp. 108–109.
422. Ullrich, pp. 365–6.
423. Dorpalen, p. 434.
424. Kershaw, p. 420.
425. Turner, *Hitler's Thirty Days to Power*, pp. 144–5, Dorpalen, p. 435.
426. Dorpalen, p. 436.
427. Turner, *Hitler's Thirty Days to Power*, pp. 150–1, 157.
428. Dorpalen, pp. 437–8.

429. Carsten, p. 393.
430. Ullrich, pp. 367–9.
431. Turner, *Hitler's Thirty Days to Power*, pp. 155–7.
432. Carsten, p. 394.
433. Dorpalen, p. 441.
434. Ullrich, p. 370.
435. Quoted in Kershaw, p. 423.

Epilogue
1. Evans, p. 311, Astore, Showalter, p. 95.
2. Goltz, *Hindenburg*, pp. 173–4.
3. Pyta, *Hindenburg*, pp. 605, 835ff., 855, Goltz, *Hindenburg*, pp. 173.
4. Dorpalen, p. 451.
5. Turner, *Hitler's Thirty Days to Power*, pp. 172–6.
6. For a full discussion of Hindenburg's political vision, *see* Pyta, 'Hindenburg and the German Right', and in particular pp. 41–3.
7. L.E. Jones, 'Taming the Nazi Beast', p. 40.
8. Carsten, p. 394, Enzenberger, pp. 119–26.
9. Carsten, p. 395.
10. Enzenberger, p. 136.
11. Tuner, *Hitler's Thirty Days to Power*, p. 163.
12. Dorpalen, pp. 448–9.
13. Ibid., pp. 450–2, Goltz, p. 172.
14. Evans, pp. 322–3, 337, Harsch, p. 228.
15. *See* Hett, pp. 186–94.
16. Dorpalen, p. 460.
17. Hauner, p. 90.
18. Dorpalen, pp. 455–6.
19. Goltz, pp. 171–3.
20. http://www.gonschior.de/weimar/Deutschland/RT8.html (accessed 28/12/20).
21. Dorpalen, p. 462.
22. Goltz, pp. 174–5.
23. Quoted in Goltz, p. 175.
24. Quoted in Dorpalen, pp. 465–6.
25. Goltz, p. 177.
26. Document 19, Anson Rabinbach, Sander L. Gilman (eds.), *The Third Reich Sourcebook*, (University of California Press: 2013), pp. 46–7.
27. Ibid., p. 180.
28. Dorpalen, p. 463.
29. Quoted in Dorpalen, p. 469.
30. Dorpalen, p. 470.
31. Ullrich, p. 444.
32. Goltz, p. 174, Dorpalen, pp. 471–5.
33. Goltz, pp. 178–9.
34. Dorpalen, pp. 476–8.
35. Ullrich, p. 465.
36. Dorpalen, pp. 479–80.
37. Goltz, pp. 180–1.
38. Ibid., p. 182.
39. Dorpalen, p. 481, Goltz, pp. 183–5.
40. Goltz, pp. 187–8.
41. Dorpalen, p. 483.

42. Goltz, pp. 193–6.
43. Chickering, pp. 172–3, Lockenour, pp. 152–4.
44. Lockenour, pp. 154–8.
45. John Wheeler-Bennett, Knaves, *Fools and Heroes, Europe Between the Wars*, (MacMillan: 1974), p. 97.
46. Quoted in Kershaw, p. 427, highlighting the prevalence of this forgery in popular history.
47. Ullrich p. 372, see also p. 852, n. 122.
48. Wheeler-Bennet, 'Ludendorff: Soldier and Politician', https://www.vqronline.org/essay/ludendorff-soldier-and-politician (accessed 29/12/20), Goodspeed, p. 247, Kershaw, p. 681.
49. Lockenour, p. 131.
50. Ibid., p. 162.
51. Chickering, pp. 172–3.
52. Lockenour, pp. 164–5.
53. Lockenour, pp. 165–9.
54. Ibid., pp. 168–9.
55. Ibid., pp. 170–2.
56. Chickering, p. 173.
57. Lockenour, p. 135ff., Hans Speier, 'Ludendorff: The German Concept of Total War', in Earle (ed.), *Makers of Modern Strategy: Military Thought from Machiavelli to Hitler*, (Princeton University Press: 1952), p. 306. *See also* Alan Kramer, 'From Great War to Fascist War', in Alonso et al. (eds.), *Fascist Warfare, 1922–1945: Aggression, Occupation, Annihilation*, Palgrave MacMillan, 2019, pp. 26–7, Chickering, pp. 173–4.
58. Chickering, pp. 176–8.
59. Erich Ludendorff, trans. Rappoport, *The Nation at War*, (Hutchinson: 1936), p. 28.
60. Ibid., pp. 36–40, 53–4.
61. Speier, pp. 315–16.
62. Ludendorff, *The Nation at War*, p. 169.
63. Chickering, p. 175.
64. Speier, p. 321.
65. Chickering, pp. 175–7, contrasted sharply by Lockenour, p. 135ff.
66. Kramer, p. 31. *See also* Miguel Alonso et al., 'Introduction', in *Fascist Warfare, 1922–1945: Aggression, Occupation, Annihilation*, (Palgrave MacMillan: 2019), p. 14 for a discussion of the ways Nazi warfare was even more radicalised than Ludendorff's total war.
67. Hauner, p. 120, Kershaw, p. 681, Ullrich, p. 372.
68. Goodspeed, p. 247.
69. Lockenour, p. 182.
70. Ibid., p. 248.
71. Parkinson, p. 229.
72. Ullrich, pp. 700–701.
73. Goodspeed, p. 248.
74. *See* https://ludendorff.info/ (accessed 29/12/20), available in four languages!
75. Tuner, *Hitler's Thirty Days to Power*, pp. 181–2, Astore, Showalter, pp. 104–105.

Further Reading and Bibliography

This volume has, for reasons of space, been unable to explore in full detail the political careers of Hindenburg and Ludendorff and makes no claim to be a comprehensive account in either case. Rather it has focused on the ways in which the two men directly and indirectly contributed to the rise of the Nazis. The following studies will provide a more in-depth picture of certain figures and events and have been hugely useful to the author. For a more full account of Ludendorff's career after 1918, in particular his post-NSDAP activities such as the Tannenberg League, Ludendorff Press and Deutsche Gotterkenntnis, see Lockenour's excellent biography *Dragonslayer* (which owing to its date of publication in April 2021, I was sadly unable to make extensive use of) and Steven Neftzger's unpublished PhD thesis 'Hail Ludendorff' (available online). Roger Chickering's chapter 'The Sore Loser' in *The Shadows of Total War* is also indispensable in studying Ludendorff's life after 1918. David King's *The Trial of Adolf Hitler* is perhaps the best of the many books on the Beer Hall Putsch and the subsequent courtroom drama. On Hindenburg's political career, Andreas Dorpalen's account is the classic work, and it remains unsurpassed for detail, even if some of his conclusions might now be questioned. Wolfram Pyta's fine biography sadly has not yet been translated into English. Larry Eugene Jones has written many excellent books and articles on Weimar politics and his monograph *Hitler versus Hindenburg* is indispensable for the events before, during and after the 1932 presidential election. Anna von der Goltz's *Hindenburg: Power, Myth and the Rise of the Nazis* provides a good overview and focuses in on the field marshal's mythical reputation and cultural and political significance. Finally, on the events of 1930–33, William L. Patch's *Heinrich Brüning and the Demise of the Weimar Republic* is an invaluable study of the beleaguered chancellor and Henry Ashby Turner Jr.'s *Hitler's Thirty Days to Power* is the best narrative of the backstairs intrigue in the Republic's final weeks.

Select Bibliography
Astore, William J., Showalter, Dennis E., *Hindenburg: Icon of German Militarism*, (Potomac: 2005).
Beck, Hermann, Jones, Larry Eugene, 'The Nazi Seizure of Power in Historical and Historiographical Perspective', in Beck, Jones (eds.), *From Weimar to Hitler: Studies in the Dissolution of the Weimar Republic and the Establishment of the Third Reich, 1932–1934*, (Berghahn: 2020).
Carsten, F.L., *The Reichswehr and Politics, 1918–1933*, (Oxford University Press: 1966).
Chickering, Roger, 'The Sore Loser: Ludendorff's Total War', Roger Chickering & Stig Förster (eds.), *The Shadows of Total War: Europe, East Asia and the United States, 1919–1939*, (Cambridge University Press: 2008).
Deist, W., 'The Military Collapse of the German Empire: The Reality Behind the Stab-in-the-Back Myth', trans. E. Feuchtwanger, *War in History*, 3, 2 (1996), 186–207.
Dornberg, John, *The Putsch That Failed, Munich 1923: Hitler's Rehearsal for Power*, (Weidenfeld & Nicolson: 1982).
Dorpalen, Andreas, *Hindenburg and the Weimar Republic*, (Princeton University Press: 1964).

Enzensberger, Hans Magnus, trans. Chalmers, *The Silences of Hammerstein*, (Seagull Books: 2017).
Eschenburg, Theodor, 'The Role of Personality in the Crisis of the Weimar Republic', in Hajo Holborn (ed.), *Republic to Reich: The Making of the Nazi Revolution*, (Vintage: 1973).
Evans, Richard J., *The Coming of the Third Reich: How the Nazis Destroyed Democracy and Seized Power in Germany*, (Penguin: 2004).
Fahrenwaldt, Matthias A., 'The Knives Are Out: The Reception of Erich Ludendorff's Memoirs in the Context of the Dolchstoß Myth, 1919–1925', *Portal Militärgeschichte* (2021), (http://portal-militaergeschichte.de/sites/default/files/pdf/fahrenwaldt_ludendorff_0.pdf).
Feuchtwanger, E.J., *From Weimar to Hitler, Germany 1918–33*, (MacMillan: 1993).
Geyer, M., 'Insurrectionary Warfare: The German Debate about a *Levée en Masse* in October 1918', *Journal of Modern History*, 73 (2001), 459–527.
Goltz, Anna von der, *Hindenburg: Power, Myth and the Rise of the Nazis*, (Oxford University Press: 2011).
Goodspeed, D.J., *Ludendorff: Solider, Dictator, Revolutionary*, (Rupert Hart-Davies: 1966).
Gordon, Harold J., *Hitler and the Beer Hall Putsch*, (Princeton University Press: 1972).
Harsch, Donna, *German Social Democracy and the Rise of Nazism*, (The University of North Carolina Press: 1993).
Hauner, Milan, *Hitler: A Chronology of his Life and Time, Second Edition*, (Palgrave MacMillan: 2008).
Hayes, Peter, 'A Question Mark with Epaulettes? Kurt von Schleicher and Weimar Politics', *Journal of Modern History*, 52 (1980), 35–65.
Hett, Benjamin Carter, *The Death of Democracy: Hitler's Rise to Power* (Windmill Books: 2019).
Hindenburg, Paul von, Charles Messenger (ed.), *The Great War*, (Frontline Books: 2013).
Jablonsky, David, *The Nazi Party in Dissolution: Hitler and the Verbotszeit, 1923–25*, (Routledge: 1989).
Jones, Larry Eugene, 'Taming the Nazi Beast: Kurt von Schleicher and the End of the Weimar Republic', in Beck, Jones (eds.), *From Weimar to Hitler: Studies in the Dissolution of the Weimar Republic and the Establishment of the Third Reich, 1932–1934*, (Berghahn: 2020).
Jones, Larry Eugene, *The German Right, 1918–1930: Political Parties, Organized Interests, and Patriotic Associations in the Struggle against Weimar Democracy*, (Cambridge University Press: 2020).
Jones, Larry Eugene, *Hitler versus Hindenburg, The 1932 Presidential Elections and the End of the Weimar Republic*, (Cambridge University Press: 2015).
Jones, Larry Eugene, 'Generational Conflict and the Problem of Political Mobilization in the Weimar Republic' in L.E. Jones, James Retallack (eds.), *Elections, Mass Politics and Social Change in Modern Germany: New Perspectives*, (Cambridge University Press: 1992).
Jones, Mark, 'Political Violence in Italy and Germany after the First World War', in Millington, Passmore (eds.), *Political Violence and Democracy in Western Europe, 1918–1940*, (Palgrave MacMillan: 2015).
Jones, Nigel, *The Birth of the Nazis: How the Freikorps Blazed a Trail for Hitler* (Robinson: 2004).
Kershaw, Ian, *Hitler, 1889–1936: Hubris*, (Penguin: 1999).
King, David, *The Trial of Adolf Hitler: The Beer Hall Putsch and the Rise of Nazi Germany*, (Pan: 2018).
Kolb, Eberhard, trans. P.S. Falla, *The Weimar Republic*, (Routledge: 1992).

Kramer, Alan, 'From Great War to Fascist War', in Miguel Alonso et al. (eds.), *Fascist Warfare, 1922–1945: Aggression, Occupation, Annihilation*, (Palgrave MacMillan: 2019).
Lee, John, *The Warlords: Hindenburg and Ludendorff*, (Weidenfeld & Nicolson: 2005).
Lockenour, Jay, *Dragonslayer: The Legend of Erich Ludendorff in the Weimar Republic and Third Reich*, (Cornell University Press: 2021).
Ludendorff, Erich, *Ludendorff's Own Story: August 1914–November 1918, The Great War, Volume II, From the Siege of Liege to the Signing of the Armistice as viewed from the Grand Headquarters of the Germany Army*, (Lucknow Books: 2012).
Ludendorff, Erich, trans. Rappoport, *The Nation at War*, (Hutchinson: 1936).
Ludendorff, Margarethe, trans. Raglan Somerset, *My Married Life with Ludendorff*, (Hutchinson:1929).
Naftzger, Steven, '"Heil Ludendorff": Erich Ludendorff and Nazism, 1925–1937', unpublished PhD thesis (2002).
Nerdinger, Winfried (ed.), trans. Jefferson Chase et al, *Munich and National Socialism: Catalogue of the Munich Documentation Centre for the History of National Socialism*, (C.H. Beck: 2015).
Orlow, Dietrich, *The History of the Nazi Party Volume 1, 1919–1933*, (David & Charles: 1971).
Parkinson, Roger, *Tormented Warrior: Ludendorff and the Supreme Command*, (Hodder & Stoughton: 1978).
Patch, William L., *Heinrich Brüning and the Dissolution of the Weimar Republic*, (Cambridge University Press:1998).
Pelz, William A., *A People's History of the German Revolution*, (Pluto Press: 2018).
Pridham, Geoffrey, *Hitler's Rise to Power: The Nazi Movement in Bavaria, 1923–33*, (Hart-Davies: 1973).
Pyta, Wolfram, 'Hindenburg and the German Right', in L.E. Jones (ed.), *The German Right in the Weimar Republic, Studies in the History of Conservatism, Nationalism, and Anti-Semitism*, (Berghahn: 2016).
Pyta, Wolfram, *Hindenburg: Herrschaft zwischen Hohenzollern und Hitler*, (Pantheon: 2009).
Röhm, Ernst, trans. Geoffrey Brooks, *The Memoirs of Ernst Röhm*, (Frontline Books: 2012).
Ross Range, Peter, *1924, The Year that made Hitler*, (Little, Brown & Company: 2016).
Schaefer, Karen, *Germany Military and the Weimar Republic: General Hans von Seekt, General Erich Ludendorff and the Rise of Hitler*, (Pen & Sword: 2020).
Speier, Hans, 'Ludendorff: The German Concept of Total War', in Edward Mead R. Earle (ed.), *Makers of Modern Strategy: Military Thought from Machiavelli to Hitler*, (Princeton University Press: 1952).
Stackelberg, Roderick, Winkle, Sally A. (eds.), *The Nazi Germany Sourcebook, an anthology of texts*, (Routledge: 2002).
Taylor, Cory, *How Hitler Was Made: Germany and the Rise of the Perfect Nazi*, (Prometheus: 2018).
Travers, Tim, *How the War was Won: Factors that led to victory in World War One*, (Pen & Sword, 2005).
Turner Jr., Henry Ashby, 'The Myth of Chancellor von Schleicher's *Querfront* Strategy', *Central European History*, 41, 4 (2008), 673–81.
Turner Jr., Henry Ashby, *Hitler's Thirty Days to Power: January 1933*, (Bloomsbury: 1996).
Ullrich, Volker trans. Jefferson Chase, *Hitler: A Biography, Volume I. Ascent*, (Vintage: 2017).
Vascik, George S., Sadler, Mark R., *The Stab-in-the-Back Myth and the Fall of the Weimar Republic, A History in Documents and Visual Sources*, (Bloomsbury: 2016).

Watson, Alexander, *Ring of Steel: Germany and Austria-Hungary at War, 1914–1918*, (Penguin: 2015).
Weitz, Eric D., *Weimar Germany: Promise and Tragedy*, (Princeton University Press: 2007).
Wheeler-Bennett, John, *Wooden Titan: Hindenburg in Twenty Years of German History, 1914–1934*, (William Morrow: 1936).
Wheeler-Bennett, John, 'Ludendorff: The Soldier and the Politician', VQR (Spring 1938), (https://www.vqronline.org/essay/ludendorff-soldier-and-politician).
Wheeler-Bennett, John, *The Nemesis of Power: The German Army in Politics, 1918-1945*, (MacMillan: 1980).

Index

1919 election to Constituent Assembly, xxxviii
1920 Reichstag election, 51–2
May 1924 Reichstag election, 98–9
December 1924 Reichstag election, 104–105
1925 presidential election, 106–18
1928 Reichstag election, 135–6
1930 Reichstag election, 146–9
1932 presidential election, 164–77
1932 Prussian State election, 180–2
July 1932 Reichstag election, 189–91
November 1932 Reichstag election, 195–9
1933 Reichstag election, 226–7
For all election results *see* 242–4

Bauer, Colonel Max, xx, xxxiii, 11, 33–4, 37, 44, 48–9, 51, 53, 57, 60
Bavarian People's Party (BVP), xvi–xvii, xli, 55, 67, 77, 98, 104–105, 122, 140, 145, 148, 158, 180, 199, 201, 220, 242
and 1925 presidential election, 107, 110, 112–15, 117–18
and 1932 presidential election, 164–6
and Schleicher, 205–206, 209
Beer Hall Putsch, 71–86
trial, 87–97
Braun, Otto, xx, 107, 112, 136, 145, 149, 154, 165, 177, 181, 190, 243
Brüning, Heinrich, xx, 139–40, 201
persuaded to form government, 139–42
relationship with Hindenburg, 141, 143–4, 153–7, 159, 176–7, 180, 183–5, 200–201, 238–40
chancellorship, 143–85
economic policy, 145–6, 150–2
and 1930 Reichstag election, 146–9
and Nazis, 178–9, 181–2, 191

and 1932 presidential election, 159–63, 165–9, 172–3, 177
ousted, 182–8
Bürgerblock, xviii, xl, 122–6, 134–5

Catholic Centre Party (Z), xvi, xviii–xix, xxxviii–xli, 5, 51, 60, 94, 122–5, 137, 144, 147, 156, 201, 226, 230, 233, 242
and 1925 presidential election, 107, 111, 115, 118
shifts rightwards, 139–41
and 1932 presidential election, 164–6
potential coalition with Nazis, 181, 183, 191, 199, 220
oppose Papen, 185–90
and Schleicher, 203, 205–206, 209, 211, 215
Christian-Nationalist Peasants' and Farmers' Party (CNBL), xviii–xix, 136, 144, 146–8, 151, 154–8, 164, 167, 169–70, 181, 191, 242
Christian Social People's Mission (CSVD), xviii–xix, 136, 146–8, 158, 164, 166, 181, 191, 242
Communists (KPD), xv, xxxviii, xl, 2, 6, 30, 64, 147, 154, 158, 179, 181, 188–91, 195, 198, 207, 211, 216, 223, 242–4
and German Revolution, 6, 30, 35, 54
and Kapp Putsch, 39, 46, 47, 50
and 1925 presidential election, 107, 115, 117
and 1932 presidential election, 160, 165, 167, 171, 173, 176
and threat of collaboration with Nazis, 201–205
Nazi repression of, 226–7
Ludendorff believes controlled by Judah & Rome, 236

Conservative People's Party (KVP), xvii–xix, 136, 144, 146–8, 158, 163–4, 166, 181, 185, 191, 242

Democrats (DDP), xvi, xviii, xxxviii, xl, 5, 20, 31, 38, 51, 60, 107, 111, 115, 121–3, 140, 164, 242
  as State Party (DStP), xix, xl, 146, 148, 158, 169, 181, 191
Duesterberg, Theodor, xx, 70, 155, 161–2, 168, 170, 173–4, 176, 243

Ebert, Friedrich, xx, xxxvii–xxxix, 14, 33, 53, 61, 65, 69, 123, 226
  and Ebert-Groener Pact, 6–8, 29, 41
  and Versailles, 16–7, 25
  and Kapp Putsch, 36–9, 46–7, 50
  and Beer Hall Putsch, 79
  death, 106, 109–10
Economic Party (WP) *see* Reich Party of the Middle Class
Ehrhardt, Hermann, xx, 36–9, 41, 45–9, 54, 57, 60–1, 63, 66, 68, 70

Frick, Wilhelm, 54, 63, 79, 90, 95, 98, 193, 209, 226

German National People's Party (DNVP), xvii–xix, xli, 19, 27, 98, 104, 135, 148, 151, 154–5, 181, 189, 195, 198, 227, 242
  and Hindenburg, 20, 24, 53, 113–14, 121–7, 138–9, 145–7, 153, 177, 194, 215, 224, 231
  and Kapp Putsch, 34, 36, 39, 51
  and 1925 presidential election, 107, 112–14, 116
  and Ludendorff, 133
  fragments, 136, 140–1, 144–5
  and 1932 presidential election, 160, 162, 164, 166, 168–9, 173–4
  and Schleicher, 206, 214
German Revolution, xxxvii–xl, 4–8, 28–31
  in Bavaria, 53–5
German Völkisch Freedom Party (DVFP), xvii, 97–100, 102, 105–106, 108

Gessler, Otto, 52, 107, 123, 135, 156, 162
Goebbels, Joseph, 164, 167, 172, 181, 186, 199–200, 210, 213, 221, 228–9
Göring, Hermann, 63, 68, 73, 83, 85, 90, 104, 157, 160, 162, 194–5, 203, 210, 213, 218, 226
Graefe, Albrecht von, xxi, 97–106, 108–109
Groener, Wilhelm, xxi, xxxviii, 36, 52, 135, 141, 144, 157, 160–2, 172, 184, 238
  and Ebert-Groener Pact, 6, 14, 29, 41
  and Hindenburg, 7–8, 16–18, 137, 141, 166, 179–80
  and Schleicher, 124, 135, 141, 154, 158, 177, 182
  and Brüning, 140–1, 157, 178–80
  bans SA, 178–80
  sacking, 182–3
Grossdeutsche Volksgemeinschaft (GVG), 97, 99, 102–105

Hammerstein-Equord, Kurt von, xxi, 179–80, 217–20, 225
Harzburg Front, xix, 155–8, 161–3, 174, 201
Hindenburg, Paul von:
  historical reputation, xxvi–xxviii, 222–4, 238–41
  origins, xxviii–xxix
  First World War career, xxx–xxxvii
  relationship with Ludendorff, xxxi–xxxii, xxxvii, 133–4, 235
  and Stab-in-the-Back myth, 1–8, 14–27
  and Versailles, 16–18
  war enquiry appearance, 19–23
  first approached to run for president, 20, 53
  writes memoirs, 23–6
  and Kapp Putsch, 52–3
  and 1925 presidential election, 112–18
  first years in power, 119–28
  and Schleicher, 124–5, 136–7, 140–1, 154, 178–9, 183, 187–8, 192, 206–209, 216–19, 240
  and Grand Coalition, 134–42
  and Brüning, 141, 143–4, 153–7, 159, 176–7, 180, 183–5, 200–201, 238–40

forms 'Hindenburg Cabinet', 143–5
and Hitler, 149, 157–8, 192–4, 196–7, 200–202, 215–21, 222–4, 226–33, 239–41
agitates for more right-wing government, 154–64
physical & mental health, 159, 170–1, 222, 226, 231
and 1932 presidential election, 164–77
tires of Brüning, 177–85
and final months of Weimar Republic, 187–221
and Papen, 187, 192, 195, 198, 207–208, 215–21
persuaded to appointment Hitler, 212–21
after Hitler's rise to power, 222–33
Hindenburg Bloc, xix, 146, 148–9, 154–6, 158, 181, 190
Hitler, Adolf, xxi, xxvi–xxvii, 56, 65–70, 243–4
origins, 57, 61–3
and Ludendorff, 58, 63–4, 66–70, 97–106, 108–12, 128–33, 234–5, 237, 239–41
and Beer Hall Putsch, 71–86
and trial, 87–97
imprisoned, 97–100, 103–104
refounds party, 105–106, 111
and 1925 presidential election, 108–11
and Hindenburg, 149, 157–8, 192–4, 196–7, 200–202, 215–21, 222–4, 226–33, 239–41
and Brüning, 148–9, 157
and the National Opposition, 155, 162
and 1932 presidential election, 160–2, 167, 173, 176
deal with Schleicher, 181–2
demands chancellorship, 193–4, 200
and Strasser affair, 204–206, 209–11
appointed chancellor, 212–21
Hugenberg, Alfred, xxi, xli, 135, 144, 153, 158, 182, 188, 201
and Young Plan Referendum, 138–9
and Brüning, 145–8, 154–5
and Harzberg, 155–6

and 1932 presidential election, 160–2, 167, 171, 173–4
and Hitler's appointment as chancellor, 214–15, 220, 222

Independent Socialists (USPD), xv, xl, 46–7, 51, 54, 242

Kahr, Gustav Ritter von, xxi, 50, 66, 231
as Bavarian Prime Minister, 55–8, 61
as Bavarian Commissioner-General, 69–70
and Beer Hall Putsch, 71–9
and Putsch trial, 87–90, 92, 94, 97
Kaiser Wilhelm II, xxx–xxxviii, 4–8, 21, 25, 32, 40, 113, 126, 175, 233
Kapp, Wolfgang, xxii, 33–5, 37–9, 42–8, 50–1, 55, 60, 63, 133
Kapp Putsch, 33–52
in Bavaria, 55
Kemnitz, Mathilde von, xxii, 89–90, 93, 102, 129–30, 132, 237–8
Kriebel, Hermann, xxii, 66, 68, 75–8, 80–3, 85, 90, 92, 104

Lossow, Otto Ritter von, xxii, 66–70, 72–81, 83, 86, 88, 92, 94
Ludendorff, Erich:
historical reputation, xxvi–xxviii, 238–41
origins, xxix–xxx
First World War career, xxx–xxxvii
relationship with Hindenburg, xxxi–xxxii, xxxvii, 133–4, 235
mental health, xxxvi, 8–11, 26, 32, 57, 71, 131–4, 233, 240
and Stab-in-the-Back myth, 1–14, 19–23, 27
relationship with Margarethe (first wife), 9, 34, 49, 57, 89, 109, 128–30
publications, 11–14, 58–60, 63, 65, 89–90, 132–3, 233–7
and Max Weber, 31–3
and Kapp Putsch, 32–53
and move to Bavaria, 57–60
and Hitler, 58, 63–4, 66–70, 97–106, 108–12, 128–33, 234–5, 237, 239–41

and NSDAP, 63–4, 66–70, 97–106, 108–12, 128–31, 233–8, 240
and Beer Hall Putsch, 69–86
and trial, 87–97
relationship with second wife, Mathilde, 89–90, 93, 102, 129–30, 132, 237–8
and struggle for control of Nazi movement, 97–106
and 1925 presidential election, 108–12
creates Tannenberg League, 128–34
after Hitler's rise to power, 233–8
Luther, Hans, xxii, 107, 122–3, 127, 133
Lüttwitz, Walther von, xxii, 33, 35–9, 42, 44–5, 47–52, 60

Marx, Wilhelm, xxii, 107, 111–18, 123–4, 126–7, 140, 164, 186, 224–5, 243
Meissner, Otto xxii, 121, 128, 140, 142, 160, 168, 183–5, 193, 201–2, 215, 218, 220, 226
Müller, Hermann, xxiii, 136–7, 139–42, 218, 240

National Opposition, xix, 138, 149–51, 153–63, 166–8, 170, 173, 183, 206, 215–16, 222, 241
National Socialist Freedom Party/Movement (NSFP/NSFB), xvii, 99, 101–107, 110, 242
National Socialists/Nazis (NSDAP), xvii, xix, 129–30, 151, 154, 180–2, 188–9
origins, 61–3
and Ludendorff, 63–4, 66–70, 97–106, 108–12, 128–31, 233–8, 240
activities during 1923 crisis, 65–71
and Beer Hall Putsch, 71–86
infighting while banned, 88, 97–106
and 1925 presidential election, 108–12
and Hindenburg, 139, 153, 160, 192–4, 200–201, 206, 215, 218–21, 224–33, 239
and Schleicher, 149–50, 178–9, 182–3, 192, 196–7, 202–206, 209, 212, 214
electoral breakthrough, 147–8
and 1932 presidential election, 161, 167–8, 173–4, 176

become largest party, 190–1
problems in late 1932, 198–200, 204–205, 209–11
recovery early 1933, 213–16
Nationalists *see* German National People's Party (DNVP)
Noske, Gustav, xxiii, 16, 30, 36–8, 41, 52, 162

Organisation Consul (OC), 57, 60–1, 66

Papen, Franz von, xxiii, 135, 143, 186, 225, 230–1, 240
appointed chancellor, 185–7
chancellorship, 187–208
and Hindenburg, 187, 192, 195, 198, 207–208, 215–21
and Prussian coup, 190
and Hitler, 193–4, 212–14, 219–21
confidence vote, 195
ousted, 203–207
persuade Hindenburg to accept Hitler, 215–16, 218, 222
People's Party (DVP), xvi, xviii–xix, xl–xli, 20, 39, 51, 53, 55, 68, 122, 135, 145–9, 177, 181, 191, 201, 206, 227, 242
and first Hindenburg candidacy, 53
and 1925 presidential election, 107, 114
and Grand Coalition, 136–41
shifts to the right, 154–8
and 1932 presidential election, 164, 166–7
support Papen, 188–9, 195, 198
Pöhner, Ernst, xxiii, 54–5, 57, 61, 63, 73, 75–6, 82, 86, 90, 92

Reich Party of the Middle Class (WP) xviii–xix, 145, 148, 150, 154–5, 158, 164, 181–2, 191, 242
Reich Rural League (RLB), xviii–xix, 144, 150, 155, 158, 164, 167, 174, 183, 214, 242
Röhm, Ernst, xxiii, 29, 45, 58, 65, 88, 90, 95, 110, 158, 193–4, 231
and Bavarian politics, 54–6, 61, 63, 66–70

and Beer Hall Putsch, 72, 80–2, 84–5
and Nazi infighting, 97–100, 103–105, 111

Scheubner-Richter, Max Erwin von, xxiii, 63, 68, 72–4, 77–8, 80–1, 83, 85
Schiele, Martin, xxiii, 121, 136, 141, 144, 147, 150, 152, 158, 184, 191
Schleicher, Kurt von, xxiv, 40, 52, 124, 135, 200, 223–4, 231
   and Hindenburg, 124–5, 136–7, 140–1, 154, 178–9, 183, 187–8, 192, 206–209, 216–19, 240
   and Brüning, 139–41, 143–5, 157–9, 177–85
   taming strategy/cooperation with Nazis, 148–50, 158–9, 160–1, 181–2, 188, 192–3, 203–206, 209–11, 214–15, 220, 225
   and 1932 presidential election, 160–3, 168, 175
   and Papen, 185–9, 192–4, 202–208, 219–20
   chancellorship, 208–21
   ousted, 212–21
Seeckt, Hans von, xxiv, 5, 36–41, 44, 48–52, 65–6, 68–70, 75, 79, 87, 124, 126, 155
Seisser, Hans Ritter von, xxiv, 55, 69–70, 73–9, 84, 87–8, 92, 94
Social Democrats (SPD), xv–xvi, xl–xli, 104, 124–6, 135, 140, 147, 188, 190, 191, 199, 242
   and German Revolution, xxxvii–xxxix, 6–7, 29–30, 54
   and Stab-in-the-Back myth 5, 7, 167
   and Ludendorff, 12, 14, 93
   and Kapp Putsch, 38, 41, 44–6, 51–2, 55
   and 1925 presidential election, 107, 111, 115, 118
   and Hindenburg, 5–7, 20, 115, 121–3, 136–7, 141–2, 159, 164–5, 167–8, 172, 174, 180, 197, 201, 224, 238
   and Brüning, xix, 145–6, 149–50, 153–4, 158, 160, 185, 188
   and 1932 presidential election, 159, 164–5, 169, 174, 177
   and Schleicher's calculations, 203–206, 212, 215–16
   Nazi repression of, 213, 226–8
Spartacists *see* Communists
Stab-in-the-Back myth, xxvi, 1–27, 31, 58, 60, 133, 167, 236, 238–41
Stahlhelm, xix, 70, 113, 118, 120–2, 127, 130, 136, 145, 147, 154–5, 216, 220, 222, 227, 243
   and 1932 presidential election, 160–2, 164, 167–70, 173–4
Strasser, Gregor, xxiv, 97–8, 100, 102–103, 105, 111, 181, 192, 204–206, 209–15, 231
Stresemann, Gustav, xxiv, xl, 68, 70, 87, 107, 111, 114, 119, 122, 137–8, 147

Tannenberg League, 129–32, 234
Treviranus, Gottfried, xvii, xxiv, 136, 140, 144, 146–7, 157, 159, 191

Völkisch-Social Bloc (VSB), xvii, 98, 103, 104
   see also National Socialist Freedom Party

Weber, Friedrich, xxv, 68, 71–2, 75, 79, 81, 83, 90, 92
Weber, Max, 31–3, 50
Weimar Coalition, xviii, 51, 53, 107, 111, 164, 181
Westarp, Kuno von, xxv, 34, 121, 123, 135–6, 138–9, 144, 146–7, 163, 166, 169, 172, 176, 181–2, 185, 188, 191